Helsinki of the Czars

Studies in Scandinavian Literature and Culture

Edited by
George C. Schoolfield
and
Robert E. Bjork

Helsinki of the Czars
Finland's Capital: 1808–1918

George C. Schoolfield

HELSINKI
OF
THE CZARS

Finland's Capital: 1808–1918

CAMDEN HOUSE

Copyright © 1996 by
CAMDEN HOUSE, INC.

Published by Camden House, Inc.
Drawer 2025
Columbia, SC 29202 USA

Printed on acid-free paper.
Binding materials are chosen for strength and
durability.

All Rights Reserved
Printed in the United States of America
First Edition

ISBN:1–57113–026–8

Library of Congress Cataloging-in-Publication Data

Schoolfield, George C.
    Helsinki of the czars : Finland's capital, 1808-1918 / George C.
Schoolfield.
        p.   cm. -- (Studies in Scandinavian literature and culture)
    Includes bibliographical references and index.
    ISBN 1-57113-026-8 (alk. paper)
    1. Helsinki (Finland) --History. 2. Finland--History--1809-1917.
I. Title.   II. Series.
DL1175.46.S36   1995
948.97' 1--dc20   95-18982
                                                                              CIP

Contents

List of Illustrations

All illustrations are from the Picture Archive of the Helsingfors City Museum.

Acknowledgements

The author wishes to thank the Finnish Literary Society for its generous financial support of the present publication; particular thanks are due to Marja-Leena Rautalin, the director of the Information Center for Finland's Literature in Helsinki, for having furthered the stipend which made publication possible. His gratitude must likewise go to the Finnish Ministry of Education for several grants during the 1980s; and to the staffs of the Helsinki City Library, the Helsinki University Library, and the Sterling Library at Yale University, as well as to the Helsinki Municipal Museum. Kerttuli Wessman of the Museum's Picture Archive has been especially gracious and helpful. Thanks are also due to Professor Kim Nilsson of the University of Wisconsin, Professor emeritus Lars Huldén and Professor Johan Wrede of the Nordic Department at the University of Helsinki, and Marianne Bargum, formerly of the Information Center for Finland's Literature and now director in chief of Söderströms förlag, as well as Soila Lehtonen, editor of *Books from Finland*. A particular debt is owed to Mona Leo for having allowed the author to examine her memoirs in manuscript, about the last days of the Civil War. Dr. Christian Gellinek merits special mention for his strong and continued interest in the project. Charles S. Fineman, West European Bibliographer at the Harvard College Library, has been quick and generous with his help, as have Professors Paul A. Bushkovitch and Vasily Rudich of Yale University. Laura Gray of the Music Department at Yale University must be warmly thanked for her aid in the preparation of the final manuscript. And great praise must go to Gloria D. Schoolfield for her concern and patience.

George C. Schoolfield
Yale University
New Haven

Preface

As EUROPEAN CITIES go, Helsingfors (in Finnish, Helsinki) has a brief history: it was founded in 1550 by edict of Gustaf Vasa, king of Sweden and Finland, with the hope of attracting some of the trade then flourishing between Russia and the Netherlands, and with the intent of establishing a rival port to the Teutonic Knights' city of Reval (Tallinn) just across the Gulf of Finland. (Almost immediately, Gustaf Vasa's creation lost one of its reasons for being; in 1561, after the dissolution of the "Deutscher Orden," Gustaf's son, Erik XIV, took Reval and northern Estonia for Sweden.) The settlement spent some ninety unhappy years at the place of its foundation, about two miles northeast of the present heart of Finland's capital, where the Vanda (Vantaa) River debouches into waters of Gammelstadsfjärden (Vanhankaupungin selkä, "Old Town Bay"). In 1640, a new town was laid out on the rocky headland of Estnässkatan (Vironniemi), corresponding roughly to the district now called Kronohagen (Kruunuhaka); here, Helsingfors-Helsinki continued to lead a life of gray unimportance, being altogether overshadowed by Åbo (Turku), Finland's ancient administrative and ecclesiastical center to the west and even by the little port of Borgå (Porvoo) to the east, a going concern since the fourteenth century. In 1713, during the Great Northern War, the town was besieged by the Russians and then burnt to the ground by the retreating Swedes; the majority of the town's inhabitants disappeared into the countryside or into Russian hands, while a few succeeded in escaping to Sweden. Nor was this the only disaster to befall the town; in the 1690's, epidemics had decimated the population, a calamity repeated in 1710, on the eve of the Russian invasion; and the wretched place which went up in military smoke in May, 1713, had been the victim of a fire (caused by civilian accident) twelve years before. The Peace of Nystad (Uusikaupunki, 1721) brought Helsingfors-Helsinki back to the control of the Swedish crown, and the process of rebuilding began; many of the returning citizens used the barracks the Russians had put up, and in 1727, that most important building, the town church (named after Queen Ulrika Eleonora of Sweden) was completed; it was destined to stand for exactly one hundred years, being removed in the great renovation after Helsingfors-Helsinki had become the capital of the czars' Grand Duchy of Finland. In Sweden's next eastern war, Helsinki-Helsingfors once again fell to the Russians: this time, on August 29, 1742, a whole Swedish army surrendered, just outside the town limits, to the Muscovites, competently and colorfully led by an Irishman named de Lacy. But now the occupation was much briefer (peace was signed in 1743), and, evidently, more humane, although not so gentle as to persuade all the townsfolk to stay at home, and in Russian care.

The great event in the eighteenth century's second half was the construction, started in 1748, of the great fortress-complex on the islands guarding the harbour's mouth, Sveaborg ("Svea's Castle," first called Viapori in Finnish, but rechristened as Suomenlinna, "Finland's Castle," after Finland became independent); it was the design of Augustin Ehrensvärd (1710–1772), "a genius able to serve the fatherland, and a heart desiring to do so," as his epitaph says. The double-edged importance of the undertaking for Helsingfors-Helsinki should be plain enough; it brought considerable new blood and some money to the town (whose population increased from 1,520 in the year of the work's beginning to 3,072 in 1800), but it seemed to condemn Helsingfors-Helsinki to be everlastingly linked to the fates of the giant in the front yard, or front waters. Extant statistics are few and unclear, but an interesting side effect of the building of Sveaborg may have been a change in the town's linguistic balance, from what was perhaps a Finnish-speaking majority (according to a frequently cited notice of 1697) to a community of unimpeachably Swedish cast in the 1780's: it must be borne in mind that Helsingfors-Helsinki lay in the center of an almost wholly Swedish-speaking coastal population, and the town, with its fortress and naval station, had an attraction both for nearby peasants and fishermen, and for seamen and artisans from Sweden proper. Furthermore, there was a liberal sprinkling of other ingredients from the Baltic mix: Germans, Estonians, and Swedes from nearby Estonia, a few Lithuanians and Latvians, and (as in the case of other southern Finnish ports) ambitious Germans from farther away. And students of the city's history have also noted the prominence of German names among the city's better families of the day: it may be that German continued to exist as the home language of some up to the eighteenth century's end, albeit Swedish, of course, was used for all public matters.

In 1800, then, prospects of Helsingfors-Helsinki seemed good enough, if not brillant: it lay in the lee of the Gibraltar of the North, it was a trade center of some importance, particularly in the export of wood, thus fulfilling the original purpose of its foundation (as a mart, a "stapelstad," a "tapulikaupunki"), and, in maritime affairs, it was a clear success, having become the most important seafaring town in the eastern part of the Kingdom of Sweden: in 1804, only Stockholm, Gothenburg, and Gävle surpassed it in tonnage. Culturally, though, it had been and was a wasteland, the magnificent designs of Ehrensvärd aside; the one author of some note to be tenuously connected with it during these centuries — Sigfridus Aronus Forsius or, sometimes, Helsingforsius (1550–1624) — spent much of his life in Uppsala (where he studied and was briefly professor of astronomy) and at Stockholm, where he had a pastorate, a post he lost amidst rumored drunkenness, squabbles with his wife, trouble with his colleagues, and involvement in the violent death of a friend; his removal from the chancel of Stockholm's Riddarholmskyrka, however, resulted officially from the "superstitious" sermons he offered his congregation and the insolence he offered his ecclesiastical superiors. After some years of misery, Sigfridus Aronus Helsingforsius was restored to limited grace, being allowed to assume a charge at Ekenäs (Tammisaari) in western Nyland (Uusimaa), where he died. Despite his vicissitudes, the poet, in his *Physica*, had been able to praise God and all his creations in some detail, even to:

> The sirens who so mirthfully
> In the ocean have their gaming.

His tenacity, and his disputaciousness, made him a worthy child of his birthplace.

It is the intention of the present book to praise, in some detail, the city of Helsingfors-Helsinki during the outsized century, from 1808 until 1917, when it was the capital of the "Grand Duchy of Finland" in the Russian empire, and then briefly to tell what befell the city in the first months of 1918. In these roughly 110 years, despite its peripheral location, it became a place of some European importance. It was one of the last cities to be created (or, rather, recreated) by the will of absolute monarchs (Alexander I and then Nicholas I), it was one of the rather few cities of any size to be shaped by the good taste of a gifted city-planner and a gifted architect, working in harmony (Albrecht Ehrenström and Carl Ludwig Engel). It housed, now and again during the "Russian time," some figures of international reputation in the arts: the poet Johan Ludvig Runeberg, the novelist, dramatist, and lyricist Aleksis Kivi, the composer Sibelius, the painters Albert Edelfelt and Axel Gallen-Kallela, the architects Eliel Saarinen and Lars Sonck. It represented a case of rivalry between language groups which, in its eccentric way, was fruitful, and which — to Finland's credit — never degenerated into bloodshed, save in some incidents of the Civil War; it likewise represented a city's linguistic transformation which (unlike Prague's, for example, or Breslau's) was not furthered by political or military events. Finally, and simply, Helsingfors-Helsinki "of the

Czars"[1] provides a fascinating if episodic drama, played out on a municipal stage whose dimensions do not overwhelm the observer.

The book's composition has been a kind of busman's holiday for the author, who is a literary historian by training and profession; he has written the book (or long appreciative essay) because he likes the place and its genius, and because he wishes to share his liking with others, not because he has any thesis to argue. In his work, he has been influenced, inevitably, by the subject of his Nordic literary research (the Swedish-language literature of Finland); but he has tried to take the "Finnish" standpoint into full and fair account. However, since the leading language of administration and culture during much of the period was Swedish, and since many, if not the majority, of the leading characters in the tale had Swedish as their mother tongue, he has used Swedish place-names and street-names throughout; Finnish equivalents are given in a glossary, as well as the Finnish and Swedish equivalents of those common names (for example, Senate Square and Society House) which it seemed more helpful to put into English.

The Anglophone reader who wishes to know more about the general annals of Finland should turn to the revised edition of the history of Finland by Eino Jutikkala and Kauko Pirinen (New York, 1974), Matti Klinge's *A Brief History of Finland* (Helsinki, 1981) and Klinge's *Let Us Be Finns : Essays on History* (Helsinki, 1990), and Fred Singleton's *A Short History of Finland* (Cambridge and New York, 1989), as well as to T.K. Derry's *A History of Scandinavia* (1979). For the twentieth century, two fairly recent books are to be recommended, D.G. Kirby, *Finland in the Twentieth Century* (1979) and Anthony F. Upton, *The Finnish Revolution 1917–1918* (1980). An account of Finland's literary development is to be found in Jaakko Ahokas' *A History of Finnish Literature* (New York, 1974), and in Sven H. Rossel, *A History of Scandinavian Literature*,

---

[1] The title of the book was suggested by Aarni Krohn's *Tsaarin Helsinki: Idyllistä itsenäisyyteen* (Helsinki, 1967: *The Czar's Helsinki: From the Idyll to Independence*), an account of the city from the 1890's to 1918, with a rich stock of photographs, including many by a pleasant adjutant of the Russian governors-general, Major-General Ivan Timiryasev, a skillful hobbyist and a devotee of the city where he spent three decades.

1870–1980 (1982). A somewhat out-of-date general bibliography (by Yrjö Aav) of books in English on Finnish matters can be found in the book edited by Sylvie Nickels, Hillar Kallas, and Philippa Friedman, *Finland: An Introduction* (New York and Washington, 1973) but it, of course, needs updating; more complete listings can be found in J. E. O. Screen's, *Finland* (Volume 31 in the World Bibliographical Series, Oxford and Santa Barbara, 1981).

I. 1808–1854

1. Disasters: Sveaborg's Fall and the Helsingfors Fire

EARLY ON SUNDAY morning, February 21, 1808, a major of Nyland's Light Infantry Battalion, Gustaf Arnkihl, reported to his brigade headquarters that Russian troops were marching on the Kingdom of Sweden's border station at Abborfors. The report was correct; the soldiers of Alexander I had, in fact, gone over the border, the Kymmene River, at five different points; and the first skirmish of the Swedish-Russian war of 1808–1809 took place at the Abberfors bridge. By the 24th the Russians were in Borgå, by the 29th at Sibbo church; a Russian major-general named von Berg went ahead to Helsingfors, ostensibly to see if an evacuation of the town could be arranged. The real purpose of his excursion was less humane: he meant to find out how many Swedish troops were in the vicinity of Helsingfors. Whatever fears the invaders may have had were allayed by von Berg's observation; an immediate advance was ordered. It began before dawn on March 2, with the Russians drawn up in two columns; the fighting was brief. The defenders assembled on the frozen North Harbor, members of the Adlercreutz Regiment, and put up some resistance against the column coming down the "winter-road" (of ice) from the north-east, but when the second Russian force advanced out of the sunrise (it marched toward Helsingfors past Högholmen, where the city's zoo is now located), the Adlercreutzers hastened toward the shelter of Sveaborg, the fortress-complex in the outer harbor. The guns of Långören protected the unhappy men, who dragged ten or eleven wounded with them, from the Cossacks. The Swedes can scarcely be censured for their behavior; their commander, Colonel Gutofski, had jumped into a sleigh and set out for Sveaborg even as the engagement continued. Luckily for the people of Helsingfors, the foe had suffered only the slightest of losses (while of the 460 Swedish soldiers in town, some 70 or 80 were missing); the Russian officers had no difficulty in keeping their troops under control. By noon, the Russian commander-in-chief, General Buxhoevden, had arrived, and the city was in Russian hands; it would remain so until December 6, 1917.

Helsingfors had become Russian, but the "island in the sea's embrace," Sveaborg, had not. The commander of the fortress, Admiral Carl Olof Cronstedt, had 6,750 fighting troops at his disposal, 734 artillery pieces on the walls of his realm, and the guns of the "skerry-fleet," laid up

in the fortress' harbor — the sheltered sound between the two main islands of the complex, Stora Östersvartö and Vargön. Cronstedt had been
warned in plenty of time that war was likely; on February 1, the Swedish
ambassador in Saint Petersburg had advised the command in Finland that
peaceful accord with Russia was impossible, and Cronstedt had shown
great industry in emptying the storehouses of Helsingfors, clearing Sveaborg's walls of snow, and removing inflammable wooden structures. Now,
with the Russians in Helsingfors, there was an even better chance for
Cronstedt to show of what stuff he was made; before March 20, when the
Russian contingent in Helsingfors was doubled, the troops of Sveaborg,
supported by their heavy guns, could very well have driven the Russians
out. But Cronstedt did nothing, saying that he had no cavalry; in all peace,
the Russians were allowed to put up their siege batteries, using them to
bombard the fortress from the 19th until the 21st of March. The psycho-
logical harm was great, although little material damage had been done; the
Swedes, softened, fell prey to a splendidly clever negotiator, Paul van
Suchtelen, sometime professor of mathematics at Leyden and general-of-
engineers in the Russian army. He proposed that the Swedes not fire in
the direction of the city (where the Russians, of course, were quartered),
promising that no batteries would be put up on a line between Sveaborg
and Helsingfors. Cronstedt and the members of his council-of-war —
councilors whom Robert Rehbinder, a prominent Åbo jurist, characterized
as "vieillards impotents, des gens nuls et sans mérite" — agreed. At the
end of March, the Russians undertook a second great cannonade; this time
an officer and five men were killed, some thirty others badly wounded, and
the spirit of the troops began to drop — not so swiftly, though, as the
spirit of their commanders. Fredrik Adolf Jägerhorn, in charge of Stora
Östersvartö and a brother of the Johan Anders Jägerhorn who had plotted
against Gustaf III years before, is supposed to have cried out, when he
caught sight of some three-pronged pikes in the hands of his men: "For
God's sake, throw them away, for if the Russians see them later on, they'll
give no mercy!" It was Jägerhorn, for the rest, who spared no argument in
advising Cronstedt to surrender.

The Russians decided that their 59 guns had done their work and repaired again to words. By April 6, a convention had been signed, between
Cronstedt and van Suchtelen, in accordance with which the fortress, its
provisions, and the skerry-fleet would be surrendered, if at least five
Swedish ships-of-the-line had not appeared off Sveaborg by noon on May
3. Meanwhile, three of the fortress' islands, Lilla Östersvartö, Västersvartö,
and Långören (whose guns had covered the retreat across the ice on the
day of the city's fall) would be given over to the Russians as a bond, and
an armistice would prevail. Those brave and loyal persons in the fortress

who looked hopefully seaward might have spared themselves the trouble; the two officers whom Cronstedt had sent off (he thought) to Stockholm with news of the convention had been detained by the Russians; the first of them reached the court of Gustaf IV Adolf only on May 3, the day that the armistice was to end. It is doubtful that the Swedes would have been able to send a fleet to Sveaborg at any event; the winter had been unusually cold, and, early in May, pack ice still blocked the sea approach to Helsingfors — something which Cronstedt, an experienced mariner, could well have foreseen. The end of the story was precisely what the Russians had expected: the Swedish banner was hauled down on May 3, and, in the next days, the Swedes marched out, the Russians marched in, "with flying standards and full music." Du Rietz, an officer loyal to Sweden, recalled that: "Everyone wept, officers, men, and their wives, curses and insults for the admiral and his council were heard . . . the previous evening, the admiral had got half-a-dozen corporals as a bodyguard; how could he be sure of their devotion, I don't know." When Cronstedt left Sveaborg on May 6, he was accorded ruffles and flourishes by his former foes; but the troops of the fortress (the Swedes among them on their way to captivity, the local forces bound for their home districts) were given verbal abuse by the citizens of Helsingfors; women refused them water, saying they were fit to drink only with swine. With some delicacy, the Russians waited until May 8 to run up their flag on Sveaborg, where they were to stay for 110 years.

Cronstedt's behavior has long been argued about by historians, professional and amateur. Finland's national poet, Johan Ludvig Runeberg, put him into a kind of eternal Coventry in *Fänrik Ståls sägner* (*The Tales of Ensign Stål*), where the old ensign's youthful listener is told to keep the name of Sveaborg's last Swedish commander silent; "Call him but shame and scorn and grief/and guilt and scourge and death." Once upon a time, Cronstedt had been a hero; Gustaf III's flag-captain at the second Battle of Svensksund, on July 9–10, 1790, he had been given credit for creating the king's sea-victory. However, like so many other Gustavians, he had not prospered in the Sweden of Duke Karl, the regent of Gustaf IV Adolf, the murdered monarch's wretched son. In December, 1801, while serving as naval secretary in the king's cabinet, Cronstedt had suddenly been ordered to assume command on Sveaborg "within three days." Although almost a child of Helsingfors — he had been born at Botby Estate near the town — Cronstedt felt no affection for the ruler he served at his splendid but drafty outpost. Furthermore, in 1808, the disgruntled admiral had as his associates men (like Jägerhorn) in patent sympathy with the besiegers; the wives of many of Sveaborg's officers were allowed to remain in Helsingfors, where they enjoyed the Russians' gallant company, and the foxy Suchtelen saw to it that the ladies described at least some of their amusements to their lonely husbands on Sveaborg. Suchtelen himself had capable advisers, themselves Finlanders: old Göran Magnus Sprengtporten, who once had dreamt of an independent Finland under Russia's protection, and Karl Henrik Klick, a leading figure in the Anjala conspiracy (of 1789 against Gustaf III), who came to Helsingfors now with the express purpose of helping the Russian cause. One must conclude that it would have taken a man of heroic character to withstand the threats and temptations to which Sveaborg's commander was subjected, from without and within. Yet Robert Rehbinder, who often saw Cronstedt in Saint Petersburg following the capitulation, observed that the admiral was "soft unto cowardice" and "as credulous as an old woman." The best that can be said for Cronstedt is that he and his contingent were isolated indeed, and that he seems to have been genuinely concerned about the fate of the many non-combatants, soldiers' wives and soldiers' children, on Sveaborg; the worst charge is that he was bought by the Russians. Decades later, Jean Sibelius, who had a quick tongue, took up the question of Cronstedt's venality in a bon mot. Hearing that a descendant, Baron Cronstedt, was trying to sell Brändö manor house (on an island east of the city's main peninsula), an edifice reputedly built by Augustin Ehrensvärd, the creator of Sveaborg, Sibelius remarked: "The same old story — Ehrensvärd builds and Cronstedt sells!" It may be worth noting that, in 1813, Cronstedt purchased another of the estates around Helsingfors, Hertonäs, with the financial support of the Emperor. The admiral spent his last days here in "bitter melancholy," and, as the Gustavian he was, transformed Hertonäs park into a work of art, including a summerhouse by the popular German architect, Carl Ludwig Engel. Cronstedt died at Hertonäs in 1820; his ghost is supposed to walk there still. The author Henrik Hildén observed that the park, as it were, lies turned away from the sea and Sveaborg.

Jägerhorn, who had been so worried about upsetting the Russians, concluded that the fall of Sveaborg made "Finland happy, did a service to Russia, and caused little harm to Sweden." The last part of his opinion may be open to doubt — in the short run — since the fortress, kept in Swedish hands, could have been a thorn in the Russian flesh as the war progressed; yet it is unlikely that Sveaborg's preservation would have caused the conflict to end differently. The last fighting took place in August, 1809, in Sweden proper; peace was concluded, and not just Helsingfors and Sveaborg, but the whole of Finland, became Russian. At the diet of Borgå, opened on March 29, 1809 (thus before the hostilities had ended), Alexander I — with Sprengtporten as his reader in Swedish — assured the estates general of Finland of his intention "to acknowledge and confirm" the laws and religion of the land. The estates (nobility, clergy, burghers, and peasants) swore fealty to him, and he held another touching little speech in French, concluding with the pious wish that "Almighty God would give him the strength and wisdom to guide this estimable people in accordance with its laws and the order of eternal justice." It was a splendid scene, albeit somewhat cramped, in Borgå's little cathedral; most of Finland's residents decided, or wishfully thought, that the Grand Duchy had a bright and better future before it. Four months later, at the diet's official conclusion on June 19, Alexander spoke again in farewell: "Finland is now raised up among the number of the nations."

The citizens of Helsingfors kept easily abreast of these stirring events in neighboring Borgå; the distinguished merchant, Erik Borgström, was the city's representative at the diet. However, Helsingfors had more immediate problems than an interpretation of Alexander's promises. The city suffered not at all when it was taken by Buxhoevden's troops; the accidents of military occupation laid it low. A stable boy named Lindqvist and a Russian soldier sat up late on the windy night of November 16, 1808; possibly, alcohol aided them in overcoming their linguistic differences. A horse belonging to Lindqvist's master was brought back at about one in the morning, and Lindqvist, none too steady, led it into a shed: Russian hussars had taken the regular stables for their own mounts. Then he gave the horse some hay, put out his lantern (which had no glass in it) by pinching off the wick, and went to bed. The trouble is that he threw the wick into the hay, and that a strong southwest wind was blowing. At five o'clock, an early-rising neighbor observed that smoke and fire were ascending from the place where these blurry events had transpired. Good-hearted souls who ran to the main Russian guard-house for help found the sentries unwilling or unable to understand the nature of the excitement, and so the alarm was sounded much too late. Lindquist was sentenced to 14 days on bread and water for his carelessness, and about a quarter of the town burned to the ground.

2. The Great Rebuilding: Ehrenström

SUBSEQUENTLY, BORGSTRÖM MADE representations to the Emperor at Borgå concerning the burden which the quartering of Russian soldiers placed on a city ravaged by fire; but the plight of Helsingfors seems at first to have left Alexander cold. Then the new governor of the provinces of Nyland and Tavastland, Gustaf Fredrik Stjernvall, lately a major in the Adlercreutz regiment and a veteran of Sveaborg's capitulation, now a faithful servant of the Russians, took matters into his own hands; he persuaded Michael Speranski, Alexander's secretary of state, to remind the Emperor of the city's present plight and future importance. A committee was formed with Finland's new governor-general, Fabian Steinheil — "Old Man" Steinheil, a member of the Baltic nobility and a Russian general — as chairman, and Stjernvall as a member. The committee met at Åbo, still the capital of Finland as it had been under the Swedish regime, in December, 1810; the people of the proud city on the Aura did not know that they sheltered vipers at their breast. Besides, the committee began its work in a way that boded ill for Helsingfors, Åbo's young rival; it chose an aging lieutenant, Anders Kocke, to make a new plan for the stricken town, the destruction of which had been so severe that it could be laid out anew. Probably unaware of the difficulty of his task, Kocke worked quickly; his plan was approved by Alexander with equal dispatch. On February 23, 1811, Alexander established a new committee — a genuine "committee of reconstruction" — whose job it was to supervise the rebuilding of Helsingfors in accordance with Kocke's plan: here, Steinheil would still supervise, but Stjernvall would be in direct charge. Kocke's blueprint offered few difficulties, since it offered few major changes in what had been before. Storgatan, "Main Street," which ran where Alexandersgatan now lies, would be broadened and continued over Gloviken, the somewhat boggy body of water cutting into the town from the north; to this purpose, Gloviken must be filled in. A predecessor of the North Esplanade, Södra Strandgatan — which had its strand-name from the proximity of Gloviken — would likewise be expanded and lengthened, and the streets running at right angles to it would be straightened and extended southward. The town marketplace, hitherto smallish, would be expanded.

The year of 1811 passed in preparatory work, including the establishment of kilns for brick and lime. An effort to transport stone from the old Swedish fortifications on the Ulrikasborg Heights annoyed the commander on Sveaborg, Gavro, who intended to use the material for a new redoubt at the same spot; the recalcitrant Gavro also refused to allow Stjernvall to press the town's vagrants, in detention on Sveaborg, into municipal work. But Stjernvall had found a mighty ally; he had captured the attention of Gustaf Mauritz Armfelt, once the favorite of Gustaf III and presently the favorite of Alexander, for a new project — that of making Helsingfors the capital of Finland. Armfelt, who had returned to his native Finland in the spring of 1811, was appointed chairman of the "Committee for Finnish Affairs" in Saint Petersburg; although himself from Åbo (his estate, Åminne, lay near the old city), he gladly insinuated the notion of a new capital into Alexander's mind. Two imperial rescripts were issued on April 18, 1812. The one of them declared Helsingfors to be the new seat of government, "because of its location nearer our capital, its splendid harbor, its inhabitants' industry and public-spirited disposition, as well as its situation, protected by the fortress of Sveaborg." Åbo, in other words, was too near to Sweden and too Swedish in its sympathies. The second rescript, sent to Steinheil on the same day, named still another Gustavian, and an old and good friend of Armfelt, as the new chairman of the building committee; thus Stjernvall was relieved, at his own request, of part of his heavy load of responsibilities. Poor Stjernvall — "the inventor of the plan to make Helsingfors the capital," as Rehbinder called him — died suddenly three years later; the "sturdy fellow," in Armfelt's words, had been worn out.

The man whom Stjernvall and Armfelt had recommended so urgently to Alexander was Johan Albrecht Ehrenström, born in Helsingfors on August 28, 1762. His mother was a Sederholm, a member of one of the little city's most respected families; in 1755–57 her elder brother, Johan Sederholm, built the handsome stone house which, one of the city's few relics of the eighteenth century, still stands beside Senate Square. As a youth, Ehrenström had been an admirer of Sprengtporten, the would-be "George Washington of Finland"; growing aware of Sprengtporten's faults and seeing the chance to follow a much more powerful protector, he switched horses, becoming the trusted private secretary of Gustaf III, and sometimes Gustaf's private spy. The king made good use of the Finlander, especially during the Russian War of 1789–90; in return, Johan Albrecht was inculcated with that refined taste which cultural historians call "Gustavian": all the monarch's intimates acquired it. After Gustaf's assassination, Ehrenström became involved in the conspiracy Armfelt had organized against Gustaf Adolf Reuterholm, the regent's favorite; arrested, Ehrenström was sentenced to death. Years later, he recalled the morning of his execution; taken to the scaffold on Nytorget in Stockholm, "he saw the block at the left, and the headsman with his upraised axe shining in the sun." It was a terrifying piece of make-believe; before starting his ride to the scaffold, Ehrenström had been informed that his sentence would be commuted at the last minute, and it was. The "traitor" spent the morning exposed in the pillory, and the next six-and-one-half years in prison, longer than either Armfelt, the cause of his trouble, or another conspirator, Johan Fredrik Aminoff — he too a Finlander and a Gustavian — who someday, as vice-chairman of the Committee for Finnish Affairs in Saint Petersburg, would do much to support his old friend and fellow culprit. Americans should note that Ehrenström, during his confinement, planned to emigrate to Pittsburgh; we may toy briefly with the vision of a Gustavian city established in the Golden Triangle. After his release, Ehrenström was employed by Gustaf IV Adolf on various missions; on one of these he had a reunion in Vienna with Armfelt and Aminoff (August 5, 1803), a scene later spread through Finland's parlors as "The Three Gustavians," an engraving made after Berton's painting by the Austrian, Johann Peter Pichler.

Upon Gustaf IV Adolf's abdication, in 1809, Ehrenström grew ever more uncomfortable in Sweden; two years later, he decided to go home to Finland, following the example of Armfelt and Aminoff. His refuge was a property of his brother-in-law, Hoplax Estate near Helsingfors; he did not suspect, he later claimed, that Helsingfors so much as had a building committee. Knowing Ehrenström's clear head and fine prose style, Armfelt asked his friend to take a look at clumsy Kocke's plans for the city. Ehrenström, already under obligation to Alexander because of a pension the Emperor granted him, could not refuse to comply with Armfelt's request; as Armfelt might have predicted, Ehrenström found Kocke's work "bare of taste and in most respects unreasonable." Then, giving rein to his eloquence, he concluded his opinion by praising the unique advantages of Helsingfors as a capital city for Finland. Alexander liked what was translated to him from Ehrenström's *Miscellaneous Remarks Concerning the Drawing of Plans for the Projected Reconstruction of the City of Helsingfors* — he liked it so much, indeed, that he echoed it in the rescript by which Helsingfors became Finland's capital.

When Ehrenström learned that he would replace Stjernvall as head of the building committee, he was enraged. He wrote to Aminoff: "When I left Sweden, I could scarcely imagine that [my move] took place in order that I might sacrifice my time and all sorts of comforts for a building committee, struggling meanwhile with troublesome citizenry." Nor was his mood improved when he discovered that his "free residence" in Helsingfors (one of the advantages of his post) was in such bad shape that he was forced to live elsewhere in the town at his own expense. But, out of a sense of duty or fear of offending Alexander, he undertook the "work of a galley slave" all the same, and performed it with superb energy and intelligence, complaining constantly. Another letter to Aminoff, from June, 1812, ran thus: "I use my feet, which are well now, to wander up hill and down dale here [the terrain of Helsingfors was anything but flat] and I long to be able to accomplish something, but I sigh at the manifold difficulties." His first summer in office appears to have been sheer misery: the military in Helsingfors, using Napoleon's invasion of Russia as its feeble excuse, refused to help in any way, and the citizens of Helsingfors were unenthusiastic about the novelties being thrust upon them. (Their hesitance is understandable: persons who had to give up their property as a result of the renovation received only a new plot of land and moving costs in recompense.) In addition, the government council in Åbo moved very slowly in granting money for the improvement of Helsingfors, the town the Emperor now so clearly favored; with the Grand Army advancing on Moscow, Alexander had no time to make Åbo's local patriots behave. The bad summer ended nicely for Ehrenström; on the way to Åbo to meet Karl Johan Bernadotte (the meeting would result in the Russo-Swedish alliance against Napoleon), Alexander stopped off at Helsingfors to see how his program prospered. Ehrenström was granted a lengthy private audience, and the two men took an immediate liking to one another, having found a point of departure in their mutual hatred for Napoleon. Wisely, Alexander heaped praise on Ehrenström for the little that had already been accomplished, praise which (Ehrenström assured Aminoff) had nothing whatsoever to do with the lofty opinion Ehrenström conceived of his master. Ehrenström had at last found his replacement for Gustaf III.

Henceforth, matters went much better for Ehrenström, although he did make an attempt to resign in 1813; at this juncture, he had not yet received any salary, finding himself compelled, instead, to spend large sums of his own money on the improvement of Helsingfors. Governor-General Steinheil, formerly so timorous about the raising of Helsingfors to its new prominence, refused Ehrenström's resignation with tact and skill; eventually, in 1816, Ehrenström was given an annual salary of 6,000 rubles, retroactive to the day on which he had begun his giant task. His champion, Armfelt, had died at Tsarskoye Selo in August, 1814; but, to put the matter cruelly, Ehrenström no longer needed Armfelt's aid. Steinheil had learned to call Ehrenström "my friend," Rehbinder — permanent secretary of the Committee for Finnish Affairs — had utter faith in him, and, in the very month of Armfelt's passing, Ehrenström got a rescript from Alexander, expressing the monarch's delight with the building committee, its chairman, and the "patriotic citizens" of Helsingfors. As another self-made man, Postmaster G. W. Ladau, said a little enviously: Ehrenström was "le roi d'Helsingfors," an epithet which may have been double-edged, if one considered Ehrenström's high-handedness.

In 1817, after five years of experience in his post, Ehrenström furnished a second city plan to the Emperor, who wrote on it simply: "Approuvé, Alexandre." Ehrenström had learned on the job, and learned well. Where Kocke had been unable to free himself from the outlines of an earlier Helsingfors, Ehrenström knew no piety for the past; in the twentieth century, Eirik Hornborg chided him for his destruction of the town's old church and churchyard (which lie beneath the stones of Senate Square), thus removing the main visible link with the eighteenth century. But Ehrenström was not a sentimental man. The classical features of *his* Helsingfors were these: 1) a broad esplanade would be drawn between the South Harbor and the southern end of Gloviken, filled in; 2) a canal would be dug between the Harbor and the new edge of Gloviken — a part of Ehrenström's plan which was never realized; 3) "Skillnadstorget" (roughly, "Separation Square") would be the connecting link between the city proper and the suburbs lying to the west and the south, suburbs divided by that splendid avenue which was to be called the Boulevard; 4) "Edbom's Plantation" (later immortalized as Kajsaniemi) would be a general "promenade and park"; 5) the little "Big Square," where the ill-fated church and graveyard lay, would be expanded into a broad "heart of the city"; 6) another great square would be laid out south of the Esplanade, "Förstadstorget" ("Suburban Square," shortly rechristened as "Kaserntorget," "Barracks Square"). It would be a city of long, straight streets; those extensions of the north-south and the east-west avenues first projected by Kocke were pleasing to the sensibilities of Ehrenström, although he had a very low opinion of Kocke himself, whom he retained as a member of the building committee only with the greatest reluctance. It was Ehrenström, of course, who had the inventiveness and the authority to carry out the often difficult task of the streets' lengthening — the avenue that would be called Unionsgatan required extensive blasting, for example — and it was Ehrenström who realized that the capital should have edifices commensurate with its status and its streets. Helsingfors must be thankful to Ehrenström for his city plans of 1812 and 1817, and the energy with which he saw to their realization; it has often been remarked that a person who left the city in 1808 would scarcely have known where he was if he returned for the first time two decades later. And Helsingfors must also be thankful to him for the care with which he chose the city's architect.

During the first years of Ehrenström's regime, private building, aided by city funds, had been carried on apace. Twenty-four stone houses had been built, 9 with 3 stories, 14 with 2 stories, and one modestly on a single floor; while, restricted to the suburbs by the express wish of Ehrenström, at once aristocratic and concerned with fire-hazards, 107 wooden houses had been constructed, 28 of them with 2 stories, 79 with one. (In 1825, anxious to fill in the new blocks at the western end of Alexandersgatan and along the Esplanade, Ehrenström had to abandon his zoning restrictions on wood.) The new stone houses, as might be expected, belonged to the city's well-to-do, among whom a certain Russian infusion was apparent: the more or less "Swedish" names of Aschan, Etholén, Govinius, Heidenstrauch, Lampa (it was a Lampa who had spotted the fire in 1808) were mingled with Kiseleff, Korostileff, Uschakoff. But where was the government to be housed, when it moved to Helsingfors? Where would the Emperor reside, on his visits to Finland, which Ehrenström hoped would be frequent? Where, in short, could one find a competent architect for official edifices? The candidates at hand were a poor lot. One was "a simple artisan, who had become a non-commissioned officer" — Truls Wannberg, who served as a foreman for the reconstruction committee. Another, in Ehrenström's acid description, was "a lieutenant of the army's fleet, who had tried to make himself into an architect by studying Wijnbladh's handbook" — Ehrenström's *bête noire*, Anders Kocke. The third was "a fortifications officer, who understands how to carry things out, but who lacks taste in the art itself." The recipient of this condescension was Pehr Granstedt, a native Swede (from Karlskrona); long active in Finland and a Russian prisoner after Sveaborg's fall, Granstedt had decided to stay in Helsingfors for good and all. It was Granstedt who, in 1813, designed the city's first "neo-classical" building, the mansion of the merchant-brothers Gabriel and Nathanael Heidenstrauch on the North Esplanade — the mansion which, almost a quarter-of-a-century later, was rebuilt by Carl Ludwig Engel as an "imperial palace," a residence for the Russian rulers on tour. (After the establishment of the Republic of Finland, it became the "presidential palace".) Through the intercession of Armfelt, Granstedt's plans were sent to Saint Petersburg, there to be inspected by the dean of Russia's architects, Giacomo Quarenghi, the Italian who had created the Hermitage Theater, Alexander's palace at Pushkin, and the Smolna Institute. Quarenghi — or his associates, for the old man was nearly blind — made some necessary corrections in Granstedt's plans; but Quarenghi, to his disgust, was paid for his services "in the Finnish fashion," i.e. the Heidenstrauchs forgot to pay him at all. Unaided by Quarenghi, Granstedt designed other private residences, on Alexandersgatan and on the North Esplanade, and in 1818 was appointed city engineer; in this capacity, he carried out the planning for the city's northwest side, "Kampen," the rocky terrain north of the Boulevard and west of Henriksgatan. There, shortly, the Russian troops would have their exercise field. Honest Granstedt was not the man to design the great buildings of Ehrenström's dream; he died in 1828, his amateur's promise fulfilled by a professional.

3. The Great Rebuilding: Engel

IF THE MISFORTUNES of war had aided in creating the new Helsingfors, they also served Ehrenström by bringing him the architect he needed. Carl Ludwig Engel was born in 1778, the son of a master bricklayer in Frederick the Great's Berlin; he learned his father's trade, took examinations in surveying (Ehrenström was also a master of this skill), and, in 1804, finished his architectural studies at the Bauakademie, where Friedrich Gilly was his teacher, and Karl Friedrich Schinkel, the creator-to-be of Prussian neo-classicism, was his fellow pupil. The collapse of the outmoded Prussian army at Jena and Auerstedt may have persuaded Engel that Berlin was hardly a promising spot for an ambitious builder whose best years were slipping away. In 1808, he got the post of city-architect in Reval, the old Hanseatic city across the Gulf of Finland from Helsingfors; in Reval, Engel built little but learned much. Nils-Erik Wickberg points out that Saint Petersburg neo-classicism found some of its best imitations in Estonia; for the first time, Engel had the chance "to confront neoclassic architecture in wood, a material he would frequently employ in Finland." Tired of his poor salary and with a family to support, Engel got a year's leave of absence from his Reval post and its "complete lack of commissions," in order to reconnoiter on the other side of the Gulf of Finland. In Åbo, he immediately found jobs to do — the best-known of them being Åbo Academy's astronomical observatory. Yet Åbo quickly lost Engel, as it did so much else; by October, 1814, Ehrenström had arranged for an interview with the German. (Engel had been called to Ehrenström's attention by still another Gustavian in Russian service, Johan Fredrik Norberg, who was spending his sunset years as the designer of the naval port in Reval.) Much impressed, Ehrenström wrote to Carl Johan Walleen, a member of the Committee for Finnish Affairs: "Yesterday I met an architect from Berlin, presently employed by Mr. Lohman in Åbo, whose talents exceed my very expectation . . . Unless such a man is situated here, in Finland's new capital, there will be no end to the piling up of new architectural mistakes and stupidities." High-handed as ever, Ehrenström dismissed Engel's obligations in Åbo, and to Lohmann, as follows: "It would be a shame if so great a capacity [as Engel's] should be buried in the petty cares of putting up sugar-refineries." Realizing that he would need still more training in the erection of capital cities, Engel went to Saint Petersburg, where he studied Quarenghi's, Cameron's, and Starov's buildings, and got a commission for a country house, to be put up at Saarela Estate near Viborg. The estate-owner was the governor-general of Finland, Fabian Steinheil. In short order, Ehrenström made successful application for Engel's appointment as architect of his committee: "his taste [Ehrenström's favorite word] is refined, he is young, industrious, and by nature mild and pleasant." Engel began his work in Helsingfors in May, 1816, and one may fairly say that it ended only with his death, in May, 1840. He is supposed to have been a man of few words, words colored, in the Swedish he was forced to learn, by his strong German accent; it is lucky that he was "mild and pleasant," otherwise he could not have got along with imperious and temperamental Ehrenström. Perhaps he had no time to be anything but gentle, interested as he was only in his work, just as he had little chance (or inclination) to put his thoughts on paper.

The first dozen years of Engel's activity were spent, naturally enough, in designing structures for the administration and the military. The Senate had to be completed, so that the transfer of the government from Åbo could be accomplished as quickly as possible; the building was located on the eastern side of the main square, or Senate Square. (Officials breed officials: wings were added in 1828 and in the 1850's.) Merchant Bock's house, across Katrinegatan from Sederholm's house, was selected to serve as the residence of the governor-general; Engel rebuilt it, adding a third floor, four Ionic columns on the facade, and, as its ceremonial heart, a magnificent arched chamber. (It did not serve as the residence for long; in 1832, another and spacious building, which Engel designed [1824] to shelter the "inspector of the Finnish military," at the corner of South Esplanade and Fabiansgatan, became the governor-general's residence, and "Bock's house" was turned into the city hall.) An early structure on Senate Square was the main-watch, "le corps de garde," which stood, handsomely and briefly (from 1819 until c. 1839–40), to the north, in front of the steps leading up to the Nikolai-Church. (Both stairs and church were nonexistent, of course, when the guard-house went up.) On the arm of land which ran out from the main peninsula toward the east, Skatudden, separating North Harbor from South Harbor, Engel designed the Naval Barracks (1816–20) in Doric style; on Förstadstorget or, now, Kaserntorget, there was placed the Barracks of the Finnish Guard (1820–24). A famous and perhaps apocryphal story is connected with its location. Portly Robert Rehbinder came to Helsingfors in order to aquaint himself with the progress Ehrenström and Engel had made. After a hearty meal, he was led out to be shown the site of the city theater, for which a space had been reserved on Förstadstorget. Rehbinder, however, decided that duty required him to look first at the place set aside for the barracks. Told that the barracks was to be located in the far west, at Sandviken on the other side of the peninsula, Rehbinder refused to undertake so long a promenade, deciding instead that the barracks would have to be put in the theater's place. (A closely reasoning critic, Yrjö Hirn, has remarked that, overloaded with food and drink or not, Rehbinder did right in putting the barracks on Förstadstorget; it became an architectural ornament of the central city, while, at Sandviken, it would have been as little visible as the Naval Barracks is on Skatudden. As for the displaced theater, it landed on the Esplanade, in the very heart of town; designed by Engel during 1826–27, it was built, very draftily, in wood. Wood was the stuff, too, for the first building by Engel intended to take care of the town's religious needs; in 1826 the

"Old Church" — white, in wood, and strangely familiar to New England eyes — was erected on the burial ground west of Skillnaden, north of the Boulevard. Its contemporary was the Holy Trinity Church, of stone, on the back slope of the knoll forming the northern limits of Senate Square; this church, again by Engel, was intended for Russian Orthodox worshippers, many of whom had come to Helsingfors of late. However, the "Old Church" (a name it has got as the oldest of the city's surviving churches) was even more necessary, for it served the town's Lutheran majority; the church from 1727, Ulrika's or Ulrika Eleanora's Church, spoiling the grandeur of Senate Square, was torn down and its wood sold at auction just a century after its dedication. All the town's Lutherans had to crowd into Engel's neatly handsome but unheated building (the theater was unheated too), warming themselves by their very numbers until the grandest of all Engel's creations, the Nikolai-Church, could be completed.

The Nikolai-Church (or "Great Church," or today, rather pompously, the "Cathedral") rose triumphant on the aforesaid knoll north of Senate Square, overshadowing the little gem which lay behind it, the Orthodox Church. Its cornerstone was laid on June 25, 1830, in connection with the celebration of the Augsburg Confession's tricentennial; by 1839, aided by a Lutheran God, work had gone so well that Engel could note: "All the external scaffolding has been taken away from the dome, which stands complete, blue with white stars . . . during the next year we can think of the interior arrangements . . . the altar, the pulpit, the organ, the bells, and so forth." One fly was in the ointment: the main-watch had to be removed, both to leave the upward sweep of the great steps free and to keep divine services from being interrupted by military commands. Engel saw the necessity of its dismantling, but recalled, regretfully, that Alexander I had commanded the creation of the guard-house's rows of columns "à la Paestum." (The guard-house, much stunted, was put up anew to the east of the imperial residence: did the employment of a few of the beloved columns placate the spirit of the departed emperor?) Meanwhile, Engel sketched the broad, steep stairway which has been the undoing of so many ceremonial processions and weak hearts; even as he did, his luck turned. A flaw was detected in the walls of the auditorium; it was feared that the weight of the mighty cupola would pull the whole structure down. Bets were placed: would the dome fall toward the rising or the setting sun? A decision humiliating to the master architect was taken: four small towers were designed which, filled with stone, would hold the monster in place. Fortunately for Engel, he passed away before this protective measure could be carried out; instead, it was the work of of his successor as director of public buildings, another German, Ernst Bernhard Lohrmann. Remembered more for his terrible temper than his professional gifts, Lohrmann was also the author of those two strange side-towers, the oversized dove-cotes flanking the great stairs: one of them contains the church's bells, too heavy for the cupola, the other balances the awful presence of the first. As for the twelve apostles perched around the Nikolai-Church's roof, they are from 1843, zinc castings from Berlin, imitations of the statues by Thor-valdsen which adorn Vor Frues Kirke in Copenhagen. This final addition to the external clutter took place, it appears, at the behest of Nicholas I, the art-loving monarch who gave the church its sometime name; the em-peror also presented an altar-painting, "The Burial of Christ" by the Rus-sian-German von Neff, as a replacement of R.W. Ekman's "Christ among the Children." (Ekman at least had the advantage of being a native of Finland; his painting, which Nicholas deemed "too childish" for his splendid church, went instead to the pleasant simplicity of the "Old Church," the homeliest of Engel's public buildings.) All these unhappy events took place, as said, after Engel's death; the Nikolai-Church was employed for public ceremonies (i.e. for the university's bicentennial jubi-lee in July, 1840) even before Engel was cold in his grave, but was not consecrated until 1852. Posterity can obtain some idea of what Engel in-tended by looking at Fredrik Tengström's lithograph of Senate Square from 1838; there the noble simplicity of Engel's concept can be detected still.

The tale of the Nikolai-Church seems all the sadder because it came at the end of a brilliant career. In 1824, Engel had been appointed director-in-chief for all the public architectural activity in Finland, as a successor to Charles Bassi, the Italian whose estimable work can be admired in Åbo; Engel's own activity outside Helsingfors is extensive, but does not belong to the present story. The building committee for which Engel had per-formed so much service was dissolved in November, 1825; it should be remembered that its architect had designed not only the public buildings already mentioned, but a good number of private houses, among them Consul Sundman's mansion, overlooking the South Harbor. The decision to transfer Åbo Academy to Helsingfors, in 1827, where it could be re-born as the Imperial Alexander-University, gave Engel a whole new field of public labor; his attention was turned now to the western side of Senate Square, using it for the University's main building, directly opposite the Senate itself: the first sketches were done in 1828, and the building was finished by 1832. Going north, up Unionsgatan, he created the University Library; his first sketches were made in 1833, but (for reasons not alto-gether apparent) they did not receive imperial approval until 1836. Of Engel's three façade-designs, Nicholas chose the one Engel liked the least; in this case, the emperor's taste was good, since the Library — completed in 1844 — turned out to be one of Europe's most handsome housings for books. Next on Unionsgatan, across from Holy Trinity, there came the "military hospital," the central part of which was intended as a school for the children of Russian soldiers — the pious innocents would have only a short walk to their chapel services; later, the complex would become a part of the university clinics. The university hospital proper, Engel's "Old Clinic," lay still farther to the north, on the other side of Unionsgatan, at the corner of Elisabetsgatan; put up in 1830–32, it was quickly expanded to meet the needs of medical education and the city's ill. The University Botanical Garden, vis-à-vis the "Old Clinic," also got the advantage of Engel's versatile pen; for its orangery, Engel experimented with the "Gothic style," as can be seen from his sketches: the orangery did not survive, although Engel's classical fountain did. In the midst of his labors on the sober clinic, Engel drew another outlying university edifice which, because of its location and its size (too small for the slopes around it and the avenue at whose end it lies), has acquired an air of romantic neglect: the Observatory, facing the southern tip of Unionsgatan, on the Ulrikasborg Heights. Finally, not very long before he died, Engel designed two buildings for frivolous ends, the "Spa House" and the "Bath House" in Brunnsparken, the new and elegant spa lying on the other side of what came to be called "Observatory Hill," in the extreme south of the city's peninsula. In fact, Engel had already contributed to the social life of Helsingfors with "Society House" on the North Esplanade, designed in 1829 and finished in 1833: Helsingfors, housing Finland's government and its university, needed ballrooms and banquet halls. "Society House" was also meant to serve as a hotel; in 1829, a shocked traveler had written a complaint to *Helsingfors Tidningar*: "I took lodging at one of the town's best inns, which nonetheless left much to be desired." Encouraged to provide appropriate shelter for the city's guests, Engel was not allowed to do his best for the most illustrious visitor of all: his cherished plan for an imperial residence near the Senate was never carried out; instead, he was instructed to improve on Granstedt's beginnings. Had Nicholas, otherwise generous with funds, concluded that his own imperial presence would cast sufficent splendor on the renovated mansion? Would his predecessor, Alexander, have commissioned an original Engel creation, had he lived? Helsingfors, after all, was the child of Alexander's will, not Nicholas's.

The capital was created, then, at Alexander's behest, and by two men, an elderly official, whose past was full of disappointments, and a German architect in search of a promising place to work. Ehrenström and Engel have received just tributes from the many authors who have written on Helsingfors. Torsten Hartman said of Ehrenström: "His cultivated taste and sense of beauty put their unmistakable mark on Finland's young capital," Nils-Erik Wickberg praised Engel: "In his architecture there is always summer and a lofty sky . . . it has epic breath." Then, taking the Dioscuri together, Wickberg put them in European context: "Their Helsingfors is a final shoot on the tree which brought forth the geometric grandeur of the baroque's city-plans — Versailles, Mannheim, Karlsruhe, Saint Petersburg." (Appropriate enthusiasm can cause inappropriately mixed metaphors.) Finally, there is Johannes Salminen's aperçu: "What is the Senate Square of Engel and Ehrenström but a dream of Hellas in Nordic stone?" Something is missing in their creation, of course, an irrational quality, perhaps, or an enigma; Helsingfors does not possess that atmosphere of almost insane tension which Rilke senses in its neighbor, Saint Petersburg, nor does it have the irreality which pervades the Russian capital in Dostoyevsky's *White Nights*. There is not much mystery even in the Helsingfors cemetery, "Western Burial Grounds," which Ehrenström and Engel laid out at Lappviken, and to which the planner was borne in 1847, seven years after the architect.

4. Alexander's Last Visit and the New Nomenclature

IT WAS ONLY natural that Alexander would want to visit the city to which he had devoted so much attention and still more money: by December, 1818, Ehrenström's committee had received 1,600,000 rubles, *not* including the special sums allotted for the construction of certain public buildings. Now, Alexander wanted to see what he had got for his money. His trip to Helsingfors in September, 1819, was a kind of final inspection, a seeing to it that everything was in readiness: for, at the beginning of next month, the Senate would begin its activities in Helsingfors, despite the efforts of Åbo to postpone the move "for all time." A rush was made to finish the Senate's new home on the Square, while its archives were stored for the time being in Ehrenström's private residence. Bock's mansion, rebuilt by Engel, was externally ready to serve as Alexander's headquarters during his visit; but, on September 9, Ehrenström still had not found sufficiently imperial furnishings. Alexander, who had stopped in Gammelstaden to freshen up, arrived in Helsingfors toward midnight on the 11th; his way into the city, along the much lengthened avenue that still, for a brief time, bore the modest name of Västra Kyrkogatan, was illuminated by torches, and there was a light in every house. The emperor had entered the city formally by passing between two pillars, lit with colored lamps,

which had been set up at Långa Bron in the north; as his carriage moved
southward toward the great square, he could perhaps catch a glimpse, if he
looked straight ahead, of the wooden pillar, likewise illuminated, erected
in his honor on the Ulrikasborg Heights, at the point shortly to be occupied by Engel's observatory. (Or it may be that even an imperial eye could
not see the enormous "A I" which topped the obelisk; a contemporary report tells us that the tower, in its proudest moment, fell victim to a "wind
from the sea.") The emperor's cavalcade swung left into the square;
Ehrenström, in a rage because other carriages had been allowed to descend the "new street" ahead of the emperor's, got his feelings soothed
when Alexander, the right word always at the ready, caught sight of him
and said: "I am charmed to see you, Monsieur Ehrenström. Many remarkable things have happened here since last we met." The crowd assembled
before the governor-general's house was similarly enthralled by the words
of greeting which Alexander, aided by an interpreter, directed to them
from the balcony. The next day, after an excursion to Sveaborg and attendance at mass in the Russian cantonments outside the city, Alexander
asked — to no one's surprise — that he be taken on a tour of Helsingfors.
Then he granted Ehrenström a private audience, examining all the
sketches ("down to the last detail," Ehrenström reported) for the city's
public buildings, completed and planned. As Alexander left, he presented
Ehrenström with a golden snuffbox, on which the emperor's portrait was
surrounded by diamonds. It was Ehrenström's greatest moment as king of
Helsingfors; in October, when Governor-General Steinheil and the Senate
appeared, Ehrenström was no longer the center of the city's new life.

Opening the northern extension of Västra Kyrkogatan for the emperor's visit, Ehrenström had proposed that the avenue be called Alexandersgatan, but Alexander refused, deciding that it should be called
Unionsgatan instead, in commemoration of the union between Russia and
Finland. (A decade later, the name, "Alexandersgatan," was bestowed on
another street, the one that ran along the south side of Senate Square, in
front of the houses of Bock and Sederholm; this street, the "Main Street"
of Swedish days, had in the meantime become "Fredsgatan" ("Peace
Street"), a name subsequently passed along to the inconspicuous road
behind the Nikolai-Church. Now, given its final title in memory of the late
emperor, it became the city's main business thoroughfare, and thus Alexander's modesty came to naught — his name is immortal in the mouths of
shoppers.) However, Alexander did have one positive request on nomenclature; the new street rather unimaginatively dubbed "Stora Aveny" ("Big
Avenue") in Kronohagen — the section off to the northwest from Senate
Square, fated to become the "Faubourg Saint Germain" of Helsingfors, in
August Schauman's hyperbole — was now to be called Elisabetsgatan after

the wife with whom Alexander was somewhat less than happy. Other streets were named, it is assumed, after Alexander's second and fourth brothers, Konstantin and Michael, who got, respectively, substantial north-south avenues, the one a few blocks east of Unionsgatan, the other a few blocks west; but poor Nicholas, the third brother, received only a small by-way of two blocks, cut by Konstantinsgatan. Justice triumphed; upon Nicholas's accession to the throne, the largest street on the eastern side of Senate Square, Tavastgatan, was rebaptized Nikolaigatan, the new emperor's old street becoming Manegegatan instead, thanks to the presence of a riding-school. (The visitor to contemporary Helsingfors will look in vain for Nicholas and Konstantin; the emperor has been replaced by a Finnish cultural hero, Snellman, the grand duke by the "Sea Customs" — "Sjötullsgatan" or "Meritullinkatu". Only Michael has survived.)

According to legend, Alexander's mother, Maria Feodorovna, provided the name for the street between, and parallel to, Nicholas and Konstantin. Some little streets south of Senate Square got their names from close to home: Sofiegatan from Engel's wife, Katrinegatan from Ehrenström's (a born Sederholm, do not forget), Helenegatan from Steinheil's daughter — or do these names come from other female relatives of the Emperor? Such unimportant mysteries do not exist when one moves away from the seat of government, toward the city's young west. Around the square where the wooden Lutheran church would be erected (on ground that had been an emergency cemetery for victims of the plague in 1710, and that again, from 1790 until 1829, had served as a burial place), the names of Russian orders of merit were used, whether because of the holiness of the plot or for simple flattery. Saint George guarded the church's park on the east, Saint Anna on the west, and Saint André and Saint Vladimir stood watch on the streets to the north. (After the establishment of the Republic, André had to give way to Elias Lönnrot, the assembler of the *Kalevala*, whose statue faces the side of Engel's great wooden creation; and Vladimir was supplanted by Kaleva, the epic's *heros eponymos*. For some reason, patriotism did not consign George and Anna to oblivion.) Elsewhere, some of the fathers of the new Helsingfors got their due in intimate fashion. The western neighbor of Unionsgatan was called Fabiansgatan, after Steinheil; in the — then — most distant reaches of inhabited Helsingfors, Robert Rehbinder got "Stora Robertsgatan" and its miniature extension, "Lilla Robertsgatan," the former of which has recently been turned into a carless promenade. Almost all the giants of the foundation were presented with a street called after their first or middle name: Armfelt with Mauritzgatan in the northwestern corner of Kronohagen, Aminoff with Fredriksgatan, lying west of Annegatan, and Ehrenström with Albertsgatan, Fredrik's parallel, a street that, especially in its southern reaches, got a bad name during the gay nineties, or even before. Lately, Ehrenström has received more fitting honor with Ehrenströmsvägen, a windswept avenue which curls around the peninsula's southeastern tip, a concession to the motorization of the capital of the Republic of Finland; it is only fair that Ehrenström be feted here, since the last names of Ehrensvärd, Armfelt, Rehbinder, and Engel were used for the nomenclature in Eira, a planned development in the southwest from the early twentieth century. During his lifetime, however, Engel had been meanly dealt with; Ludvigsgatan is a street but a block long, south of Skillnaden, in a quarter neither fish nor fowl, a street as dwarflike as its neighbor, Richardsgatan, which honors Richard de la Chapelle, a member of the Senate's financial department.

Imagination seems to have run out in this and other parts of town. Ludvigsgatan runs into one of the angles of the inverted and (more or less) isosceles triangle called "Trekanten," created by the extension of Georgsgatan; its official name was "Förstadstorget," "Suburban Square" again, a title transferred to it from the square where the barracks had been erected. The street forming the base of the inverted triangle, the first southern parallel of the Boulevard, was Nylandsgatan, called after the province in which Helsingfors lies. The southern extension of Michaelsgatan (to be respelled in the course of time as Mikael) was Högbergsgatan, "High Hill Street," because it went — like so many of its brothers in the rocky terrain — over a sizable knoll; the same is true, one may guess, of Berggatan, "Hill Street," which went between the two blocks, each with its promontory, called "The Camel" and "The Elk." Berggatan had its beginning in "Regeringsgatan," "Government Street," which led into the heart of government, Senate Square. "Glogatan" reminded the city of the boggy dent in its side, Glo Bay, and showed how far the bay's waters very recently had come; the streets hopefully stretching out, at least on paper, over the inlet's filled-in expanse were called Brunnsgatan (a spring, "Globrunnen," was its central feature), Vilhelmsgatan (perhaps after Otto Vilhelm Klinckowström, another Gustavian whose very special role in Helsingfors will subsequently be described), and Hagasundsgatan, named after the "sound" ("sund"), flanked by enclosed pastures ("hage, hagar"), which had formed part of Glo Bay. In modern Helsingfors, Brunnsgatan is the most dangerous of all pedestrian crossings (it can be avoided by taking a tunnel with perils of its own), Vilhelmsgatan is but a stump of itself, and Hagasundsgatan's poetic name has given way to Central Street.

Alexandersgatan, Brunnsgatan, and (before its truncation) Vilhelmsgatan all met the major road that led to the northwest, Henriksgatan — Henry's Street East and Henry's Street West, with a strip of green in between. One would like to think that the gemination was so entitled out of patriotism and piety, after Finland's patron saint; instead, it was a tribute to the middle name of Rehbinder, whose good work in Saint Petersburg had perhaps aided Helsingfors more than any heavenly intervention by the converter of Finland's pagans. Now, as every visitor to Helsingfors knows, the green strip has wholly disappeared, and Henrik has given way to Mannerheim, whose statue rises — not unlike a mounted traffic policeman — at about the point where "Esbo tollgate" stood at the time of great rebuilding. The brazen Mannerheim gazes, if he looks to the right, at the Helsingfors bus terminal, on the site of the Russian caserne (named Åbo Barracks) that was thrown together in the 1830's — a dismal complex quite unlike Engel's two military creations, the Naval Barracks on Skatudden and the Guards' Barracks, the quarters of the "Finnish Sharpshooter Battalion of the Lifeguards." German artillery caused a fire which destroyed most of Åbo Barracks in the Civil War of 1918; bus travelers may still admire its remnants, if they wish to do so.

5. Foreigners, Russian and Academic

THE RUSSIAN SOLDIERS of Åbo Barracks gave little to Helsingfors, save that they afforded the citizens the chance to watch the brutal methods of the Czar's drillmasters; the Russian merchants, who came to Helsingfors in goodly numbers after the war, gave a great deal. Some of the more substantial ones among them belonged to families long familiar with the Finnish lay of the land; they had resided in that part of eastern Finland, "Old Finland" it was called, which had been Russian since the treaties of Nystad (1721) and Åbo (1743), and which now was "reunited," under the Russian aegis, with the Grand Duchy. The Kiseleffs, who owned the sugar refinery on Tölö Bay, are a good example, the Sinebrychoffs another. Nikolai Sinebrychoff had come to Helsingfors in 1819, from Kymmene parish in Viborg's "county," and forthwith had founded the classical brewery of the city at Sandviken. Nikolai's younger brother Paul distinguished himself by the role he played in the establishment of "Tölö's health springs," the first of those spas which helped transform Helsingfors from a provincial town into a city able to attract what the modern world calls the tourist trade. Sinebrychoff was seconded in this interest by Yegor Uschakoff, the son of still another prominent Russian merchant and entrepreneur.

If these Russians and others like them were considered not quite *comme il faut* by aristocratic circles (who found it very easy to get on with

Czarist officials and officers), Helsingfors still had every reason to be
thankful for their genial presence. When shares were sold for the establishment of the new theater in 1825, Fabian Steinheil, the governor-
general, Uschakoff senior, and Ivan Korostileff, grocer and building contractor, purchased the most — five each, followed by Ehrenström with
four. It should be noted that the theatrical passion of early Russian mercantile families, several of which became Swedicized and absorbed into the
city's permanent picture, did not abate with the passing of the years: Nikolai Kiseleff (whose mother was a Sahlstedt, a member of a Helsingfors
Swedish clan) was a moving force in the construction of the new stone
theater in the 1850's, and its director during the golden age of the late
1860's and 1870's: Swedish-language drama in Helsingfors never had a
more devoted patron. Still another Nikolai, a Sinebrychoff, the son of Paul
(who expanded the family brewery), eventually withdrew from business
altogether, devoting himself to the commodoreship of Nyland's Yacht
Club; his brother Paul nurtured the firm, married the actress Fanny
Grahn, and became a major collector of art. The generalizations on the
Helsingfors Russians to be found in the memoirs of Anders Ramsay and
August Schauman (neither author forgetful of his distinguished "Swedish"
background) are a little misleading; the Russian merchants were all, perhaps, "good-natured, simple and modest men," but the Kiseleffs and the
Sinebrychoffs were scarcely "strange to the interests of the city and the
country." The memoirists both quote, not uncondescendingly, the
schoolboy rhyme about the Russian merchants:

> Baranoff and Tabunoff,
> Duldin! Duldin!
> Uschanoff and Jablokoff,
> Koroloff and Durakoff,
> Scharin! Scharin!

Both Ramsay and Schauman, writing toward century's end, seem anxious
to show that such fellows, "long-bearded, dressed in kaftans lined with
fox-pelts," and speaking broken Swedish, were disappearing from the city;
certainly the old stronghold of the poorer ones among them (and the
Jewish ones), the "narinka" on Nikolaigatan, had been taken away, transferred into the vicinity of Åbo Barracks. A distinguished descendant of one
of the solid Russian families, Herman Koroleff, himself the author of a
memoir more generous in tone than those just mentioned, is ready to
admit that many of the smaller businessmen were alien birds indeed,
whose passing from the scene was not much lamented. Yet a distinction
must be made between those who became assimilated, "Russian in name,
Swedish in language and thought" (to quote Koroleff), and those who did
not. Nineteenth century Helsingfors owed much of its vitality to the for-

mer group, and much of its color to the latter — "good-natured, simple, and modest men." There could be worse epitaphs.

In 1827, all of a sudden, Helsingfors received still another novel element — novel, at least, to a town which hitherto had only the most rudimentary intellectual life. Once again, as so often in the city's history, disaster (in this case, not its own) was turned to profit. On September 4–5, 1827, Åbo became the victim of a fire far worse than that which had struck Helsingfors nineteen years before: about three-quarters of its houses were destroyed. The new emperor, Nicholas, seeing the chance to stifle the Swedish sympathies supposedly rampant at Åbo Academy, moved quickly. While the members of the Academy's consistory were meeting in Engel's observatory (which had escaped the holocaust) in order to consider means of repaying J.C.Frenckell, the Academy's printer, for the losses he had suffered, a mounted courier from Saint Petersburg arrived. It was October 25, 1827; four days earlier Nicholas had issued a manifesto, in accordance with which the Academy should be moved to Helsingfors, so that it might enjoy "the advantage of a closer connection with the country's government and higher authorities." In memory of Finland's "unforgettable benefactor," the institution was now to be called the "Imperial Alexander's University in Finland." The academy's professors, already stunned by the loss of homes and private libraries, were unable to greet the emperor's generosity with unmixed joy; and the burghers of the town, seeing their remaining treasure thus summarily taken away, were less happy still. A new year's ode of 1829, printed in *Åbo Underrättelser*, the town's newspaper, made no bones about it:

> Why, in care's hour, did you flee from our town,
> Oh learning's sun, which warmed and lighted all?
> Now in another place you send your proud rays down,
> Since fate itself, it seems, decreed our fall.

The poet, one Carl Johan Luthström, knew very well how rhetorical his question was; there was nothing town or gown could do to change Nicholas's decision. In September, 1828, the teachers from Åbo reassembled in Helsingfors, and at the beginning of the next month opening ceremonies were held. The omnipresent Rehbinder, as the university's *pro tempore* chancellor (a substitute for the real chancellor, the Czarevitch Alexander, who was only ten years old), spoke in Swedish, and the *pro tempore* vice-chancellor, Alexander Amatus Thesleff, a native of Viborg and commander of the Russian troops in Finland, spoke in German. The following day two new professors were installed, Johan Gabriel Linsén in eloquence (i.e. Latin literature) and Johan Jacob Tengström, who had become a Hegelian during a trip to Germany, in philosophy; both men were destined to become lights of the university in its new surroundings — an ambiguous compliment, since the performance of the professorial body during its first decades in Helsingfors was less than brilliant. Yet the troubles confronting the faculty should not be forgotten: the lack of proper living accommodations, the lack of a proper library, and, worst, the difficulty of becoming accustomed to a town which had not a shred of academic tradition. The professors vented their feelings in the often repeated pun on the new capital's name, "Svältingfors" ("Starving-fors"); and even their offspring were infected with nostalgic misery. Vilhelm Lagus, the son of a law professor, recalled that: "For a long time, the very name of Helsingfors awakened a certain horror among us children, linked as it was to the memory of the Åbo fire."

The acquisition of homes, private and academic, slowly turned the refugees into satisfied citizens of Helsingfors: Professor Lagus put up a house on the "Triangle" — a "genuine professor's house," a neighbor boy remembered — and the slope running down to Skillnaden shortly got the name, "Lagi Backe," "Lagus' Hill," a popular spot for tobogganing. Likewise, Engel's university building on Senate Square was completed; it was consecrated to its academic mission in June, 1832. Young Vilhelm Lagus (and the rest of the city's populace) enjoyed the academic processions, the cannon salutes, and the music; inside the "Solemn Hall" of the University, Professor Linsén showed, in Swedish, that he was worthy of being professor of eloquence, and Professor Soloviev spoke at length on Russia's literature and culture. Some choruses, the blame for which may be put at Linsén's door, were sung, choruses wherein Alexander's generosity and that of "his noble brother" were eulogized: "Both harvest tears of thankfulness." The products of the university, however, were more interesting than the professors; at the "promotion" (graduation) of medical doctors, Elias Lönnrot and Frans Johan Rabbe were among the recipients of degrees: Lönnrot had already begun his wilderness travels in search of ancient song, and Rabbe would play a considerable role in the history of Helsingfors. On June 21, the masters of arts were graduated, and to the eye of August Schauman's memory, they were much grander than "nowadays" — i.e., in the 1880's: "All in tight uniform dress-coats with stiff, gilded collars, knee breeches, silk stockings, and shoes with golden buckles." Among those so finely dressed was Tengström's disciple in Hegelianism, Johan Vilhelm Snellman (known for his sharp tongue and his stubbornness even then), and Fredrik Cygnaeus, the plump son of the bishop of the Lutheran congregations in Russia, and himself destined to become a cultural bishop for Helsingfors. The song to the young *magistres* was from the pen of the witty Johan Jakob Nervander, "adjunkt" (something like an associate professor) in mathematics and physics, and a versifier to boot; the events were described for the Helsingfors public and

posterity by a "docent" (assistant professor) in Latin, Johan Ludvig Runeberg, who had the reputation of possessing the most creative literary mind
among the young lions. Recently, Runeberg had married Fredrika Tengström, the niece of the archbishop of Åbo and Professor Tengström's
cousin. Needing extra income, the docent had become a newspaper editor
on the side; it was in this capacity that he told of the academic events just
described.

6. Intellectual Life: Runeberg Appears

TWO NEWSPAPERS HAD been established in Helsingfors at the close of the
previous decade — *Tidningar från Helsingfors* (*News from Helsingfors*), a
short-lived product of Frenckell's printing house, removed to the capital
with the academy; and *Helsingfors Tidningar* of the bookdealer Gustaf
Otto Wasenius, a paper which would achieve brilliance only when
Zacharias (Zachris) Topelius became its editor in 1846. There also existed
Finlands Allmänna Tidning [*Finland's General Newspaper*], but it was
the government's official organ, dry as a bone. Thus the city needed a paper able to provide something of interest for its new intellectual class; undaunted, Frenckell founded *Helsingfors Morgonblad* (*Helsingfors Morning
Paper*), with Runeberg at its helm. As might be expected, it had a strongly
literary air about it; the paper of Wasenius, as time went on, sought to
reach a larger audience. The *Morgonblad* became the mouthpiece, if that
inelegant term may be used for a paper which played so distinguished a
role in Finland's cultural history, for the "Saturday Society" or the
"Kronohagen Society," called thus after the section of the city where its
members lived. The kernel of the club was composed of old friends who
had been students together in Åbo — Runeberg, Snellman, Cygnaeus,
Nervander, the lachrymose theologian Bengt Olof Lille, the physician Lars
Isak Ahlstubbe, and the jurist Johan Jakob Nordström, the last-named so
sparkling that he almost outshone Nervander. New aquaintances from
Helsingfors were another physician, Mårten Lindfors, and someone who
may most easily be called a polyhistor, Axel Laurell. Sometimes Lönnrot
was present, and sometimes a younger man who shared Lönnrot's passion
for Finno-Ugric studies, Mathias Alexander Castrén. They talked, they argued, they read their works aloud, they criticized; Fredrika Runeberg, who
provided refreshments when the Society met at the newlyweds' lodgings,
spoke of her husband's club with admiration unusual in a housewife: "No
theme was too high or too low to be touched upon, vitality and passion

prevailed everywhere, and a genuine fireworks display of genius and wit occurred, glittering, flaming, burning." The men around the table did more than provide a pioneer display of intellectuality for Helsingfors, which had never seen the likes of the Kronohagen Society before. From its meetings there arose the idea of a formally organized Finnish Literary Society; founded in 1831, its purpose was the encouragement of literary activity in Finnish, a tongue which only a few of its initial members spoke well, and its first project was the publication of Lönnrot's initial version of the *Kalevala* (1835). This was a service to the whole nation; for the city proper, the Saturday Society provided another gift, suggested perhaps by Mårten Lindfors. It called attention to the fact that Helsingfors badly needed a private school, set up in accordance with modern pedagogical principles. The result was the Helsingfors Lyceum, which began its first term on March 15, 1831, the day before the Finnish Literary Society began its life. The director of the school was Axel Laurell; Runeberg and Nervander (and, a little later, Snellman) were on its faculty, and its first enrolled pupil was Robert Tengström, a son of the philosopher and a "filius" in whom high hopes were placed. Lindfors (or was it Nervander who conceived the idea of a lyceum?) was not quite accurate in his claim that Helsingfors had no "modern school". In 1829, Johan Henrik Avellan — a historian removed to the capital from Åbo, a man already ancient of days but young in ideas — had founded a school meant to go far beyond what the city's old "trivial school" could offer; but the "Avellan School" passed away in 1832, the same year as its inventor. The new school of Laurell combined the elementary school and the more advanced years into an organic whole; it had teachers in subjects rather than the old-fashioned class-teacher, expected to be a jack-of-all-trades; it attempted to avoid rote learning; it punished by confinement instead of thrashing. (Later reports from the Borgå Gymnasium would indicate that the great Runeberg, proud of his strong arm, did not preserve the last-named reform.) When the Helsingfors Lyceum died in 1891, its obituaries took fitting notice of the role it had played in making the capital a city of genuinely distinguished schools.

Johan Ludvig Runeberg remained in Helsingfors as long as he could. In 1833, the "adjunktur" ("associate professorship") in Greek and Roman literature at the university became vacant, as a result of the advance of Axel Gabriel Sjöström — poetaster, alcoholic, and sometime editor of the failed *Tidningar från Helsingfors* — to the professorship of Greek. The comedy of insignificance rewarded went on; of the two applicants for the "adjunktur", docents Runeberg and Gyldén, the latter was chosen — "one of the greatest mistakes . . . ever made at Finland's university," Werner Söderhjelm said. Fourteen years afterwards, Nils Abraham Gyldén became the wretched Sjöström's successor in the professorship; Runeberg had long since moved to Borgå, lured away by a lectorship in classical languages and a regular salary. At the farewell party given for him on May 8, 1837, before his departure from the capital, Runeberg said that he would always preserve a loving memory of the university where he had learned "to see life in bright colors rather than dark," a generous valedictory in consideration of what happened. The festival went on until six in the morning, and those students still able to walk accompanied Runeberg a part of his way home; they knew, if the faculty did not, that he was already Finland's most famous poet, a man to whom even haughty Sweden paid regard. The decade in Helsingfors, despite economic and scholary cares, had seen the establishment of his literary reputation: his *Dikter* (*Poems*) had come out in 1830, his epyllion in hexameters on Finnish peasant life, *Elgskyttarne* (*The Elk Hunters*), in 1832, a second and still more original collection of verse in 1833, his *Hanna* in 1836, the idyll of a country parsonage. Surely he had found the intellectual ambiance of his club stimulating, as he did the editorship of a newspaper, where he could express himself on matters of literary criticism. But it would not be correct to say that he got his deepest inspiration from Helsingfors; instead, it was his memories of country life on which he drew. Where does the new city appear in his work? He cannot have failed to be attracted by Engel's neoclassical buildings: they followed, as it were, the same stylistic spirit as his verse. Yet he was not a city man; remarkably self-sufficent, he did not need the university air in order to continue his production, and the countryside, to which Borgå was the next, best thing, provided a simplicity that not even Engel's Helsingfors possessed. Maybe the "Peasant Boy" of Runeberg's poem ("Bondgossen") speaks for his creator: the boy would perhaps find "a reward for hard work and loyality in the nearby town," but he "cannot yearn to go there." The poem was written in 1832, just prior to the university's display of bad judgment. Helsingfors lost by the error, but Finland's literature may have gained.

7. Nicholas Appears

IN 1830–31, FEELINGS in Helsingfors had been very mixed with regard to the Polish uprising. The Finnish Guards had marched off to partake in the campaign against the rebels; nine-year-old Vilhelm Lagus — he recalled the scene in his memoirs, written after his retirement from a varied academic career — had enjoyed the battalion's farewell parade and prayer on

Barracks Square, even though he and the rest of the crowd had suffered
dreadfully from the January cold. Followed by the cheers of their countrymen, the Guards did well, fighting bravely at the storm of Warsaw,
where they lost, among others, a young officer named Schybergson, a half-
brother of the tutor of the Lagus boys. The report of his bloody death (his
arm and shoulder were torn away by a cannon ball) brought the war home
to Helsingfors, as did the news that many of the guardsmen had been
felled by disease; yet surprisingly few peple reflected on the paradox of
Finlanders giving their lives for Russia against Polish insurrectionists.
Nonetheless, if the Guards, commanded by one of the ubiquitous Ramsays
(Anders Edvard, a model soldier who had won the trust of Czar Nicholas
during the Decembrist conspiracy), richly demonstrated the loyalty of
Finland to its new master, there were other Finlanders more interested in
Poland's freedom. Nils Gustaf von Schoultz, whom the British would later
hang at Fort Henry in Ontario for his part in the Upper Canadian rebellion, won his spurs on the barricades at Warsaw, defiantly shouting some
lines from Tegnér's poem on Charles XII ("Out of the way, Muscovites! /
Now we shall test / The bite of Swedish steel") at his compatriots under
the Czar's banners. And August Myhrberg — "the lofty son of Northern
snows," Topelius would call him in a poem written after the old soldier's
death (1867), a poem having exclusively to do, *nota bene*, with
Myhrberg's exploits in Attica — battled as hard for the Poles against the
Russians as he had for the Greeks against the Turks.

    In academic circles, demonstrations for the Polish cause had less
blood-and-thunder about them, but were no less dangerous, all things
considered. On the evening of December 16, 1830, some students who
had just passed their examinations celebrated the event at Menn's Inn,
near the south wing of the Senate, still the university's temporary home. A
few younger teachers, among them the poet Runeberg, the physicist, versifier and wit J.J. Nervander, and the mathematician Tulindberg were also
present, the last-named, it was thought, only in body: he appeared to have
gone to sleep on a sofa. Two weeks earlier, the Polish uprising had begun
with the attack on Grand Duke Konstantin's palace in Warsaw and his
flight; the students proposed a "skål" for the Poles, to the dismay of
Runeberg who foresaw the consequences. The young man who proposed
the toast was hushed; it was decided to let the matter die in silence. But
Tulindberg had only been playing possum; annoyed at Runeberg because
the poet had thrown a snowball at his high hat, anxious to get Nervander,
his rival for the associate professorship in mathematics, out of the way,
Tulindberg denounced his colleagues to an official at the governor-
general's office as sympathizers with the Poles. The report quickly found
its way to Czar Nicholas, who was forever ready to believe the worst of

universities; he demanded that all the participants in the affair be put into the Russian army as privates. That good spirit, Robert Rehbinder, protector of Finland's interests at the Saint Petersburg court, persuaded the Czar to let him carry out an investigation on the spot. Runeberg, questioned, explained that the dregs in the glass were called "polacken," "the Pole"; thus political offense was not intended. Rehbinder, whose native tongue was Swedish, smiled at the report but passed it along to Nicholas; by some miracle, or Rehbinder's charm, the Czar was mollified. Instead of entering the Russian army, Runeberg entered the bonds of matrimony; his marriage to Fredrika took place only a month after these stirring events. The suggestion has been made that Runeberg's poem, "The Grave at Perho," · was granted only second prize by the Swedish Academy in the competition of 1831 because Karl Johan of Sweden did not wish to offend his friend, Nicholas — Swedish neutrality must be preserved at all costs, and the armed raiders in the bloody poem were pretty plainly Cossacks. Likewise, the "toast for the Poles" may have been remembered by anxious minds in Helsingfors when the question of Runeberg's academic promotion came up; August Schauman's characterization of the age of Nicholas in Helsingfors as a "time of uncertainty and even fear" is surely correct if applied to important circles in the university and the government. Certainly it was a milieu in which such wretches as a Tulindberg could be spawned; the informer's story would be repeated in the "Tamelander case" and the "Tölö affair" of 1855. As for Tulindberg, he got his comeuppance; prematurely aged, he sat beside the refreshment stand on the Esplanade, amusing strollers with antics born of advanced alcoholism: he shared his bench with imaginary goblins.

Hardly had the episode of the toast been consumed as a fuel for gossip when another and even more serious event involving the students and the Russians took place; once again, the former paid no heed to the vulgar warning one of their professors had uttered: "a fart in Helsingfors sounds like a cannon shot in Saint Petersburg." On Russian Easter Eve, in 1831, a band of students amused themselves by harassing the celebrants and worshippers in the Church of the Holy Trinity on Unionsgatan; stones were thrown through the windows of the church, and the officiating priest, trying to remonstrate with the rioters, was told to go home and shave off his beard. The university's rector, old Gustaf Gabriel Hällström, arrived only after the damage had been done. The student body was commanded to undergo inspection "by nations" (the student clubs, comprised according to provincial background) in order that the person who had manhandled one of the church's deacons could be identified and punished. Police-sergeant Eklöf, nicknamed "The Sausage," was dead sure that the culprit was a student, although plenty of non-academic onlookers (and participants) had been at the church on the holy night. All the "nations" save the Ostrobothnians, out on an excursion when the decision was announced, had time to decide that they would refuse to obey. Hällström — who may have well been nettled at the students' failure to follow his standing advice, "Run away when you see officers of the law" — did his utmost to make the Ostrobothnians comply; he collided head on with young J.V. Snellman, hysterically stubborn, who ranted and wept: in later life, Snellman would employ similar talents in his struggle to make Finland a monolingual — i.e. Finnish-speaking — entity. Clever Docent Nervander saved face for both sides, pointing out that, having protested, it was now the duty of the Ostrobothnians to prove their innocence by participating in the line-up. Unluckily, Eklöf could not find the culprit among the students; the entire student body, concluding that it had been insulted, announced that it would not attend classes during the autumn term. Nicholas was enraged, and Rehbinder let it be known that he was unwilling to pull the academic chestnuts out of the fire again. The cholera, raging through Helsingfors during late summer, saved the students from carrying out their pledge: the university remained officially closed for reasons of health. It is impossible not to agree with Rehbinder's disgusted judgment on the Easter Riot; it was an "attentat sacrilége et barbare." In his relations with the university at Helsingfors, Nicholas proved (if it needed proving) that he was a most unenlightened despot; yet his opponents, the students, demonstrated to the full their own ability to make uncalled-for trouble (the year before they had almost provoked a riot at the new theater) and their arrogant blindness to the religious sensibilities of others. In his diary for December, 1833, Zachris Topelius noted that he had visited the Russian church and found its worshippers "crude and, in my opinion, very little pious." He was going on 16; time and Russian favors would teach him some tolerance.

Nicholas first visited Helsingfors in August, 1830, when he reviewed the Guard, conversed in Russian with some students, and elevated Governor-General Zakrevsky and his wife to "Count and Countess of Finland." Three years later, the Czar decided that it was high time for him to have another look at the city which had given him a loyal regiment and a myriad of problems. In fairness, it must be remembered that the Czar's "wise and generous concern for Finland's learned culture," as the university's consistory put it in a message of thanks, *did* deserve gratitude; Nicholas had approved all requests for funds to increase the library's holdings, and his tampering with the plans of his great architect, Engel, demonstrated not only authoritarianism but genuine interest. In June, 1833, he and his Czarina, Alexandra, arrived in Helsingfors harbor, borne by the steamboat *Ischora*; the *Ischora* had made local history on May 30, 1833, when it became almost the first steam-propeller vessel to enter Helsingfors harbor, as it brought Prince Menshikov, successor to Zakrevsky, to his new post. (A pioneer Swedish sidewheeler, the *Stockholm*, had put in at Helsingfors on its way to Saint Petersburg in August, 1824.) At 6:30 on the morning of June 10, the *Ischora*, adorned with imperial eagles, pulled up alongside the "South Quay," which had been covered with red carpets. The Czar was somewhat fat, according to the observant Topelius, and sun-burned; his helpmate was simply dressed, "like the wife of an artisan from the city," and her face had something touchingly good-natured about it. Shortly after his disembarkation the Czar addressed the students at the university, thanking them "for the good behavior shown thus far." This white lie must have placed too much of a strain on the naturally autocratic Nicholas; his good nature collapsed during a slovenly parade of the Finnish Guard, and its commander, the faithful Ramsay, got a public dressing-down. A great ball was held in the evening, and Senate Square was illuminated by 2,000 lamps — the reception accorded the late Alexander some years before was thus outdone, in illumination if not affection. The next morning the *Ischora* carried the imperial pair away again; it had the misfortune of running aground as it puffed out of the harbor, giving the "Emperor's Shallows" their name. The visit also left another permanent memento in Helsingfors: a granite shaft, "the Empress's Stone," the imperial eagle roosting on its point, was erected at the spot where Alexandra first set her foot upon Finland's soil. It was designed by Engel himself and unveiled on Nicholas's name-day, December 18, 1835. Another loyal postcript to the great visit had already been written on the Czar's name-day of 1833: Society House had its official opening with a subscription ball for 400 guests. The Czar's bust was the ballroom's central ornament, and above his plaster head one beheld his "lofty monogram and the imperial coat of arms." During the soupé, a toast to his absent majesty was proposed; it was downed amidst "prolonged hurrahs." Then a poem by Professor Linsén, whose official rhetoric seemed unescapable, was sung by the assembled company. It began:

> Hail, Nicholas, hail!
> Great, happy, and blessed,
> Hail, father of our land!

Could Nicholas have asked for truer subjects than these, the imperial visit still relatively fresh in their memories? Nicholas's June excursion to Helsingfors had been a great success, no doubt about it. Yet his own thoughts on that occasion may have gone back with some regretful fondness to the trip of August, 1830, when, without Alexandra Feodorovna in tow, he had had the chance to chat with Agrafina Zakrevskaya, the governor-general's wife, whom envious tongues called a "Cleopatra and Mag-

dalene in one person," and when he had fallen in love — if one gives cre-
dence to the romantic tale — with Aurora Stjernvall, reputedly the most
beautiful woman in Finland. The same year, Aurora went to the court in
Saint Petersburg as lady-in-waiting to the empress; loyal observers insisted
that she had got the appointment in May, before Nicholas met her.

8. The Sea

THE APPEARANCE OF Nicholas, with his spouse, was reassuring, then, to
the people of Helsingfors; the Czar was a devoted father of the land, even
as he was usually a devoted husband. However, the imperial couple's
mode of locomotion was as important for the development of Helsingfors
as were the visitors themselves; or, to put it another way, if the cargo was
precious, so was the container. Helsingfors had long been a port of some
importance; just before the separation of Finland from Sweden, it had the
fourth largest merchant fleet — after Stockholm, Gothenburg, and
Gävle — of the cities in the Swedish realm. This pre-eminence was lost, for
a variety of causes, in the years after the union with Russia: in 1826,
Helsingfors, now competing only with Finnish ports, came in third, and,
by 1852, reckoning the size of shipping by tonnage, it had gone down to
tenth. But, during the same period, the voyages made by the bearer of the
Helsingfors ensign grew ever longer and more adventurous. In 1831, a
ship from the city made it to Brazil, in the 1840's, vessels of the merchant
fleet sailed around Africa to the East Indies, and, on the eve of the Crimean War, it was generally expected that a new golden age of Helsingfors
shipping, resembling that of the last Swedish days, lay just over the hori-
zon. The prospect pleased the merchants of the city who were also the
principal ship-owners, men such as C.W. Lindeberg, the owner of the
Finland (208 tons), the largest Helsingfors ship of the 1830's, and the
Brenners, who had the *Phoenix* (257 tons), the leviathan of the 1840's.
No mistake about it: Helsingfors was a city of the sea; the forest of masts
to be detected in the background of Vilhelm Le Moine's watercolor from
1822, or in Vladimir Svertshkoff's lithograph from 1843, is not misleading. In some ways, Helsingfors was like the Norwegian coastal towns of
Alexander Kielland's novels: the sailors' huts on Skatudden resembled the
tumble-down West End of Kielland's Stavanger, the shipowners' houses,
around South Harbor, resembled the roomy establishment, containing offices and residence, of Kielland's Consul Garman. And there is a prefigu-
ration of the Kielland atmosphere, wind and waves, in the letter where

Topelius describes for his fiancée the autumn storms which rage along Finland's southern coast: "Inside the very harbor the waves are frothing white, and I had difficulty in catching my breath and keeping my feet when, at noon, I climbed up on the Ulrikasborg Heights to look at the sea. A handsome little schooner sank here, right beside the dockyard, the masts were swept overboard, the wreckage floated all around. A great many yachts and small boats have been smashed against the quays, and the waves are swirling over the Market Place itself [and around the Empress's Stone, Topelius might have added]. I am supposed to pass along greetings from Jakob Kerrman. He came in safely yesterday with Consul Sundman's ship, the *Afrika*, which he undertook to bring back from Cadiz, since the captain was ill." One can almost hear Kielland's Skipper Worse make his famous entry: "I come late, Herr Consul, but I come well!"

Beside this romantic world of sail, however, a different kind of romance arose, thanks to the *Ischora* and its younger siblings. In June, 1836, a sidewheeler, dutifully named *Menshikov* after the governor-general, slid down the ways in Åbo, and was towed over to Norrköping in Sweden, where it got a 90 horsepower steam engine. In May, 1837, its sister-ship, built in England, arrived at Åbo; it was called *Storfursten* (*The Grand Duke*), its captain was W.S. Palén, and it was put in traffic on the line Åbo-Helsingfors-Reval-Saint Petersburg: the whole tour, from home port to home port, took about two weeks. From 1839, the *Menshikov*, first used on the Åbo-Helsingfors route, doubled *Storfursten*'s itinerary, so popular had the "Russian traffic" become; and, in 1842, a British-built steamship, the *Finland*, subsequently rechristened the *Victoria*, in order to avoid confusion with Lindeberg's three-master, went into service between the capitals, Stockholm, Helsingfors, and Saint Petersburg, without stops in Åbo or Reval. The people of Helsingfors could now congratulate themselves upon their entry into the great world of international steam; the effect upon the passenger traffic to the city was astonishing. In 1836, only about 600 persons had entered or left the city by sea, in 1839, the number was 2,268, in 1850, 7,000. Little August Schauman cast an enraptured eye on the steamers, naturally enough; when *Storfursten* tied up at Helsingfors for the first time, August was Johny-on-the-spot, beholding the admirable Palén, brass megaphone in hand, on the bridge, the two English engineers in their white leather coveralls, the strange machinery, the elegant salons. Schauman's family took him along on one of the day-excursions the new ships made to Reval, and the boy's happiness was complete: he had sailed on the marvel of the age. For those who could not afford the Reval voyage, which appears to have been accompanied by obligatory sea-sickness, there were other and cheaper ways to get a taste of paradise: in 1837, a steam-sloop was purchased from Sweden, where (because of the genius of an immigrant from Shropshire, Samuel Owen) building techniques were assumed to be at an almost British level of excellence. The sloop, christened the *Lentäjä* (Finnish for "Flyer"), could carry 25 to 30 passengers, and served as the link to Sveaborg during the iceless season; the Russian military, its principal patrons, immediately dubbed it *Lentyai* or "Lazybones." The Sveaborg trade was not very profitable, however, since the people of Helsingfors were not allowed to visit the fortress, and, in consequence, knew it about as well as they did the moon; in order to make a profit, the *Lentäjä* sailed, in the mornings, from South Harbor to a distant world of delights called Brunnsparken, about which more shortly. Another possibility for getting back to Sveaborg (as tippling Russian officers well knew) was a boat driven variously by sail or oar, depending on the weather; its telltale nickname was the German-Swedish "Katern," or "Hangover." Local traffic was also served, in the 1840's by the "crank-sloops," in which the sidewheels were turned by hand. These oddities, *Kävijä* ("Visitor") and *Juoksija* ("Runner"), were likewise used on the routes to Sveaborg and Brunnsparken.

Coastal traffic by steam was the initial property, from 1839, of the *Helsingfors*, a vessel greeted with considerable local pride, since both hull and machinery were of Finnish manufacture; but its performance soon taught its passengers that patriotism had got the upper hand over wisdom. The *Union*, bought at auction for the Helsingfors fleet in 1844, after a beginning as the *Uleåborg* on the Gulf of Bothnia, turned out better in the coastal routes to the east, to Borgå, Lovisa, Fredrikshamn, and Viborg; its hull was Finnish-built, but its heart, the engine, was fortunately Swedish. If the saga of the *Helsingfors* was a disappointment, and that of the *Union* a qualified success, then another Helsingfors steamer, the *Hengist*, was a triumph: it was made by German shipwrights. The *Hengist* was bought in Bremen by the Helsingfors firm, Henrik Borgström and Company, in 1850, and was as solid as its owners — a thoroughly modern ship, its hull of iron, its engine, 60 horsepower, turning not sidewheels but stern propellers. Contrary to initial plans, which called for a route between Saint Petersburg and sub-arctic Torneå, at the top of the Gulf of Bothnia, the *Hengist* was assigned to a line of far greater cultural importance, the route from Helsingfors to Lübeck and the continent. Transferred in 1852 to the Finnish-Lübeck Company, the *Hengist* flew the merchant flag of the Holstein city from then on; but it struck a blow against the most stubborn foe of Finland's capital and its shipping: the winter that closed the harbor from November until April or May, cutting Helsingfors off from the western world. At the end of November, 1852, the *Hengist* plowed its way into the harbor through ice already seven inches thick, simultaneously opening the way for two brigantines; it bore the crews of three other ships crushed by ice. Nor was this performance enough; having unloaded, the powerful *Hengist* made its way through the ice once again, bound for its new home-port on the Trave. The winter isolation of Helsingfors, and Finland, was not permanently broken, however, until 1877, when a more or less regular winter traffic was established between Hangö, a new town southwest of Helsingfors with a harbor frozen only a relatively short time, and Stockholm. By 1890, after having hired the Danish icebreaker *Bryderen* on an experimental basis, the Finnish government acquired an icebreaker of its own, the *Murtaja* — a "Breaker" like the Dane.

9. The Parks

IN ONE OF his *Lastuja* (*Shavings*) — those sketches, short stories, and prose poems which perhaps offer the best of his work — Juhani Aho wrote that there is no beating the Finnish climate: "Springtime cold first and then autumn frost — meanwhile many of our fondest hopes have frozen, and our boldest dreams have perished." Yet in the last years of the 1830's and throughout the 1840's Helsingfors became a summer city, and beheld a realization of the boldest of dreams. During the city's rebuilding, after Alexander I had decided to make it the worthy capital of his newly acquired Grand Duchy of Finland, a young man from Lovisa, Henrik Borgström, had set up "a wholesale and retail business in manufactured and colonial wares"; he was a relative of the Erik Borgström who had represented Helsingfors at the Diet of Borgå in 1809, when Alexander generously and ambiguously proclaimed his intention "to guide this estimable people [the Finns] according to its laws and the order of eternal justice." Borgström the younger was an immediate success as a businessman; in 1834 he founded the tobacco factory which, with its 57 employees, was one of the city's leading concerns, and the largest undertaking of its kind in Finland. But the admirable Borgström was not only interested in making money; he also cared about his adopted city's welfare. In the very year of his factory's establishment, he persuaded a group of prominent citizens to form a company for the creation of a spa in the southern reaches of the peninsula on which the city lay, "a region quite unknown to the inhabitants of the town in general." Czar Nicholas himself graciously took thirty shares (at 100 rubles a share), and so there was no difficulty in selling the others. The apothecary Conrad Appelgren essayed the laying-out of the avenues and paths of what would be called Brunnsparken; the "Bath-House" and the Spa were designed by the great Engel, and, thanks to the financial boldness of Borgström, Appelgren, a merchant prince named Etholén, and Etholén's rival, Consul Sundman, the two buildings were ready to be opened on June 5, 1838.

A rich collection of medical waters had also been provided, the work of Pehr Adolf von Bonsdorff, who held the university's chair of chemistry, and Victor Hartwall, a former student of Sweden's Berzelius. The two had started the production of mineral waters in 1831, during the cholera epidemic, and thus were ready and willing to provide the necessary ingredients for Brunnsparken's "Carlsbad apparatus." Stouthearted guests even could bathe in the open sea from an island lying off the park, an island to which they were taken by boat; this arrangement proved inconvenient, and, in 1839, a regular bathing-beach was set up on the mainland. (Since the 1820's daring swimmers had breasted these southern waters of Helsingfors, inspired by academic example: Nils Abraham af Ursin of the medical faculty, followed lemming-like by his students, was wont to cast himself into the waves from a promontory known even today as "Ursin's Cliff.") The pleasantly shaded walks in the park itself, the twenty-five different kind of baths (salt-water baths, mineral baths, sulphur baths), the assortment of waters for internal consumption, the view over the sea, and the chance, on rare warm days, of risking one's life in it — all these charms had an immediate appeal; the park's direction had taken its motto from the *General Rules for the Use of Mineral Waters*, distributed to all patrons: "The soul's diet is as important as the body's." The affluent citizens of Helsingfors learned that they could reach the paradise either by water on the *Lentäjä*, or by land — a new road had been laid out which led from South Harbor to the park's gate. "Distant Brunnsparken" had the additional charm of seeming far away to people who lived in Kronohagen, where the government buildings were; indeed, at the end of the century, one still talked of moving to "far-off Brunnsparken" — the modern suburban dweller has an entirely different sense of distance from that of his ancestors.

The new spa, however, was meant to appeal not only to the cream of Helsingfors, but to those members of the Russian aristocracy, both genuine Slav and from the Baltic lands, who could not go to "foreign" resorts because of the edicts of Nicholas. Helsingfors was easy to visit now, by steamboat from Saint Petersburg or Reval, and had the added advantage (even aristocratic housewives like to find bargains) of offering certain goods, because of customs regulations, at a lower price than the Russian ones. Borgström's venture was bound to succeed: Brunnsparken was a going concern even before the decision had been taken to build "Brunnshuset," "The Spa House," the park's main edifice. In the summer of 1836, the following description of a city transformed appeared in

Helsingfors Morgonblad, the young newspaper edited by the poet Runeberg: "During the last several weeks Helsingfors has not been as empty
and desolate as it usually is in the summertime. During promenades one
hears not only Finnish, Russian, and our own Finno-Swedish, so displeas-
ing to native Swedish ears, but also, not infrequently, the mellifluous
Stockholm dialect, and even this 'Spanish of the North' is eclipsed by
genuine Spanish and sweet-sounding Italian. Helsingfors has never before
been visited by so many foreigners as this summer, and I do not exagger-
ate if I say that we get them by the ship-load. The steamer *Alexander
Nikolaievitch* brought over no less than fifty-some Estonian and Livlan-
dian noblemen from Reval, come here to have a look at our fair capital."
The foreign visitors found the people — those with whom they came into
contact — to their liking; the Russian Bulgarin wrote: "Life in Helsingfors
is pleasant, since the upper classes are communicative and hospitable."

The delights of Brunnsparken were often described during its golden
age, which lasted until the eve of the Crimean War. In January, 1843,
Zachris Topelius, now the gifted editor of *Helsingfors Tidningar*, had begun his long series of *causeries*, the *Letters to Lieutnant Leopold in Grusia*:
Leopold was a fiction, an officer serving (like so many real sons of Finland)
with the Russian army in the Caucasus, and Topelius kept him abreast of
conditions in the homeland. By 1849, Leopold, risen to major, was informed that "the traffic of foreigners, drinking, eating, and amusing themselves, is greater than ever before. Princes, princesses, generals, [and]
millionaires . . . are nothing out of the ordinary here." Three years earlier,
Leopold, then a captain, had learned that moneyed folk were drawn to
Brunnsparken even from Irkutsk in Siberia; imported virtuosi played for
the guests as they made merry ("such exertions [at the table] can have an
effect on even the sturdiest nature"), and "they live only for the hour; the
happiness of champagne knows no tomorrow." There was, in fact, no
Finnish tomorrow for this high society; the cholera epidemic of 1853
frightened it, and the outbreak of war kept it at home. As heir to the
throne, Alexander (II) had been an honored guest at Brunnsparken in
May, 1842, when Governor-General Thesleff arranged a "soirée dansante"
for him, with two military bands outside Brunnshuset and an orchestra inside; but as Czar, the liberal Alexander allowed Russians to go abroad, as
Nicholas had in the last years of his reign, and thus Brunnsparken's days of
glory ended.

Not all the guests at the party had decided to leave: the land east of the
park became a favorite site for the erection of splendid villas. Princess
Zeneida Yusupova, unusually wealthy even for a visiting Russian, commissioned a mansion from Anders Fredrik Granstedt, a son of the Per
Granstedt who botched Heidenstrauch's mansion a few decades before.

Zeneida called her home "Rauhaniemi," "Peace Point"; Finnish house-names were fashionable just then, but did not customarily bear witness to any larger knowledge of the language on the owner's part. Rauhaniemi looked out across the bay to Långören, the island in the Sveaborg fortress-complex where prisoners were kept. Thereby hangs a tale of old Helsing-fors: Zeneida's lover (or her husband, in more moral versions) was con-fined on Långören, but his jailers were lenient: gossipy Augusta Krook tells how Zeneida was always seen dancing with the same young man, his hair shorn convict-fashion, at the city's balls. An extravagant version says that Zeneida had a tunnel dug underneath the waves, so that she could indulge her passions at will, a tale no more credible than the rumor which put the late Alexander I, Finland's darling, on Långören as a prisoner after his mysterious demise at Taganrog. Coming to the home of Zeneida's neighbor, one treads on firmer ground; it was what the Russian professor, Jakob Grot, described as "Rabbe's handsome stone house, put up in a Gothic style." "Kalliolinna," "Stonecliff Castle," was the creation of Dr. Frans Johan Rabbe, the director of Brunnsparken. Rabbe, who was a wit, called his house "my boyhood's final prank"; in fact, it was the scene of highly serious activities. Rabbe was an active member of the Finnish Liter-ary Society; whenever they were not in Karelia or farther afield, the Finno-Ugrists Lönnrot and Castrén were welcome guests at Kalliolinna, from the high tower of which — as Grot added — "one gets a wonderful view of the city." Rabbe could see other things from his castle, too; according to Anders Ramsay's *chronique scandaleuse*, the doctor had a hard time keep-ing Princess Yusupova from resuming the naughty habits (including the recruitment of "living statues," very lightly clad, for her garden parties) she had practised once upon a time in Saint Petersburg's more tolerant world. Russian wealth and Russian mores vanished; but eastern Brunnsparken remained a delightful and exclusive place to live. It was here, for example, that the veteran orator and esthete, Fredrik Cygnaeus, decided to settle down in the 1870's, calling his villa "Fredrikshamn" ("Fredrik's Harbor," after himself and the little coastal town east of Helsingfors), and describing it as "a hut on a windswept cliff beside the Gulf of Finland" — perhaps the only occasion in Cygnaeus' long rhetori-cal career when he employed litotes. (Today the villa houses the "Cygnaeus Gallery," a collection of paintings and bric-à-brac from the Golden Age of Helsingfors.)

As for Brunnsparken itself, its charm survived the end of its days as a spa. Of its two great buildings, the one, the "Bath-House," became in time a sanctuary for budding authors and painters: Helene Schjerfbeck and Maria Wiik had a virginal studio here in the 1800's before they became the best-known of Finland's lady-painters, and the ferocious T.K. Sallinen used an atelier in the building for artistic and erotic purposes some twenty years later. The bath-house was destroyed by a Russian air-raid in 1944; as for "Brunnshuset," it still stands, a restaurant and night club. Of the men associated with the founding of Brunnsparken, Henrik Borgström continued to play a role as a Maecenas, and a creator of green spots in the city. After 1848, he was the leading spirit in the establishment of Djurgården, a watering place and park north of Tölö Bay. The watering place came to nothing; the park remains the city's largest. Upon Borgström's death in 1883, a bust of the generous man, by Walter Runeberg, the poet's son, was put up in this second park of his, which, despite its name ("Animal Park"), still has no beasts on display, but rather a profusion of hearty strollers. Bonsdorff, the concocter of the mineral waters on which Brunnsparken's initial popularity was built, had a less happy fate: he died before Brunnsparken was fairly underway. In his report on Brunnsparken from 1839, Grot laments that the formula of Bondorff's waters had perished with the man himself: "Everyone admonished him not to conceal so precious a piece of information, but he replied . . . that perhaps he would write something about it in good time. Now Bonsdorff is dead, and his secret has been lost to humanity." Grot had forgotten the sorcerer's assistant, who shared the secret. The practical-minded Hartwall brewed mineral waters of even greater potency; the consumer was warned to let the carbonization evaporate a little before drinking, in order to avoid "Eingenommenheit des Kopfes," a condition so terrible that Hartwall could describe it only in German. Grown wealthy, Hartwall passed away in 1857; his factory took up the production of simpler beverages, such as lemonade, and it was not long until Hartwall's kiosk became a source of refreshment for thirsty folk on the Esplanade in the city's center. Today Bonsdorff is remembered only in the annals of science; the bottles of Hartwall are everywhere in Finland. (However, there would be a plethora of other Bonsdorffs, physicians, academicians, soldiers, to keep the family's name at the fore.)

Analytical for once, Ramsay says that "if the 1840's were the great age of Brunnsparken, they were likewise the great age of Kajsaniemi," and "if Brunnsparken was the gathering place of an international and aristocratic society, then Kajsaniemi played the same role for the 'national intelligensia'." The land which was to be christened Kajsaniemi comprised a grassy arm pushing out into Tölö Bay north of the center of town. It had long been a grazing ground for the cattle of Helsingfors; a map of 1775 calls it, appropriately, "Old Town Pasture." Then the Masons laid out a garden on the site, for out-of-door meetings, and planned to put up an orphanage nearby; an air of enlightened endeavor begins to hang over the meadows. A monument to these praiseworthy Masonic deeds (the lodge-brothers sold their garden's products for the support of poor children) is still to be seen in the park: the tombstone of Major Fredrik Granatenhjelm, who was buried here in 1784, after leaving his wealth to the needy; the inscription, which does not give Granatenhjelm's name, suits a man who put action higher than words. "Just as the world knows who rests here / So God knows what he has done / And Wretches bless his memory." The little wretches of the proposed children's home never got its shelter, since it was never built; instead, placed in private families, they received their keep from the funds Granatenhjelm and the garden had so generously provided. During the great rebuilding of Helsingfors, the city-planner Ehrenström conceived a plan for the transformation of the land into a "General Promenade" or "Society Garden," and Engel, devoted as ever to simple beauty, continued what Ehrenström had begun: in 1829, the part of the land lying nearest to Unionsgatan became the university's Botanical Gardens, designed by Engel, the rest became a "promenade," as Ehrenström had hoped. (The Masons, by the way, had left the scene in 1822, their society forbidden by imperial edict; all that remained of them was Granatenhjelm's grave and a long stone block, supposed to have been used as a table during their meetings.)

Now a new genius enters: not a Mason or an architect, but a cook from Kristinehamn in Värmland, Catharina Christina Wahllund. (Or Walund or Wahlund: she was not sure; her friends called her Cajsa). Like so many Swedes of higher birth than hers, she decided that a fortune was to be made in Alexander's El Dorado; she went east to Finland in 1810. In Åbo, she quickly got a reputation as a gifted restauratrice, and was given the management of the New Society House which was the ill-fated capital's pride and joy — she was about 40 years old when she received this signal honor. She did not allow loyalty to the city on the Aura to get in the way of Finland's progress or hers; she followed the Senate to Helsingfors, when the government was transferred thither from Åbo, and became the owner of a little hotel off Senate Square. Robert Rehbinder, visiting from Saint Petersburg, was a contented guest, as were old Carl Erik Mannerheim (the general's great-grandfather) and Otto Vilhelm Klinckowström, the last-named a recently arrived Swede, like Cajsa herself, albeit of bluer blood and lower character. In 1837, using her connections, Cajsa was given permission to establish an inn at the tip of the land which had such mixed memories, of cattle, Masons, and orphans; her establishment, enclosed by verandas, and with water on three sides, became the legendary "Kajsaniemi värdshus," the "inn at Cajsa's point," known for its splendid food, its abundance of drink, and the endless conversations held within its walls, or, weather sometimes permitting, on its porches. Unlike Brunnsparken, it was a year-round undertaking; unlike Brunnshuset, it had a cozy and congenial atmosphere, its tone set by Cajsa's own generous self. Jakob Grot, the Russian professor, was quick to notice the change that came over Brunnshuset when Cajsa, who had briefly been in charge of its buffet, was replaced by a professional hotelier from Germany: "He's put everything into the best possible order, it's all handsome and splendid; but how can we help missing the simplicity we once knew, and your patriarchal [sic] hospitality, you splendid old woman?" She had the pleasant habit of being delighted at her guests' enjoyment of her food and drink; she extended credit in an almost reckless way; on her nameday (November 25) she treated her regular customers, who were legion, at her own expense. These customers, the students in particular, rewarded her well: they renamed the whole of the park after her, "Kajsaniemi," a homely mixture of Swedish nickname and Finnish topographical designation; and on her reputed birthday, May 1 (the day on which, for the rest, Scandinavian university students hopefully celebrate springtime's coming), her admirers assembled to serenade her. It was the beginning of a tradition; the Swedish-language chorus of the university, "Akademiska sångföreningen," opened the May in Kajsaniemi each year. The power and the glory lasted only a brief time for Cajsa; she died in July, 1843, at the estimated age of 72.

The business was continued, in Cajsa's spirit, by her adoptive daughter, Emilie Myhrman, except for a two-year closing during the Crimean War. This hiatus in the life of Cajsa's inn occasioned a long-winded valedictory by the fledgling journalist August Schauman, in which he catalogued the charms he thought were past: "It is strange how an inn — a real inn — can acquire not only so much trust, but also such genuine devotion and love among all classes, men and women, matrons and girls, fathers and sons — and acquire it from such a dour people as the Finns." (Schauman was writing at a juncture when it was still possible, barely possible, to say "Finn" and mean "citizen of Finland" without reference to language.) Concluding, Schauman decided that a certain "aura of innocence" lay over the whole Kajsaniemi experience, and he was right: it was the innocence of a would-be nation's cultural youth. When Mamsell Myhrman died, a decade-and-a-half after Schauman's premature lament, times had become very different. Because of the new railroad, whose embankment came down the western side of Kajsaniemi, toward Karl Edelfelt's "Gothic" station (built on land created by filling in Glo Bay, the shallow lower extension of Tölö Bay), the view from the restaurant's verandas was impaired, and its peace was destroyed; and, because of the new railroad, the population of Helsingfors was growing by leaps and bounds. The city's idyllic age was over. Students who, twenty or thirty years before, had toasted the beauties of the Finnish tongue in Cajsa's inn, all the while speaking Swedish, were now divided into two camps. From the 1870's on, the Finnish speakers (and singers) repaired to "Alphyddan" in Djurgården (that is, to "Alppila" in Eläintarha) for their First of May celebration, while the Swedes stayed true to Kajsaniemi. (Later still, the Finns assembled in Brunnsparken's — Kaivopuisto's — elegant confines.) Not that Kajsaniemi lost all its charm or its patrons immediately after the railroad's coming; the swans still swam happily in their pool, a left-over from Glo Bay, at the park's southern boundary, and, even in the 1880's Zachris Topelius, unforgetful of the dear, dead days beyond recall, remained devoted to the inn and its surroundings. Whenever the old man came into Helsingfors from his home at Björkudden, he put up at Vilhelmsbad Hotel, on the edge of the park, a short stroll from the inn itself. But what would Topelius say about Kajsaniemi as it is today, grimy, its trees nearly gone, the swans long since disappeared? There lies some sort of injustice in the fact that aristocratic Brunnsparken, even now, lets one sense what it was before; Kajsaniemi does not.

One last park from the days of the idyll must be adduced: Hesperia, on the western side of Tölö Bay, across from Kajsaniemi. Hesperia was of different stuff from her sisters — the park owned a rowdy popularity growing out of the kind of entertainment it offered: fireworks, acrobats, tightrope walkers, and a carousel belonging to Monsieur Platanoff: "moved by human power, with Platanoff enthroned in its center, it went round and round to the tune of the Tölö Polka. And there was also . . . a giant ferris wheel, painted green, sky-high." The park had a restaurant, too, "Tölö Inn," where Russian officers and raffish folk from the town gambled and drank — Hesperia was not far from the great Russian cantonment on Västra Henriksgatan. The most dramatic event in the park's entertainment history is the great fire of September, 1847. Jean Baptiste Magento, the fireworks expert, was preparing a display of Roman candles in a room at the inn when his materials suddenly became ignited; he ran out into the safety of the park, but, thinking his wife was still inside, dashed back into the building again. Standing in the middle of the flames, he caught sight of her on the lawn; he escaped a second time, plunging into the waters of the bay, and died of burns four days later. The inn, however, was quickly rebuilt, and became the scene for another tale of devotion: a Russian officer's servant, interrogated by the police about the games his notorious master played in the inn, repeated the word "fortepiano" again and again. Such tragedies and puzzles confronted the keepers of law and order who were summoned to Hesperia, and they were summoned often.

Hesperia provides a puzzle, too, for the historian of Helsingfors: what prompted Carl Johan Walleen, the "procurator" of the Senate and a man of exquisite taste, to choose the strand-property immediately south of turbulent Hesperia as the site for his "representative villa"? The mansion, designed by E.B. Lohrmann, was one of the architect's most felicitous imitations of Engel's style; called Hagasund, it housed not only Walleen but his extensive library and his several objets d'art. As far as we know, the proximity of Hesperia did not bother Walleen, who spent his summers in the country; but he cannot have ignored the reminder of new and more vulgar times which the railroad provided, here as at Kajsaniemi: it passed uncomfortably close to the lawns of Hagasund. Walleen had to suffer the iron horse as his neighbor until his death in 1867; in 1902, Hagasund came into the ownership of the city of Helsingfors, as stipulated in the will of Walleen's favorite and most beautiful stepdaughter, Aurora Stjernvall-Demidov-Karamzin, and in 1912 was fitted out as the city's museum, freight and passenger yards easily visible, and audible, from its rear windows.

10. High Society

NEAR THE END of his residence in Helsingfors, in 1850, Grot wrote to his friend Pletnyov: "When one observes social life here, one cannot avoid remarking how much luxury has increased during the [past] ten years . . . Of that simplicity in manners and mores you once found here [Pletnyov had visited Helsingfors a decade before], not a trace remains." Now, Grot could well have added that it was the example of his own fellow-countrymen at Brunnsparken which had led Helsingfors society down the primrose path — a path it took, however, most willingly. The saga of the beautiful stepdaughters of Carl Johan Walleen is a case in point. Their actual father had been a field officer in the Swedish army and, for the Russians, an energetic governor of Viborg province; their uncle was the Stjernvall who had been Ehrenström's predecessor in the rebuilding of Helsingfors. Father and uncle died in the same year, 1815, apparently of overwork for Finland's sake; the widow of Governor Stjernvall married Walleen, whose talents were social rather than administrative. The girls, growing up, sought broader horizons than those of simple Finland. Emilie was so fair that Lermontov courted her, writing a poem in praise of her beauty; she married a Russian nobleman, the owner of vast estates, and died in Russia, still young. Unfortunate Aline lost her teeth in a sleighing accident, and so could not compete on the Russian market; she had to content herself with a middle-aged Portugese count, resident in Denmark, a prize that, in the long run, made her very happy. The loveliest of the

three, though, was Aurora, who crept out from underneath the over-
turned sleigh with her already legendary beauty unmarred; the head injuries she suffered were easily concealed.

The tale of the Czar's passion for Aurora, when he was so briefly a
grass widower in Helsingfors, has already been told; whatever the truth of
the episode is (and the argument that Nicholas was generally a model of
marital fidelity can also be used to underscore the magic of Aurora's
charms), her sojourn at the Saint Petersburg court culminated in her engagement to a dreamy nobleman, Alexander Muhanov; he died even as
the wedding party awaited him in Finland. Having reached the desperate
age of 26, Aurora decided that she must console herself with Pavel Nikolaievitch Demidov, reputedly "the richest man in all the Russias," and as
eccentric as he was wealthy: he had the strange habit of washing his hands
every time he touched metal. (Aurora could have chosen honest Carl
Gustaf Mannerheim, the entomologist, in Demidov's stead; but Carl
Gustaf was too Swedish and too wooden for her tastes.) The wedding
took place in Helsingfors: it was a double ceremony, with the Lutheran
portion in Engel's wooden church, the Orthodox in the chapel of Åbo
Barracks; the bridegroom, who was ill, had to be carried through both
performances. Kind observers expressed the hope that Demidov was not
beset by his usual complaint, kidney stones. The couple had one child,
Pavel junior or Paul; Aurora's sister-in-law remarked that the boy's birth
"must be regarded almost as a miracle." In 1840, Pavel the elder passed
away; the serenity of the union had frequently been shaken by his insane
jealousy of Aurora, which led him, with oriental zeal, to post eunuchs at
her bedroom door.

Aurora returned to Helsingfors from Russia, the wealthiest of widows;
it can be a measure of her resources that her little son was provided with a
personal physician, Sten Eduard Sjöman, who, for his services, received
6,000 rubles a year, a furnished apartment, a staff of servants, and free
laundry. The "season" of 1841–42 in Helsingfors is reputed to have been
the most brilliant the town had ever seen, or would see, in large part as a
result of Aurora's presence. As usual, men cast themselves at her feet. One
of her victims was Xavier Marmier, a French travel writer preparing a book
on Finland, who is said to have been a "Nordic god" in appearance and
deportment. Another admirer was the son of Gustaf Mauritz Armfelt, Alexander; as the director of Finland's bank, he had been a leading figure in
Helsingfors during the later 1820's and early 1830's, and now was on the
verge of replacing Robert Rehbinder (who died in the spring of 1841) as
Finland's chief protector and spokesman at the court in Saint Petersburg.
Recently widowed himself, Alexander Armfelt would surely have been a
good catch for Aurora, and she for him (what a constellation of beauty,

wealth, cleverness, and political power!); but Aurora decided to marry a Russian once again. This time the lucky man was younger than she, by five years, André Karamzin, a son of the great historian and heir to none of his father's qualities: a professional soldier, André had the reputation of being lazy in everything save love, with at least three illegitimate children to his credit. How could he resist Aurora, with her still dazzling looks, her incredible wealth, and her inclination to coddle him? (She was obsessed with fears about his health, a neurosis resulting from her experiences with Muhanov and Demidov.) The couple set out on an extended honeymoon, which took them to Paris; there André became a member of the Jockey Club, the organization that later gained musical immortality by organizing the riot at *Tannhäuser*'s French premiere. The February Revolution of 1848 sent the Karamzins back to the peace, or somnolence, of Finland; staying at Villa Hagasund in the winter of 1851–52, André repented his sins and underwent a religious awakening — in the nick of time. The magnificent if tiring life of moves between Saint Petersburg, Helsingfors, and Träskända, the estate Aurora had purchased from her stepfather, was interrupted by the outbreak of the Crimean War. André hastened to the colors, and, in the spring of 1854 endured a fate prefiguring General Custer's; ignoring the advice of more experienced subordinate officers, he attacked a Turkish force much larger than his own. He fell, and 129 of his men with him; the Turks mutilated the slain, and the corpse which was returned to Saint Petersburg could scarcely be recognized.

This hideous event, coupled with the precocious erotomania of her son Paul, convinced Aurora that she had best devote her fortune to charity, and her life to prayer. In 1867, she established the Deaconess Institute, a hospital on Christian principles, one of the first of her many good deeds for the poor, the infirm, and the sick of Helsingfors. The vestibule of Hagasund was crowded each day with suppliants, never turned away empty-handed, and the mansion became popularly known as Karamzin's villa. Yet what was it that Helsingfors remembered best about Aurora? The unabating charity she practised during her long old age (she died in 1902), the loveliness that turned the head of a Czar, or her altogether un-Finnish riches? In a story of Runar Schildt from 1919, an old man, a poor upholsterer, remembers what his late wife's nickname had been in her days of youth: "Her friends called her 'the Karamzin horse,' because once upon a time there had been a woman here in the city whose name was Karamzin, and she had the handsomest and the fastest horses in all the world."

If Aurora Karamzin was the fair goddess of Helsingfors, investing even her animals with beauty after she had lost it, then Otto Vilhelm Klinckowström was its devil, a spirit eternally negative, albeit so scatterbrained that he emerges only as a second-rate Mephisto. (Judging by the evidence

of letters and behavior, neither Aurora nor Otto Vilhelm was exceedingly
bright; but it does not take intelligence to become a legend in one's own
time.) Ehrenström has often been called "the last Gustavian," and the ap-
pellation is intended to imply that he represented the grace, elegance, and
rationalism of Gustaf III; Klinckowström, born in Sweden in 1778, had
the Gustavian qualities too, but in him they were perverted. He was a wit,
but he used his cutting tongue (unlike, say, his opponent, Lars Gabriel
von Haartman) to exclusively destructive ends; he was a patron of the arts,
but his taste inevitably went awry; he enjoyed life, but destroyed others in
the process of his enjoyment. His advancement in the Swedish army had
been rapid; his fine figure made him the pride of the royal household's
dragoons and, with his quick retorts added, the favorite of highly placed
ladies; at 21 he became the chamberlain of Fredrika, the bride of the unhappy Gustaf IV Adolf, at 22 he was chevalier to Charlotta, the jolly
Duchess of Södermanland. However, his charm soon got him into trouble: a young woman of good family, seduced by him after the usual promises of matrimony, threw herself over the parapet of Stockholm's Norrbro
just as a detachment of the Horse Guards was cantering past, Klinckowström in command. Wit did not help him this time, and the officer had to
leave Sweden for friendlier climes; friendly they were: in Naples he met
Lady Sara Brooke, whose husband was off at the Peninsula Wars with
Wellesley. Lady Sara found Otto Wilhelm irresistible, so much, indeed,
that their son could be legitimized only three years after his birth, by his
parents' marriage in Stockholm.

In 1816, Klinckowström moved to Finland, a nice refuge for Swedish
noblemen not altogether successful in the homeland; he quickly got himself appointed — thanks again to repartee — as chamberlain at the court in
Saint Petersburg. His term as provincial governor in Viborg was darkened
(or brightened, depending on the point of view) by his divorce from Lady
Sara, who had come to detest him, as he did her: she had a violent temper,
which her residence in the Finnish backlands can scarcely have improved,
and he could not leave the servant girls alone. (Yet Sara never remarried;
remaining in Finland, the vain and puffy beauty died of a burst blood vessel, incurred while being laced into a corset for an amateur theatrical performance.) Freed of his better half and appointed a member of the Senate,
Klinckowström settled down in Helsingfors; his fortunes improved still
more when his great and good friend from Saint Petersburg days, Prince
Menshikov, was appointed governor-general of Finland in 1833, a post
the prince held mostly in absentia until 1855. That Klinckowström was
charged with such tasks as the furnishing of the Heidenstrauch mansion in
its new capacity as imperial residence, and with the design of uniforms for
the Grand Duchy's officials, came as no surprise; he had a professional in-

terest in expensive trappings. However, even the patient Finlanders were amazed when he was appointed general of engineers in 1841, in command of Finland's land and water communications; it is a credit to the sound financial planning of Lars Gabriel von Haartman and the technical skills of the Baltic-German, Carl von Rosenkampff, that the Saima Canal, the project to connect the interior of eastern Finland with the sea, could be begun (1846) during Klinckowström's term in office. Some thanks must be given, too, to Klinckowström's other pursuits, which frequently kept him from his desk; in the 1830's, for example, we know that he preferred to spend as much time as possible with "La Belle," a modiste whom he had set up in business. In subsequent years, he became distracted by compulsory domestic bliss; at the age of 62, he was forced to marry one Elisabeth Krause, reader in German to the Czar's sister, Helena Pavlovna. The punishment seems crueler than the one legend has visited upon him. The story goes that he dared not to be alone when the clock struck midnight, else he would see that unhappy maid of Stockholm as she cast herself into the icy waters, and would hear her cry "Farewell, Klinckowström!"

During his days of power Klinckowström opposed the Finnish currency reform which won a sobriquet, "Silver Lasse," for its inventor, von Haartman. Also, a native Swede, Klinckowström openly despised the innocent beginnings of Finnish national-cultural enthusiasm; but he was too unsystematic, too frivolous, to do any lasting damage. Klinckowström's main concern, Anders Ramsay concluded (and the naughty memoirist could well interpret Klinckowström's nature, to which he had a certain affinity), was to maintain himself in imperial favor, "so that he could continue to enjoy the epicurean life." In Helsingfors, where Klinckowström pretended to be Ehrenström's successor, the traces of his activity vanished long before the century ended. A lover of large gardens, like the other Gustavians, he designed a "plantation," open to the public, in Röddälden, a dell west of the Ulrikasborg Heights; shortly, however, he rented it to the Finnish Guards for use as a target range. On the north side of Elisabeth Square, in Kronohagen, he built a "palace" for himself and his treasures — an art collection bought without plan, a library in which only the pornography had been assembled with care; the "palace" had gardens overlooking North Harbor. After Klinckowström's death, in 1850, the house and grounds were purchased by the state and turned into a military academy; in time, the academy was torn down to make way for Nyland's Barracks and its draftees.

Writing in the 1880's, August Schauman had these memories of the autocrats' Kronohagen: "For all its aristocratic inhabitants, Kronohagen could not boast of any distinctive mansions until Baron Klinckowström put up his remarkable structure in the Gothic style . . . and laid out his

new garden . . . Opposite this courtier (a by no means uninfluential man
in his own right), another and much mightier gentleman dwelt from 1840
on, Baron Lars Gabriel von Haartman, up whose staircase there came
every day whole squadrons of people seeking official jobs or the state's
aid — as they climbed their knees trembled and shook, for they knew that
they would shortly stand before 'His Holy Terror's' countenance, and in
its features, contorted in approval or disfavor, they would perceive either
the light of their future or the dark grave of their hope."

Lars Gabriel von Haartman's good deeds for Finland were many; two
major efforts — the furtherance of the Saima Canal and the currency reform — have already been named, and the tidying up of Finland's chaotic
customs regulations was a third. Indeed, he had spent his whole life in the
service of his homeland, as secretary and then member of the old Committee for Finnish Affairs in Saint Petersburg, as Robert Rehbinder's right-
hand man, as provincial governor in southwestern Finland, and finally as
head of the Senate's treasury department, in which role he is said to have
ruled all Finland from his apartment in Kronohagen. The more awe-
inspiring of his nicknames, "His Holy Terror" ("Hans Förskräcklighet"),
tells much about his autocratic ways and his personal peculiarities, even as
"Silver Lasse" reveals the bedazzlement of a populace aware of his mone-
tary policies but unable to comprehend them. That terrifying manner of
his does not redound entirely to his discredit: he suffered from chronic
overwork, chronic nervous tension, chronic bad health, and fits of twitch-
ing and coughing beset him when he was in the throes of decision or,
simply, annoyance. In the opinion of Professor Grot, one of the few who
could approach his chambers as a guest and not a petitioner, he was an
extremely keen-minded man, interested in everything, down to the frictions surrounding Russian instruction at the university; and von Haartman's correspondence and travel diaries support Grot's judgment. In the
opinion of liberal-minded critics, however (and such voices were heard
more and more frequently during the 1850's), von Haartman was a petty
tyrant who enjoyed wielding the might concentrated in his hands, and
who, in the last analysis, was more mindful of the privileges of his little
and powerful class than he was of Finland's future: he envisioned that future as a painless absorption into "la mère patrie," Russia. In this connection, his hospitality toward Grot — who, once a popular teacher at the
university, found his academic duties ever more burdensome because of a
growing anti-Russian spirit on the students' part — could be misinter-
preted, or interpreted in a special way. Von Haartman left his post in
1858, disgusted at his collisions with another autocrat, Governor-General
Berg, whose high-handedness was ameliorated neither by competence nor
devotion, and dismayed at the prospect of a convening of Finland's diet

under the aegis of the new and (relatively) liberal Czar Alexander II; he died the next year.

Reflecting on the Helsingfors he had known as a boyish student and youthful newspaper editor, Topelius told how society had been divided into layers quite separate from one another. "High society, few in numbers, had its evening gatherings, the military had its own, the lower officials theirs, and then came the university, the burghers, and the artisans; as for the workers, they had nothing but their taverns." Contact occurred, to be sure, between "high society" — either members of the old Finno-Swedish nobility, like von Haartman, or recent arrivals like Klinckow-ström — and certain other elements; the aristocrats took pains to be friendly toward Russian officialdom in Helsingfors, while less favored citizens, possessing little authority, were not so worried about losing it. The sturdy book-dealer, Gustaf Otto Wasenius, betrayed what he, and people like him, thought of the aristocracy when he wrote to an Åbo friend about a "picnic" which members of his circle had decided to hold, forgetful that the date chosen, December 2, was the anniversary of Czar Nicholas's coronation. (By "picnic," Wasenius meant a dance where sandwiches were served.) "The event has caused a disturbance among the elegant folk, since the day's solemn import, to which we hadn't given a single thought . . . , compels them to be all dressed up, in full uniform, etc. We members of the plebeian mob laugh at the political considerations which the aristocracy tries to assign to even the smallest matter; and, despite all sorts of hints, we can't be persuaded to change the date." The more cultured, wealthy, and vocal members of the middle class, such as Borgström, Kiseleff, Sederholm, Wasenius, the students at the university (the diary of young Topelius is filled with outbursts against "bent-backs" and "servile pussy-footers"), and the professors, insofar as their semi-official position allowed it (or their lack of high birth: some few were genuine bluebloods) — all were critical of the aristocracy and its airs; they deemed it too haughty toward fellow Finlanders, and too ready to lick Russian boots. (Given the chance, of course, bourgeoisie and academe gladly joined in the cheers for Nicholas and other visiting notables.) Nonetheless, the aristocracy served as a handy target for feelings that might otherwise have been directed at Russia itself, and it was safer to sneer at Klinckow-ström than at his crony and master Menshikov. Also, in the professors' case, their dislike for the aristocracy stemmed in part from injured vanity. "Students cannot take part in [social life] because it is too expensive for them," Carl Daniel von Haartman told Grot, "and the professors feel perhaps that in the salons of Helsingfors they are not shown enough respect . . . Matters were different in Åbo [where the Academy had been a prime source of local pride]; there the most outstanding professors were welcome everywhere." (A half-brother of Lars Gabriel, Carl Daniel — surgeon, professor of medicine, patrician — could afford to dissect his colleagues' motives.) Similar feelings of pride can be detected among other and simpler folk who found their way, however fleetingly, into the halls of society. A tale is told about an encounter at a "picnic" in Society House between a lieutenant of the Finnish Guards, freshly returned from heroic acts of suppression in Poland, and a well-to-do butcher. (The butcher must have been an outstanding man in his line, otherwise he would not have been able to gain entrance for himself and his family to the "picnic," a word now used for a "public ball" — "public" in the sense that high officials, professors, students, officers, and particularly respectable or affluent members of the middle class could attend.) The lieutenant exclaimed, in a loud voice: "Why, there are butchers here," and the butcher replied, with a bow: "Don't be afraid, lieutenant, I don't have my knife with me." The anecdote may be taken as a bold expression of contempt on the citizenry's part toward the Czar's well-born hirelings; more likely, though, it shows nothing more revolutionary than honest value asserting itself. Peace was kept, by the way, and etiquette was directed at these balls by a person with the joking title of "dance councillor," who "in his manner . . . was a caricatured reminiscence of the Gustavian times and their *gentillesse* and *complaisance*." The good spirit's name was Carl Magnus Gripenberg; his "genteel calves and skinny legs, / His back bending in a thousand waves" were active until the 1850's. The words are taken from a piece of contemporary Helsingfors doggerel: people could poke fun at Gripenberg, yet his effeminate being kept gentility alive on those unusual occasions when some of the disparate elements of the city's society had the chance to meet on the dance floor and at the buffet.

11. The University's Golden Age

THERE TOOK PLACE, however, one love feast without parallel and almost without blemish; Gripenberg's pacific services were not needed this time. The event was the bicentennial celebration of the founding of Åbo Academy, brought into the world by Per Brahe in 1640 and moved to Helsingfors in 1827; now, from July 14 until July 20, 1840, the capital experienced academic and (within proper limits) patriotic delirium, a delirium carefully prepared. The placing of the ceremonies outside the university term kept scholarly pursuits from interfering with the festival. The guardian hand of Rehbinder, still chancellor *pro tempore*, rested this last time over the university he had so often aided; and the university's rector was Dr. Ursin, whose interest in reckless aquatic sports was coupled with the organizer's cool mind. As for transportation, the new steamboats made travel from Saint Petersburg and the Baltic lands easy; the Stockholm line was in operation as well, although the university had been warned against inviting too many Swedes. But, Swedes present or absent, the university's aula could not contain all the guests summoned to the ceremonies. Happily, Engel's great Nikolai-Church had reached a stage which enabled it to be used instead.

The opening day, July 14, began with an assembly in the Senate chambers, a short parade over the square to the church, and orations in its auditorium, where the plaster was not yet dry: orations in Latin by Ursin, in Swedish by Linsén, and Russian by Soloviev, as well as music (a welcome change) directed by a young German named Fredrik Pacius. Then there came a march across town to Engel's handsome wooden church for divine services, and an orderly return, still in ranks, to the university's aula, where a select audience could hear deputies from Dorpat and Kiev extend greetings in Baltic-German or Russified Latin; Ursin retorted in his Finno-Swedish pronunciation of the same noble tongue. The reward for the survivors of these physical and linguistic trials was a dinner at Society House. The next day the jurists' graduation took place, wholly in Swedish, affording the audience a measure of relief; the law faculty's new red hats, ordered for the occasion, added to the entertainment. On Friday, the 16th, the theologians had their turn, while the evenings' great event — an intentional juxtaposition? — was a giant ball for 1,400 people at Society House, arranged by the merchant union of Helsingfors and attended by all the well-heeled Russians who were taking the waters at Brunnsparken. Saturday was the day of the medical promotion; Israel Hwasser, the Swede who had been professor of medicine at Åbo and, very briefly, at Helsingfors before he was called to the greater financial and academic rewards of Uppsala, was heaped with honors intended to make him regret his choice of homelands. Sunday was not a day of rest, but was devoted to the "masters' banquet" at Brunnsparken, where the guests of honor were a Finlander who had migrated to Sweden in 1811, the poet Frans Mikael Franzén, and the theologian Gustaf Gadolin, who, faithful to the past, had elected to stay in Åbo upon the university's move to Helsingfors. On Monday, the graduation for the philosophical faculty took place; the old gentlemen Franzén and Gadolin were again the center of attention, as "jubilee masters" of fifty years' standing, and honorary doctorates were given to Rehbinder, "Finland's best support," to the grimacing Lars Gabriel von Haartman, to Grot's friend Pletnyov, rector of the university in Saint Petersburg, to the mineralogist Nils Nordenskiöld, a chief star of the university at Helsingfors, and to other more or less distinguished scholars from Russia and from Finland. That night the great "masters' ball" was held at Society House; its belle was Rosina von Haartman, Carl Daniel's daughter, Lars Gabriel's niece, and Franzén's granddaughter, "kransbinderska" ("coronaria," "binder of wreaths") at the ceremonies earlier in the day, a young lady who enchanted everyone she met, including Grot. She was good, she was beautiful, she was intelligent, this Euphrosyne, and, a quality that especially appealed to the Russian: "it seemed as though she would deeply scorn the vanity and the pomp" of the gilded world of Helsingfors. Grot's own qualifications as *officier de liaison* of the festival were ideal: the grandson of a Lutheran from Holstein, who had been pastor of Saint Catherine's Church in Saint Petersburg, young Grot had first come to Helsingfors as a summer guest at Brunnsparken in 1838. Learning Swedish quickly, he had become the friend of Cygnaeus, and, through him, of Runeberg. Now he would be rewarded for his services; wise Rehbinder had chosen him as Soloviev's successor in the chair of Russian at the university. On Sunday, July 18, a dinner was given by the Russian representatives for Finland's intelligensia: Franzén, Runeberg, Lönnrot were among the stars in attendance. The main topic of table discussion was an annual, to be published in a double edition, in Swedish for Finland and Sweden, in Russian for Russia. Contributions were to be solicited from the major literary men of both language realms; Grot was to serve as editor and translator. The annual appeared only once, in 1842; among other things, it contained the poem of Franzén on his "Journey to the Celebration of 1840," apostrophizing the new city in which the happy events had taken place:

> What a splendid town, as little like the past's
> As butterfly is like the chrysalis! —
> Arisen here in haste, as Thebes once rose
> To chords of Amphion's harp.

The sentiments expressed in Franzén's pseudo-classic strophe are correct; Helsingfors was a freshly born and, in its way, a splendid city. When the dancing ended on the final night, those who had arranged the jubilee had good reason to be satisfied both with their work and its municipal setting.

There had been sour notes in the chorus of happiness. The very invitation of Franzén — who would come, officially, as the representative of the Swedish Academy — had caused worries, not least on the part of poor old Thesleff, the university's eternally apprehensive vice-chancellor. After all, Franzén was a living link with Finland's Swedish past, and a famous poet who had decided not to live in Finland under Russian rule. Rector Ursin was able to calm Thesleff's fears; however, Thesleff could have said after the event that first impulses are the right ones. A horde of students waited half-a-day outside Tölö Inn for Franzén, coming by coach from Åbo; the authorities feared that they were inspired by anti-Russian sentiments. Once arrived, crotchety Franzén got into a dispute with a Russian guest, Muzovskiy, court preacher from Saint Petersburg. Overwhelmed by the pomp and circumstance, the prelate observed that: "I have been abroad a great deal; in other places there's more action and less ceremony." Franzén, who was bishop of Härnösand, retorted that there was surely no lack of ceremonies in the Russian church, but he had his doubts as to whether any meaning lay behind them. (Discovering this exchange, one's sneaking sympathies go to Muzorskiy, who must have been very hot and very tired.) Another Russian who had a bad time was the long-suffering Soloviev, shortly to be replaced by Grot; young Topelius, who had scampered from event to event all week long, becoming a *magister* himself on Monday, confided to his diary that at the banquet on the very first night: "Eduard [af] Brunér [a classical philologist] got mixed up between Soloviev's nose and the port-wine bottle — both had the same crimson color and were equally full of the juices of Bacchus. Brunér — usually the most peaceable man under the sun — grabbed Soloviev by the nose. Soloviev sounded the alarm, and Brunér had to go home for a good sleep." Funny stories both, but also symptomatic ones: the harmony of the bicentennial would vanish all too quickly, and Grot, worn out by demonstrations against him on the part of a student body grown ever more nationalistic in its attitudes, would withdraw to Russia (in 1852), where he became a distinguished scholar of Russian literature and history. Russia never again had a cultural representative of Grot's calibre and tact in Helsingfors, and Finland never again had so well-informed and understanding a spokesman in Russia. "See," Grot wrote on the eve of the bicentennial, "the people of Finland are of this sort — not yet removed from nature's bosom, living in poverty . . . they are wealthy only in inner merits, and seek nothing else. At home in Russia, people have no idea of what the Finns are like, and often say, after a fleeting acquaintance, 'Quel mauvais genre!'" In the same jubilee-summer, Grot composed his portrait of Elias Lönnrot, the compiler of the *Kalevala*, a portrait which concludes: "He seems not even to suspect that he has any virtues; instead, he believes that everyone else is more important than he is."

Grot was only one of the university's ornaments. The old guard from Åbo had begun to pass away, and their professorships were taken by men who had reached intellectual maturity in the new capital, although they had begun their academic training at the "cradle of Finland's culture," now abandoned. Gabriel Rein, an assistant in the academy's library when the Åbo fire took place, had risked his life to save something of the holdings. In Helsingfors, he became known as a young scholar unafraid —

within reason's bounds — of Saint Petersburg; a nationalist who made no
bones about it, he had studied Finnish even in his Åbo days, and had un-
successfully competed for the university's new lectorship in Finnish, established in 1829. Five years later, Rein became professor of history; his field
of research had become, and would remain, the annals of Finland. J.J.
Nordström was named professor of law the same year — the brilliant man
who introduced the red hats at the bicentennial; his more enduring fame
lies in his historical study of Swedish law, a topic of the greatest importance for contemporary Finland: Alexander I, during the generous days at
Borgå, had promised to respect the land's "religion and basic laws" which,
of course, were Swedish. Rein and Nordström were natural spokesmen for
the new and mildly independent spirit of the university's consistory; Rein
was rewarded for his devotion to Finland by election as the university's
rector in 1848, the right man, surely, to defend academic freedom during
the hard times to come — the news from Paris and Berlin and Vienna had
confirmed Nicholas in his worst fears about liberal thought. Nordström,
however, followed a call to Uppsala in 1846, tired of his battles with
Rector Ursin, whose practical turn of mind and desire to please higher
authority kept him from understanding matters of principle. Ursin had
failed to gain re-election as rector in 1845; but his defeat came too late to
save Nordström for Finland. (Nordström left Finland by the same ship as
Professor Tengström's son Robert, the marvelous "filius" of whom so
much was hoped: Robert died in Paris in November 1847, twenty-three
years old.) Another light of the university was J.J. Nervander, who once
had illuminated the Saturday Society; he was appointed professor of physics in 1845 but death took him early, too, at forty-three in 1848: his wit
had won him many admirers and many enemies, chief among the latter the
"old men," the conservatives of the university's faculty. Other quondam
members of the Saturday Society had preceded Nervander into the professorial ranks: Axel Laurell as professor of dogmatics in 1835, B.O. Lille as
professor of church history in 1840. The medical faculty had good reason
to be proud of another of Runeberg's friends, Immanuel Ilmoni, a man of
simple beginnings — his father was a parish clerk at Nummis, in the Nyland backwoods — who became the star pupil of Israel Hwasser, Sweden's
Benjamin Rush; at Hwasser's suggestion, Ilmoni applied for and received
the chair of theoretical and practical medicine in 1834. A practical doctor
Ilmoni surely was, with his interest in epidemics, which ravaged Helsingfors so often in these years; and, as might be expected of a student of
Hwasser, he had other concerns as well, instructing colleagues in their
moral duties with his pamphlet, *Om läkarens yrke och pligter* (*Concerning
the Profession and Duties of the Physician*, 1847), and working on a history
of disease in the North. He was in the midst of the fourth part when he

died in April, 1856, of the typhus. It had been Ilmoni, for the rest, who tried to keep Runeberg in Helsingfors by proposing that the university create a professorship in "esthetics and modern literature"; the post was indeed created, but well-nigh two decades too late, in 1854.

These men and others — the legal historian Johan Philip Palmén, another defender of the Swedish code, and the theologian Frans Ludvig Schauman (the considerably older brother of the omnipresent August), a distinguished scholar of Finland's ecclesiastical law and, more important, a major figure in the renaissance of constitutionalism during the liberal reign of Alexander II — stood in painful contrast to certain of their fellows: Axel Gabriel Sjöström, poor teacher, failed editor, bad poet, mediocre but indefatigable translator; Carl Axel Gottlund, lector in Finnish from 1839 on (there was no professorship until 1850), whose good will was outbalanced by his eccentricity — he wrote an epic in seventeen cantos, *Runola*, for the bicentennial, for which not even Finnish literary historians can find anything good to say, save the fact that it was written in Finnish and was thus a pioneer work; and, last but not least, the *pro tempore* vice-chancellor himself, Alexander Amatus Thesleff, who provided comic relief. Thesleff liked to visit his professors' lectures; on such a pedagogical reconnaissance he once interrupted Gabriel Rein, in order to tell (in his broken Swedish: he came from a German-speaking Viborg clan) about his adventures in the Napoleonic Wars. Asked by a group of students for permission to celebrate the hundredth anniversary of the birth (1739) of Henrik Gabriel Porthan, the great pioneer of Finland's cultural history, Thesleff replied: "Why do the gentlemen want to celebrate the memory of that old Swedish professor? There must be something better to celebrate." His foot in his mouth, Thesleff at least had the excuse of his military background; however, Germund Fredrik Aminoff, named professor of philosophy in 1849 despite (or because of) the fact that his rival for the post was the brilliant Snellman, could not claim the old soldier's innocence of intellectual matters. Aminoff is remembered for his observation on the Berlin uprising of March, 1848 ("Who could have thought that Prussia was so demoralized?"), and the fact that not even his abject loyalty could keep Nicholas, who mistrusted "philosophy" as "a bringer of dangerous ideas," from abolishing the chair, in 1852, as a part of the humanities (see page 118). Aminoff was not left unemployed; he returned to the position as censor he had held before his academic appointment.

Something else should be remembered about the university in the 1840's, too: many of its promising young men were far away. Returning to Finland in 1842 after his long sojourn in Sweden and Germany, Snellman had briefly held private lectures in his capacity as docent: by the autumn of 1843 he had moved to distant Kuopio, to make a living there as a school director. To be sure, it could be claimed that his spirit was not absent from Helsingfors: his *Läran om staten* (*The Doctrine of the State*, 1842), which argued that a "national spirit" is the only basis for a nation's life, was widely read; and, in 1844, he founded two papers, *Maamiehen ystävä* (*The Countryman's Friend*) for Finnish readers in the countryside, and *Saima*, in Swedish, for the nation's cultured class. The readers of *Saima* were told, again and again, that they must work not only for the elevation of Finnish into the ranks of the "cultural languages," but that they must be prepared, in time, to sacrifice Swedish, their own mother tongue, in order that national unity might be achieved. In result of its nationalism, *Saima* was killed by government edict in 1846; in 1847, Snellman began his *Litteraturblad för allmän medborgerlig bildning* (*Literary Paper for General Civic Education*), where he continued to preach the doctrine of "one language, one people." (Switzerland, of course, was anathema to him.) Snellman's friend Cygnaeus, now school director in Helsingfors and docent, likewise left the city in 1843, but bound for more interesting spots than Kuopio; he made his grand tour of the continent, supported by the university's "Alexander fellowship." Filled to the brim with Europe's culture, he would return in 1847. Meanwhile, his cousin Uno Cygnaeus had gone traveling in another direction; an ordained minister, he had been appointed in 1839 as pastor of the Lutheran communicants in Russian Alaska, with headquarters at Sitka, where he stayed a biblical seven years, consoling his brethren in the faith and collecting specimens of Alaska's and Siberia's wildlife, which he generously gave to the university upon his return. (The most prominent member of Uno's congregation, by the way, had been Arvid Adolf Etholén, member of a Helsingfors mercantile family and Russian naval officer, who was governor of the emperor's North American properties during these years.) The Finno-Ugric scholar, Mathias Alexander Castrén, had been absent on a research trip to Siberia and Finnish Lapland since 1841; he returned in 1844, holding well-attended lectures on Finnish grammar to the university's students — after Gottlund, there was surely room for improvement, and Castrén was an imposing man and an imposing scholar. In February, 1845, he fled civilization again, setting out on the last of his expeditions. Topelius saw him on the eve of departure: "Lönnrot and Castrén started out yesterday, the one for Kuopio, the other for Siberia and perhaps even for Altai — he's going in order to find the original home of the Finnish people, and he hopes to be able to prove that we are closely related to a ninth of the human race. For such a goal, it's worth sacrificing one's life and health . . ." As for Lönnrot, he was enjoying a leave of absence from his medical post at Kajana in the far north, in order to continue his philological and folkloristic researches. His permanent settlement in Helsingfors would not come until 1853, when he was named professor of the Finnish language as Castrén's successor: Castrén had surely made the sacrifices mentioned by Topelius, holding the newly created professorship only for a short time, from 1851 until his death of tuberculosis on May 7, 1852.

In 1839 another promising young docent had been appointed. Georg August Wallin, from Åland, the islands which lie toward Sweden off Finland's southwestern tip. Wallin was an orientalist, following thus in the footsteps of Petter Forsskål, a son of Helsingfors who had died in Arabia Felix in 1762, as a member of a Danish expedition. In 1840–42, Wallin resided in Saint Petersburg, perfecting his knowledge of Turkish, Persian, and Arabic; then he took up his academic duties in Helsingfors again, at the same time studying medicine. It was his intention to make his way through the forbidden lands of the east on the strength of a physician's skills, and this is precisely what he did, aided, to be sure, by the Alexander fellowship, like Fredrik Cygnaeus before him; Wallin's accounts of his travels through Egypt, Northern Arabia, Persia, and Syria won him the attention of Sir Henry Rawlinson and a prize from London's Royal Geographical Society. Returning to Helsingfors in 1850, he gave lessons in English, since he had to support a widowed mother and sister; Schauman, a prospective tutee, tells how he found Wallin dressed in Arab garb — a surprising sight in an apartment on Högbergsgatan, and one which hinted that Wallin was not altogether ready to cease being "Abdul-Walî," healer of suffering nomads. T.E. Lawrence would have similar difficulties in accommodating himself to western life. The "twin heroes of Finland's scholarship," Wallin and Castrén, published their qualifying studies for their respective professorships within three days of one another, in October, 1850, and received their posts almost simultaneously; broken in health by his journey, like Castrén, Wallin shared Castrén's death-year, too. Disappointed by a contretemps in negotiations concerning a new expedition to Arabia and, he hoped, to Turkestan, Wallin succumbed to a heart ailment in October, 1852. (Syphilis may have played a role as well.)

12. A Passion for Finnish

THE REAL ARABIA Felix of the young, however, lay much closer at hand, in Finland's interior. At the graduation ceremonies for masters of arts, on June 21, 1844, busy Topelius declaimed an extremely lengthy "song" or ode which took note of nationalistic stirrings in other lands:

By Ireland's streams, in Hungary's and Bohemia's fields,
A cry is raised that peoples may grow young
By their own strength, and cast off what they've borrowed;
In Suomi's fells the cry has echoed loud.

The climax put Snellman's demand for a single national spirit, born out of a single language, into verse:

One folk! One land! One tongue! One wisdom and one song!

It sounded quite splendid, and aroused guilty consciences as well as patriotic passions. In his diary, Topelius reproached himself for his lack of knowledge of Finnish; the lines just quoted — and all of the other works of Topelius — were composed in Swedish. Yet Topelius was the son of an Ostrobothnian physician who had been a pioneer in the collection of Finnish folksongs. Contemporaries of Topelius who spent their childhood in Helsingfors heard no Finnish at all, or very little; the city lay in a Swedish-speaking coastal region, and thus the supply of labor closest to hand had Swedish as its mother tongue. The burghers of the town had of course mostly been Swedish-speaking, as were the officials and academicans who arrived after the capital's transfer. The Finns who came from the interior learned Swedish (and became "Swedicized") for their own advantage, and their children's. Mixed marriages, between Finno-Swedes and Finns, were frequent, at the lower end of the social scale, and the offspring of these unions quite naturally learned the dominant language of the city as their main tongue, acquiring the "useless" words of their Finnish parent only incidentally or not at all. A keen investigator of the sociology of Helsingfors, Heikki Waris, has studied the enrollments in the catechism classes of the Lutheran "Swedish-Finnish congregation" of Helsingfors, the city's principal religious body: in 1841–45 there was an average of 223 Swedish-speaking and 40 Finnish-speaking children enrolled, in 1846–50 the figures were 226 and 42, in 1851–55, 256 and 26. Anders Ramsay tells how embarrassed he was when in 1848, he was sent from his Helsingfors home to the gymnasium in Åbo, and could only stammer "Mitä?" ("What?") upon hearing Finnish spoken "for the first time between respectable people." The forthright Schauman confesses: "For me, as for almost all Helsingfors children, Finnish had been . . . a completely foreign tongue. We had no doubt heard considerable Finnish, but we'd never read a word of it, and no one had suggested that we ought to learn the language." As matters turned out, Ramsay went to his grave, in the twentieth century, without having acquired Finnish; like so many other idealists of his time (and practical-minded people from a later age), Schauman spent summer vacations in the country in order to master the mysterious tongue. The lectures of Castrén had been inspiring but all too scholarly; it was only

upon Lönnrot's succession to the Finnish throne at the university that instruction in academe treated Finnish as a living organism. Lönnrot came
from Sammatti in northwestern Nyland, close to the birthplace of Immanuel Ilmoni, and in his case, as in Ilmoni's, the home language had
been Finnish.

The enthusiasm of Swedish-speaking academic youth for Finnish is
admirable, although one must surmise that, in it, patriotism was not infrequently coupled with a search for the mildly exotic and a romantic admiration of the noble savage. Setting off to Savolax for the summer,
Schauman wrote that he was 19 years old, leaving home for the first time,
"in order to get to know my own land and my own people and its own
language." It was 1845; by the end of the 1850's Schauman, as the editor
of the newspaper *Papperslyktan* (*The Paper Lantern*), had begun to have
second thoughts about his youthful passion; he had been brought up
short by the fanaticism with which Snellman, and others, proclaimed their
message — that Swedish must vanish from Finland altogether for the nation's good. Pointing to the example of Switzerland, Schauman dared to
rejoin that Swedish had a rightful place, and a valuable one, in Finland's
future — a piece of boldness which roused Snellman to some of his cruelest polemics. (No doubt about it: Snellman was a master of Swedish, the
language he intended to remove.) But in the 1840's, "people still lived in
a linguistic state of innocence. Zeal for the Finnish language was general;
Finnish was considered to be the mother tongue even of those who had
spoken Swedish from their earliest years and had never learned Finnish at
all thereafter." The words are by a man of a later generation. Axel Lille
(1848–1921), the son of Runeberg's friend, B.O. Lille, and, as the century wore on, one of the great champions of the rights of the Swedish language and of Finno-Swedish culture in Finland. Lille may very well have
been thinking, as he wrote, of a case such as that of the irascible Sven
Gabriel Elmgren, the disciple of Snellman who took over the editorship of
the *Litteraturblad* in 1850, continuing the cry for "one language, one
spirit" with a bad temper indistinguishable from that of his master. Elmgren confided his innermost thoughts to his diary in Swedish and, as secretary of the Finnish Literary Society (1846–1861), conducted the
organization's meetings and kept its records in the same tongue; he was
from the Swedish-speaking community of Pargas, near Åbo, and Finnish
remained an insurmountable obstacle for him, save in the world of dreams.
Another zealot, less Finnish than even Elmgren, was Fredrik Berndtson, a
native Swede from Falun, who had come to Finland in the 1840's, quickly
writing verse about the Finnish backwoods and getting an appointment as
docent in esthetics in 1847. Together with Elmgren, he became the editor
of Runeberg's old *Helsingfors Morgonblad*, now simply called *Morgon-*

bladet and turned into still another mouthpiece for Snellman's ideas; but subsequently, marrying a senator's daughter, Berndtson dumped his acquired patriotic and Finnish pastimes, and became editor of the government organ, *Finlands Allmänna Tidning*, and a section chief in the governor-general's office.

Not very long after coming to Finland, Berndtson had served as the editor of *Necken* (*The Water-Sprite*), the country's first poetic almanac, which appeared at Christmas, 1844, with contributions by figures already familiar (Cygnaeus, B.O. Lille, Nervander, Topelius) and recent debutants (Emil von Quanten, Carl Wilhelm Törnegren, Herman Kellgren). Having hailed Finland in "Suomi's Song," the tubercular von Quanten left Helsingfors for a voyage to the East Indies; then he settled in Stockholm, where he became a leader in those "Scandinavianist" circles which hoped for a return of Finland to Sweden, or at least to the Swedish sphere of influence. Von Quanten's pure-blooded Finnish enthusiasm was thus short-lived, as was that of Törnegren, who with his *Teckning af den svenska vitterhetens äldre öden i Finland intill Franzén* (*Description of the Older Fortunes of Swedish Letters in Finland until Franzén*, 1849) established a Swedish literary canon for Finland — a modest sign of reaction against "Fennomane" claims. Kellgren, a gifted linguist whose speciality was Sanskrit, had no difficulty in transforming his Finnish passion into a working knowledge of the tongue; in 1847, he published a Finnish grammar intended for a German public, thinking in this fashion to spread the gospel abroad. And he tried to win Finland's Swedish hearts as well, using blandishment rather than Snellman's sarcasm. With Robert Tengström, the "filius" of Johan Jacob, and Karl Konstantin Tigerstedt, Kellgren had issued three volumes of a *Fosterländskt Album* (*Patriotic Album*), in the first of which he included translations of Estonian and Finnish folksongs (from the *Kanteletar*) and presented the Estonian epic, *Kalevi poeg*, and Tengström made a long, popular presentation of the *Kalevala*. (The second volume contained still more translations from the *Kanteletar*, as well as essays on such topics and questions as "I hvad förhållande står språket till nationaliteten?" ["In what relationship does language stand to nationality?"], "Om den Svenska bildningens förhållande till det Finska" [Concerning the Swedish culture's relationship to the Finnish"], and "I hvad mon uppfyller Finska språket fordringarne af ett språkideal?" ["To what extent does the Finnish language fulfil the demands of a language ideal?"]. Then, in 1847, the third volume offered not just retellings of Estonian and Finnish folktales, and specimens of historical songs such as, e.g. "The Murder of Bishop Henry," but samples of "Tschudisk" [Ingrian, Vepsian, Vodian, Livonian], Zyryan, and Lappish songs — the Finno-Ugric realm was rapidly being expanded. Nestled among further essays at the volume's close was the first complete printing of Runeberg's "Vårt land.") Tigerstedt offered a compilation of views of medieval Finns and Finland provided by the Norse sagas. The Tengströms, son and father, had both contributed to the second volume (1845) of another patriotic journal, *Joukahainen*, in Swedish, of course, but named after Väinämöinen's rival singer in the *Kalevala*, and issued irregularly by the Ostrobothnian "division" of the university; here, the younger Tengström had written of "The Finnish people as presented in the *Kalevala*," and Topelius asked a pertinent question with the essay, "Do the Finnish people have a history?" (He answered himself by deciding that the period of what he called "the Swedish occupation," from 1157 until 1809, had been "a time of schooling, which served as an intermediary between the Finnish people's antiquity and their future"; the Finns had a "history" only since then, thanks to the "generosity and wise guarantees of two monarchs" — the kind of wishful thinking about Finland's special place in the Russian empire, it might be added, which future generations, after Topelius, would have cause to regret.) Interestingly, Fredrik Cygnaeus — whose highfalutin verse and melodramatic prose (about Marie Antoinette and *le procès du collier*!) had constituted much of *Joukahainen*'s first volume (1843) — engaged in sympathy with the Irish cause here, in the long poem, "Erin har sorg" ["Erin Laments"], on the British government's arrest of the aged Daniel O'Connell. And in the same year as this issue of *Joukahainen*, Tengström junior published a *Finsk antologi*, still another effort to present a systematic selection of Finnish folk poetry in translation (by M.A. Castrén, Kellgren, Bengt Olof Lille, and himself), arranged in sections, early epic songs, early lyric songs, more recent folksongs. The would-be patriots who, inspired by all this attractive and easy material in their mother tongue, wanted to settle down to the hard job of mastering the details of Finnish, could turn to the new grammar (1847) by Fabian Collan, intended primarily for use in schools, where Finnish now was introduced as a subject for instruction. As the "curator" (faculty advisor) of the Savolax "nation," the hunchback Collan — writing essays on Finnish mythology — had been an active propagandist for Finnish at the university even before the bloom of the 1840's; like Snellman, financial considerations had forced him to leave Helsingfors in 1844, to become a teacher of history at the new Kuopio gymnasium. Having also been entrusted with the teaching of Finnish, as he says in his introduction, "the author, like many another teacher, had more than sufficiently felt the lack of a usable handbook for the grammar." It was a kind of homecoming for him (his father had been pastor at Idensalmi, north of Kuopio), and he was enormously successful. By 1850 he was called back to Helsingfors and an associate professorship in philosophy, but died a year later. (Arvid Järnefelt

gave Collan a handsome vignette in his recounting of his father's memories of a visit to Kuopio in *Vanhempieni-romaani* [*My Parents' Novel*,
1927–29]: "the widely traveled, ruthless lector, who, having been exiled
from the capital, had begun to blow his fireman's trumpet.")

As editor of *Helsingfors Morgonblad* (1841–44), Fabian Collan had
won the praise of Snellman, who said that, while others talked about Finnish matters, Collan did something about them with his paper. Certain of
Collan's contempories were willing to go still further: they undertook the
supremely difficult task of providing Finland's capital with a newspaper in
the language now so admired in intellectual circles, albeit so little used. In
1846, the eccentric Gottlund tried to found a weekly, *Suomalainen* (*The
Finn*), aimed at the educated reader, but the censors quickly killed it; undaunted, he tried again, with *Suomi* (*Finland*). It was also meant to come
out every week, but its appearance grew more and more sporadic, and in
1849 it perished too, without the censors' aid. The reasons for its demise
are readily discovered; the "cultured readers" of Finnish in Helsingfors
were few, and Gottlund's bizarre personality put its stamp both on the paper's materials and its language — a "Savolax dialect" of Gottlund's own
concoction. Also, *Suomi*'s death was hastened by the foundation, in 1847,
of *Suometar* (*The Finnish Woman*, an ideal figure like 'Germania'); it began as a feeble weekly, with only 258 subscribers in its first year, but prospered with time, and was able to boast of 4,600 subscribers by 1856. After
another decade, it too passed away; yet it can be regarded as the parent of
a major Finnish paper, founded in 1869, which survived until 1991 —
Uusi Suometar, the "new" *Suometar*, called *Uusi Suomi* from 1919 on.
The moving spirit in *Suometar*, was Paul (or Paavo) Tikkanen, the son of a
well-to-do peasant, who had come down to the university in 1841, making a name for himself with translations of Runeberg and the Danish romantic Oehlenschläger. Tikkanen surrounded himself, editing *Suometar*,
with associates who likewise had come from the Finnish-speaking hinterland: young August Ahlquist, who had made Finnish renderings of Franzén, Runeberg, and the brightest lights from Sweden, Tégner, Stagnelius,
and C.J.L. Almqvist; D.E.D. Europaeus, a disciple and aide of Lönnrot;
and Anders Warelius, a many-sided man, ethnologist, philologist and lexi-
cographer, who — like his colleagues — knew the Finnish people and
their needs. It was Tikkanen's policy to appeal both to the "cultured
reader" and to a broader public, a novel program for those days.

Still another Finn whose name got brief but telling attention during
these years was Anders Räty from Sordavala on the shores of Lake Ladoga,
in the far east of Finland; his translation of the Wiliam Tell episode from
the elder Dumas' *Impressions de Voyage* is supposed, according to tradition, to have been the occasion for the infamous "Finnish language re-

script" of 1850. On April 8, the censorship statutes were complemented thus: "in the Finnish language only such [publications] may be issued which . . . possess, both in their spirit of composition and their manner of presentation, simple religious edification or economic application as their aim; on the other hand, it is absolutely forbidden to make public in print, in the Finnish language, political news or crimes which have been committed abroad." "The publication of novels in Finnish" was also forbidden, "whether they be original works or translations, not even excepting those works whose publication the censors might allow in other languages." The intent of this proclamation — a representative flower of the final years of Nicholas's reign — was to shield the Finnish masses from foreign contamination, contamination in particular from the revolutionary spirit of 1848–49; in a way, the rescript could be taken as a compliment, a result of an imperial belief in that essential innocence of the Finnish spirit which Grot so much admired, of which Runeberg sang and Topelius boasted. The prohibition was so patently silly that it was quietly withdrawn after a while; it must have become clear even to Russian officialdom that the dangerous faction in the land — if it possessed a dangerous faction at all — was its intelligensia, Swedish-speaking. During the months when the rescript was sternly applied, *Suometar* could not appear; it took a dramatic farewell of its readers with the cry, "Eläköön Suomi ja sen kansa!" — "Long live Finland and its people!" The main result of the rescript had been to make the Finnish language doubly dear to its admirers; a secondary effect was the strain it put upon those countless Finnish hearts which wanted to love Nicholas, the "mild monarch" of Topelius' wishful words. As a matter of fact, administrative delay caused a strange constellation of events; what was taken with the one hand was returned with the other. The proposed professorship in Finnish had won the warm support of old Thesleff, of all people, and he did what he could to see its realization before his retirement in 1847; on March 22, 1850, the plan was given to the Senate with Nicholas's stamp of approval — only two weeks before the appearance of the language rescript. A year later, Castrén received his certificate of appointment to the professorship from none other than Alexander, Nicholas's son, heir to the Russian throne. The Russians were of two minds about Finnish. On the one hand, they feared that the faithful Finns might lose their purity of spirit if they read about Tell's crossbow and Gessner's apple; on the other, they had come to realize that Finnish, encouraged to just the right degree, would be a handy weapon for breaking the power of Finland's Swedish speakers, and all that they stood for in the land.

13. 1848 and "Our Country"

IN 1848, CARL Johan Walleen wrote to Aline, the least fair of his step-daughters: "It is strange that our land will be the only one in the whole of Europe to enjoy complete peace at the present." Not so strange, if one remembers Finland's isolation; not so strange, if one remembers the alacrity with which Russian rule had been accepted in 1809; not so strange, if one remembers the devotion to Alexander and his promises. Even the students had learned to swallow certain measures without too much grumbling; in 1832, mindful of the lesson of Russian Easter, Rehbinder had "granted" them a prescribed uniform. By doing so, he in fact complied with the wishes of the dandies among them who thought to rival the military in nattiness of appearance but he also knew that the uniform made them readily identifiable as students in case of trouble. (They were forever suspect; when a gendarme was found dead, it was immediately assumed that he had fallen prey to academic marauders. An autopsy showed that he had died of a stroke.) But, uniformed or not (and the regulation was not applied very stringently), the students remained especially sensitive to oppression, real and fancied. Kellgren wrote to his father that he refused to study law, since a jurist's duty in Finland "is to further the assimilation of our poor fatherland into Russia"; and even loyal Topelius composed a *Marseillaise* in which he proclaimed that, if the Finns forgot Swedish culture, it would not be for Russia's sake. Demonstrations took place against the gentlemanly Grot, because his requirements in the obligatory Russian section of the bachelor's examination were deemed to be too stern; a member of the Ostrobothnian "nation" got himself suspended by shouting "Vivat Polonia" in one of the city's hotels; and August Ahlqvist received the same penalty because, at Kajsaniemi Inn, he denounced those students as traitors who applied for stipends to study Russian in the great motherland. Otto Vilhelm Klinckowström capped his dismal career by reporting the young firebrand's remark to the proper authorities. (Ahlqvist's reasoning had not been faulty: the recipients of such stipends had to promise that they would teach Russian for at least five years in Finland's schools upon their return, thus rendering the Russian cause a valuable service.) Sometimes the students were given mass punishment. In the 1830's they had inaugurated the pleasant custom of celebrating their "Flora Festival," a well lubricated descendant of the Roman Floralia, on May 13, a pendant to May 1 with a slightly improved chance of clement weather. On one such Flora-day, a "toast to the Fatherland," not listed in the program, was proposed — legend says by Snellman; the awful news reached official ears, and neither Pipping, the circumspect rector of the time, nor Ursin, his equally careful successor, wished to arouse Thesleff's ire by requesting that the festivals be continued. The students kept the memory of Flora-day alive, having carefully wrapped it in nostalgia.

On December 9, 1847, the recently appointed governor of Nyland, Major-General Johan Mauritz Nordenstam, was designated as dear old Thesleff's successor in the latter's university post. A native of Stockholm, Nordenstam was no stranger to Finland; his father had settled in the Grand Duchy after taking part in the campaign of 1808–09, and the younger Nordenstam had received his cadet training in the military school of Haapaniemi, which was moved during Nordenstam's days to Fredrikshamn. Having been appointed an ensign in the Russian army, Nordenstam was immediately put on Finnish service; somehow the ambitious youth found time to father an illegitimate child, none other than our August Ahlqvist, with a servant girl. Then, still bursting with energy, Nordenstam was off to the wars in the Caucasus, where he became known as a brave and conscientious officer. A fine figure of a man, he came to Helsingfors with the reputation (some peccadilloes aside) of being a chivalrous sort as well; the students took to him immediately, and he quickly conquered the innermost corners of their hearts by allowing the resumption of the Flora Festival.

The celebration, on May 13, 1848, has so often been described that it is encrusted with myth and legend; the chain of events appears to have been the following. At 3:00 p.m. on the great day, the student body moved off along Unionsgatan from the university, its voice raised in song. "A great many droskies and other vehicles followed the procession; in a number of them there sat patients ill with the ague who, though pale and weak, did not wish to miss the festivities." At Long Bridge the band of the Finnish Guards — whose players, otherwise, found so much employment at the city's numberless balls — was waiting in formation; and here, for the first time, "Vårt Land," "Our Country," destined to become the national anthem of Finland, was sung by the Academic Song Club, accompanied by the band. The premiere took place in the original Swedish; the Finnish translation, "Maamme," was not yet ready. The text was by Johan Ludvig Runeberg, and had first been sung on November 9, 1846, at the annual festival of the Ostrobothnian "division," in a setting by Fredrik August Ehrström, who had composed melodies for other Runeberg texts; his music, in fact, was published as an appendix to the third volume of the *Fosterländskt Album,* but was sharply criticized — by Axel Gabriel Ingelius, among others. (The poem would then become the opening canto of Runeberg's *Fänrik Ståls sägner*, Part One, which appeared in its entirely on December 14, 1848 — a date to remember, since *The Tales of Ensign Stål*, about the war of 1808–09, became Finland's national poem, a patriotic monument.) Runeberg himself had also tried his hand at the composition, and his setting was performed at Borgå on December 3, 1846, the 500th anniversary of the town's founding. It had been written down and harmonized by the music teacher at Borgå Gymnasium, Carl Fredrik Blom, and was performed by the town chorus, augmented with boys from Runeberg's and Blom's institution. For this glorious Floralia, however, Fredrik Pacius — the university music teacher, director of the Academic Song Union, and the leading musical figure of Helsingfors — had been asked to do a professional job. Not knowing that fate had its eye and ear upon him, and given only four days of writing time, Pacius had taken his task (he recalled later) "rather lightly." What troubles there were arose in performance and not composition; his singers could not master the rhythm of the opening phrase, which to this day is often sung wrong. An experienced musician, Pacius also made a hasty band arrangement; professional cornetists are a more dependable lot than amateur tenors — and, besides, the performance was to be out of doors.

A good deal of confusion, in result of overheated or faulty memories, beclouds the immortal events at Long Bridge and Gumtäkt Meadow, the parade's destination. The several singings of "Our Country" by or on the bridge — were they planned or not? Did Pacius, muttering "Better safe than sorry," intend to hold this opening rehearsal, or had a patriotic frenzy seized the academic singers even before they could lift the cup at Gumtäkt? As for the bandmaster's identity, that too has been hidden from us; Pacius' daughter Maria Collan-Beaurain, and the noted Helsingfors music critic of a later day, Karl Fredrik Wasenius, thought that it was Adolf Fredrik Leander, the Gilmore and Sousa of Helsingfors during the 1870's and 1880's, but their notion merely proves how myths are formed around great men — in 1848 Leander was only a cadet hornist in the band, a boy of fourteen. At the command, then, of a bandmaster forever unknown, the parade fell in again, and made its way, somewhat thirsty, to the place of the academic festival, a part of Johan von Bonsdorff's estate, which he had placed at the students' disposal. Thirteen tents had been put up; "a number of tables with 'wet wares' of all sorts in elegant goblets, as well as benches and sofas placed here and there, offered refreshment and rest"; at the outset, there was mead, drunk from two colossal horns — Viking horns, not tubas. Music was everywhere; the Guards' band had a rival on the field, the musicians of the Finnish Naval Establishment. Games were played, songs sung, and "the feminine onlookers soon learned that they had nothing to fear from the students." (Had prior experience taught them to expect anything but the most exquisite deportment?) Silence fell; the formal toasts had to be offered. They were eight in number, according to the somewhat dizzy memory of Topelius; first to Nicholas, then to his son Alexander, then to Prince Menshikov, combined with his popular deputy, Rokassovsky, and the "imperial senate for Finland," then to Vice-Chancellor Nordenstam, then to Rector Lagus, near the end of his administrative trials, then to the university's teachers, then to all the officials present and other guests, and then — to Finland. The final toast was proposed by Fredrik Cygnaeus, recently returned from the grand tour and with his large self swathed in a Venetian cape. Cygnaeus talked for more than an hour, and as he stood bathed in the setting sun (some tired souls in the audience must have wished that it would hasten in its fall), he reminded his listeners how lucky they were to have been born in Finland. In the crowd every eye was moist. After Cygnaeus had at last run down, the survivors showed their staying power by singing "Our Country" over and over again. No one cared that its tune, like that of Silcher's beer-garden favorite, *Die Lorelei*, suffered from the esthetic fault of descending even as the text soared skyward: "No height is lifted toward the heaven's edge . . . that's dearer than our Northern home, . . . than this our fathers' loam." The singers were drunk on love of country, and perhaps, a little on modest self-compliment:

> Our land is poor, shall thus remain
> For him who gold desires!

Finally, one is relieved to report, a supper of cold food was devoured, as the moon — which had risen during Cygnaeus' peroration — hung over Gumtäkt. Nordenstam thanked the students for the evening's pleasures in such eloquent terms that they carried him on their shoulders to his coach; he had the advantage over the late Thesleff of speaking Swedish with native fluency. The events of the evening were given poetic immortality by Topelius in a poem, "Finland's Name," which he published in his paper a week later:

> Oh youth, it is your mother's name,
> The dearest 'mongst the dear;
> She gave you life, and it she claims;
> Now swear, oh youth, while light remains,
> Her honor to revere.

August Mannerheim, Carl Gustaf's effeminate brother, a member of high society and a feared caricaturist, gave the day another kind of immortality with his cartoon of fat Cygnaeus and skinny Topelius on the podium, a cheering throng before them and a fullblown muse preparing to crown Cygnaeus' shaggy mane and Topelius' thinner locks.

14. Peaceful Intermezzo I: Pacius and Music

BEFORE THE ARRIVAL of Fredrik Pacius, there had been a musical life — but only of sorts — in Helsingfors. In the 1780's Bernhard Henrik Crusell, a boy from Nurmijärvi, had become a bandsman on Sveaborg, whence he went on to Stockholm and a career as one of Europe's great clarinet virtuosi. Sveaborg had again given the city a kind of musical distinction at the beginning of the Russian period. Ludvig von Heiden, commander of Sveaborg from 1815 to 1823, was a lover of music and, like Esterhazy, supported an orchestra of some distinction. Its first conductor was a Pole, Joseph Tadeucz Tvaryansky; when Tvaryansky was lured to the mainland by the bandmaster's post in the Finnish Guards, he was replaced by another Pole, Johan Christoffer Downer. Suddenly von Heiden was called to Saint Petersburg, charged with involvement in certain peculations at his fortress; his patron gone, Downer likewise departed — for Åbo and its cathedral. He left Helsingfors too soon; the removal of the academy to Helsingfors meant that its musical traditions must also be transplanted. In 1833 an Academic Musical Society was founded in Helsingfors; its leader was Fredrik August Ehrström, the sometime seaman who put Runeberg to music. The Society arranged concerts, both vocal and instrumental, for the university and the capital at large. The city's concert life was also enlivened for a while by the presence of an Austrian named Josef Gehring who, like Ehrström, had come to Helsingfors from Åbo, where he had begun his Finnish musical career; Gehring was the founder of a so-called "permanent musical society" which collapsed upon the departure of the restless musician for Saint Petersburg and its brighter prospects. Another musical gift from Åbo was the Swedish cellist, Carl Vilhelm Salgé, music teacher at the academy since 1811; Downer had briefly been his assistant, during 1826–27. Salgé was indeed a man who needed assistance; when Salgé and Downer, a violinist, made a concert tour to Saint Petersburg, Downer discovered that his partner was more devoted to the bottle than to duets.

The death of Salgé in 1833 left the position of university music teacher, long open in fact, open in theory too. Perhaps Salgé's colleague Downer should have had the job, as a reward for what he had endured from Salgé; but it went instead to Fredrik Pacius, a first violinist in the Royal Orchestra at Stockholm. Vice-Chancellor Thesleff, whose German blood seems to have made him a good judge of musical accomplishment if not academic freedom, liked Pacius, as did Henrik Borgström, whose devotion to the city's cultural life, as Topelius remarked, "would have made him a Lorenzo dei Medici, had he lived in Florence." The Academic Musical Society was changed into a simple "Musical Society," in order to win broader support, with Pacius as its director; on Good Friday, 1835, it performed Ludwig Spohr's *Die vier letzten Dinge*, and Topelius — present, of course — became ecstatic: "At the 'Heilig, heilig, heilig, ist Gott der Herr,' a nameless feeling streamed through the depths of my heart." (Topelius was certainly not constrained by any sophistication in musical matters; hearing an oboist perform at Borgström's house, he decided that the man played well, but that, as an instrument, the oboe was a "poor and squeaky" thing, not good for much.) With a new name and a new leader, the Musical Society still could not survive; it was dissolved in 1838, like Gehring's group before it. Pacius deduced that choral music, allowing amateur participation, might win steadier support than instrumental undertakings. He established a general "Song Society" which was to take part in the performance of those oratorios the nineteenth century affected to love so much; then he saw to the creation, in 1838, of the "Akademiska sångsällskapet," the "Academic Song Society," which was redubbed "Akademiska sångföreningen" or "The Academic Song Club." The men's choir, heavy with tradition, exists until this very day; Pacius was its director until 1846, and remained its supreme authority throughout his life.

As events had showed, Friedrich (or, Swedicized, Fredrik) Pacius was the right man at the right place. The son of a well-to-do and cultured Hamburg wine-dealer, he had got a proper education both in school and at home; in his father's house he acquired that personal solidity, and a concomitant respect for the same quality in others, which were of immeasurable value to him as he dealt with Helsingfors merchants. He had been a gifted student of Ludwig Spohr, whose music he never stopped playing in later life, and was altogether capable of appearing as a violin soloist on the concert stage; yet, again, his talent was not so great that it made him restless. Nor, having come to Helsingfors in 1835 as the university's music teacher, did he want to leave the nest he built; in 1842, he married Nina Martin, the daughter of a good Helsingfors family, into which he had been introduced by Professor Gadolin, his landlord during his first years in Finland. Pacius spoke Swedish fluently and correctly, although with an accent often smiled at, and thus was able to move easily in literary and academic circles; Topelius and Cygnaeus were not only his collaborators but his personal friends, he got on well with Lönnrot, despite the fact that he was decidedly and vocally "Scandinavian" rather than "Finnish" in his sympathies, and he even managed to be on good terms with Snellman. Among his intimates were Vilhelm Lagus, the philologist and son of the university's sometime rector; Alexander Collan, a brother of Fabian and Karl, a gifted physician; and Berndt Otto Schauman, an eccentric but distinguished member of the gifted Schauman tribe. With "a long, pale face, shadowed by a rich growth of hair, . . . a white slender hand," and a terrible temper, Pacius was what the nineteenth century thought a musician should be; but he was a charmer only within the bounds of propriety (Emilie Björkstén, Runeberg's "own beloved," was genteelly fond of him). The temper was balanced by a sense of humor, and a readiness to forgive and forget, which surely made his musical life, surrounded by talented amateurs, the easier to live, and the favor of the amateurs' prosperous relatives the easier to keep. He concertized together with his violin pupil, Leonhard Borgström, Henrik's son; whatever tolerance he had to muster was rewarded immmediately by Borgström senior and, forty-odd years later, by Leonhard's aid in the founding of the Helsingfors Musical Institute (1882). He was patient in his tutoring of Anna, Ulla, and Adolf Wasenius for their roles in his opera *Kung Carls jagt* (*King Charles' Hunt*); at the party following the premiere their father, Gustaf Otto, started off the collection for a new theater in Helsingfors with a gift of 500 rubles. There is a sad coda to the story; the old consul fell ill immediately thereafter, and, as he drifted into death, his children were unable to take part in the performances any longer. The main role, the king's, was entrusted to a schoolboy whose voice had matured early, Carl Robert Mannerheim. The stage-king's son, in turn, would some day be the marshal of Finland and its president.

Pacius had his detractors, it is true. His faithfulness to Spohr led a newspaper to remark that people had heard *Die vier letzten Ding*e until it was coming out of their ears, and the *littérateur* and composer Axel Gabriel Ingelius had many a hard word for his conducting, his violin-playing, and, last but no means least, the derivative nature of his compositions. Ingelius, a chronic failure in the arts, may have been envious of Pacius' success: after years of disappointment and alcoholism, this author of chaotic musical novels, reduced to piano-tuning, died a classical Finnish death, frozen in a snowbank; but the modern observer is inclined to agree with Ingelius' judgment on Pacius the composer, and to suspect that his choral and, especially, his orchestral concerts left much to be desired. Of course, it was not the fault of Pacius that the few professional players in Helsingfors were mostly foreigners who, for one reason or another, including the inability to meet continental standards, had found their way to what was an out-of-the-way corner of the North. And Pacius himself knew his limitations as a composer; he wrote to his brother that: "You know I have no great pretensions as a writer of music." The score of *Kung Carls jagt*, with its huntsmen's choruses, could scarcely have come into being without the aid of Weber's *Freischütz*. But *Helsingfors Tidningar* was right when it said that the opera represented "the . . . victory of music in Finland, and a whole future lies in the fact."

When Ferruccio Busoni came to Helsingfors in 1888 as piano teacher at the Musical Institute, Pacius was still very much alive; history records that he was rude toward the young virtuoso. The old German had long since become one of Finland's national monuments, and every schoolchild could sing "Our Country" and another patriotic hymn, "Suomi's Song," to von Quanten's words, and perhaps even the Pacius setting of the opening canto of *Fänrik Stål's* second part, "The Soldier Boy," a militarist's delight. Furthermore, he had created the "Age of Pacius" in the musical life of Helsingfors, and of Finland.

Lacking Pacius' talents as organizer and composer, lacking his reasonably high standards of performance, Helsingfors would have had to content itself during the century's middle decades with the vagaries of local talent and the treats provided by travelling virtuosi — of whom a good many appeared, for Helsingfors made a profitable stopover between Saint Petersburg and Stockholm. Ole Bull came in 1838, Jenny Lind in 1843; the soprano lured Runeberg away from his summer home at Kroksnäs, and inspired B.O. Lille both to tears and, apparently, romantic love: he wrote sentimental verses to her, even as Hans Christian Andersen had. Other artists came too — the Schmidts from Amsterdam, who performed trombone duets, Franz Schalk from Austria, a virtuoso on a vanishing instrument, the basset horn, and the aging Hermann Levy, another Austrian, for whom Beethoven is supposed to have written the infamous fourth-horn part in the slow movement of the Ninth. A more staple fare was provided by the several opera companies which turned up not infrequently at the theater Engel had built: Schultz's (also a theatrical troupe), Madame Kesteloot's, whose directress and star had seen better days in Germany, Hornicke's, in which the director himself appears to have been something of a vocal phenomenon, since he dared to sing both baritone (Don Giovanni, Fra Diavolo, Zampa) and tenor roles (Masaniello). It may be that his audience was not able to detect subtle differences; *Morgonbladet* speaks expressly of his splendid tenor voice. Surely, Helsingfors was lucky when it got the services and knowledge of Pacius, who provided the ingredients of a musical tradition. It was much too early to think seriously of export; yet some of the songs of Pacius did find their way to Germany, and a local soprano, Johanna von Schoultz, made a name for herself by singing the Finnish folksong, "Tuoll' on mun kultani," throughout Scandinavia and in southern Europe, where briefly, she was a feted Amina and Rosina. Beset by tuberculosis, she abandoned the great world, retiring to Helsingfors, obscurity and death.

15. Peaceful Intermezzo II: Actors Bad and Good

IN HELSINGFORS TIDNINGAR for October 29, 1851, Zachris Topelius had published the introduction to a series of novellas which would follow the fortunes of the Bertelskiölds — sometime Ostrobothnian farmers, the Bertilas, whose first notable representative was enobled on the battle-field — from the days of the Thirty Years' War to the beginning of the reign of Gustaf III. (Gustaf Bertila was, in fact, the love child of Gustaf II Adolf and a lovely maiden, who had been sent by her well-to-do peasant father to the court at Stockholm.) The series received the title, *Fältskärns berättelser* (*The Tales of a Field-Surgeon*) because, like the verse tales of Runeberg's Ensign Stål, it is told by a veteran of the last days of Swedish control in Finland. The work's publication would not be concluded until 1866; it became a piece of national literature, second in popularity only to Runeberg's epic, of which the latter half appeared in 1860. Determined to give Finland an account of its glorious history in prose fiction, Topelius also felt the call to offer a national opera (to be sure, with some musical aid) and a national drama. He would be Finland's Scott, its Carl Maria von Weber, and its Schiller, all rolled into one. The musical deed was accom-plished when, on March 24, 1852, the opera *Kung Carls jagt*, with text by Topelius (and, as said above, music by Pacius) received its premiere: de-spite the 74 rehearsals, Pacius is said to have looked "as pale as a con-demned man" upon ascending the podium to confront his amateur company. *Kung Carls jagt* told a story about the visit of Charles XI of Sweden to Åland and the quelling of a conspiracy against him; in the li-bretto, Charles is not the cold and unimaginative monarch of Merimée's *Vision de Charles XI*, but a boyish and romantic charmer — even as he is in one of the cycles of *Fältskärns berättelser*. The audience loved Charles, and it loved the tributes the opera paid to Finland still more; as the king sailed off into the sunset, in the finale, a chorus sang about his unwilling departure from Finland's strand ("that dear land, that beloved land"). Af-ter the last hurrahs from the stage and the auditorium, Pacius was crowned with a laurel wreath, and both cast and audience, wild with na-tional exultation, sang "Our Country." A party was given at Society House for the participants; the composer and the poet, according to one story, had to drink a "toast of brotherhood" a hundred times. Hardened though he was to Finnish alcoholic habits, the ceremony was too much for

Topelius, and he departed early, leaving his German colleague to be lionized alone. It was a fitting triumph for Pacius; a solo victory of Topelius, in his efforts to create a national drama for Finland, came a year later, when his play, *Regina von Emmeritz*, based on a tale in *Fältskärns berättelser*, was given its first performance.

Through the columns of *Helsingfors Tidningar*, Topelius had long since taken up the question of the acquisition of a permanent theatrical troupe for Helsingfors. In the spring of 1843, he wrote: "Why don't we possess a national theater, or even a single theatrical talent, we can call our own? You reply that we are too serious for that. Well, why don't we try the tragedy?" It was not surprising that music had to go through hard times in Helsingfors; but the theater, by reasonable expectations, should have been off to a strong start. Ehrenström, the truest of Gustavians, was a friend of the drama; by 1813, Helsingfors already had a temporary theater, an artillery shed in Kronohagen. The shed was extensively rebuilt to suit its new purpose; Ehrenström boasted that its auditorium was the most beautiful in all of Finland. (The competition was very thin.) The first troupe was Johann Gappmeyer's, come from Saint Petersburg by way of Reval, and playing in German; its repertoire was comprised of farces interlarded with serious stuff — the inevitable Kotzebue, Schiller, and a Shakespeare much revised. Other bands, including some from Sweden, followed. During the year of mourning for Alexander I (1826), theatrical performances were forbidden; life on the Helsingfors boards was splendidly reborn with the troupe, German again, of Johann Arnold Schultz, which had the honor of inaugurating the new and terribly uncomfortable theater of Engel, in the Esplanade, with a performance of Kotzebue's *Die Korsen* on March 9, 1827. The Schultz troupe favored Helsingfors by its presence fairly steadily until 1834, when its leader decided that he could endure no more. The problems he confronted were many, and not just those caused by the devil of theatrical accidents: Carl Gustaf Mannerheim, attending a farewell performance in December, 1827, looked aloft to see a Cupid peering down at the audience, prepared to sprinkle messages of thankful goodbye upon its collective head; "but when Cupid was about to emerge through the hole in the ceiling where the chandelier is hoisted up and down, the poor fellow got caught and had to stay there for half an hour before help came." The attendance at the stage plays given by the troupe was necessarily limited; in Helsingfors, a German play would attract, usually, German-speaking officers from Sveaborg, members of the aristocracy and academe, and those merchants who were at home in the lingua franca of the Baltic. Schultz must have given his operas in order to attract a larger audience; as every American knows, the true friend of opera does not need to understand the libretto. But the temperature in the

building was a more dangerous foe than mishap or foreign tongue; Jac-
quette Jägerhorn told a friend: "I haven't been at the theater for two
weeks, as I ascribe the rheumatic pangs, to which I have once again fallen
prey . . . to a spectacle [there], and for this reason I've almost taken a
pledge not to visit the place during the cold seasons of the year." Schultz
gave up, to be succeeded by other brave Germans: Weylandt, a virile Robert the Devil in Meyerbeer's opera (but shortly thereafter a pathetic victim
of demon rum), and his colleagues from the German theater of the Saint
Petersburg court, the tenor Köcher and the comedian Mohr. In connection with the last-named, it is pleasant to record that he helped to make
the sober citizens of Helsingfors (doubtless less sober than Topelius rhet-
orically claimed they were) acquainted with the Viennese comedies of the
immortal Nestroy. The German companies — inclining more and more to
opera, as time went on — came to the end of their rope in the 1840's.
Not even the lovely pair of sisters, the Reithmeyers of Hornicke's troupe,
could save them. The elder, Julia, won hearts both as a female (in Bellini's
Norma) and a male (Romeo in Bellini's *I Capuletti ed i Montecchi*); and
Johanna, an alto and younger, captured something more valuable, a proposal of marriage (promptly accepted) from the young physician, Georg
Wallgren. The Reithmeyer charm worked wonders, but it could not stem
the tide that demanded theatrical performances in Swedish, the mother
tongue of the majority of the audience.

The Swedish troupes, which alternated with the Germans and eventually replaced them altogether, came directly from Sweden and spoke
Swedish accordingly; the effect was that of a British company appearing
before an American audience. The most important of these troupes in the
1830's was led by Carl Vilhelm Westerlund, who knew how to carry an
unsophisticated public along by force of histrionics. Westerlund's wife and
leading lady was a rare bird, a speaker of Finland-Swedish who became a
star of Finland's Swedish stage, where the audiences, with the snobbish-
ness born of an inferiority complex, believed that they got less than their
money's worth if they heard their native accent from the boards. Marie
Silfvan-Westerlund had begun as a nubile ticket seller for Bonuvier's
Swedish troupe, when it had its own theater in Åbo, in the days before the
great fire; marrying one of its members, Evert Lemke, she let him train her
in proper Swedish diction and the dramatic arts. Then after some twelve
years, she divorced Lemke, replacing him with the energetic Westerlund.
Happily, Lemke was not cast aside; he stayed on with the newlyweds and
their band, in consequence of a divorce-settlement which promised him
(as the wronged party) support for the rest of his natural life. The repertoire of the Westerlunds was considerably more respectable than their private behavior: they did Gustavian and post-Gustavian plays from

Stockholm, they did Calderón, Schiller, and Kotzebue, they did the new French dramatist Scribe and the Austrian Franz Grillparzer. It was Grillparzer's *Sappho* which brought Madam Silfvan-Westerlund, grown ever more corpulent, to a fall: "for when, with a paper lyre in her hand, she threw herself down from the cliffs into the waves, flat footed, the boards gave out a horrible crash." Her size and the new steamboats (which could bring over first-rate guests from Sweden) put an end to the Westerlund era; the great actor settled down as a brewer and restaurant-owner in subarctic Uleåborg, and faithful Lemke was his bookkeeper.

The visitors from Sweden introduced a new and somewhat better time; in the summer of 1836, members of "The Royal Swedish Theater" appeared, with Emilie Högqvist — the great Swedish Ophelia of her day — as their star, then came the Torsslows, the brothers Deland, and Edvard Stjernström. The Torsslows were performers of the first magnitude and, as in the case of Miss Högqvist, their occasional visits let the people of Helsingfors find out how subtle good professionals could be. The Delands, the many-sided Pierre (who created the role of Magnus Drakenhjelm in *Efter femtio år* [*Fifty Years Later*] of Topelius), and the comedian Fredrik, were not of the same stature as the Torsslows, but they were ready to give Helsingfors more of their time. Topelius characterized Pierre, his wife, and their three daughters thus: "Vivacity, finesse, proportion, and, at the same time, a cultivated manner of speech [were] the qualities" which distinguished them. As for Fredrik, he was more popular even than the dignified Pierrre, introducing the Helsingfors audience to the new Stockholm farces of August Blanche; he also turned the pioneer play of Fredrik Berndtson, *Friaren från Åbo* (*The Suitor from Åbo*), into a boxoffice success, aided by the fact that it had a setting in Kajsaniemi. Stjernström, as gifted an administrator as he was an actor, knew the way to theatrical success in the Grand Duchy, which he had visited before; he organized a troupe expressly for a sojourn in Finland, appearing first, for experience's sake, in Åbo, Viborg, and Borgå, and then settling down in the capital. The Stjernström players were in Helsingfors from 1851 to 1853; the artistic pinnacle of their engagement was the staging of still another Berndtson play, *Ur lifvets strid* (*From Life's Strife*), about the War of 1808–09, and *Regina von Emmeritz* of Topelius, in which Stjernström himself played Gustaf Adolf and Fru Lagerqvist, a beauty well-known to Helsingfors audiences from the days of the Deland company, played the heroine.

The triumphant premiere of *Regina* took place on April 13, 1853; theater-goers in Helsingfors had just had time to catch their breath after *Kung Carls jagt*. The play's success consoled Topelius for the critical buffeting (especially at the hands of Fredrik Cygnaeus) his initial dramatic

venture, *Efter femtio år*, had received the previous spring. (The public had
liked the earlier play, however; in its main character, the old Gustavian
Drakenhjelm, they thought they saw their sometime *arbiter voluptatis*, the
late Otto Vilhelm Klinckowström.) Enjoying the applause, Topelius was
nonetheless dissatisfied with the performance Fru Lagerqvist gave in this
first Finnish tragedy; she was "as beautiful as a picture, and as stiff." Regina became a touchstone for Finland's actresses; Hedvig Charlotte
Forsman-Raa, and Ida Reis-Brander both tried their hand at it, and only
the great Ida Aalberg, appearing in the role in Finnish translation in 1882–
83, got Topelius' full approval. Of course, Topelius had presented them
with a hard job; Regina is the faithful Franconian Catholic who, misled by
the evil Jesuit Hieronymus, gets the assignment of murdering Gustaf
Adolf, a deed to which she at first looks forward. Love spoils her potential
for assassination; she becomes enamoured of the Swedish Lion, and, by
the fifth act, can find no way out of her dilemma save death. As contemporary critics were quick to remark, too much of Regina's torment, in this
novella converted to play, takes place inside her, unrevealed to the audience; Topelius himself understood the nature of the fault, and revised the
drama before it was printed in 1854 , a quarter of a century later, he was
still tinkering with it. Today, it is difficult to find the "demoniac air of the
darkhaired sulphur-flower" Eino Leino once descried in Regina — to be
sure, in an ironic context. And if Regina herself has grown pale, her men-
tor, the vicious Jesuit, has become utterly ludicrous. It does not matter;
Topelius had given Finland a serious play on a theme that was somehow
very Finnish, too, although the action takes place in Germany, the theme
of loyality and treachery. Whether the contemporary public pondered the
play's drift, is another story; they were probably content to see the Swedish king surrounded by officers of the Finnish Horse, and to hear the
sounds of "The Finnish Cavalry's March in the Thirty Years' War" as the
final curtain went down.

16. Nicholas's Twilight

THE HONEYMOON WITH Nordenstam ended all too quickly. Nicholas got
word of the Viennese students' role in the Austrian uprising, and Nordenstam immediately received orders to instruct his charges that, although
they were true Finns, they should never forget that they were also "His
Imperial Majesty's subjects." Granting himself unlimited disciplinary
power, the hero of the Caucasus decided to make sure of the students'

loyalty; the academic uniforms, hitherto donned by the students whenever the spirit moved them, now had to be worn in public at all times. Next, taking a leaf from the sister university at Dorpat, in Russian Estonia, Nordenstam appointed an academic "inspector," whose job it was to look after the behavior of the young gentlemen. The inspector turned out to be one Baron Hjärne — an unusually stupid man, according to Grot, and a well-known roué. These characteristics, to be sure, may have helped Hjärne and the students in getting along with one another; the baron had sown so many wild oats of his own that he possessed neither the energy nor the desire to be a stern father. His six assistants were more to be feared; they were a police force in miniature, even in their dress, "a blue uniform with shiny buttons," and their weapon, a short black staff with an ivory tip. The traditional "student nations" (or "divisions," as they were now called in Helsingfors) were dissolved because of their reputation as breeding grounds for trouble; the students would be split up among the academic faculties, in accordance with their fields of study. The deanships of the various faculties no longer would rotate among the professors; instead, the chancellor himself — in other words, Alexander, the heir of the imperial throne — would choose the deans. The "philosophical faculty" was split into two parts, the "historical-philological" and the "physical-mathematical" faculties; and the dangerous professorship of philosophy was abolished — or rather, transferred to the faculty of law, where the students with philosophical inclinations could feast on "the law of nations" and "moral philosophy." The university statutes of 1852 contained some valuable reforms: they called for careful planning of lectures and examinations, a simplification of the university's finances, and the appointment of a *consistorium plenum*, made up of the rector and the two or three eldest members of each faculty, in order to free the other professors from administrative burdens — a sacrifice, as it were, of the few for the many. However, these improvements could not hide what the reactionary spirit in Saint Petersburg had wrought. Nicholas was the source of it all, and Nordenstam was his agent on the scene; but the operative evil genius was Casimir von Kothen, native of Finland, Russian officer, and presently (he was Menshikov's trusted favorite) governor of Viborg province. Von Kothen was reputed to have been the moving force behind the suppression of Snellman's *Saima* and the Finnish language rescript of 1850; now this dangerously active man turned his attention to Finland's university, pulling the more liberal Alexander Armfelt and Carl Gustaf Mannerheim along behind him — the former was secretary of state for Finnish affairs, the latter (who would rather have given his time to his entomology) the chairman of the committee appointed to revise the university's statutes. Helsingfors had not heard the last of von Kothen.

On January 20, 1851, Grot wrote to Pletnyov that "a great deal of animosity prevails toward Nordenstam," a good soldier who carried out his orders with zeal. Nordenstam's critics remarked that behavior learned while roughing it in the Caucasus was scarcely appropriate in academic circles; the students struck back with what weapons they had. Nine days before Grot composed his letter, Vice Chancellor Nordenstam had held a ball to celebrate Alexander's 25 years as chancellor of the university, a post in which the Czarevitch had begun at the age of seven. The ball was preceded, as usual, by academic festivities; Cygnaeus wrote a poem in twelve strophes beginning "Per Brahe's spirit stood upon a silver cloud," Pacius wove a cantata out of part of the text, Professor Ilmoni made a speech, and the program was opened and closed, unaccountably, with Mendelssohn's *Wedding March*. A dinner for 200 guests was held at Society House, and during the ball itself all domiciles belonging to the university's teachers and employees had candles in their windows: a transparency painted by B.A. Godenhjelm, an instructor at the new Finnish Art Association, hung over the facade of the university's main building. Yet all was not well, despite these manifold signs of loyalty; forty students, handpicked by Rector Rein to attend the ball, did not appear. Poor Rein had been informed of the boycott in advance, as had Lars Gabriel von Haartman, who made Rein writhe by a lecture on the hideous punishments awaiting the culprits and their institution; Rein tried to reason with the students, but they refused to give in. However they did make an effort to show that their ill will was directed at Nordenstam and not at Alexander; they assembled at Kajsaniemi (indoors) to toast the chancellor, and then stood before the university building, singing the Russian national anthem and "Our Country." The penalties for their stubbornness were less serious than von Haartman had thought; Alexander decided that the offenders should be suspended until the end of the term, but Nordenstam himself — he *did* have a chivalrous side — asked the Czarevitch to pardon them instead. Alexander agreed, announcing his generosity in the speech he made to the student body on his visit to the university in March 1851. So overwhelmed were the students by this gesture, and by Alexander's ability to say "I thank you" in Swedish when they had sung "Our Country" for him, that they subsequently accepted the statutes of 1852, and the obligatory uniforms, more gracefully than otherwise might have been the case. Disillusioned by the fickleness of his charges, Nordenstam obtained release from his office in September, 1855 — the request was granted by the sometime chancellor and new emperor, Alexander II. The regulations concerning uniforms were relaxed in 1860, in keeping with the liberal spirit of Alexander's reign, and the "student divisions," which had led an illegal existence ever since they had been forbidden, were allowed to come out of hiding in 1868.

In the twilight of Nicholas's despotism, Helsingfors was a martial and gloomy place. The French traveler, Léouzon Le Duc, was struck by the air the city had of being a military camp: "In the morning, the sound of the drum and the bugle awakens its inhabitants and, from the exercise fields lying beyond the walls, one hears the repeated commands of the officers and the sounds of firearms." Two of the military establishments were nominally Finland's, of course, the Finnish Guards and the sailors; but they were also as much the instruments of the emperor's will as the Russian troops — infantry, artillery, Cossacks — quartered in the city, not to forget the large contingent on Sveaborg. Usually so sanguine, Ramsay remembered the times thus: "it was as if the skies were wholly covered by dark thunderclouds, one had the sensation of being enclosed from every side." Hopes were raised, only to fall again; the deaths of the university's young heroes, Castrén and Wallin, did not fail to have an effect, and it should not be forgotten that they occurred in the year the university's new statutes were initiated. These academic tragedies took place against a background of civil disaster; the cholera epidemic of 1853 was even worse than the dreadful one of 1831, and Sven Elmgren told in his diary about the panic that spread over the city. Spirits got some cause to rise again in the early months of 1854, when first Lönnrot, then Cygnaeus, then Topelius (the last-named on a special appointment) held the inaugural lectures for their professorships at the university; the caretakers of Finland's culture had just got official recognition. (There is a touching vignette about Lönnrot's appointment; two hundred students marched to his house, to congratulate and serenade him, and found the simple man on skis, about to take his daily exercise.) Lönnrot replaced Castrén; in the fall of 1854, Wallin's post was filled, too, by Herman Kellgren, an appointment which aroused something less than general enthusiasm — his enemies considered the new professor of oriental literature to be "a charlatan, a hypocrite, and a selfish schemer." Whatever his personal qualities, Kellgren deserved respect for what he had done to advance the cause of Finnish; he had served for a while as an editor of *Suometar*, and, again in the company of his brother-in-law Tikkanen, had been the co-owner of "Öhman's Bookstore," a venture with the express purpose of making books in Finnish available to the public. Surviving the censor's order of 1850, the bookstore was forced to close by the economic difficulties attendant upon the Crimean War. Nor did Kellgren himself live much longer; he died in 1856, at the age of 34. Death seemed to side against Finland: the case of the family of old Professor Tengström would prove it. He had lost his son Robert in 1847, one of his daughters was married to M.A. Castrén, another to Kellgren — both became young widows. Then, in 1857, Helena Maria, the daughter who was Tikkanen's wife and good genius, died in childbirth; and, four months after, Tikkanen's home was destroyed by fire. These catastrophes, together with the financial difficulties which must pursue a man dedicated to furthering the cause of Finnish in the Helsingfors of the middle nineteenth century, caused Tikkanen to lose his mind; he ended his days as a patient at Helsingfors' insane asylum beside Lappviken — as had his contemporary, the young Finnish historian, Johan Esaias Waaranen.

Nevertheless there was some light in the darkness, radiated not least by a man with very good reason to be devoted to Emperor Nicholas. In 1852, Zachris Topelius was about to be lost to Helsingfors, like Runeberg before him. In order to acquire a sure income for his family and himself, Topelius had twice applied for a position in history at Vasa, and his second effort, made in the spring of 1852, met with success; as the result of a fire in Vasa, the school was moved to Jakobstad, a tiny town on the Gulf of Bothnia north of the first-named city. Even though he came from those far-off reaches, Topelius called the new site a "Van Dieman's Land." Upon Nicholas's last visit to Helsingfors in 1854, Fredrik Cygnaeus decided that he must do what he could to save Topelius for the capital. His customary self-confidence enhanced by his own new professorship, Cygnaeus approached Alexander Armfelt with the half-joking proposal that Topelius be named lecturer in Swedish at Helsingfors University. Armfelt committed one of the few daring deeds in his careful life by suggesting to the chancellor — i.e. Alexander, the heir to the throne — that Topelius be appointed professor extraordinary in Finland's history, a subject which was not a part of the university's regular curriculum and a post for which Topelius possessed no particular scholarly qualifications. Chancellor Alexander gave assent, assent all the more notable in the light of what Topelius had recently done to foster a Finnish national consciousness. Here, as later, Alexander demonstrated that special talent he had for handling the Grand Duchy — encouragement in mild doses, rather than oppression, was the policy by which he would win an affection greater even than that granted his uncle, Alexander I.

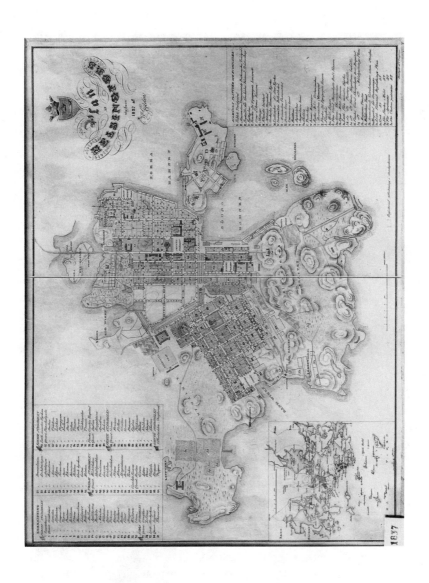

1. Map of Helsingfors (Helsinki), 1837.
(Helsingfors City Museum)

*2. Senate Square, Nikolai-Church, and the University Library.
Lithograph by F. Liewendahl, 1851. (Helsingfors City Museum)*

3. View from the Tower of the Nikolai-Church toward Skatudden and the Uspenski Cathedral. Photograph by E. Hoffers, 1866. (Helsingfors City Museum)

4. View from Kronohagen toward the Finnish Naval Barracks on Skatudden in the 1860's. (Helsingfors City Museum)

5. The Yusupoff Mansion in Brunnsparken in the 1860's.
(Helsingfors City Museum)

*6. Skatudden, 1868. Photograph by L.A. Hårdh.
(Helsingfors City Museum)*

7. Västra Henriksgatan 6, Eugen Hoffers' photographic studio, c. 1870. Presently Mannerheimvägen 2. (Helsingfors City Museum)

8. Åbo Barracks and Arcadia Theater on Västra Henriksgatan.
Photograph c. 1870. (Helsingfors City Museum)

9. *Market Place. Drosky drivers beside the Empress' Stone during the 1880's. Photograph by Charles Riis and Co. (Helsingfors City Museum)*

10. Strollers on the Runeberg Esplanade in the 1890's. Runeberg's statue and the rear side of Swedish Theater in the background. (Helsingfors City Museum)

11. Imperial Alexander's Theater, Boulevard 23–25 (later the home of Finnish Opera). Photograph by Charles Riis and Co., c. 1900. (Helsingfors City Museum)

12. Governor-General Bobrikov's Funeral Cortège, June, 1904.
(Helsingfors City Museum)

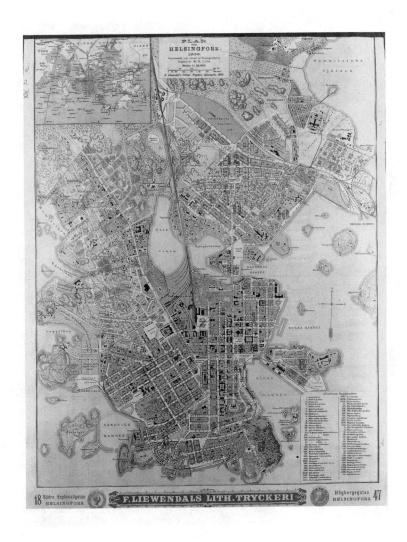

13. W. O. Lille's Map of Helsingfors (Helsinki), 1909.
(Helsingfors City Museum)

14. *Fish Market in the South Harbor. Uspenski Cathedral in the*
background. Photograph by Signe Brander, 1912.
(Helsingfors City Museum)

II. 1854–1898

1. The Crimean War

IN THE SPRING of 1853, Prince Menshikov — the eternally absent governor-general of Finland — was dispatched to Constantinople as the emissary of Nicholas, there to inform the Sultan that the Czar of all the Russias intended to protect the Greek Christians of Turkey. By October, the Turks had declared war on Russia, and in November the British and French governments entered into an alliance with their Moslem friends. Three months more, and the sea-powers opened hostilities against Nicholas, too; Finland's coast lay open to attack by their ships. Sveaborg suddenly came alive, and Konstantin, Nicholas's second son and Grand Admiral of the Russian navy, arrived to inspect the fortress in February, 1854; a month later, he appeared again, followed directly by his father. The diarist Sven Elmgren recalled that Helsingfors had not welcomed Nicholas since 1833, in the wake of the Polish insurgence; rediscovered, the city fell into its customary "imperial delirium." There were still no railroads; Nicholas came by sleigh from Saint Petersburg, and on the night of March 13, the faithful people of Helsingfors waited for him in a heavy fog. After a false alarm, which turned out to be the chief constable of Helsinge parish in full regalia, the Czar and his entourage swept down Unionsgatan by torchlight, just as Nicholas's brother, Alexander I, had done four decades earlier. Giving priority to the institution he trusted the least, Nicholas visited the university at noon the next day. Pains were taken to seat students with new academic uniforms in the front rows of the aula, and Alexander Armfelt, Nicholas's minister of state for Finnish affairs, arrived ahead of time to tell the youths that they were expected to cheer. Cheer they did; unfortunately, very few of them understood Nicholas's speech, and so they gave vent to their patriotism, as instructed, at what they assumed to be the end of the imperial address. They were in error. Perplexed at the enthusiastic interruption, the ruler of a good part of the world continued to the genuine conclusion of his text, whereupon he got another salvo of hurrahs. In the afternoon, Nicholas visited the buildings (among them the Nikolai-Church, the hospitals, the observatory, the library) which had been finished since his last visit to Helsingfors, and then, the evening come, he appeared on the balcony of his palace to thank the students who had vouchsafed him a torchlight parade, a performance of the Russian national anthem, "God Shield the Czar," in Finnish, and, to be sure, "Our Country." The second and final day of the visit was devoted to military tasks. Instead of being left at home to defend their native coast, the Finnish Guards were on orders to leave directly for service in Russia, and so they must be reviewed on Senate Square; having spent the afternoon in an inspection of Sveaborg, Nicholas left Helsingfors at 5:30 in the afternoon. He was a sick man during this last swift junket; upon his death, a year later, the university mourned him — with words by Cygnaeus, "The last and quiet strife was at an end," and music by the equally indefatigable Pacius, an oratorio which made "the Christian Emperor" seem another Godfrey of Bouillon, another Gustaf Adolf. In *Helsingfors Tidningar*, Topelius predicted that tears would be shed for Nicholas "in every Finnish hut." A young natural scientist named Thiodolf Saelan observed a different species of weeping: "Happiness glistened in every eye . . . we could breathe freely at last."

Two weeks after Nicholas said goodbye to Helsingfors, the British and the French made their official declaration of war, the Admirality already having dispatched Sir Charles Napier and his squadron to the Baltic. On April 8, 1854, the first British ship was sighted off Helsingfors, and on May 19–20 a series of small engagements took place at the approaches to Ekenäs, a coastal town in western Nyland. The British landing parties were driven off, and the losses on shore were light: a major and three men were killed when a steam-frigate ran aground opposite a shore battery and, making the best of a bad situation, blew the Finnish battery to pieces with its broadsides before it pulled free. The affair had sentimental overtones: faithful old A.E. Ramsay, the veteran of the storming of Warsaw, commanded the defenders, and Finnish sharpshooters stood side by side with Russian grenadiers on the shore. The Russo-Finnish artist Vladimir Svertshkoff was quick to immortalize "the battle of Vitsand" in a painting; in verse, Topelius moved with even greater speed. The readers of *Helsingfors Tidningar* were informed, in "The First Drop of Blood," that "the pirates" should remember the lesson of Vitsand:

> The ancient heart of Finland throbs for God and fatherland,
> In faith unto our duty and with weapons in our hand!

(Topelius never included the militant poem in any collection of his verse; however, it achieved wide international currency, not only in Sweden but in English, French, and German translations, the last made by none other than the young Swiss Conrad Ferdinand Meyer, someday to be one of the great symbolist poets in the German language.) The feelings of Topelius were certainly not shared in all circles. The skeptical newspaperman, August Schauman, called the war "a heavy duty," for which it was difficult to muster enthusiasm; and there were even those advocates of a Scandinavian union, such as Emil von Quanten in his Stockholm exile, who hoped that Sweden would enter the fighting on the Allied side, an act which, after victory, would cause Finland to be detached from the Russian empire.

Whatever their opinion of the conflict, the people of Helsingfors could not ignore present realities. The Finnish Guard long remained on garrison duty in western Russia, not returning to Helsingfors until six months after peace was concluded; sanitary conditions were so bad that disease killed far more Finnish soldiers than the enemy would have. Meanwhile, unit upon unit of Russian troops streamed into Helsingfors: grenadiers, the Grodno hussars, artillery, engineers, cossacks; the city had a hard time finding quarters for the soldiers not swallowed up by Sveaborg. Still, the Russian presence must have been a comfort, for the British displayed their skill with raids on Brahestad and Uleåborg, on the Gulf of Bothnia. Admiral Plumridge — "Admiral Plundering" — had easy pickings among Finland's coastal shipping, and Napier's fleet was sighted off Sveaborg. Particularly frightening was "a giant ship of the line with two stacks and the admiral's ensign," which, the watchers on the Ulrikasborg Heights decided, must be the flagship, *The Duke of Wellington*. As Sveaborg restored its neglected defences — the Russian admiral Arkas could scarcely believe his eyes upon beholding the disrepair — the greatest action of the first summer's war in the Baltic took place, the bombardment of Bomarsund Fortress on Åland, ending with the citadel's capitulation on August 16. Panic in Helsingfors, fed by this news, got more fuel when, later in the month, three forts on the southern part of Hangö peninsula were blown up at the order of their own commander. The autumn brought some surcease, and winter ice finally forced the Allies to lift their blockade. The total tonnage of the Helsingfors mercantile fleet had gone down by 60%; the city, accustomed to get a good part of its food and fuel from the skerry dwellers, found reason to complain about the Russian directive which forbade people living west of Porkala to sail to Helsingfors: the prohibition was designed not to protect the skerry-folk from the English, but to keep them from selling fresh provisions (and, maybe, fresh information) to the foe. In Helsingfors, too, before the ice set in, the populace had made wry comments about "our brave fleet," which did not venture away from the shelter of Sveaborg's guns; its officers evidently "did not wish to risk such a precious force, so important for the land's defence." The navy's principal activity took place on land. At their barracks on Skatudden, the future mariners of the First Naval Division were trained by means of infantry drill; a newly constituted "Second Naval Division," housed in the empty quarters of the Finnish Guards, had trouble in filling its ranks. Although plenty of seamen were out of work because of the blockade, they preferred idleness to military discipline.

As the bad year of 1854 came to a close, Rokassovsky, the acting governor-general, applied for release from his position, reasoning that he was more a man of peace than of arms. The request was granted, to the general unhappiness of Helsingfors, which had formed the warmest affection for the good and simple man. A propempticon in Swedish, by Professor B.O. Lille, the poet for all seasons, expressed the wish that he would soon return, a wish to be fulfilled sooner than anyone imagined. Rokassovsky's wartime replacement, Friedrich Wilhelm Berg, a nobleman from Livonia, was a fire-eater who had served against Napoleon and helped to subdue the Poles; in 1849, he had been on loan to the Austrian emperor in the cowing of the Hungarian rebels. Anxious to display his vitality to Helsingfors, Berg let the orders tumble from his mouth so rapidly that they contradicted one another; his subordinates noticed that he rouged his cheeks, and that he owned a set of wigs, with gray threads among the brown, which represented a progression, in their various lengths, from one haircut to the next. After a while, the people of Helsingfors learned to detest him; at first, they had been impressed by the energy with which he set up batteries on Stora Räntan, in the waters just off Brunnsparken, and in the park itself, at the same time laying out a roundabout system of back-roads and bridges to connect the island batteries east and west of town, on Sandhamn and Drumsö, to the mainland. Another preparatory measure was the mining of the harbor channels; unfortunately, the only victim of the mines was a little steamer attached to Berg's own harbor command. Otherwise, the crews of the British steam sloops made a sport of fishing the dangerous objects out of the water. These nautical adventures took place once the ice had melted. Prior to that usually anticipated but now dreaded event, the nervous people of Helsingfors were distracted by the news of Nicholas's death and the subsequent report that Alexander II had removed the supercilious Menshikov from his governor-generalship, so long held in absentia. Berg, already in Helsingfors, became Menshikov's successor.

Once warm weather arrived, the combined Allied fleets, commanded by Richard Saunders Dundas and Charles Penaud, made their presence felt all along Finland's southern coast. The summer was unusually fine, and strollers enjoyed the breezes on Observatory Hill, at the same time keeping a lookout for enemy ships. The Allies sharpened their skills by attacking smaller fortified points to the east of the capital: Fort Slava, near what later became the town of Kotka, was sent sky high, the batteries on Sandhamn (the eastern anchor of the Helsingfors system of defence) were reconnoitered from close in, and, on July 5, the fort at Lovisa was destroyed. (At the same time, by accident, the little town itself caught fire; the blame lay with the distraught residents of Lovisa themselves. The British navy, indeed, offered to send its jacktars ashore, to aid in putting out the blaze; but the citizens — remembering Plumridge's exploits of the year before — refused to accept the helping hand, and so Lovisa went up in smoke.) Then came August, and the turn of Helsingfors to suffer. By the evening of August 7, more than 70 vessels were assembled off Sveaborg; on the morning of the 9th, after divine services on board the British vessels, the bombardment began. Allied ships of the line lay farthest out, cannonboats darted closer to the fortress, back and forth among the floating batteries (likewise Allied), and the French dared to station a mortar section on Abrahamsholm, under the very nose of the Russians. The guns of Sveaborg, it was quickly discovered, could not reach the ships of the line, and hit the cannonboats but seldom; the British and French shells, however, had no difficulty in reaching Sveaborg and in setting its wooden buildings afire. The bombardment continued all day long, and, at night, Congreve rockets flew through the air; wounded from Sveaborg were brought to the South Harbor by boat, under the cover of darkness, and were then transported to the New Clinic on Unionsgatan. The civilians, not comforted by the order that there must be a barrel or two of water on every roof, spent the night in the open air, terrified lest they be caught in a sudden blaze. Some went to Kajsaniemi, some simply sat on the greensward in the middle of Henriksgatan, and some, the most vigorous or the most frightened, rowed out to Högholmen, putting up a regular tent city. The brave and the curious trooped southward, up the slope of Observatory Hill, following the excellent example of Berg himself, who had a look-out post there. Some souls were especially cool, or slaves of habit: at the opening of the bombardment, Dr. Rabbe drank his morning coffee with friends on the terrace of Kalliolinna, overlooking the harbor and Professor Matthias Akiander, ignoring his 53 years and the hostile shells, took his customary dip off Brunnsparken — all alone. Akiander, a specialist in Russian studies, was the son of a Finnish peasant; by his swim he lived up to the highest ideals of Finnish stubbornness.

The next day and the next night the bombardment continued; suddenly, at five in the morning on the 11th, it ceased, but the fleet lay in position until the 13th, when it sailed away. Berg had a gift for statistics if not generalship; he estimated that, during the 46 hours of shelling, about 17,000 shots had been fired by the busy foe, including 3,000 against the Sandhamn batteries and 1,000 against those on Drumsö. The damage done to Sveaborg was great, but the French newspaper report, "Sveaborg n'existe plus," was surely an exaggeration. As for Helsingfors itself, which depended (as the anti-Russian Schauman observed) on the gentlemanliness of the foe for its survival, it got a few accidental shells or fragments thereof. A corner of the Bath House in Brunnsparken was hit, the stairs of the casino were damaged; the shells had been intended for a nearby battery. Watching with ever-jaundiced eye the fortunes of high and low, Elmgren reported that some humble cottages were likewise struck: the house of Lind the cabinet-maker at the south end of Georgsgatan, chimney-sweep Ringvall's place on Stora Robertsgatan. The story that a Russian soldier picked up a bomb beside the imperial palace, only to drop it again — to his undoing — is touching but unlikely; the palace, on the North Esplanade, lay outside the line of fire. It is difficult to make out what losses of life the defenders suffered; Finland's official newspaper spoke of 260 killed and wounded — on Sveaborg, at the coastal batteries, and among the crews of the Russian ships *Rossija* and *Hesekiel*; Elmgren mentions a larger figure, 400. Genuine Finnish casualties were very light; among the sailors of the First Naval Division, manning the guns on Sandhamn, one Finn was killed and nine were wounded, and on Drumsö, where General Ramsay once again was in charge, a single member of the Finnish Grenadier-Sharpshooters, the veterans of Vitsand, is supposed to have fallen. The Russians took the brunt of the assault; yet they could console themselves with the knowledge that they had saved ammunition: learning that the guns of Sveaborg were ineffectual, Berg had ordered them to cease fire early in the attack.

The most gallant tale to emerge from the whole affair concerned a Russian, too; told by Ramsay's nephew, Anders, about old Ramsay's defence command on Drumsö, it is too good to be passed over in silence. Once upon a time, a wealthy and youthful millionaire, Prince Tscherkasi, forgetful of his lovely wife, conceived a burning passion for a dancer at the Moscow opera. The dancer refused to listen to his pleas, and so — behaving like Tolstoy's Anatole Kuragin — he kidnapped her; still adamant, the poor girl was murdered and her body thrown out of the window of the prince's palace. Influential friends got his sentence, deportation to Siberia, changed to forced enlistment as a private in the Russian army; his regiment was sent to Helsingfors at the beginning of the war. Since his ever faithful wife had followed him, he was allowed to rent Villa Hagasund, empty at the time, as a residence; he reported for duty now and then at the nearby Åbo Barracks on Henriksgatan. His regiment was dispatched to Drumsö during the attack on Sveaborg; in the engagement between ship and shore, he so distinguished himself that he was promoted out of the ranks by the generous Alexander. But Tscherkasi had had enough of military hardships; he resigned forthwith from his new commission. Whatever the authenticity of Ramsay's story may be — and it sounds a little like a variant on the legend of Princess Yusupova and her lover — it shows how things sometimes turn out better than anyone has the right to expect. The same may be said about Helsingfors itself. By August 16, the weather became rainy, and the city took up its old ways; "moves back into town continue without abate," Elmgren curtly told his diary. Sebastopol fell a month later; but Sveaborg — no particular thanks to anyone — had stayed in Russian hands. In April, 1856, the Crimean War ended with the Peace of Paris.

2. Tamelander and Tölö

NICHOLAS'S DEATH AND Alexander's accession to the throne did not mean that the political climate of Helsingfors changed overnight; nor did the loyal, or passive, behavior of the citizenry during the bombardment of Sveaborg calm all fears in the official heart. The university in particular was still regarded with suspicion, and snide tongues said that Berg kept a closer watch on its students than he had on the Allied fleet. Unluckily for Berg's peace of mind, he had lost a useful assistant in Nordenstam who, his request for release from his academic post having been accepted, now devoted all his energies to his job as chief-of-staff for the troops stationed in Finland. Johan Reinhold Munck, his successor as vice-chancellor, was also a product of the Russian military, but less the disciplinarian. Munck had been a protégé of Rehbinder, imbibing the spirit of that good man at the Rehbinder menage in Saint Petersburg; although forced, as a young officer, to do some dirty work in the suppression of the Decembrist plot — he had served at the execution of the condemned revolutionaries — Munck had become something of a liberal, and a close friend to boot, of young Alexander. The trust which the new emperor felt for Munck surely aided the latter in protecting the university during the second half of the 1850's. And Munck had another qualification for his new post; falling into disfavor with Nicholas, he had been shoved off in 1843 to the command of the Finnish Cadet School at Fredrikshamn, and there had learned the art of dealing firmly but fairly with the young.

Even as he arrived in Helsingfors, in October, 1855, Munck was put to the test. One Oskar Tamelander, a student — remembered by the not unprejudiced Anders Ramsay as "a flatterer and affected in a coquettish and effeminate way" — was discovered to be a spy in the service of Berg. Wartime regulations had made it difficult to obtain a passport for travel to Sweden; but Tamelander, whose father was a high postal official, had made frequent trips thither. In connection with these trips, he offered his services to student friends as a courier; their correspondence with Sweden, he pointed out, would be safe in his hands. But that was just where the catch lay; the letters entrusted to Tamelander, both outbound and in, made their way through the governor-general's offices, where they were opened, read, and sealed again. The particular aim of this espionage was to gain information about "Scandinavianist" tendencies in the student body — that is, sympathies for the plan to free Finland from Russia for re-incorporation, in one way or another, into the Swedish sphere of influence. Tamelander took special pains to make contact with Emil von Quanten, now — as a "refugee" in Stockholm — a leading light among the journalists who wrote for Swedish newspapers about conditions in Finland. Eventually, the amateur agent made the mistake of asking von Quanten whether he could not be hired into Russian service; by means of a clever device, von Quanten let his compatriots in Finland know what Tamelander apparently was up to. Proof of his guilt was subsequently provided by the vigilant and courageous Baron Edvard Walleen, an official in Berg's own chancellery. The university had opened late that year, as a result of the semi-evacuation of Helsingfors; not guessing that his game was revealed, Tamelander returned to Finland with his load of letters and other communications, all of which took the customary route over Berg's desk to their addressees. A commission of students was formed, let by the "curator" of the "historical-philological faculty" to which Tamelander belonged; it summoned Tamelander, confronted him with the evidence, and got him to confess. In his distress, he tried to shove the blame onto Alexander Wulffert, the postal director, claiming the latter had seduced him with promises of a diplomatic career. The commission demanded that Tamelander be removed from the rolls both of his "faculty" and the university as a whole, thinking perhaps to visit him with a punishment of oblivion not unlike that which Runeberg had dealt to Admiral Cronstedt. Having investigated the matter, Munck agreed wholeheartedly with the commission's findings. Caught in an embarrassing posture, Berg had to abandon Tamelander publicly, while privately seeing to it that he got a minor post in distant Moscow. Eventually Tamelander returned to Finland, and passed away in obscurity; Wulffert attempted to make a martyr of himself, as Elmgren tartly remarked, "by throwing stones through his own windows," and by arguing that Tamelander was a liar, plain and simple. Luckier than Tamelander, Wulffert was quickly freed from the isolation with which Helsingfors surrounded him; he died of a stroke at his desk in December, 1855.

In this sordid affair, the forces of good had emerged with a pleasant little victory, thanks in no small part to Munck's unequivocal stand. Within a month, the new vice-chancellor got a second chance to prove himself. On November 30, 1855, Saint Andrew's Day, four students decided to celebrate the name they held in common, Anders, with a banquet for themselves and their friends at Tölö Inn. The company numbered 28, hosts and guests; musical fare was provided by the band of the First Naval Division and a quartet of singers from the university. A good time was had by all; the pinnacle of the entertainment was a series of toasts, led by Karl Wetterhoff, the life of the party. He began with a reference to the sardines on the table, put into connection with Victor Emmanuel, the King of Sardinia, who had taken sides against Russia. Wetterhoff's flights of imagination seemed anti-Allied enough in their tone; he parodied Palmerston's speech on the capture of the Russian fortresses on Åland, ending with a loud "skål" for Victoria, her doubtful morals, and her lover, Napoleon. A paronomasiac fervor came over Wetterhoff's listeners, and they began punning: Sultan Abdu-l-Mejid was wittily converted into "Abdul med skeden," "Abdul with the spoon"; reflections were made on the names of the generals opposing one another in the Crimea, Pélissier and Tulubyev (the one recalling a greatcoat lined with fur, the other a sheepskin coat); Canrobert, marshal of France, got his due with a toast to a Helsingfors wine-merchant, Robert Carger, nicknamed "Kann-Robert" ("Tankard-Robert"). The students forgot the lunatic sensitivity of their Russian masters; casting all caution aside, they offered a tribute to one of the guests, Edvard Bergh, whose name sounded precisely like that of the governor-general. Answering the toast, young Bergh catalogued a number of differences between himself and his semi-namesake. In conclusion, someone saluted Wulffert of the postal service.

It would have been difficult for anyone in the room to ignore the toasts; the naval bandsmen blew a fanfare before each of them. The waiters did not serve during the speeches, and could devote their full attention to what was said, as could the musicians — who were, in addition, subject to Russian military law. Still another attentive listener at the feast was an outside guest, a young officer from the Russian Guards. The news of what had happened got out very quickly; the waiters, the bandmaster, some of his men, and the officer were summoned to bear witness against the students. To what extend the bandmaster and the lieutenant tattled willingly, and how much coercion was used, has never become clear; enchanted by the mystery, the novelist Tavaststjerna employed the mildly tragic figure of the officer as a partial model for the hero of his novel, *En patriot utan fosterland* (*A Patriot without a Fatherland*, 1896). Berg was delighted that he had been given an opportunity to take revenge for the humiliation just suffered in the Tamelander affair; hearing the names of the culprits, he cried out in German, his mother tongue: "Why, they're all old acquaintances!" An investigation was swiftly arranged and punishment as swiftly meted out. Munck himself asked for heavier sentences than those originally suggested: for example, the two-year suspension given Wetterhoff was transformed into suspension "forever," suspensions of one year were extended to two, and the innocent members of the male quartet were barred from the university's halls for a term. Two guests who held quasi-faculty posts, Gustaf Ehrström, the "curator" of the law faculty, and Adolf Nordenskiöld, holder of the same title in the "physical-mathematical" faculty, were stripped of their curatorships, and Nordenskiöld, as well, lost both an appointment he had been given in the government's department of mines and a travel grant. Munck's action was by no means indefensible; the students had not shown any particular good sense in what they did and said, since they knew that Russia was still at war, and that her forces had been forced to evacuate Sebastopol less than three months before. The jest about Canrobert was particularly ill-considered, since the Frenchman had recently been in Stockholm, attempting to persuade the Swedes to abandon their neutrality; the students of Helsingfors were already in hot water because of their suspected Scandinavianism. Munck may have reasoned the stern measures would put a stop to such dangerous nonsense, and help to preserve the new emperor's large store of good will for Finland's university. It is worth noting that both Munck's professors and a majority of the students from the "philological-historical" faculty supported him. Wetterhoff's lifetime suspension was now reduced to three years, but he refused to wait and went over to Sweden, making a career as a fairly successful publicist, editor, and foreign correspondent. Nordenskiöld, a son of the mineralogist, went off to Berlin, to study with his father's Prussian colleagues and friends.

That Alexander's favor had not been lost was proved, shortly, by the appointment of Snellman as professor in a strange field entitled "moral teachings and the system of science," a disguise under which the former professorship of philosophy would now be resurrected. (During the last few years Snellman had earned his bread as an employee in Henrik Borgström's enterprises, another good deed of this northern Lorenzo.) The students, delighted at the appointment, gave Snellman a serenade; in his speech of thanks, he stated that he had got the position without concessions being asked or given. Alexander came to the university on March 28, 1856, his first imperial visit; in return for the student's songs, he managed to come up with another of his Swedish phrases, "Jag tackar herrarna" — "I thank the gentlemen." He seems not to have known that the text of one of the songs, "Suomi's Song," was by Emil von Quanten, the Finnish leader of Stockholm's anti-Russian camp.

3. Alexander's University

THE CORONATION OF Alexander II took place in Moscow on September 7, 1856; thirteen days later the university at Helsingfors celebrated the event with a program arranged by Gabriel Rein, the university's rector magnificus, who mistakenly assumed that he had his stormiest years in the post behind him. The intent of the coronation-program was to demonstrate that Finland was by no means as badly off under the Russian yoke as Stockholm's press had recently argued — that, on the contrary, it had become a much better place during the almost half-a-century of Russian rule. The speakers were the theologian Frans Ludvig Schauman in Swedish, Edvard af Brunér in Latin (he who had tweaked the nose of the Russian professor, Soloviev, at the university's bicentennial), Carl Gustaf Borg in Finnish (continuing a practice of Finnish academic oration initiated at the memorial service for Nicholas), and the inescapable Bengt Olof Lille in Swedish verse. Schauman's speech was the most carefully listened to and the boldest. He called attention to the "laws and cultural institutions" which Finland had received as a "heritage" from Sweden, and his words reached a climax with the statement that: "one of the most important provisions in the country's constitution" provided for representatives of the four estates to meet, "upon being summoned by the regent," in "parliaments or diets." The speech was printed without alteration, since the university had the right of censorship over its own publications. The public censors could forbid its sale; but Governor-General Berg had sense enough not to order them to do so, the contents of the oration already having become well-known. Alexander got to read Schauman's speech in Russian, and was reminded that the diet had not met since the honeymoon days in Borgå in 1809; the delivery of the reminder was worth the price paid by Munck, Rein, and Schauman, who incurred the emperor's personal displeasure for certain passages in what, considering the situation, was a remarkably free-spirited document. Schauman's oration, however, almost called down the threat of an infinitely more severe penalty on the university itself: the removal of this academic hotbed of liberalism from Helsingfors to some provincial town, or its division into special schools, to be distributed throughout the country. How poorly some of Finland's most influential aristocrats understood the university's role as a national institution was shown by Alexander Armfelt, still minister of state for Finnish affairs in Saint Petersburg, and his assistant, Carl Emil Knut Stjernvall-Walleen: they approved the scheme, reputedly the brainchild of still another Finlander, Casimir von Kothen. Ludicrously, the move foundered on Berg's opposition — not the result of sudden enlightenment on the governor-general's part, but of his resolve to keep the university under his watchful eye.

Berg's relations with his academy had already been strained by the Tamelander affair, and by Tölö Inn. The old soldier's tribulations continued when, in May, 1857, a graduation was held for the first *magistres* produced by the new "historical-philological" and "physical-mathematical" faculties, created in the recent revision of university structure. In addition, Runeberg would be made doctor of theology, and the 700th anniversary of the introduction of Christianity to Finland would be celebrated. Vice-Chancellor Munck had approved the invitation of five representatives of the student body at Uppsala; Johan Axel Nyblaeus from Lund, professor of "practical philosophy," was also present. At a farewell party given for the Swedes, the hotspur Nordenskiöld, returned from Berlin to be awarded both master's and doctor's degrees, let his Scandinavian spirit get the better of him; he praised Finland's Swedish past more warmly than he did its Russian present. Professor Fredrik Cygnaeus decided that Nordenskiöld's words had unduly inflamed the audience; he sought to calm the listeners (and to indulge his own oratorical mania) by denying that Finland was "a golden nest of thralldom," as a Swedish journalist had called it. Nordenskiöld was not assuaged by Cygnaeus' rhetoric; dashing back to the podium, where Cygnaeus still stood, he shouted: "He does not speak for us!", and the audience took up the cry. Berg got the bad news quickly; Rein was summoned, but even dressing down the university's rector did not make the governor-general feel better. He ought, he said, to hang Nordenskiöld in front of the university. (No one could deny that Senate Square would be an impressive spot for a public execution.) Nordenskiöld went to his family's summer place; there a lackey of Berg informed him that he must ask for pardon immediately, or leave Finland. Taking the latter alternative, Nordenskiöld set out immediately for Sweden; when he returned to Helsingfors in the 1880's, after his voyages with the *Vega*, he was a world-famous explorer, the discoverer of the Northeast Passage and long since a Swedish citizen.

The skirmishes between the university and Berg claimed another victim, an elderly one, in 1858. The students had begun the collection of funds for a "Student Union" — a plan not realized, for the rest, until 1870, when the building (with the self-congratulatory inscription, "Spei suae patria dedit") was formally opened. A lottery was undertaken by the ladies of the city, led by Baroness Munck herself; professors gave public lectures, the proceeds of which went to the project; and a "triple quartet" of student singers traveled the length and breadth of Finland, demonstrating the musical advantages the university had brought the homeland. In Helsingfors, a student dramatic society decided to arrange a benefit program at Oelze's Salon. Since the world was about to celebrate the centennial of Schiller's birth, some scenes from *Don Carlos* were given; one wonders if the great address on freedom of thought by the Marquis of Posa was included. In Finnish the student actors offered Pietari Hannikainen's comedy, *Silmänkääntäjä* (*The Conjurer*), a play which had already become something of a Finnish classic, *faute de mieux*, since its premiere in far-off Villmanstrand a decade before. (Its rendering by the students now, in 1858, could be considered the first performance of a Finnish work on a Helsingfors stage, if one disregards *Finska flickan, eller hittebarnet på kyrkogården* [*The Finnish Girl or The Foundling in the Churchyard*], a Swedish-language play in three acts with "couplets and melodramas in the Finnish language" given by Westerlund's troupe on February 8, 1833.) The main piece of the students' dramatic evening, however, was a farce, *Dramatiskt ditt och datt* (*Dramatic Hodgepodge*), written by that bright, wealthy, and improvident student, Carl Robert Mannerheim, known to Helsingfors because of his sudden advance from stand-in to star in *Kung Carls jagt*, six years before. The structure of Mannerheim's opusculum, in which the author was also director and main performer, was simple enough: two plays within a play. A student dramatic society comes to Sordavala, the Karelian town on Lake Ladoga, and performs "Donna Sol, or Love, Revenge, and Death," together with the quasi-opera, "The Ancestors," pleasing both the entrepreneur, a Karelian-Russian merchant, and the naive audience on stage. The audience in Oelze's Salon was likewise amused, but after four performances, the command came from Saint Petersburg to desist. Berg had taken offence, first of all, at certain descriptive references in the play: Finland, for example, was called "a poor and oppressed land." Furthermore, cogent personal reasons existed for Berg's displeasure. He was married to an Italian lady, Leopoldina Cicogna, the widow of a Count Arconi; an ardent mass-goer, she wanted Helsingfors to have a Roman Catholic church. (She got what she wanted; on September 17, 1860, the little red-brick Saint Henry's, opposite the entrance to Brunnsparken, was consecrated in the presence of Countess Berg and her husband.) Very likely, the students who conceived *Dramatiskt ditt och datt* had made fun in private of the Countess, her nationality, and her religion; ridicule is a weapon often used against a hated master, and the students of Helsingfors had never displayed the ecumenical spirit. Carl Gustaf Estlander, the disciple of Cygnaeus, recalled that "The Ancestors" in Mannerheim's farce was generally taken to be a satire on Berg's recent ennoblement (as an Austrian count in 1849, and a Finnish one in 1856) and

on his Countess's ancient ancestry; a student named Leo Mechelin —
someday to be called "king of Helsingfors," as Ehrenström had once
been — delivered the chief forebear's role from a catafalque "with a sepul-
chral bass voice of unusual depth and strength." Berg decided to use the
uproar caused by Mannerheim's impudence to get the liberal Munck's
scalp; instead of Munck, however, Rector Rein was dismissed, charged
with dereliction of duty. Although Rein had approved the play, he had not
read it himself, leaving the task of censorship up to some older students.
Plainly, their taste was different from Berg's.

Things went immediately downhill for Berg after the row over
Dramatiskt ditt och datt. In the spring of 1860, another graduation was
held, and, once again, catastrophe ensued; it is not surprising that Berg
suggested the permanent cancellation of these ceremonies, "at which
scandals always take place." Once again, the graduation was to be held by
the historical-philological and physical-mathematical faculties; the honored
guests this time were two former Finlanders, resident for decades in Sweden, Gustaf Adolf Montgomery, a veteran and historian of the war of
1808–09, and the jurist, Professor Johan Jakob Nordström. Fears to the
contrary, their presence at the ceremony caused no difficulties; the trouble
arose at the graduation ball, traditionally held by the new *magistres* and to
which they invited the highest dignitaries of the state and their families.
Feeling their oats, the *magistres* decided this time to choose only those
persons with whom they had personal associations; the detested governor-
general was omitted from their guest-list. As usual, Berg got immediate
wind of what was planned, and took advantage of the newly installed telegraph line between Helsingfors and Saint Petersburg to ask for instruc-
tions. The reply was in full accord with his own wishes; the ball must be
forbidden. Louis Kleineh, the owner of Helsingfors' best hotel, modestly
called Kleineh's, and, since 1843, the manager of Society House, was in
despair, since all arrangements had been made for the souper and ball at
the latter establishment; the young ladies of Helsingfors were no less unhappy. Then Carl Magnus Creutz of Malmgård — estate owner, historian,
and public-spirited man — got a bright idea. The roles could be reversed,
the *magistres* and other students could be invited to the ball by those
good citizens who would have been their guests, and Berg could do
nothing to stop these "private" revelries. Living just across the Esplanade
from Society House, the governor-general watched the celebration — held
same time, same place as announced — from his front window. The studied insult caused Berg, beside himself with rage, to go too far: he tried to
persuade Saint Petersburg that the ball provided evidence of a revolutionary spirit. Munck assured Alexander Armfelt that Berg was utterly mis-
taken, and Armfelt, entertaining a low opinion of the ineffectual defender

of Sveaborg, was delighted to believe the vice-chancellor. Berg was given leave of absence, a leave ending, in November, 1861, with his retirement, in preparation for the return of the popular Rokassovsky.

Rokassovsky bore the official message that the estates should convene again, as soon as the Senate could make necessary arrangements. Constitutionality was established; the diet was opened in September, 1863, in the presence of Alexander, the good emperor. The university's students — previously concerned with championing Finland against Nicholas's despotism — could devote themselves to other pursuits, internecine warfare chief among them. In Mannerheim's *Ditt och datt*, there had been jesting about Snellman and his excessively pro-Finnish *Litteraturblad*; one of the actors, made up as Snellman, stood in the lobby prior to the performance. Getting wind of the *lèse-majesté*, a band of serious-minded Snellman-supporters — Thiodolf Rein, the rector's son, among them — had tried to disturb the final performance. In his *Litteraturblad*, Snellman subsequently attacked those Finlanders who went to Sweden ("they are buried as far as Finland is concerned"), and defended Cygnaeus for his part in Nordenskiöld's exile. Devotion to Alexander, one of whose first academic acts in Finland was the long overdue appointment of Snellman to a professorship, may have encouraged the imperial favorite in these sentiments; but underlying them was Snellman's Hegelian philosophy of national and linguistic identity. "Until the two languages have become one common tongue [Finnish], bearing witness to the fact that the national spirit has been united," there could be no Finnish nation. Returning from a trip abroad, August Schauman grew aware that Snellman's disciples were ready to turn the master's teachings into practice. Earlier, Schauman had "never heard a word of hatred against Finland's Swedish culture"; now (it was the autumn of 1858) he was present when "an unusually gifted and cultured young man" argued that "the entire Swedish element must leave the country" or become Fennicized. "A whole new race had grown up around Snellman's lecture platform." The members of the race were given a nomenclature which told much about their zeal; in Swedish they were called "fennomaner," of which the English "Fennomaniacs" would be an all too drastic translation ("Fennomanes" is preferable); in Finnish, the tongue of which some of them had only an embarrassingly poor command, they were called "Finnish zealots," or, more flatteringly, "those with a Finnish spirit."

The language war, which would rend the university, lay just ahead; the old unity, nurtured by Nicholas's despotism and blooming one last time during the transition to Alexander's "lofty and humane mode of thought," as Rector Rein rather wistfully called it, was dead. Yet it should not be forgotten that the university also led a "normal" life in these years, untouched by questions of national and academic freedom. Students lived on credit and were greeted, at their favorite café, Catani's, by the owner's friendly query: "Has a letter come with money from papa?" An Italian-Swiss, Florio Theodor Catani had plenty of opportunity to practice his Swedish with this sentence. One wonders if the students tried to get credit elsewhere, too, at the notorious "Green Villa," an inn and bordello lying across Tölö Bay from the relatively innocent verandas of Kajsaniemi; even the high-minded youths of Topelius' student-novella, *Vincent Vågbry-taren* (*Vincent Breakwater*), knew where the "Green Villa" was, although Topelius takes neither them nor his gentle readers inside, and gives the place the air of a nocturnal short-order restaurant. Yet students did purchase something more than victuals "of a mediocre quality" there; for one thing, they sometimes acquired veneral disease, which they (and others, non-academicians) could also get at the cheaper and more dangerous houses in Rödbergen, a section of ill repute south and east of Sinebrychoff's brewery and gardens, and north of the Finnish Guards' target range. Some faculty members, too, marched to a different drum from that of Lönnrot, Cygnaeus, Snellman, Rein. The professor of astronomy, Fredrik Wohlstedt, is a case in point. He could perhaps have excused his eccentric behavior with a reference to the curse which seemed to hang over his chair. Its first holder, Henrik Johan Walbeck, had shot himself in the new observatory at Åbo, five years before the university was moved to Helsingfors; Walbeck's successor, the Baltic-German Fredrik Argelander, the first to reign in Engel's observatory at Helsingfors, was so talented that Friedrich Wilhelm IV lured him to Bonn. After Argelander came his student Gustaf Lundahl, professor at 28 and dead at 30; Wohlstedt followed the unfortunate youth, and proved to be more entertaining to the city's gossips than he was helpful to his students. Brutal toward his family, he had also conceived a hatred, monomaniacally proclaimed, of pastors and of Euclid's geometry; death released him from his madness, if it was that, in 1861, when he was not yet 50. "The event is sad, for he was a skillful astronomer, a well-meaning man, and one who lived only for his science. Of course, he was a little one-sided and confused, and in his youth had been something of a carouser; his lust for spirits increased during his final year." It was as kind an obituary as Wohlstedt could have hoped for.

4. The Idyll and Its Shadows

THE GERMAN NOVELIST Wilhelm Raabe liked to use the motto "Look toward the stars, but pay attention to the streets." It was not easy to do the latter in Helsingfors of the 1850's. In a latitude where days are very short for a good part of the year — the city lies, as its inhabitants boastfully and regretfully remark, 43 kilometers north of Greenland's southern tip — street-lighting should have been of particular importance, but reports from the century's earlier decades have a medieval sound: well-to-do persons going abroad at night had a servant perched on the back of their carriage, a lantern in his hand, those on foot were preceded by a light-bearing maid, and the poor had to carry their own illumination. The situation was bad enough before the Crimean War, because the traditional Finnish restraint toward the fair sex vanished under the cover of darkness; in the immediate post-war years, the dangers increased (blame was laid on the sailors of the Russian fleet), and the murder of a citizen named Henrik Otto Renfors, one April night, aroused particular indignation. Violent death in the streets was not unknown, but the victims had been less prominent or even anonymous — seamen or laborers or, to take a single case, the unfortunate Swedish bell-founder who, having revealed the secrets of his craft under the influence of alcohol, was made to disappear by a sinister brazier known only as "O," about whom "people had many ugly stories to tell." Long, long ago, Governor-general Zakrevsky, upset not least by the transfer of Åbo's students to Helsingfors, had attempted to improve the city's rudimentary police force; his expensive plans had been opposed by the citizenry. Already groaning beneath the incidental costs of the great rebuilding, they claimed to be content with the age-old institution of the night-watchman; at the end of the 1850's, as Augusta Krook recalled, these picturesque fellows still walked the streets, calling: "The clock's struck ten: May God's strong hand / Protect our town from fire and brand." No one protected merchant Renfors, but his death might be regarded as sacrificial; eagerly displaying his well-known energy, Berg demanded a reform of the police department, a task begun a decade before by General Nordenstam in his capacity as governor of Nyland province. Now, in 1861, the force was radically augmented and modernized, getting 3 inspectors, 8 chief constables, and 40 constables, to whom 16 deputies were then added; their assignment was not only to "fight against the more refined depravity which at present is winning entrance among the lower classes of our population," but also to aid the fire department, likewise increased and revised, in battling the blazes which so often threatened the city.

It cannot be denied that some of the fires, such as the one of October, 1846, had provided impressive entertainment; the burning of the sheds beside the Bath House, illuminating the whole of Brunnsparken and Observatory Hill, had given Magnus von Wright the subject of a watercolor. Amusement and art notwithstanding, there was always the danger that the whole of Helsingfors would go up in smoke; in the second of the fires (of April and June 1858) which ruined editor Paavo Tikkanen of *Suometar*, it looked momentarily as though Tikkanen's Kronohagen neighbors would be rendered homeless too. Kronohagen was saved, one would like to think, by the inspiring presence of Governor-general Berg and Governor Samuel Antell of Nyland, and by the fact that a fortuitous breeze blew the flames toward North Harbor. Like Renfors' murder, the Kronohagen fire of 1858 aided the city: Helsingfors — "this little Saint Petersburg" — learned that it must provide the essentials for safer municipal living. The job of the police, and the firemen, was made easier by the sudden illumination of the streets of Helsingfors. The oil-lamps, erected in a very desultory way during the earlier decades, were simply not up to the job, as Nordenstam had declared in a wise opinion, often forgotten even as one remembers his mishandling of the university. By 1860, a gas-illumination company, headed by Feodor Kiseleff, the son of a Russian merchant who had come to Helsingfors in 1811, was established; its headquarters was a mighty castle across from Åbo Barracks and somewhat south of the patrician Walleen's Villa Hagasund, which thus got another unsuitable neighbor. The gaslights burned for the first time in Helsingfors streets on a Wednesday, November 14; two weeks later, Elmgren, a doubting Thomas, was forced to concede that "the gaslights grew perceptibly brighter on the following days, and now people are satisfied with their shine." Also, Elmgren went on to say, people were happy about the election of Abraham Lincoln, the report of which had just arrived from America. For a long while the gaslights remained the object of marveling attention. When they were installed in the Nikolai-Church, Swedish speakers even attended the early (Finnish) services on New Year's morning in order to admire their steady light.

The town made bright by Kiseleff junior and company was very different from the place Kiseleff senior had found; however, its appearance had changed rather little since the completion of the great rebuilding. In the wake of Engel's death (1840), few new public edifices had come into being — most important, perhaps, were Lappviken's insane asylum, by Engel's disciple, Anders Fredrik Granstedt, and the so-called "New Clinic" and Anatomical Institute of the university by the German Lohrmann, Engel's successor as director of public construction. Lohrmann also created the Post Office (1853) on Nikolaigatan, whose facade that looks cramped and unimaginative — a reflection of Lohrmann's epigonic spirit. As for private construction, the office which had extended interest-free loans for this purpose had ceased to exist in 1855, "since the city, except for a small number of plots, is presently finished." Seen in sunlight, the "finished city" must have been a pleasant place to behold; like the official works of Engel, the homes in the new capital — some of stone, many more of wood, a few large, the most modest — had a beauty born of simplicity. The wealthy could hire a trained architect: Engel himself (although he was so busy with public charges that he could do little in this line), the Granstedts, father and son, Jean Wiik, Carl Johan Edvard Gustavson, Lohrmann. Yet the mass-creators of homes in the city were the Andstens, a family of master-masons and tile-oven-makers which had seven representatives in Helsingfors during the days of the "renovation" and its aftermath; Nils-Erik Wickberg, a leading authority on the city's architectural history, has estimated that they built at least 300 houses. These long, low buildings, of wood, with their entrance not from the street but from the side or back, have substantially vanished from Helsingfors; an impression of what they looked like in greater numbers may be gained by an excursion to Borgå, where conditions for survival of the Andsten house (or its imitations) have been more favorable. The dwellings designed by the Andstens fitted nicely into the stage-setting Ehrenström and Engel had created, being only a "popular variant" on Engel's neo-classicism. They were part and parcel of the "airy, light garden-city," with its straight streets, small parks, and simple fronts, that lives on in the paintings and watercolors of Magnus von Wright, and (reduced to shades of gray) in the panoramic photographs made by the German photographer Hoffers. Helsingfors was an idyll, its buildings white or yellow or in light pastels, topped by black or red roofs, and backed by the large plots which, required by statute to keep fires from spreading, allowed the cultivation of gardens or even small orchards in the city's very heart. Every year the idyll was covered for a long, long time by ice and snow; but, every year, this frigid covering fled away, in April, if Helsingfors was lucky, "and the city lay there fine and polished, liberated on police order from all the remaining traces of snow, and looking as if it had nothing to do save await the arrival of springtime." Karl August Tavaststjerna's words are from the novel, *Barndomsvänner* (*Childhood Friends*) of 1886; they could as well describe the Helsingfors — "our pretty little town" to Topelius — of a generation before.

An idyll, it provided a modest and sometimes idyllic life. Most civil servants and professors owned their own homes, "the equipment and arrangement of which, even in the more elegant parts of town, were very much the same. On the street, a longish main building, inside the yard a smaller house with a couple of rooms for living purposes (to be rented out to bachelors, students or not) and a baker's room, together with a long row of sheds — stalls, a cow-shed, a coach-house, a store-house, and a garden . . . Such an establishment, a 'gård,' was occupied by a single family; one could live there in a spacious and comfortable way, left alone by others and in a half-rustic fashion . . .": August Schauman, born in 1826, remembered the "patriarchal" Helsingfors of his youth in this way. The homes were almost entirely self-sufficient, and, if they had their own wells (as many did), then they could claim utter independence of the world outside, in a pinch. The patriarchal style was attractive, certainly, yet it could not survive in a municipality; it had begun to change , and even to vanish, by the middle of the century. As the detail-work in his historical narratives proved, Topelius loved the past and its apparently wholesome simplicity; but he was aware that the idyll could be uncomfortable or downright dangerous. In *Helsingfors Tidningar* for 1858 there appeared an article by his hand which pierced the pleasant veil: "Is there a single larger dwelling here which possesses something as simple, as useful, indeed as indispensible as a bathroom of its own? Is there a single building here, save the public bathhouses, which has even the slightest trace of water conduits? How many people could spare themselves the promenade, so cruel in our climate, to an outhouse in the wintertime?" (The article continued, by the way, with a remark showing that even the advantages of the idyll had not been possessed by the poor: "And how many, in the beautiful part of the year, could enjoy a balcony, a flower bed, or even a covered stair?") Topelius was not the first to call attention to the lack of water-and-sewage service in Helsingfors; the public wells, located here and there in the city, had long been given horrified attention by physicians, who rightly considered their water to be a chief source of the epidemics of cholera and typhus that were the city's bane. In 1841, Dr. von Haartman had made an extensive report on the wretched condition of the city's public and private water-sources; but even a von Haartman could not fight indifference at every social level, coupled, among the influential, with another attitude: "I thought that cholera . . . attacked only the worse sort of people," Marie Teetgens wrote, upon hearing a shocking report to the contrary. A quarter-of-a-century passed; in 1866, the city's government, rejecting the proposal of its municipal engineer that a number of deeper wells be dug, gave him permission to add a single new public well to those already extant. At last, the city's growing population — and the fire chief's observation that a water-supply would help to save valuable property — forced the hand of the city's elders; a Norwegian-born teacher at the Technical School, Endre Lekve, was asked to work out a practicable and not too expensive plan, which he did, recommending that the water be taken from the Vanda River, the site of Gustaf Vasa's Old Helsingfors. In 1872, the building of the system was undertaken by a private German firm, Neptunus of Berlin, three years later Neptunus sold the project to the city of Helsingfors, and at last, in 1878, the venture was completed. The city's wells had almost reached the end of their days: "Globrunnen," at the junction of Brunnsgatan and Hagasundsgatan, which drew its waters, one queasily guesses, from the subterranean bog left over by Glo Bay; its heir, likewise called "Globrunnen," in front of the Old Student House (then very new), covered by a quaint little structure; the wells on Kampen, on Barracks Square, at Skillnaden; and the other members of the dirty and picturesque tribe. Death did not come from a single, sure blow: the authorities had to allow the use of private wells in sections not yet reached by the waterworks, and it is recorded that, as late as 1914, wells were closed in such "outlying" regions as Tölö. A story from the city's heart has it that an old lady on Södra Magasinsgatan, who had long supplied the crones of her neighborhood with water from her well, objected violently to its sealing, with the pointed argument that *her* clientele had lived to a ripe age. Enraged at the belated and unreasonable sternness of officialdom, she departed from Helsingfors, never to return.

So, in the 1870's, twenty years after he had uttered his call for water-pipes and sewers in *Helsingfors Tidningar*, Topelius beheld the beginning of the fulfilment of his first wish. As for the second, it was realized with even greater slowness. If the city's medical men had long since known the danger of the wells, they also knew that there was a need for public drainage better than that provided by open trenches — such as the ditch which ran down to the harbor along the northern end of Barracks Square. Even the poor folk on Skatudden dimly realized that some connection might exist between their noisome outhouses and the "kurrisfeber" (typhus) which decimated them. Some gestures had been made in the direction of a subterranean sewer network, especially — and of direst necessity — around "Gloet," but the primitive nature of the undertaking may be deduced from the fact that the pipes were of wood. A system employing glazed brick pipe was planned and its installation was begun in 1878; the project was so far from completion by the middle 1880's that 200 lots within the old city limits were still not joined to it. However, the city's new sections — for example, the "worker's district" of Berghäll, first opened up in 1887–89, with its streets named "First Line," "Second Line," and so on, in imitation of Saint Petersburg — received both sewage and water conduits from the beginning. Topelius' accompanying dream of inside toilets was infinitely harder to turn into reality. The public objected to them because they allowed the deposit of human wastes directly into the sewers, and then without delay into the once pure waters of the sea; this charge was brought against the toilets of the Grönqvist Building, the architectural marvel of Helsingfors in the 1880's. By the building statutes of 1895, water-closets were allowed only if cesspools were simultaneously installed. By 1902, thirteen of the city's public buildings had been equipped with toilets, and then, by 1910, a great leap forward had occured: 32% of the city's apartments were in proud possession of water closets. The fate of the waters surrounding Helsingfors, to be sure, was still a matter of concern, and would remain so.

One of the poorest and least sanitary sections of Helsingfors, Skatudden, was at the same time its quaintest. As the city expanded in the 1860's and 1870's, it was decided that the shanty town covering the rocky point should be razed, and that Skatudden — already the home of such institutions as the Naval Division's barracks and the prison — should be made wholly respectable. The knoll at Skatudden's western end had just received an ornament which contrasted decoratively with the shacks, yet which found their proximity embarrassing. As the Russian Orthodox community in Helsingfors had grown, the Holy Trinity Church at Unionsgatan no longer could contain the worshippers; between 1861 and 1869, a brick pile was erected on Skatudden, with donations from various sources, including 20,000 rubles from Alexander. Dedicated to the assumption of the Holy Virgin, it was called the Uspenski Cathedral, and its gilded onion-dome rose in rivalry to the cupola of Engel's Lutheran masterpiece on Senate Square. The destruction of the neighboring huts took place during the next decade, and at the same time as the removal of a center-city eyesore, the flea market, from Nikolaigatan to the edges of the exercise field behind Åbo Barracks. For the most part, the people of Skatudden moved to Rödbergen in the southwest, as raffish and rocky as their former abode, but less exposed to the public eye. The respectable populace of Helsingfors had a sentimental affection for old Skatudden, although it would not have dreamed of residing there. A local artist, Rudolf Waldemar Åkerblom, published an album of India ink drawings, *Minnen från Skatudden eller det Helsingfors som går* (*Memories of Skatudden, or the Helsingfors Which is Passing*, 1873), which shows the slapdash charm of Skatudden's muddy lanes and tumbledown hovels without reminding the gentle reader too keenly of the misery bred under these conditions. Following Åkerblom's success, a genuine son of Skatudden (as Åkerblom was not), Victor Pettersson the elder, filled the pages of the newspaper *Hufvudstadsbladet* with his tales, which then came out in book form, *Bilder ur Skatuddslifvet i forna dagar* (*Pictures from Skatudden Life in Former Days*, 1881) and *Den gamle polisgevaldigerns berättelser: Bilder ur Helsingforslifvet* (*The Old Police Constable's Tales: Pictures from Helsingfors Life*, 1884). It would be unfair to criticize the middleclass audience too harshly for the appeal it found in Pettersson's stories; they were also read, with nostalgic gusto, by sometime inhabitants of the place. In 1886, the latter established their own club for the preservation of their memories, the "Association of Former Dwellers on Skatudden."

Undeniably, some romance did cling to Skatudden, provided one did not look too closely. It has been theorized that the population there at the end of the 1860's was the "oldest" in the city, a remnant of the Swedish seafarers who had been a Helsingfors mainstay in the days when it was a port and little else. Government officials and academicians were latecomers, compared to the sailors and sailors' widows on the promontory. Skatudden was an out-of-door museum; Helsingfors had looked this way before the rebuilding by Ehrenström and Engel straightened and broadened the streets, and introduced the empire style in its several varieties and prices. New elements had come to Skatudden, of course. The barracks on the north shore, the most austere of Engel's creations, had been used by Russian troops before the formal establishment of the Finnish Naval Division in 1830; and Russian soldiers who had served out their time settled down in the shacks of the island — for it had become an island in the 1840's because of the canal blasted through the narrow neck between North and South Harbors. (The Russians, returning to the barracks during the Crimean War, decided in 1861 to make Skatudden into a naval base, a decision hastening the removal of its poor folk; the base was put into full operation with the disbanding of the Finnish Naval Division in 1880, and, from then until 1918, the Russian element on Skatudden grew ever stronger.) But, as said, Swedish-speaking seamen had predominated in the old days, providing the crews for the ships of the Helsingfors owners, who had storehouses along Skatudden's shores. According to Victor Pettersson's son, like his father a journalist and an admirer of the past, these nautical families were the community's backbone — "hard-working and industrious people, simple but happy and satisfied with their lot"; those who did not go to sea could find work at Borgström's tobacco factory, across the canal. Their lot, however satisfied they may have been with it, was a hard one: the nearest wells were on the mainland, at the juncture of Brunnsgatan and Hagasundsgatan, and at the far end of Alexandersgatan — a long, long walk with a full bucket; for laundry, the women went to the shallows of what they called "Paraviken," a name taken from the Finnish "poro," dregs or sludge. The people of Skatudden, despite the healthy salt air," were the easiest victims of epidemic disease; whole families were wiped out, and the corpses were put on display in the yards — a grisly custom, albeit intended to allow a show of respect by the mourners. "Big swarms of flies flew around the bodies, and had a party . . ." As for bathing, there was Osipoff's sauna, beside the prison; no distinction was made between the sexes, but this was also the practice in Finland's countryside. In some contrast to the vaunted moral purity of the rustic sauna (it was there, Axel Gallen-Kallela said, that he discovered the sanctity of the nude human body), the tone at Osipoff's seems now and again to have become orgiastic. Prisoners were brought to Osipoff's to bathe, twelve at a time; their leg irons allowed them to pull their trousers down but not to take them off. As the center of community entertainment, Osipoff's had a rival in Utter's house, a goal of Russian sailors on the hunt for "flikuski"; Skatudden's linguistic makeup is shown by their blithe mishandling of the Swedish "flicka," "girl." Other inns rivaled Utter's, and a cottage industry was carried on by widows who found whoring a way of survival; respectable gentlemen risked robbery or worse in order to visit them. Here a sociological excursus might be made: Rödbergen and the adjacent tract around Sandviken had long been a *locus classicus* for organized prostitution in Helsingfors, and the bordellos had such exotic names as Alhambra, Mesopotamia, Philadelphia, London, Paris, and The Green Hell. On Skatudden, such ventures were usually of a homelier nature, bearing witness to the independent Viking heritage of the people.

Nor was education of a different and better sort neglected on the promontory; the fact that Skatudden possessed a school would indicate that Victor Pettersson was right about the soundness of the native stock. In order to pass the time between voyages, a ship's mate named Carl Johan Granberg (born in 1787) maintained an elementary school for the children of seamen; leaving the sea in 1842, he gave himself wholeheartedly to education. Granberg had "the first mixed school" in Helsingfors, boys and girls in the same classes; he also helped older boys prepare for the mate's examination, straightforward youths, one guesses, resembling the heroes of Pettersson's tales. Upon his death, in 1868 — immediately before the death of old Skatudden itself — Granberg was followed to his grave by a procession of grateful sailors, some of them bearing the merchant flags beneath which Granberg had sailed. It is estimated that several hundred pupils passed through his classroom; one of them was the elder Pettersson himself, another had been a poor boy from Nurmijärvi in northern Nyland, Alexis Stenvall, whose native tongue was Finnish. As Aleksis Kivi, he would write the tragedy *Kullervo*, the comedy *Nummisuutarit* (*The Heath Shoemakers*), and the novel *Seitsemän veljestä* (*Seven Brothers*), works that are the cornerstones of Finnish literature.

One cannot help admiring the close awareness displayed by Topelius, in the columns of *Helsingfors Tidningar*, of the material deprivation suffered by the poor and the lower middle class. In the article on the necessities and comforts of life, quoted above, he went on to discuss a matter as pressing as the need for water and sanitation. Helsingfors had a housing shortage; it had existed even before the Crimean War, and now it had become acute. "After the fire [resulting from the bombardment], Sveaborg sent more than a hundred families to the city, as well as unmarried military men and the chief-of-staff with his functionaries." The minor civil servants of Helsingfors were up against it: "Can a man pay a third or a fourth of his salary for bare walls?" Elsewhere, Topelius observes that the poor, compared to the struggling officials just mentioned, are even worse off: "A very small part of the working class in Helsingfors owns its homes; some of them dwell above the ground in little wooden huts, and some below," renting cellar rooms; in proportion, "the lower working class pays far more dearly for its wretched dwellings than do people of position [for their homes]." The most shameful example of the exploitation of the poor was furnished by a Russian-born landlord, Michael Antipoff, although it should scarcely be concluded that natives of Finland did not indulge in similar practices. Antipoff had acquired his original capital with a food store on one of the city's best streets, for which he had been granted a franchise in 1864; using this money, he put up his notorious "stone castles" near the city's center. The largest of these tenements was at Nylandsgatan 34–36, with 115 rooms; pleased at his gains, Antipoff built several somewhat smaller versions of the original design. The plan of operation was simple: to crowd as many people as possible into every room, and to collect the rent every Sunday morning. It has been estimated that, at the beginning of the 1880's, an average of 5.9 to 6.7 persons lived in each of Antipoff's rooms, and that the owner — who liked to describe himself as a "warmhearted man" — received about 40,000 marks a year in rents. The hygienic conditions were beyond description, as was the disrepair; Antipoff excused himself by claiming that his tenants were inherently dirty and destructive. In his memoirs, the artist Åkerblom says simply that "Antipoff's house on Nylandsgatan was a hangout for all the dregs in the city," and it was true that Antipoff sheltered doubtful characters under his roofs. Upon the condemnation of the tenements in the 1890's, the population moved for the most part to Berghäll and Sörnäs; the police were unhappy at the disappearance of Antipoff's establishments, since they afforded an excellent point of departure for any criminal investigation.

Yet, many of Antipoff's unfortunates would surely have done better if they could; some were displaced residents of Skatudden, others were unskilled laborers come in from the country after the great famine of 1867–

68, hoping to find a job in the suddenly expanding factories of Helsingfors. Energetic folk moved on to the "sound and healthy dwellings" for
workers which lined the way to Lappvik asylum, in the section of town
called "Lugnet" ("Calm"); here stood a housing project with a total of 79
rooms and, in 1870, about 300 occupants. On Västra Chausséen, again
not so far away from that ever more isolated landmark of opulence, Villa
Hagasund, three of "Tallgren's houses" were erected, double-storied and
containing 150 "apartments" of one room each. (Did the mistress of Villa
Hagasund, Aurora Karamzin, learn to know the misfortunes of the poor
by observing the folk at Tallgren's, across the highway?) In one of Tallgren's houses, on March 12, 1881, the day before the assassination of Alexander II, Väinö Thomasson was born; as Väinö Tanner, he became
director of Elanto (Finland's great co-operative enterprise) and a major
social-democratic politician; his clearest memory of his birthplace was of
the "gigantic armies of bed-bugs," which his parents eventually found un-
bearable. Healthy housing indeed: in the 1870's, another concern,
"Helsingfors Joint Stock Dwellings," was created, a more serious effort to
ameliorate the situation of the city's workers; Heikki Waris observes that
its founders were not members of the older Helsingfors establishment, but
men who themselves were recent arrivals, representatives of the city's new
industries. Their "company villas" were located near the Russian training
field, on "Kampen," and on Tavastvägen, in the far northeast. One project
was given the hopeful name, "Villa Surutoin" ("Free from care"); heaven
knows that laborers needed to retire to a Sanssouci at night, for they spent
their long days under bad conditions in a bad climate. At the printing establishment of Theodor Sederholm, a humane man and concerned with
his employees' lot, the following mortality record can be found: of the 21
young typesetters employed there in 1876, 13 were dead a decade-and-a-
half later, 10 of tuberculosis.

5. The Railroad

THE CAUSE OF the city's expansion was, before all else, the railroad. Writing in 1858, as the question of a railroad for Finland was debated, Topelius made a prophecy: "Twenty years from now, when a railroad net . . .
leads hither, Helsingfors will have perhaps 40,000 inhabitants." The fore-
cast about population was correct; the city's size increased from 15,212 on
the rolls of the "Finnish and Swedish congregation" in 1855 to 18,718 in
1860. By 1870, 28,519 souls were listed in the church registries; in the

same year, a first official census was taken, which indicated that the total population was 32,000, including the members of the Russian garrison, and by 1875, the total population was about 35,000, almost twice what it is estimated to have been on the eve of the Crimean War, ten times what it had been in 1810. (The total population of 1880 was 43,142; in 1890, it was 65,535; in 1900 it had climbed to 93,217.) However, Topelius miscalculated the speed of the railroad's progress. Visiting Finland in 1856, Alexander had presented the Senate with a program for the economic development of the Grand Duchy, in which the railroad played a considerable part. The next year, Knut Stjernvall, a product of the Russian army's corps of engineers, began the planning of Finland's first railroad, over the 108 kilometers from Helsingfors to Tavastehus; Knut's brother, Claes Alfred, had already proposed a "horse-railway" for a part of the route in 1849. The pace of work was not breath-taking, a surprise in consideration of the fact that such energetic fellows as Nordenstam and Berg were interested in the project; but only Stjernvall, a veteran of the building of the line between Saint Petersburg and Moscow, knew much about railroading.

At last the day of the trial run arrived, January 31, 1862; the invited guests were told to be at the new station on Brunnsgatan at 5:30 in the morning. Surrounded by winter darkness, they were packed into a passenger coach by the conductor, a former color-sergeant of the Finnish Guards; General Stjernvall clambered onto the tender, commanding all he surveyed, and his assistants took their positions on the locomotive proper — it was named *Lemminkäinen*, after the amorous hero of the *Kalevala*. Pleasure was combined with business; the train's freight cars carried a load for Tavastehus, where the brave band arrived at 11:20 A.M., amidst cheers. On the return trip, a stopover was made at Hyvinge; here one of those scenes of the high iron took place which make one wonder how the railroad's several inauguration trips (the ceremony became obligatory) were ever completed: "The rest-pause at Hyvinge was used by the travelers to express, with still another glass, their personal enthusiasm and that of the whole fatherland for General Stjernvall and his men." The railroad openings now followed one another with some dispatch; the spur to Sörnäs was finished by the beginning of 1863, providing Helsingfors with the first of its dockside switching lines, and, seven years after that, the line from Riihimäki (a junction on the Helsingfors-Tavastehus run) to Saint Petersburg was done, again with Stjernvall in charge: the event passed without celebration, out of respect for the victims of the great famine. In 1872, the railroad down to Hangö was finished, joining its more or less ice-free harbor with the capital; in 1874, the line connecting Kervo and Borgå was laid (enabling people of Runeberg's town to come to Helsingfors by rail, albeit circuitously); in 1876 Åbo was joined to

Helsingfors, again in a very round-about way, by the extension of the Tavastehus line to Tammerfors, and the running of a division from the midpoint of that line, Toijala, down to Åbo. The businessmen of Helsingfors regarded the Hangö, Borgå, and Åbo lines with some distaste, since the railroad enabled these harbor towns to compete successfully with the capital, in import as well as in export. By 1883 the Ostrobothnian coastal line to Vasa was opened (the first trip was "an official banquet all the way"), followed by an extension, three years later, to Uleåborg, a section of track in whose dedication Topelius took part; in the 1890's still more lines were added, east and west. The pioneer of Finland's railroading, Stjernvall, had proved that blood will out; he was a grand-nephew of the Stjernvalls who had worked themselves to death for Finland at the opening of the Russian period. Becoming a favorite railroad advisor of Czars Alexander II and III, he was with the latter when the imperial train was wrecked at Borki in October, 1889; Stjernvall received injuries from which he never fully recovered, although he lived on, in Helsingfors and at his Lindnäs estate, until century's end.

The railroad service began modestly: an 1866 guidebook to Helsingfors notes that the passenger train for Tavastehus left the capital every afternoon at 4:00, arriving three-and-one-half hours later; the Tavastehus-Helsingfors run began at 6:15 in the morning, a time chosen for the convenience of those who wished to spend a part of the day in the big city. (Poor people could also make the trip in the third-class cars attached to the freight trains.) At first the income from the line was not as great as had been hoped, and during the famine years the passenger traffic sank below the level of 1863, an early peak, when 23,977 tickets were sold for the trip to Helsingfors. But even habitual pessimists turned sanguine. Witness Sven Elmgren: "One can already see that Helsingfors city has acquired new life since the building of the railroad began . . . Structures appropriate to a metropolis have gone up here during the last few years, perhaps in part because of the railroad." The railroad made it much easier to get into the city; if a traveler from the interior could reach Tavastehus — or, shortly, some other interior point — by water in this land of a thousand lakes, then the remainder of the journey was swift. More than 60% of the migration into Helsingfors had come, in the 1850's, from Nyland, a province with a large Swedish-speaking population; this proportion decreased steadily as the rest of the country was joined to the capital by lake-steamer and rail. By 1880–82, Nyland's contribution was but 41%; by 1900, 32.7%. (The figures become still more meaningful if one recalls that the migration to Helsingfors often took place by stages: from the Tavastland countryside, say, to the Nyland countryside, and then into the city.) In the novella by the Finno-Swede, Runar Schildt, "Sinande källor" ("Failing Sources,"

1918), the main figure — an archivist whose dream it is to write a study of 18th century Finland, when Swedish culture had no rival in the land — reflects on the fate of the capital: "I have lived through two invasions in the city of my childhood. The first of them came from the north, and there's very little to say about it, it had to happen." The archivist (whose profession is symptomatic) means the invasion of Finnish-speaking workers, and not workers alone, who reached Helsingfors by means of Stjern-vall's railroads. The story takes place sometime during the last decade of the Russian period: presently the "second invasion" comes from the east, from a Russia determined to deprive Finland once and for all of its special status. Schildt's hero goes on to confess that he feels a special affinity to Prague — a statement not without its irony. Like Helsingfors, Prague had changed its cultural and linguistic character as industry drew in cheap labor from the countryside. Czech slowly displaced German, even as Finnish would slowly displace Swedish.

6. Industrious Men

IN THE INDUSTRIALIZATION of Helsingfors, not only the laborers but the owners themselves came from outside of town: a phenomenon resembling that of the great rebuilding, where energy and initiative had often seemed to be the exclusive property of men either not native to Finland or long absent from it. Exceptions existed, of course, as they had in earlier days; at the head of the city's new private bank, "Föreningsbanken i Finland," ("The Union Bank in Finland"), a Borgström sat, Henrik the younger, a brother of the violinist Leonhard. (A gifted financier, Henrik was killed by a fall from a horse when he was 35 years old; he had learned about money from Fabian Langenskiöld, von Haartman's successor at the head of the financial department and the creator of a new currency for Finland, in marks and pennies, rather than rubles and kopeks.) Like the Borgströms, the Sundmans and the Sederholms and the Waseniuses remained active in the world of industry and mercantile endeavor; but now they were joined by others come in through the hawsehole: Wilhelm Andsten who, beginning as an apprentice in the building trade, became the owner of a large factory for tile products, or Fredrik Wilhelm Grönqvist, who started on the way to his wagon works as a mere smith's apprentice, or A.E. Jürgens, a tailor's apprentice who came to own a clothing factory. Others were outsiders by virtue of nationality: Russians such as F.F. Tschetschulin, the owner of the famous harbor steamboat, "Tschetschulin's joy-machine," as the impudent folk of Helsingfors called it, and a brickmaker whose products won medals in international competitions; or native Swedes such as Johan Wecksell, who had come to Åbo as a young man, settled there as a hat maker, and, in 1864, moved his concern to Helsingfors. Another notable, Oscar Osberg, was the son of an immigrant coppersmith from Sweden; he founded the firm of "Osberg and Bade" (August Bade was a German from Reval), a "mechanical factory" which, employing 800 people, was the largest of Helsingfors' industries in the 1870's. An entire Swedish firm, Rörstrand's, moved to Finland and to the banks of the Vanda River in 1874, founding a porcelain and fayence factory, complete with workers' dwellings because of its distance from the city; later, taking an exotic new name from the section in which it was located, it became the world-famous Arabia ceramic concern.

Germans played a surprisingly large part in the burgeoning city; they were at once so prosperous and pious that on November 6, 1864 — the 232nd anniversary of the Battle of Lützen, when Gustaf Adolf and numerous other Swedes and Finns fell for the sake of German Protestantism — they could witness the consecration of their own "German Church," on the end of Unionsgatan near the Observatory. (Many non-Germans began to visit the church for the sake of the sermons to be heard there, which according to Rafael Hertzberg had "a content directly applicable to practical life.") Georg Rieks, who had begun his Finnish career as a master in Carl Sundman's carpet factory, set up his own concern in 1858, eventually cornering the Finnish market with his low-priced wares, and exporting to Russia; Sundman sold out to the Russian Jürjeff, who provided rugs for a more refined taste. From Kassel, Ferdinand Tilgmann came to Finland by way of Sweden, and established the lithography workshop which, since 1871, has been in the same location — hard by Gamla Kyrkan, on Lönnrotsgatan (formerly Andrégatan). A Holsteiner, Franz Georg Stockmann had been brought to Finland by the owner of Notsjö's glass works, Adolf Törngren, to serve a bookkeeper; then the energetic Stockmann was moved into Helsingfors, to take charge of a "glass and hardware" store, an outlet for Notsjö products. Take charge he did, eventually buying the store from Törngren — who, nothing loath, went on to become the industrial leader of another growing city, Tammerfors. By the 1870's, Stockmann, broken Swedish and all, was one of the city's leading merchants, and his store, at the corner of Unionsgatan and Alexandersgatan, just off Senate Square, had already become a Helsingfors institution. Another Lübecker, Gustaf Paulig, came over to Finland a little later than Stockmann; his coffee firm, starting humbly in 1876, grew into the greatest in all the land.

Helsingfors was a place where men willing to work hard, and with some special talent, could do well: this was richly demonstrated by the young lions who appeared in the 1870's — Karl Renlund, for example, an Ostrobothnian whose education consisted of a few years in Gamlakarleby's elementary school. By 1884, 34 years old, Renlund became sole owner of the iron-business in whose founding, as "a wholesale establishment for colonial goods, American petroleum, and iron wares," he had had a part ten years before. Or Gabriel Vilhelm Sohlberg, the plater, who at 25 set up a workshop in a shed behind Högbergsgatan 17, and made his fortune producing the new iron roofplates; in the 1890's he chanced upon another popular specialty, milk cans. Or the Swiss engineer, Robert Huber, sent to Helsingfors as a representative of Neptunus, the Berlin firm entrusted with the construction of the water-system: he remained to head the first "installation firm" in Finland, a key figure in the building boom. Or Julius Tallberg, son of an Åbo prison-clerk and a man said to have begun his Helsingfors career as a blacksmith on Broholmen; if one is to believe portraits and eyewitnesses, the mighty frame came to bear a goodly load of fat. A youthful 23, Tallberg established a construction firm, in conjunction with a contractor named Heikel and another of the Kiseleff's, Constantin, as the firm's architect; this was 1880: within seven years the company sailed under Tallberg's flag alone, and became a major factor in the transformation of Helsingfors from an "insignificant little town" (as Harald Hornborg said it still was in the century's last decade) to a metropolis, albeit in miniature. Nor did one have to be young to find a niche in the growing city: August Fredrik Soldan, born in Karelia in 1817, had become a Russian officer, instructor in chemistry for the corps of engineers. Sent to Giessen for further study, he decided he did not want to return to Russia, "that enormous prison"; he went to Paris, Norway, and Sweden, where, pursued by Czarist agents, he took ship for America. Under the anagram "Dalson" he mapped the topography and geology of coal fields around Pottsville and Mauch Chunk, Pennsylvania, (and spread knowledge of the *Kalevala* among his American friends): he returned to Finland only after the Alexandrian thaw was well under way. Now he began a second career, becoming the head of Finland's mint and providing suggestion upon suggestion for the development of Finland's new industries, a service for which he was rewarded with the chairmanship of Finland's Industrial Union and, after his death in 1885, with a biography (from 1901) by his son-in-law, the author Juhani Aho, written in Swedish by the master of Finnish prose and given the telling title: "A Man of Ideas." Another citizen of Helsingfors with an American career behind him was Lars Thiodolf Krogius from Pyttis, at the extreme eastern end of Finland's Swedish-speaking coastal settlements. A nautical product of the

Finnish Cadet School, Krogius was taken prisoner by the British in the Crimean War; having increased his knowledge of English if not his affection for Englishmen, he served as an officer on American ships and became imperial courier between Washington and Saint Petersburg. Back in Finland, he was appointed director of Helsingfors' navigation school, and simultaneously was the commander, for a time, of passenger ships on the Stockholm-Helsingfors-Saint Petersburg run. His entrance into Helsingfors commercial life occurred when he was 40, in 1872, upon the establishment of the shipping line that bears his name. His other great contribution to the city was his directorship of the Finnish Steamship Company (the FÅA, as it was called, from its Swedish name: Finska Ångfartygs Aktiebolag), founded in 1883. The FÅA quickly became the city's and the country's largest shipping company, adding the ocean-steamers *Sirius* (694.49 tons) and *Orion* (691.25 tons) to the Helsingfors register, vessels intended for regular traffic between Finland and Hull.

7. The Exposition of 1876

IN ORDER TO show what progress industry and commerce had made in Finland, it was decided in 1874 — on a suggestion arising in Åbo, of all places — that an industrial exhibition be held in Helsingfors. The leading figures in the plan were Oscar Osberg and August Bade, practical industrialists both, together with their engineering colleague and business rival, John Didrik Stenberg; a "mechanical workshop," purchased at Hagnäs five years before by John Didrik's father, the merchant Johan Daniel Stenberg, was offering Osberg and Bade serious competition. Names with an older prestige were provided by Frans Vilhelm von Frenckell and Fredrik Idestam, leaders of Finland's booming paper and wood industries. Hereupon a directorship was established, including the gentlemen already cited and others: a Borgström, of course (Leonhard), a Wasenius, the Norwegian Lehve of water-conduit fame, Georg Strömberg from the railroads, Walfrid Spåre from Finland's telegraph system, and such prominent noblemen as Constantin Linder and Carl Robert Mannerheim, neither of them fallen as yet on the evil days which would make them outcasts: the one as a result of too great devotion to the Russians, the other from too great devotion to the gaming table. Among the representatives of cultural life were Rector Alfred Kihlman of the Swedish Normal Lyceum and Robert Lagerborg, editor of *Helsingfors Dagblad* — both the school and the paper were fairly new and surely lustrous ornaments of the city. A site in

Brunnsparken was chosen for the exhibition, and the most fashionable architect of the day, Theodor Höijer, was given the task of designing the main building, a wooden edifice to be located north of and adjoining Brunnshuset; the building would have four exhibit halls, with the largest of them, jutting out to the west, especially designed for the display of machinery. Carl Kämp, the director of the restaurant in Brunnshuset, saw to it that his establishment was refurbished and enlarged for the great event, and Helsingfors' favorite baker, Fredrik Ekberg — the owner of the popular confectioner's shop then on Alexandersgatan — got the concession for the veranda on the back of Höijer's monumental but impermanent building; Sinebrychoff opened a "beer pavilion" with waitresses in national Finnish dress, and Hartwall's, aiming at a somewhat less hearty crowd, built itself a large soft-drink stand at the entrance to the park, across from the Roman Catholic church. The directorship decided that Brunnshuset and Ekberg's might be beyond the means of a simpler folk, and so a "second-class restaurant" was created, nestled up against the separate shed erected for the display of agricultural implements. On the premises of Brunnshuset (where 25 extra waiters, from Stockholm and Copenhagen, had been installed) music was to be provided by a 42-piece band from Austria; outdoors, one could delight in the inevitable bandsmen of the Finnish Guard.

The grand opening took place on July 1, 1876, after the exposition's pièce de résistance, an entire train — locomotive, tender, mail-car of new design, and box-car — had been shoved into position. The contents of Höijer's gingerbread house may not have rivaled the exhibits at the Philadelphia Centennial, opened simultaneously halfway around the world; but they were impressive enough in their variety. Fourteen chief "classes" of displays were on hand, from the "beaux arts" (architecture, painting, and sculpture) to "chemical and pharmaceutical preparations, coloring matter, foodstuffs, and beverages," from "forestry, hunting, and fishing" to "products of domestic crafts"; if the visitor grew tired of these works (and others) of Finnish hearts, hands, and minds, he could turn to the appendant exhibit of foreign agricultural machines which opened a week after the aboriginal displays. The Finnish patriot could feel pride at what he saw of his country's present; furthermore, he was tempted to linger before the mementoes of its recent and glorious past: the main hall was adorned with busts of Runeberg, Lönnrot, Cygnaeus, Alexander Armfelt, the late composer Filip von Schantz, and the late jurist, Johan Vilhelm Rosenberg, whose lectures, Om riksdagar (On Parliaments, 1863) had been a guide for the members of the recently revived Diet. The patriot could also be reminded of another Finland, slowly passing away: the university's students had assembled a large ethnographic collection, with life-size figures in authentic regional costumes, and cabins brought from the backwoods to Brunnsparken's civilized confines. Reading descriptions of the exhibits and examining contemporary photographs, one gains the impression of a jumble, of terrible overcrowding; yet this condition may have appealed to the time's taste for gimcracks — the more objects to be dusted, the more respectable the home. The exposition's resemblance to a mauve-decade parlor was heightened by the potted palms stuck into bits of left-over floor space; the "art hall" had as its center piece " a gigantic feather-palm surrounded by other exotic green plants." The vegetation, in turn, was encircled by the works of "the father of Finnish sculpture," Carl Aeneas Sjöstrand, and his pupils, Walter Runeberg and Johan Takanen, by 250 paintings from Finland's artists, by architects' sketches ranging from Åbo classicism (Bassi) to the present, and by the innumerable projects, drawings, and arithmetic exercise books of a hundred Finnish schools.

At the start, attendance figures were discouraging: only some 2,000 people came during the first six days. Tickets were expensive and complicated: if one attended on the days when the full band of 42 Austrian musicians performed, then the entrance cost 4 marks; when only half the musicians were at their desks, the price was 3, and on Sundays (no Austrians at all), the price went down to a mark. Another difficulty was that the Swedish catalogue was ready for the opening of the fair, but the Finnish version was delayed until the end of July — a bad mistake, if one remembers national tensions in general, and the undertaking's express intent of drawing a good part of its public from the countryside. Then as now, finally, Helsingfors did not have enough hotel rooms for travelers. In short order, the exhibition's shaky finances were bolstered by a savior come from afar: Alexander, who arrived on July 14 with Empress Maria Alexandrovna, Crown-Prince Alexander, the latter's wife, Dagmar (a princess of Denmark, and, after her conversion to the Greek Orthodox Church, renamed Maria Feodorovna), and the emperor's daughter Maria. The last-named had her husband, Alfred Duke of Edinburgh, in tow: Queen Victoria's son was an added attraction for the people of Helsingfors. The imperial entourage went determinedly through all the displays, even stopping off at Sinebrychoff's to quaff some democratic beer. The emperor expressed an interest in Walter Runeberg's "Psyche with Jupiter's Eagle," but momentarily satisfied his collector's hunger by buying a more portable objet d'art, Hjalmar Munsterhjelm's "Moonshine Night in the Finnish Skerries"; his son thankfully received a gift from Jyväskylä's teachers' seminary, a rocking chair. Two days later, the royal ladies returned for some serious shopping, and their appearances clinched the exhibition's success; at its closing on September 16, a total of 93,039 persons had attended, and the press rejoiced to announce that Finnish honesty had been as triumphant as Finnish industry and art. "Save for the cases of pick-pocketing, committed during the imperial visit by sharpers from abroad," nothing had happened that required the attention of the police. Höijer's great hall was dismantled within two months after the exposition closed; no traces of the fair remained except in grateful memories.

8. The Press, Liberal and Otherwise

THE "GENERAL EXPOSITION of Finnish industry and art in Helsingfors" of 1876 indicated that the city felt safe and happy, an expression of confidence in self and situation. The sudden expansion of the city's press (without whose interest the exposition would probably never have come into being) was a similar sign. For a short time, from the beginning of 1865 until May 30, 1867, Finland had possessed a kind of freedom of the press: the practice of censorship before printing was temporarily discontinued; but even during the brief liberation, the newspapers spoke — the result of long training — with great restraint. Censorship or not, the Helsingfors press displayed a great fecundity (and almost as great a mortality) in the 1860's. Topelius left *Helsingfors Tidningar* in 1861; five years later, the once excellent paper was dead, having spent its decline in the hands of Fennomanes who used it as a Swedish-language organ for their program. Paavo Tikkanen and his friends, with their *Suometar*, were regarded as too liberal and too luke-warm in their Finnish enthusiasms by the so-called "Young Fennomanes," led by Yrjö Koskinen (*né* Georg Forsman) — a disciple of Snellman who had trained himself to write a scholarly and learned Finnish in a process which he himself termed "a descent into hell." It was a hard job to make the "young" language walk the ordered ways of factual prose. *Suometar* ceased publication at the end of 1866, preceded into death by the short-lived *Päivätär* (*The Day's Daughter*, 1863–65), an organ clearly intended to express liberal thoughts in Finnish and founded by the idealist Ernst Linder; Linder's Swedish paper of similar tendencies, *Barometern*, had lasted not a year (1861). Yrjö Koskinen had tried to oppose liberalism and Swedishness with his own *Helsingin Uutiset* (*Helsinki News*) of 1863, but it was likewise short-lived. The result of this filling of the stage with newspaper corpses, particularly ones that had spoken Finnish, was that in 1867–68 — the years of the great famine — Helsingfors had no Finnish paper at all; it is sad coincidence that Ernst Linder, whose efforts to establish a genuinely liberal Finnish paper were ahead of their time, died of typhus, a disease attendant upon the famine, after having set up a hospital near his estate for victims of the epidemic.

Liberalism turned out to be a commodity in Swedish. In 1862, a new Swedish-language paper had begun, Robert Lagerborg's *Helsingfors Dagblad* (*Helsingfors Daily*), which appeared six times a week until 1871, and then seven, thus becoming the first full-week paper in Finland and in Scandinavia. The *Dagblad* was also Finland's "first European paper," speaking with some candor about Finland's relations to Russia; Lagerborg believed that the constitutional principles embraced by Alexander II would henceforth be respected. The paper's policy resembled the character of its editor, who had been an officer in the Russian army and the Finnish Guards before entering the journalistic world: "He was firm but conciliatory, and had not a trace of that specifically Finnish pedantry which characterizes so many of us." (The author of the valedictory could very well have been making a comparison with Koskinen.) Also, Lagerborg had attracted able helpers: Anders Chydenius, a descendant and namesake of the great eighteenth-century national economist (1729–1803), and a "learned journalist" whose specialties, naturally enough, were politics and economics, and Theodor Sederholm, an experienced littérateur, publisher, and editor, who possessed "an internationalism rarely voiced in the Finland of his day." (As a publisher, Sederholm had tried to widen the horizons of the Finnish-speaking public by a magazine designed in imitation of the German *Über Land und Meer*, a kind of *National Geographic*; his effort, imitatively entitled *Maiden ja merien takaa* [*Beyond Seas and Lands*], had failed, for lack of interested readers. Like *Päivätär*, it had come too soon.) The story of Lagerborg, his gifted friends, and his excellent paper ends sadly: Sederholm and Lagerborg died before they were 50, the one in 1881, the other in 1882. Foreseeing his death, Lagerborg had handpicked a brilliant successor, Robert Castrén, the philologist's son; Castrén passed away within a year of his accession to the editorship, not yet 32 years old. An effort was made to save the paper, by Chydenius and the liberal politician, Leo Mechelin, but both the *Dagblad* and Mechelin's party were caught between the fronts of the language conflict, grown ever more bitter. *Helsingfors Dagblad* ceased publication in 1889. As Jac. Ahrenberg remarked, "its economy had always been weak"; it was, quite simply, too intelligent for its time.

In 1864, the capital had got another Swedish paper, *Hufvudstadsbladet* (*The Capital's Paper*), less brilliant than the *Dagblad* but much hardier, with August Schauman in charge. The paper's finances immediately became as solid as those of the *Dagblad* were shaky; its direct appeal was to the core (but not for long) of the inhabitants of Helsingfors, the Swedish-speaking middle class. It was well edited; widely known as "Skägg-

August" ("Beard-August") because of his theatrical appearance, Schauman knew how to win readers and how not to overtax them. In the little novel on Helsingfors life, *Statsrådet* (*The Councillor of State*) by "Jung Junior" (Rafael Hertzberg), a custodian in a government office spends his day bent in dull fascination over his copy of *Hufvudstadsbladet*. The paper also became the country's leader with respect to announcements and advertisements: "if one was looking for tenants, or had lost something — even a run-away dog — then it could be put in the classified columns of *Hufvudstadsbladet*," wrote Väinö Tanner, proving, by his complaint, that the Swedish hegemony in the Helsingfors of the 1890's extended even unto the lost-and-found department. *Hufvudstadsbladet* was a useful paper, interesting and, above all, moderate: it espoused the Swedish cause, within limits, it preached liberalism, within limits: nothing in excess. Purchased in 1885 by Arthur Frenckell of the printing-and-paper family, it became a 'national' Finland-Swedish paper. The hewing to the Horatian formula worked: the paper survives to this day, as the chief organ of Finland's Swedish population.

As for the Finns, they got their paper too; but *aurea mediocritas* had nothing to do with it. In 1869, *Uusi Suometar* was founded; its creators were Yrjö Koskinen, of whom a witness once remarked that it was miraculous "how so frail a figure could contain so much hatred of Finland's Swedish-speaking population," his brother Jaakko Forsman, whose only halfway deed was the Fennicizing of his name, and the "bear of Kangasala," Agathon Meurman, who — like Snellman — delighted even as he offended, so pungent were his expressions of distaste for Finland's Swedes. In later life, he became a thankful object of interview for journalists who wanted to give their readers a shock. Discussing the "Swedish Party," founded in the 1880's to protect the Swedish cause, Meurman told a newspaperman from Stockholm, Otto von Zweigbergk, that it was: "A little party of officials, who want to keep the jobs for themselves . . . a genuine upper-class party, which you join here in Finland when your purse swells and you want to be genteel. All the Jews and the gypsies in the country naturally count themselves among the party's members too." Whatever can be said against the logic of Meurman's arguments, the grand sweep of his insults makes them somehow memorable. In addition to its brain-trust, *Uusi Suometar* had, after 1870, a chief editor who possessed both a native fluency in Finnish (as the brothers Koskinen-Forsman did not) and practical journalistic experience: Viktor Löfberg, who had worked for Sederholm's *Maiden ja merien takaa* and *Wiborgs Tidning* before taking the post he held for 36 years. (In 1906 he became Viktori Lounasmaa, changing his name — as so many other enthusiasts did — on the centennial of Snellman's birth.) Borne along by Finnish nationalism and carefully steered by Löfberg, *Uusi Suometar* prospered: by 1885, it was printed in 6,200 copies, by 1900, in 12,000 on weekdays and 15,000 on Sundays. Tanner tells how his father swore by the paper; it was surely the chief reading matter in most simpler Finnish-speaking homes, and had to be subscribed to as a matter of course by the growing band of "cultured Finnish families."

Others who wished to stand in well with the followers of Yrjö Koskinen subscribed to *Uusi Suometar* whether they read it or not. That is one of the points made by "Jung Junior" in his satire on Helsingfors of the 1880's. The maid of the "councillor of state," a dignitary freshly returned to Finland after long service in Russia, enters the parlor with two Swedish papers and *Uusi Suometar*. "'What in heaven's name shall we do with this?' [the councillor's] wife cried, spreading out the Finnish paper on the table. 'Who's going to read it? . . . I'm not familiar with the language, and, besides, it's really nothing . . . too immature and even crude'." Yet her ambitious husband carefully leaves the paper lying on display, to give visiting Finnish enthusiasts the feeling that he is on their side. In addition, Helsingfors still had papers written in Swedish but intended to present the Fennomane point-of-view. In 1872, *Morgonbladet: Tidning för Politik, Ekonomi och Litteratur* (*The Morning Paper: Newspaper for Politics, Economics, and Literature*) was founded; its editor was an Ostrobothnian named August Hagman, a schoolmaster by trade (his sister, Lucina, was a pioneer in the establishment of Finnish-language schools in Helsingfors) and in spirit. Its reporting techniques, or lack of them, inspired a Helsingfors bon mot; "What's in *Dagbladet* today will be in *Morgonbladet* tomorrow." (The joke plays upon Swedish "i dag," "today," and "i morgon," "tomorrow.") Hagman did not hesitate to borrow stories from the liberal foe, castigating him all the while. *Morgonbladet* died in 1884, after having given old Snellman the chance for a last flail, in Swedish, at Swedish-speakers and at liberals: recalling the halcyon days when Lagerborg's *Dagblad* still provided a prime and living target, Snellman said: "the liberals shot up out of every garbage heap, swiftly as toadstools in a summer rain." Such a paper as *Morgonbladet* was itself a left-over from former times, since the number of Swedish readers who wanted to be fed pro-Finnish arguments had dwindled; its successor, *Finland*, continued the antiquated fight for a few more years, until 1895. *Finland*'s main distinction lay in its having the aging Meurman and the aged Topelius among its contributors, the latter recalling the Helsingfors of 50 years before, where Swedish-speakers, as yet unthreatened, could enjoy the luxury of feeling guilty about their mother tongue and its riches.

A new generation of Finland's Swedes had decided that Snellman was wrong — that they need not abandon language and tradition in response

to a theory. By example and argument, Axel Olof Freudenthal, then docent in "Old Norse Language and Antiquities" at the university, had
served as the inspiration for a paper, *Vikingen* (*The Viking*), which had the
clear intent of protecting the rights of Swedish speakers. Some aspect of
the *Viking* program were admirable; like Freudenthal himself, it was determined to make the well-to-do Swedes of the city aware of the existence
of their linguistic brothers in the countryside: with heavy but justified
irony, Freudenthal remarked that cultured Finno-Swedes idealized the
Finnish peasant while regarding the Finno-Swedish farmer and fisherman,
less exotic, as something of a bore. The scolding and anti-liberalism of
Vikingen (in which it closely resembled its Finnish opposite numbers) did
not win it many friends, and it lasted but four years, from 1870 until
1874. Then, in 1876, the publication of *Finsk Tidskrift* (*Finnish Journal*)
began. The journal was the child of Carl Gustaf Estlander, Fredrik Cygnaeus' successor as professor of esthetics and modern literature at the university; it was intended to be a continuing object lesson in the importance
of the Swedish strain in Finland's culture, especially as a link to western
European civilization. The lesson has survived; *Finsk Tidskrift* is not only
the oldest of Finland's journals but has reached an age greater than any of
Sweden's literary magazines. In the pages of *Finsk Tidskrift* for 1887, Estlander published the essay, "My Position in the Language Question,"
which summarized his arguments; with Swedish gone, there would occur
"a shift in sympathies from the west to the east, although in the beginning
[the Finns] might think they had only cast off their former chains." Elsewhere and earlier, Estlander issued a study which mixes cultural arrogance
with a sense of undeserved estrangement. In "Ubi patria, ibi bene" the
patriotic tag is to be taken in reverse; Estlander argues for a self-
preservative "Ubi bene, ibi patria": "If a man is denied what he deems
most essential for his soul by his fatherland, then he must break a thousand tender bonds, and steer his fortune's vessel to a foreign shore."
Luckily for Finland, neither Estlander nor other Swedish-speakers of his
generation followed the suggestion; instead, they stayed at their post. (In
Helsingfors of the 1870's and 1880's such heroism did not entail many
sacrifices.) Nonetheless, Estlander's fears now had a great many secret
sharers, who found comfort and protection in the newspaper that came
into being in 1882, with Axel Lille, a sometime editor of *Vikingen*, at its
head. Thanks to editor Lille, the son of the poetaster, Bengt Olof, *Nya
Pressen* (*The New Press*) quickly became something more than the organ of
a political group (the newly consolidated "Swedish Party"); the paper had
a first-rate music critic in Karl Flodin, a drama critic with both style and
knowledge in Hjalmar Neiglick, and a standard of news coverage able to
satisfy readers pampered by *Helsingfors Dagblad*. Its determined anti-

Russian policy, once the powers in Saint Petersburg had fairly embarked upon their project of Russification, resulted in the paper's becoming the first in Helsingfors to be "forbidden forever." This happened in 1900; it was revived in 1905, but never again regained its former intellectual or financial heights. Perhaps Lille thought of these events when, in his book on the Swedes of Finland, he wrote: "With a self-forgetfulness and a readiness for sacrifice which was never fully appreciated by Finnish speakers, the Swedish Party [and *Nya Pressen*] cast itself into the battle against Russian imperialism."

A fair-minded man, Axel Lille readily acknowledged the role that the Finns — the "young Finns," to be distinguished from the "young Fennomanes" of a generation before, now grown old — had played in the same battle. In 1889, the capital got its second large Finnish-language paper, *Päivälehti* (*The Daily Paper*), which began with a subscription list of 4,000. Arguing for the rights of Finnish in Finland, *Päivälehti* nonetheless followed a program rather different from that of *Uusi Suometar*: it was liberal, it was not afraid to stand up to the Russians (blunt Meurman had accused his Finnish-zealot contemporaries of being cowardly and "licking Russian boots"), and it devoted far more attention than the older paper to matters of music, art, and literature. Its cultural interests were not surprising, in consideration of the fact that its chief editor, Eero Erkko, was himself a man of belletristic ambitions, and a brother of the poet Juhana Henrik Erkko, who became a contributor to the paper. Other literary brother-pairs were attached to *Päivälehti* as well: Juhani Aho-Brofeldt and his brother Pekka Brofeldt, Casimir and Eino Leino. In addition, its stable contained Arvid Järnefelt, whose family was constantly busy in the service of the new Finnish culture; Teuvo Pakkala, who longed for and wrote about his Uleåborg home, even as he lived in "foreign" Helsingfors; the travel writer and then historical novelist Santeri Ivalo; and Santeri Alkio who, like Pakkala, was at his best when he thought of the region from which he had sprung, southern Ostrobothnia. The publication of *Päivälehti* was forbidden in 1904; it was resurrected a few months later as *Helsingin Sanomat* (*Helsinki News*), again under Erkko's leadership, and in time grew to be the largest paper in Helsingfors, and of the whole of Finland. The Finnish-speaking population of Helsingfors had come of age upon the establishment of *Päivälehti*; the paper had a companion in the journal *Valvoja* (*The Watchman*), which had even stronger academic ties than did its model, Estlander's *Finsk Tidskrift*. *Valvoja* was founded in 1881, and Johan Richard Danielson-Kalmari was its first editor, Thiodolf Rein its second, and Ernst Gustaf Palmén its third, all three professors at the university and writers in Finnish by idealistic choice rather than necessity. A world away from the academic *Valvoja*, which was intended, as

Rein said, to achieve "a humanization of Fennomania," another public organ in Finnish was born, *Työmies* (*The Working Man*). The title had been briefly used by *Uusi Suometar* for a little ancillary sheet, edited by a committee drawn from Helsingfors' Workers Union, an organization created by the progressive factory owner, Victor von Wright, who was also the legally responsible editor of the bulletin. The first and somewhat anemic *Työmies* ceased publication in 1889, and von Wright left the union he had created, unhappy with its steadily more radical ideas. Resurrected in 1895, *Työmies* became an organ of the social democrats, and, under the editorship of Edvard Valpas-Hänninen, preached class war with an obstinacy hypnotizing for its devoted readers and monotonously frightening for outsiders. Valpas-Hänninen found a ready audience in the industrial sections of Helsingfors, Berghäll, Sörnäs, Hermanstad, and Majstad, as well as far beyond the boundaries of the capital; his editorship — surely an object lesson in the effect rhetoric can have — ended with the brief realization of his visions during the Civil War and his flight to the Soviet Union after the White victory in that conflict. (There, he fell afoul of radical Bolsheviks because he was not extreme enough; returning to Finland, he was sentenced to life in prison but was pardoned in fairly short order.)

9. Finnish versus Swedish

IN 1894, OTTO von Zweigbergk wrote: "The censors in Helsinfors are three in number and, between them, have a heavy task . . . All the four large daily papers of the capital, *Nya Pressen*, *Hufvudstadsbladet*, *Uusi Suometar* and *Päivälehti*, are morning papers. At 6 A.M. daily, the representatives of the various sheets have to report to their respective censors, who . . . must accord or deny the endorsement necessary for the printing and distribution of the paper. Since a number of trains depart for the country as early as 8, it has become the practice for the representatives of the press to get the inspection finished by 7 at the latest." The passage tells much about the difficulties under which Finland's press had to operate; it also shows how the composition of the city had changed: in 1867–68, no Finnish-language papers, in 1894, two of the four major papers are in Finnish. Statistics will give a picture of what had happened: in 1870, the population had consisted of 18,323 persons who gave Swedish as their "chief tongue," 8,308 with Finnish, 3,878 with Russian, 562 with German, and an interesting 1,042 with "other tongue" indicated. Thus Swedish had 57% of the populace and Finnish 25.9%; it should be remembered, however, that, especially in the Finnish group, many approached bilingualism. They were the products of mixed marriages, or of Swedification brought about by school attendance and encouraged by the predominance of Swedish in the city's life. Tanner, belonging to a somewhat later time, tells how he easily acquired the useful skill of speaking Swedish by conversations with the inmates of the Swedish Girl's Shelter, one of Aurora Karamzin's innumerable charities, across the street from his home on Lappviksgatan. "My whole life through, I've profited from this ability, especially as I compare my position with that of the 'pure Finns,' who came from the country to school. For the rest, you couldn't get along in the Helsingfors of those days [Tanner means the turn of the century] without passable knowledge of Swedish — that's how Swedish the city was." In 1880, the Swedes represented 52.3% of the population, the Finns 34%, the Russians 9.6%, and the German and others 4.1%; in 1890, the Swedes had 45.6%, the Finns 45.5% — figures corresponding nicely to the division of the four newspapers between Finnish and Swedish. By 1900, the Swedes had slipped into second place, 42.5% over against 50.7%; at the same time, it is worth noting, some 42% of the Swedes claimed at least some mastery of Finnish, with only 30% of the Finns making a similar boast about Swedish: workers recently arrived from the country could now get along in their factory jobs using their native tongue alone. In 1910, the Swedes had sunk to 35.1% of the population, the Finns had risen to 59.2%. No wonder Schildt's archivist felt that the springs of life were drying up, although a man of his station could spend his life in Helsingfors without having to say much in Finnish; and no wonder that the panic which besets upholsterer Wilenius in Schildt's "Karamsinska hästen" ("The Karamzin Horse"), as his wife lies dying, is intensified by the old man's awareness of being linguistically alone in his poor neighborhood: "There was no lack of neighbors . . . but he scarcely knew them. He was weak in the Finnish they spoke, almost all of them."

To a degree, language distribution went by city section; in the nineteenth century's closing decades the older parts of town had a clear Swedish supremacy, the Finns predominated north of Long Bridge and around Gräsviken, in the west. A rude bilingualism flourished in those places where the Swedish labor force had not yet drowned in the Finnish sea. In Rödbergen and Berghäll, "both Swedish and Finnish could be heard from the mouths of women and children, on the stairs and in the yards, while the men spoke both languages at work"; the rocky nests north of Åbo Barracks heard a different kind of linguistic contamination, according to Yrjö Weilin: "Russian soldiers and Finnish idlers led the lazy life together, in which fights and knifings were a constant factor." Among "the better sort of people," the convention of speaking Swedish died very hard, however

Finnish the speakers may have been in their hearts. From a Viborg German family, but the most ardent of Finnish enthusiasts, Julius Krohn recalled his efforts, made sometime in the 1850's, to get Paavo Tikkanen, Fredrik Polén (a Fennomane publicist), and Erik Rudbeck (alias Eero Salmelainen, the collector of Finnish folktales), to converse in Finnish; they laughed at him. Even the iron-willed Yrjö Koskinen liked to slip back into Swedish, as if into a comfortable old shoe; meeting Vilhelm Floman, a fellow enthusiast, Yrjö Koskinen is supposed to have said: "hyvää päivää, hyvää päivää" ("good day, good day") in Finnish, and then to have gone on in Swedish: "How are you, as the Swedes say." The transition completed, the Fennomanes could continue their conversation in the tongue they commanded and detested. Of course, Swedish pride may have polished this tale, told many decades after the fact by Alma Söderhjelm (who, Finland's "first female professor," at the re-instituted Åbo Akademi in the 1920's and 1930's, is said never to have taken the trouble to learn Finnish well). Another piece from the same body-of-legend concerns Fanny Churberg, the founder of "The Friends of Finnish Handwork," who "could do everything possible for the Finnish cause save — learn Finnish." Wits claimed that Fanny's brother, Karl Waldemar Churberg, had been driven out of his mind by his efforts to translate the world's classics into Finnish; one day in March, 1889, he walked up to Jaakko Forsman of *Uusi Suometar* and shot him. Lightly wounded but badly surprised, Forsman could only mumble, when asked about the doer of the deed: "My friend, Waldemar Churberg." Something comical even pertained to the magnificent idealist and sometime Russian general, August Alexander Järnefelt, and his wife, born a Clodt von Jürgensburg; these descendants of the Baltic nobility turned their home at Albertsgatan 28 into a center for Finnish culture in Helsingfors. An air of superheated enthusiasm surrounded the Järnefelts; their home provided a sanctuary not least for Finnish intellectuals recently arrived in unfriendly Helsingfors from up country. The Järnefelt children — the author Arvid, the painter Eero, and the composer Armas — could almost have created a Finnish culture among themselves, even without the aid of Jean Sibelius, who married their sister Aino. (Arvid Järnefelt left a monument in particular to his mother's cultural and linguistic devotion, and sacrifice, in his *Vanhempieni-romaani* [*My Parents' Novel*].)

Well-born idealists and their gifted guests could ignore the ripples of laughter; poorer (and more genuine) Finns had to endure worse humiliations. According to V.A. Koskenniemi, poet and professor, Finnish-speakers were refused service in stores or restaurants as late as the first decade of the present century, while another professorial witness, Rafael Koskimies, says "that Finns would speak Swedish [in public places] simply for the sake of harmony." (Times indeed have changed.) Finns had to confront the fact (and confront it they did with ever decreasing patience) that, in Helsingfors, they were second-rate — sometimes in the eyes of their own group; a winged word among Finnish servants was: "A real gentleman speaks Swedish." Everyday life taught the Finnish-speaker where he stood; and, if he was thoughtful enough to look beyond single events to controlling systems, he came upon the same prejudices, better organized. In 1873, the administration of Helsingfors was revised, in conjunction with a general reform of municipal government in Finland: representatives to the city council were to be elected for three-year periods. Since the right to vote was dependent upon the amount of taxes paid, the wealthier citizens of Helsingfors were over-represented: although a third of the city's population was already Finnish-speaking, only three of the 48 members of the council had Finnish as their mother tongue. (Council members were not elected by universal suffrage until 1917.) Concluding that they had a disproportionately small voice in the government of the city where they lived, Finnish-speakers could also deduce that they had no position in the world of commerce and finance. Industrialists and merchants were Swedish-speaking (or German or Russian) almost to a man; in Victor Pettersson's Christmas calendars, for example, there are very few advertisers with Finnish names. A bank of clearly Finnish orientation was not established until 1889, the "Kansallis-Osake-Pankki," which was described thus in the newspaper *Finland* by Agathon Meurman: "Hitherto, a kind of patrician or aristocratic atmosphere has been maintained in our larger banks, estranged from a large mass of the people"; the new K-O-P would maintain "a popular attitude and character."

The establishment of the bank, the flourishing Finnish-language press, the attainment (in 1890) of numerical equality, the foundation of Finnish upper schools — all these things served to make Finns surer of themselves in Helsingfors than they had ever been before. Nevertheless, one can discover a multitude of signs that they were not yet at home in the city. The new literature from the Finnish side of the language line talks about nostalgia for the country life the Finnish-speaker has left behind, and fear of the city in which he or she has landed; the themes are as common as are those of isolation and sterility in Finno-Swedish letters. Juhani Aho's sturdy Wilhelmiina Wäisänen (in the tale bearing her name) rides a train bound north from Helsingfors, on the way home to see her relatives: she has made a place for herself in the city by hard and dependable service to a Swedish-speaking family. The eldest son has tried to seduce her, but she has put a stop to it, realizing that "his intentions were not good"; a worker from Sörnäs has good intentions, to be sure, but drowns them in drink. Now, Wilhelmiina's one aim is to save money, a sure weapon by which to keep her self-respect; Helsingfors will not destroy her, but it has given her emotional calluses. One is not so sure about the survival of Antti, the student on his way to the capital and its university in Aho's *Helsinkiin* (*To Helsingfors*). From a well-to-do family in Kuopio, Antti is full of enthusiasm for his home language, Finnish, and his youthful national culture. On the steamer which bears Antti down the lakes to the railroad at Villmanstrand, he hears the captain, who speaks bad Finnish, proclaim a program of "Swedish academic schools and Finnish trade schools." Quite understandably, the boy feels insulted both for his own sake and that of his cause; on the other hand, Antti himself willingly uses Swedish in order to make a social impression. Arriving in Helsingfors at last, he is swallowed up by the sinful city, a fate of innocent Finns to be found not only elsewhere in Aho (for example, in the story of the drunken Antero, with his soiled student's cap, who makes "A Last Attempt" to get out of the mire), but in the novels of Maila Talvio. Although her *Niniven lapset* (*The Children of Niniveh*) appeared in 1915, the beginning of the narration falls in the last years of the previous century, when the Ståhle family, Finnish-speaking and prosperous, comes to Helsingfors. It would take much too long to recount the processes by which the Ståhles fall prey to Niniveh on the Baltic; let it suffice to describe the scene in which, after a foundling has been deposited in the living room of the Ståhle apartment, family members debate the baby's parentage. Is it the father's - a man still vital by virtue of his country heritage? Does it belong to his son Leo, who, his "Ståhle" translated into the Finnish "Teräs" ("Steel"), has become a kind of journalistic crook? Or to the second son, Daniel, not yet entered upon the clergyman's career for which his biblical name has destined him? Or to Ståhle's daughter Otteli, a singer of doubtful talents and morals, purchased by an elderly Finno-Swede? Seldom have the wages of sin and the perils of life in a still heavily Finno-Swedish milieu been depicted in so melodramatic and confusing a way. One point is clear enough: the Ståhles should have remained in their country home. In the sketch called "Maan sydämeen" ("To The Country's Heart") — by which he means some small town in the interior — Aho describes Helsingfors thus: "Our capital is surely quite beautiful, and we can be proud when foreigners praise it . . . as they walk along the way between Skatudden bridge and Swedish Theater . . . a part of town that not only reminds one of a foreign country: it is, in fact, a piece of a foreign world. . . . It seems as though we are not really at home here, as if we were surrounded more by foreigners than by our own race." Helsingfors was a dangerous place for honest Finns, but they were determined to capture it all the same.

The Swedes of Helsingfors were not about to surrender; it must be remembered that Schildt's archivist and upholsterer, paralyzed in isolation,

are late figures, living their fictional life on the eve of the Civil War of
1918. In an earlier and more confident age, many Swedes felt precisely as
did Casimir von Kothen, the vice-chancellor of the university from 1869
until 1873, who believed that the country (not merely its capital) must
remain in Finno-Swedish hands, both because the Swedes of Finland had
the skills and the traditions, and because they formed such an excellent
link between Russia and Scandinavia. (Russia's advantage and the vested
interests of his own class were foremost, one fears, in von Kothen's mind.)
At the other extreme from von Kothen were liberals of the stripe of Thiodolf Rein, Professor Gabriel Rein's eldest son, who saw the Finnish advance as the righting of old wrongs (the language rescript of 1863 had at
last given Finnish an official part in the governmental structure) but who
were opposed to throwing out the child with the bath water: "Every language group in our country ought to have the right to use its tongue not
only privately but in public life." (Snellman's more conciliatory pupil, he
eventually wrote the standard biography of the great zealot.) In between,
there were thoughtful souls — some of them have already been mentioned — who feared that too ready an acceptance of Finnish claims, for
whatever reason, would result in the disappearance of the land's most precious cultural heritage. At their best, these men were the champions, in
Jac. Ahrenberg's phrase, "of Swedish culture, not of Swedishness *quand
même*"; as Finno-Swedes, they felt out of place in Sweden proper, and yet
they knew, like the student leader Ivar August Heikel, "that he whose
mother tongue and culture are Swedish is not a 'Finn,' as an inaccurate
nomenclature would cause him to believe." (Heikel, who later became
professor of Greek literature at Helsingfors, was careful with words.) With
Estlander, they asserted that "they did not intend to sacrifice Swedish language and culture, either for their own or their children's benefit." In
Helsingfors, the benefit to be had from going Finnish lay more in the future than in the present; Helsingfors' new Swedish Club was founded in
1881, "in order to comprise a connecting link between those persons who
have realized that the Swedish tongue is their mother tongue, and that
they belong to a Swedish nationality." Were all its members as concerned
with this noble and reasonable goal as they were with preserving certain
social and financial advantages and privileges? Better to keep the finger in
the dike as long as possible.

It was often charged, from the Finnish side, that a certain aristocratic,
or quasi-aristocratic aura hung over the Swedish Party; however much one
might sympathize (in retrospect) with the well-thought-out standpoint of
Estlander and Heikel and Axel Lille, one cannot help enjoying the scene
enacted in "Riddarhuset" in 1894, and described by Otto von Zweigbergk. The "House of Nobles" was the Italian Renaissance home which

the "noble estate" had commissioned for itself, to a design by Georg Theodor Policron Chiewitz. In 1860, the nobles generously asked Alexander II to allow the little *palazzo*, in its park, to be used as a meeting-place for all the estates, and it was employed until Gustaf Nyström's "Ständerhuset" ("House of Estates") was completed in 1891. During the intervening years the non-nobles at the plenary sessions could scarcely forget whose guests they were; the scutcheons of the noble families of Finland decorated the walls of the main hall, "that magnificent room of rectangular form." On the day described by the Swedish journalist, a young man somewhat dizzyingly named Yrjö Koskinen Yrjö-Koskinen (his father, the arch-Fennomane, had been ennobled as Yrjö Sakari Yrjö-Koskinen) spoke Finnish from the floor, the first time it had ever happened. "The members of the estate looked as if they had no idea of what was being said, and the stenographers put down their pens." The magnificent Victor Magnus von Born, a Swedish paladin, arose, "pale and determined," to announce that he did not understand. The marshal of the house asked young Yrjö-Koskinen to translate into Swedish; he refused. Arising a second time, the silver-tongued von Born said that what had occurred was tantamount to a breaking of the law since, according to statute 26 of the nobles' estate, "'the official tongue of the land shall be employed,' and, at the time the statutes were composed, that tongue was Swedish and Swedish alone." Von Born's arguments failed, Yrjö-Koskinen prevailed, and even von Zweigbergk, generally on the side of the Finno-Swedes in his report, applauded the Finn's obstreperousness. Enjoying von Born's discomfiture, one should still keep the home truths in mind which Kasten Antell, the leader of von Born's Swedish Party, delivered to von Zweigbergk: "The cultured classes of Finland know that the old Swedish culture must be preserved if Finland is to remain a free land . . . no one realizes better than the Russians that Swedish culture is the greatest barrier to the Russification of Finland." (The clarity and courage of Antell's judgment had to be respected; a vice-chairman of the Helsingfors city council, he had expressed his dismay at the unfairly small representation of Finns in that body.) Time would shortly prove that there were many more Finno-Swedes of the cast of Antell, Lille, and the great constitutionalist, Leo Mechelin, than there were Russian errand boys — a von Kothen, a Constantin Linder, the latter a brother, surprisingly, of the liberal Ernst Linder. (And still another liberal surprise turns up in connection with Constantin Linder: his first wife, Marie, née Mussin-Pushkin, intelligently reared by her maternal aunt, Aurora Karamzin [see Chapter I], struck a pioneer blow for woman's liberation in Finland with her novel, *En kvinna av vår tid* [*A Woman of Our Time*, 1867]. She died before she was thirty,

and before Constantin, aided by his enormous wealth, had begun to climb
the rungs of the Saint Petersburg court.)

Beyond the ken of the "Swedish cultured class," the city's Swedish
speakers of modest means and modest horizons lived out their lives, apparently not overmuch concerned about the fate of their linguistic group.
Judging by the popular literature they consumed, they disliked immorality,
luxury, and Russian connections, not Finnish-speakers. The tales of F.J.
Valbäck, the editor of the simple Swedish paper, *Folkvännen* (*The People's
Friend*, 1876–1891), usually pass the Finns by in silence; in Valbäck's ro-
manticized depiction of Helsingfors life, *En afton i Kajsaniemi* (*An Evening at Kajsaniemi*, 1892), the hero is Albert, an honest Swedish seaman,
the villain "the slippery, furtive Javetz, employed at the governor-general's
office," the heroine sweet Maria, whose father, Colonel Danielsson, a man
filled with class prejudice, becomes convinced at tale's end that Albert,
made captain of the full rigger *Gustaf Vasa*, is worthy of Maria's hand, and
Javetz is not. A little farther up the scale of literary value, Rafael
Hertzberg, writing under the pseudonym of "Sphinx" about *Helsingfors-
Monaco* (1887), has as his heroine the poor but honest school-teacher,
Olga Berggren, and his worst blackguard is the factory-owner Frisk, whose
"cultured Swedish home" is a den of over-stuffed iniquity: "Between the
bookcases [where the pages of the unbound books are not cut, and the
bound books are not read] there hung a bad oilprint, showing Cleopatra
as she let the serpent bite her bared breast. Opposite it was the factory
owner's portrait, in a broad, quilted frame, obviously done by a beginner's
hand. Above the writing desk, with its splendid utensils of white marble
and bronze, there was still another oleograph, of a naked woman partially
concealing herself behind a light blue curtain." The novel's weakling hero,
torn between Frisk's vulgar world and the virtuous charms of Olga, ends
by shooting himself after some final reverses at the gaming tables of Monaco.

In "Daniel Sten's" *Luba* (1889) — the masculine pseudonym belonged
to Ina Lange, a concert pianist — the cast again includes familiar and admirable Finno-Swedes types, the modest Dr. Collin, the hard-working and
unappreciated Lina. They wait upon Lina's sister Luba, whose unfulfilled
ambitions and erotic needs have turned her into a hysterical paralytic.
Scornful of normal virtues, Luba gets her come-uppance in a roundabout
way. She is cured by the Christian virility of one Pastor Lämmanen, who
has already won a large following among Helsingfors ladies incapable of
understanding a word of his Finnish sermons; but, having married the rev-
erend gentleman, Luba dies of shock upon discovering that he has a child
fathered on a coarse Finnish girl. The prolific Konni Zilliacus, in *I societeten: En Helsingfors-berättelse* (*In Society: A Helsingfors Tale*, 1894), of-

fers a main figure with several points of resemblance to Lämmanen: he comes from the Finnish up-country, and he has had a child with a Finnish girl, willing and sensuous. But unlike Lämmanen, who makes no effort to conceal his origins, Lieutenant Henry Krause, late of the Russian army, dislikes being reminded that he was once little "Rausin Heikki" of Kuopio. Meeting an honest and likable Finnish gentleman from his past, Councillor Walkonen of Joensuu, Krause's "loose, shapeless lips formed themselves into a pained smile," and he pretends not to notice that old Walkonen is talking to him at all. A wealthy man, Krause is on the lookout for a suitable bride; unfortunately, he is not acceptable in Helsingfors society because of the stories current about his shady dealings in lumber and (it is strongly implied) his Russified personal tastes. Rejected by Hilma Tornhjelm, who realizes that Krause is trying to acquire her for the sake of her family connections, the lieutenant finds a replacement, the daughter of an unscrupulous councillor-of-state not unlike the faintly corrupt hero of the anonymous *Statsrådet*. In the books of Lange and Zilliacus (intended, by the way, for a more sophisticated public than are the stories of Valbäck or Victor Pettersson), a vague condescension toward Finns is balanced by the critical representation of a Swedish-speaker (Luba) in the one case and by the genially honest Finn Walkonen in the other. Open dislike, of a kind occasionally to be found in Finno-Swedish literature after the turn of the century, is missing; rather, the reader is lured into thinking flattering thoughts about himself, or what he imagines himself to be.

10. Schools

AS THE CENTURY came to an end, the Swedish-speaker in Helsingfors had only begun to feel threatened by his Finnish fellow citizens; the business world was his, the more attractive sections of town were his, and in the schools — which so readily could become a sore point — he was still the master. The old modes of public elementary schooling, the "exchange-schools" (where senior pupils helped beginners) and the "poor schools," had been replaced, in the 1860's, by the new folk-schools, a general and uniform system of basic education created primarily as a result of the efforts of the quondam Alaskan pastor, Uno Cygnaeus, "the father of the folk-school in Finland," on the national scene, and the university's professor of pedagogy, Zacharias Joachim Cleve, on the local one. By 1868, six folk-schools were already in operation in Helsingfors, in which were enrolled 154 Swedish-speaking and 70 Finnish-speaking children. (In the now extinct exchange-schools, instruction had been solely in Swedish until 1857, when, on Snellman's urging, instruction was begun in Finnish as well; the first teacher of this language persuasion was a pedagogue from Jyväskylä, Jaakko Länkelä, who also, shortly after his arrival in Helsingfors, founded a Finnish private school.) The development of the city's folk-schools in the ensuing decades met with no serious problems; under the direction of Victor Öhberg from 1871, a sacristan's son from Pernå in eastern Nyland (born a Swedish-speaker, but one who had long lived in Finnish regions), the system flourished; when Öhberg retired in 1901, the schools had 219 teachers and more than 7,000 pupils, as compared to the 23 teachers and 1,000 students of thirty years before. For his building program, Öhberg was able to obtain the services of the city's best architects; "Annegatans folkskola" is representative of what Öhberg accomplished in this line, designed by Gustaf Nyström and reputedly the first school in Finland to have electric lights. (Until 1968, the building was still in happy use as a Swedish folk-school.) But the school on Annegatan, a "palace-like edifice," and others of its handsome kind caused discontent among the Finns, whose children by 1901 represented three-fifths of the city's elementary-school pupils. The Swedish-speakers, they claimed, got the fine, new buildings of stone, and the Finns had to endure more crowded and less attractive quarters of wood. The critics of Öhberg seem to have been particularly incensed by the fact that the school-director was a close friend of Axel Olof Freudenthal, the sometime leader of the Viking-circle and the most vigilant guardian of Swedish interests at the middle and lower levels of society.

The city had so many lyceums by the 1880's that Rafael Hertzberg could make the following statement in his guide to Helsingfors: "Proportionately, probably no city in the world can compare with Helsingfors in its wealth of educational institutions." The lyceums and equivalent institutions had had a development not unlike that of the folk-schools: the needs of both Swedish and Finnish children were attended to, but the Finns could argue, now and again, that they drew the shorter straw. An initial scandal had, justifiably, embittered the Finns and given the best elements in the Swedish world a chance to live up to their often proclaimed ideals of fairness and justice. In 1864, the "Normallyceum" (later to have its name appropriately augmented as "Svenska normallyceum") was founded, a school which, during the first thirty-odd years of its existence, produced such notable men-of-the-future as the painter Albert Edelfelt, the physicist Theodor Homén, the sociologist Eduard Westermarck, the physician Richard Faltin, and Pehr Evind Svinhufvud, president of the Republic of Finland. (If truth be told, Faltin had a low opinion of the education he received there, but he was a notoriously critical sort.) The "Normallyceum," beginning with only two classes, had a full program by 1868, when it sent its first products to the university; in order to develop a parallel course of instruction in Finnish, the school's inspector, the above-mentioned Cleve — from Rantasalmi in the eastern lake country, and a friend of Finnish culture — had instituted a first and second class where Finnish was the instrument of instruction. Consequently, a third class was requested, but the Senate refused to allocate money for it. The villain of the piece was Casimir von Kothen, from 1870 director of the newly constituted school-board of Finland; von Kothen's attitude was that of the captain on the boat which carried Aho's student, Antti, toward Helsingfors — Finns needed only a "practical education." (Von Kothen demanded "applicable skills," of a certain kind, for Swedes as well; it was at his instigation that the "Svenska reallyceum" was established for boys who might enter government service. Here Russian had 35 instruction hours and French 31, as compared to 12 for Finnish and 8 for Swedish *as a subject* — Swedish, of course, was the general vehicle of instruction.) Private parties in Helsingfors paid for the continuation of the Finnish program at the "Normallyceum"; but, in 1871, von Kothen struck another blow; when an additional Finnish class was applied for, von Kothen declared that the whole program should be moved to Tavastehus, leaving the capital without a Finnish-language lyceum. The order was carried out; Tavastehus became a center of Finnish education, and, in 1876, the "Suomalainen normaalilyseo" there received a boy who would turn out to be the most famous of all its pupils — Johan Julius Christian Sibelius, the child of a Swedish-speaking home.

The idea of an advanced Finnish-language school for Helsingfors could not readily be killed, however: Colonel (later General) Alexander Järnefelt, Yrjö Koskinen, Thiodolf Rein, Carl Gustaf von Essen (professor of practical theology and noted wit), and Karl Ferdinand Ignatius (geographer and notorious Fennomane) tried to get official permission to support at least one class by private means, as before. Failing to win approval of this modest request for the "Normallyceum," they decided upon a much bolder plan: the establishment of a whole new private school in Helsingfors, "Suomalainen alkeisopisto" ("Finnish Elementary School," a misleading title), opened in 1871. The survival of the school became a matter of honor for Finnish enthusiasts: the biggest single donation came from Antti Ahlström, the first major industrialist of clearly Finnish provenience (whose chief field of activity, nota bene, was not Swedish-dominated Helsingfors but Björneborg on the west coast); he was in alliance with Agathon Meurman (the giver of the initial donation), Waldemar Churberg, Julius Krohn, and Z.J. Cleve, the last undaunted by his earlier experiences. The Finnish-speaking public-at-large sent in small contributions of money, rings, and other jewelry; persons who were not directly supporters of the Finnish cause contributed as well: for example, the anonymous "Swedish-speaking person," who called his gift "a gesture of justice." By 1878, the school had got its own building; by 1879, its first graduates went to the university; and, by 1886, it was transformed into "Suomalainen normaalilyseo," a state institution. It was so crowded that, in 1891, the "Suomalainen realilyseo" was established to help bear the burden; with its "practical course," it likewise became enormously popular. Young women who spoke Finnish (or wanted to speak it) had their needs attended to, after 1869, by the "Suomalainen tyttökoulu" ("Finnish Girls School"), one good deed among the many of the industrialist John Daniel Stenberg, and a tribute to his simple Finnish beginnings; the pedagogical inspiration came from Bernhard Fredrik Godenhjelm, the son of the pioneer Finnish painter Berndt Abraham Godenhjelm and an indefatigable supplier of textbooks for the new Finnish schools. Following the modern notion of upper schools for boys and girls together, imported from Scandinavia proper, the reform was instituted, on the Finnish side, by Lucina Hagman's "Suomalainen yhteiskoulu" ("Finnish Combined School") on Georgsgatan. The school, established in 1886, got a special reputation as a place where the children of cultured Finnish families, and of those Swedes who wanted their children to get a Finnish secondary education, could find a happy home. One of its pupils was Henning Söderhjelm, son of Professor Werner Söderhjelm, the university's all-around man in modern philology and literary history. Henning, who was enrolled at the school in 1896, entered its doors in obedience to a parental point-of-view already somewhat outdated; ten years later, his brother was sent to a Swedish school, since the Söderhjelms had now decided that "it was the Swedish side that needed support."

The Finnish schoolboys, feeling their oats, enjoyed their new importance whenever they could. Väinö Tanner tells how he and his comrades from "Suomalainen realilyseo" carried on regular wars with the boys from Swedish schools, and, in order to show that their patriotism knew no bias, also terrorized the Russian schoolboys who attended the "Alexandersgymnasium," the proud creation of Governor-General Adlerberg and of the Emperor himself. Bertel Gripenberg, a Finno-Swedish poet-to-be, became the victim of his father's highly theoretical Finnish passions; put into "Suomalainen normaalilyseo," he suffered endless indignities as "a member of the Swedish upper class": "[The Finnish boys] could not stand the fact that I was more cleanly and better dressed than they, it was their greatest pleasure to make fun of me . . . and to soil and ruin my clothes." After an unpleasant interlude at the cadet-school in Fredrikshamn, where the brutal comrades this time were members of his own

social and language group, young Gripenberg at last found happiness in
the "Nya svenska läroverket" ("The New Swedish Secondary School"), a
fashionable place founded in 1880, "where one was a gentleman and
sometimes even a snob." Young Söderhjelm corroborated this opinion;
the people from "Lärkan" were particularly condescending toward the
pupils at "Suomalainen yhteiskoulu," perhaps because the student bodies
were recruited from the same social class (which meant that the boys getting a Swedish education could regard their opposite members as oppor-
tunists or renegades), and because "Nya svenska läroverket," after some
discussion, had remained aristocratically masculine. The argument, however, led to the departure of Pastor Karl Theodor Broberg from "Nya
svenska läroverket" and the establishment of "Läroverket för gossar och
flickor" ("The Secondary School for Boys and Girls"), a healthier arrangement, Broberg was convinced. The school, which produced the classic author of Swedish Helsingfors, Runar Schildt, had to meet formidable
difficulties during its early years: Yrjö-Koskinen the elder, now the chief of
the Senate's ecclesiastical department, detested mixed education almost as
much as he did the prospect of survival for Swedish Finland. Founded in
1883, "Broberg's school" got state support only in 1889. Disagreement
within Broberg's teaching corps (idealists are seldom prepared to com-
promise) had ended in defections and the establishment of two other co-
educational schools, of which one passed away after 15 years (Augusta
Pipping's "Lyceum för gossar och flickor"), while the other, "Nya svenska
samskolan" ("The New Swedish Combined School"), popularly called for
many years by the name of its second director, Dr. Albin Lönnbeck, survived. Yrjö-Koskinen feared that mixed education would make the boys
effeminate, a fear contradicted by the record of the Lönnbeck school's
alumni: 17 of them were members of the "Pathfinder" group, the kernel
of the "jägare" ("light infantrymen") who trained in Germany from 1915
to 1917 and supplied a number of junior officers for the White Army
during Finland's Civil War in 1918.

Helsingfors had its Swedish-language schools for girls alone, too: the
ancient "Svenska fruntimmersskolan" (the translation, "The Swedish
Women's School," loses something of the old-fashioned flavor), founded
in 1844 for "the daughters of cultured parents"; "Svenska privata läroverket för flickor," which from 1870 provided a second educational harbor
for proper young ladies; and, from 1889, "Privata svenska flickskolan,"
which showed signs of the times by preparing its pupils for the university.
(Brave souls had taken independent steps toward the university almost two
decades before: Marie Tschetschulin, the daughter of the Russian industrialist, had passed the student's examination, granting university admis-
sion, in 1870, followed three years later by Emma Irene Åström, who

then, in 1882, became the first woman to win a master's degree in Finland.) By the middle of the 1880's secondary school girls were a noticeable and noisy part of the Helsingfors scene; Rafael Hertzberg says that the Boulevard in those days was called "Jungfrustigen" ("The Maiden's Walk," an imitation of Hamburg's "Jungfernstieg") because three girls' schools and a combined school were located on it. (In actual fact, the name had long belonged to another street, the southern extension of Kaserngatan.) Hertzberg must have liked what he saw, since he bacame a champion of women's rights in Finland.

At its western end, the Boulevard lost its girlish air altogether: there, it formed the south side of Sandvik Square, having Sinebrychoff's brewery immediately beside it. Across the square, to the north, lay a Russian military hospital, and on the square's eastern side a sprawling building was put up to house the new Polytechnical Institute. It had begun modestly enough, as a "Technical-Practical School," and its main figure had been the Norwegian Lehve, brought to Helsingfors from his studies in Germany to become one of its first teachers. By 1877, the "Polytechnical School" (renamed in an effort to show how it had been transformed from a mere training school into an engineering academy) moved into the house which Frans Anatolius Sjöström had designed; another two years, and the "School" was promoted to a full-fledged "Institute." The Institute grew rapidly, even as Finnish industry did, and by 1886 its entrance requirements matched those of the university. Its glory was its architectural department, where Sjöström himself was a teacher, with the budding sculptor Ville Vallgren and the budding author Karl August Tavaststjerna in his classes; in 1880, Sjöström was joined on the faculty by Gustaf Nyström, his former student, who created so many of the university's and the government's new buildings during the closing decades of the century. The gifted Sjöström died young, in 1885 just after his 45th birthday, his dream of erecting a great House of Estates on Observatory Hill unrealized; the plan was carried out by Nyström instead, and the building was located on Nikolaigatan, in the city proper — less picturesque than Observatory Hill, but more practical. A lesson in practicality was also taught by the yellow building on Sandvik Square, not just in the material of its studies but in the nature of its enrollments; unintentionally, the Polytechnical Institute became a living illustration of von Kothen's plans for educational division — or, at any rate, of his notion that Finns were particularly suited for technical training.

The first lectures in Finnish at the Institute were held in 1887, but the Finns entering the school had already outdistanced the Swedes in numbers — a proportionate growth much more rapid than that of the university proper. In 1908, when the institute's enrollment consisted of 209

Finnish-speaking and 136 Swedish-speaking students, it was accorded the same academic dignity as the university itself, under the new title "Finlands tekniska högskola" or "Suomen teknillinen korkeakoulu"; its first rector was Gustaf Nyström.

11. The University Again: Finns and Finno-Swedes

IN 1873, CASIMIR von Kothen had asked for a leave-of-absence from the directorship of the school department and the vice-chancellorship at the university; the leave was terminal, for he used it to obtain release from all his Finnish obligations. Retiring to Mecklenburg, in the empire of his admired Bismarck, he died in 1880, mourned by few who had known him. His replacement was a sometime academician, the jurist Johan Filip Palmén, and so the unfortunate tradition was broken by which military men held the vice-chancellorship of the university. Before his departure, von Kothen had become as unpopular among the students of the university as he was among the Finnish enthusiasts and fair-minded Swedes of the world at large. Consistently petty, he had made efforts to keep Marie Tschetschulin from taking her examination (here he was quashed by Alexander, who was proud that a girl of Russian origin led the way), and had spoiled a student plan to buy a tombstone for a captain from the War of 1808–09; confiscating the money already collected, he forbade a benefit party in the new Student Union. Plainly, von Kothen was a man meant to serve a Nicholas, not an Alexander; once he had passed from the scene, the university entered a period of rapid and relatively unhampered growth, with 642 students in 1875–76, and 2,015 in 1895–96. As specialization increased, fields of learning were divided: the professorship of anatomy was split into chairs of anatomy and physiology, the law faculty acquired five new professorships by the same process. The professorship of Finnish language and literature, a position whose fate was of widespread interest, had been held from 1863 until 1888 by August Ahlqvist. (Because of his reasonableness, Ahlqvist was ill regarded in radical Finnish circles; he was also disliked on more cogent grounds, having denied the greatness of Aleksis Kivi.) Upon Ahlqvist's becoming emeritus, the chair was divided into a professorship of "language and literature," awarded to the young Emil Nestor Setälä, another brilliant product of the "Normaalilyseo" at Tavastehus and the author of a Finnish grammar while still a schoolboy, and a professorship of Finno-Ugric philology; the latter went to an older colleague, Arvid Genetz, who — like Mathias Alexander Castrén in past decades — had rummaged through Siberia, looking for relatives of the Finnish people. Julius Krohn had finally been named "extraordinary professor" of Finnish and comparative folklore, a post made a permanent part of the academic schedule in 1908, with Kaarle Krohn, his son, as its holder. ("Extraordinary professorships" were temporary, in that they were withdrawn after the retirement or death of the incumbent.) Seeing how other disciplines flourished, one may be surprised to note that the university got around to appointing a docent of Romance philology only in 1889, Werner Söderhjelm, who then became (in 1894) "extraordinary" professor of Germanic and Romance philology. A docent in Germanic philology was appointed for the first time in 1892; in 1898, the "extraordinary" professorship of Germanic and Romance was made "regular," a permanent academic post, thus achieving complete academic respectability for the disciplines in question. By 1910 the two fields, yoked together all too long, were finally divorced, Söderhjelm getting Romance as his own bailiwick. (Ever on the lookout for new podiums to conquer, Söderhjelm changed to a professorship of "domestic and general literature" in 1913.) A certain skepticism about novel areas of knowledge could be detected even in the medical faculty, forced by public demand to take cognizance of discoveries on the continent: it generously appointed "extraordinary professors," consoled by the thought that the posts could be dissolved if their specialties turned out to have only transitory interest.

Looking at the academic appointments of these years, one might conclude that Finnish was well taken care of; but it was on the language front that the university underwent its most serious stress and strain. The establishment of Finnish advanced schools, with larger classes (and, if one is to believe Aho, more industrious and ambitious pupils) than their Swedish counterparts, was bound to result in a larger Finnish university enrollment; by 1887, there were more Finnish-speaking than Swedish-speaking students at the university, although it was not until 1895 that the country had as many Finnish as Swedish schools — thirteen of each — qualified to send students to the academic pinnacle in Helsingfors. Finnish students were understandably eager to aid the cause of their native tongue. Some of the student "divisions," recently made legal again, were outspokenly Fennomane (those of Ostrobothnia, Tavastland, and Savolax), and Finnish passions in the first-named brought about a withdrawal of the Swedish-speakers who, led by young Ivar Heikel, established a Swedish Ostrobothnian organization. The "West Finns," the students from Viborg province, and Freudenthal's Nylanders were predominantly pro-Swedish — the first two "divisions" had a preponderance of young men from Åbo and Viborg, where there was still a Swedish hegemony, and from the estates of the Åbo hinterland and Karelia. By 1875, the Finns had formed a storm troop for the Fennicizing of the university, the "Suomalainen nuija" (the "Finnish club" or "cudgel," with echoes of the "Nuijasota," the "Club War," a peasant uprising of the 1590's): they could present one very telling argument for their pugnaciousness and their discontent — that the Finnish language was employed ridiculously little in the university's lectures and in its public functions. The appointment of Yrjö-Koskinen (who won his academic spurs with a study on the "Club War" written in Finnish) as professor of general history in 1863 had been particularly encouraging, since he lectured in Finnish, was faculty adviser of the Ostrobothnian "division" (1868–71), and did whatever else he could for Finnish interests during his eleven years (from 1871 until 1882) as dean of the historical-philological faculty. One understands his intolerance better if one remembers what he was up against.

By the stipulations of Alexander's language ordinance of August 1, 1863, the first official step toward the granting the Finnish language its proper place in national life (a "cornerstone of the Finnish people's future," as the ordinance's actual creator, Snellman, called it), members of the theological and legal faculties, as well as the professor of pedagogy, were to possess "a full knowledge of Finnish, and to be able to lecture in the language"; they were given nine years, until 1872, to acquire such competence. But they were not compelled to lecture in Finnish; and other faculty members were required only to be able to understand the contents of Finnish written material. (The university language statute was intended as an aid to compliance with the imperial decision that, by 1883, Finnish should enjoy equal rank with Swedish in all matters directly concerning the Finnish-speaking population.) In 1892, medical students submitted a complaint to the university's consistory to the effect that Finnish was not used at all by their teachers; after much argument, the consistory announced, on January 10, 1894, that hereafter anyone seeking a teaching position in any faculty should demonstrate the ability "to employ Finnish in speech and written word" and "to instruct and examine in this tongue."

Ten years before, August Ahlqvist had run up the flag by giving the "registration address" (for term's opening) in Finnish — a notable gesture, since he had just begun his tenure as university rector (1884–87); in 1893, E.N. Setälä, the freshly baked professor of Finnish language and literature, had enlivened the university's consistory (the equivalent of the American academic senate) by speaking Finnish there for the first time. Still, no absolute command existed that Finnish be employed in lecturing; at the new century's beginning it was estimated that about one-third of the university's instruction was carried out, voluntarily, in Finnish: the language was predominant in the theological faculty, which drew its audi-

ence heavily from country homes, while in the more sophisticated historical-philological section the division appears to have been half and half.
Something was awry in the linguistic proportions of faculty and students:
in 1905, two-thirds of faculty considered themselves to be native speakers
of Swedish, two-thirds of the students came from a Finnish milieu. A
question of generations was involved here: as yet, Finnish intellectuals did
not exist in sufficient numbers to supply the faculty's needs, and those
Swedish-speaking academic families which had served the university for
decades could not very well be expected to abandon their traditions overnight. Only the new university statutes of 1924 would give Finnish its
place in the sun as "the language of the university"; the Finns could pi-
ously remark that the Swedes, after all, now had their own institution, Åbo
Academy, freshly reconstituted on its old home grounds in 1918. Whatever the fairness was of the measures by which the Swedish language was
so drastically reduced in employment at Helsingfors' university after the
establishment of the Republic of Finland, it must be regarded as a blessing
that the change came as late as it did: the quality of instruction would very
likely have suffered if the Swedish-speaking old guard had been forced to
try Finnish. Koskenniemi, himself a member of the young Finnish academic generation, recalls how regrettable it was that the art historian Johan Jakob Tikkanen — Paavo Tikkanen's son, and a superbly witty
lecturer in Swedish — spoiled his later years of academic work by speaking
Finnish, a tongue in which, despite his antecedents, he was simply not at
home.

Within the student body, the frictions made themselves felt again and
again. The energy that once had gone into tormenting the representatives
of the despot Nicholas now was expended upon linguistic foes. The tide
came and went: the 1880's, calm on the political front, saw particularly
violent displays of bad feeling; the 1890's, with the beginning of Russification, had a more harmonious spirit — at least, this was what Alma
Söderhjelm thought, who was able to compare her university experiences
with those of her older brother Werner. In the 1880's a Swedish-speaking
Ostrobothnian ejected the bust of Yrjö-Koskinen from a hall where I.A.
Heikel's followers were about to have their meeting — even in plaster, this
chief Finnish devil was unwelcome. For their part, the Finns gave some
remarkable exhibitions of their famed inflexibility, arousing a similar quality in their Finno-Swedish foes.

The tenth anniversary of the Student Union's opening was to be celebrated on November 26, 1880. Complicated disputes preceded the event.
All hands agreed that the main speech would be held in Finnish, but a
second address, a salute to the ladies of Helsingfors who had done so
much, by way of bazaars and benefit balls, to pay for the house — that was

a harder nut to crack. The members of a radical Finnish group, the mysterious KPT, demanded that Finnish be the language of the salute, too; the Fennomanes of the "Nuija," which the KPT fanatics had deserted as being too moderate, countered with the gentlemanly and accurate observation that the well-born ladies of Helsingfors, in great majority, understood Swedish and Swedish alone. (The initials of the KPT might mean "Koko Programmi Toimeen," "The whole program to be realized," or, more ominously, "Kansan Pyhä Tahto," "The people's holy will.") At last, good manners and Swedish won; but it was hard to find a man to deliver the speech. Valfrid Vasenius, a moderate in the language question, was persuaded to appear; consenting, he discovered that he had become suspect to Finn and Finno-Swede alike. On the festive evening, all went well for a while: J.R. Danielson (the new professor of general history, later to become Danielson-Kalmari) told the tale of the Student Union in Finnish, the language in which the opening musical number, a setting of Schiller's "Die Künstler," had also been performed. Then the orchestra struck up "Our Country," and the student-singers kept silent as clams, an example followed, evidently out of consternation, by the public at large. What had happened was that the Finnish majority at the festival had deemed it unpatriotic to sing Runeberg's national hymn in the original text; the Swedes had refused to agree to a performance in Finnish translation alone; and so it had been decided that the singing of the words, in whatever tongue, be omitted from the program. The omission, known to the students in advance, had caused many Swedish enthusiasts, and moderates, to stay away from the celebration altogether.

Did anyone listen to the speech of gratitude, so much argued about in advance, which Vasenius then delivered? It seems unlikely: the shock had been too great, and the event was not soon forgotten. In his book on Helsingfors, from 1888, Rafael Hertzberg wrote: "From that day on, one [could] notice that the Student Union, after having been a center of the city's social life for a decade, [had] lost this position. If some day it should happen that the language war in student circles loses its bitter nature, then the Student Union once again will play a role in the students' common life." Hertzberg saw little likelihood of such a reconciliation. "Once again, on this May 1 [in 1888], the new Finnish student choir, 'Ylioppilaskunnan laulajat,' and 'Akademiska sångföreningen' each chose its own path to do honor to the fatherland." Koskimies claims that the Swedes, far more than the Finns, lacked good will in the language questions; yet, "Akademiska sångföreningen" had been bilingual until P.J. Hannikainen founded the "Ylioppilaskunnan laulajat" in 1882. Patriotism had gone a long way — in the wrong direction — since the Flora festival of 1848 when "Our Country" was first performed. *Helsingfors*, a little paper that in its attitudes was the forerunner of Lille's *Nya Pressen*, passed the following judgment on the fiasco at the Student Union: "[The Finnish students] are ashamed to sing our national song in the language which belonged both to Runeberg and all those who have done the most for Finland." Hard words, but not without a grain of accuracy in them.

12. The Theater Cultures: Swedish Amusement, Finnish Inspiration

THE RIVALRY BETWEEN the language groups took more fruitful forms in the performing arts. It is probably not a coincidence that the Swedish theater life of Helsingfors had a golden age at a time when the language struggles at the university were particularly bitter, and when, all of a sudden, a Finnish theater had been stamped out of the earth. After *Kung Carls jagt* (and *Regina*) had had their premieres, the leading citizens of Helsingfors decided to create, as Topelius said, "a lasting monument to the 24th of March, 1852, by building a theater of stone in the capital of Finland." (The poet's opinion, of course, was born of national pride, not personal vanity.) The architect entrusted with the design was again G.T.P. Chiewitz, a native Swede (with Polish blood) who had come over to Åbo in the early 1850's: his other masterpiece was the aforementioned "House of the Nobles." Work on the new theater was slowed down by the violent opposition of Agathon Meurman, who observed that Helsingfors had subscribed more money for its stage than the whole land had for the amelioration of poverty. Conversely, the theater got a powerful shove toward completion from Alexander II who, visiting Helsingfors in March, 1856, looked at Engel's old wooden theater and said: "C'est une bicoque" ("It's a hovel"). The chagrin of his cultured listeners was almost too great to bear. The project sprang alive again, shares were sold, and a board of directors was elected: Samuel Antell, governor of Nyland, at its head, Feodor Kiseleff and Mayor Carl Brummer in charge of finances, and Fredrik Cygnaeus running the artistic side of things. The grand opening took place on November 28, 1860; the work for the festive occasion was by a familiar team, Pacius and Topelius. Their child was called *Prinsessan af Cypern* (*The Princess of Cyprus*); the altogether remarkable action carries Lemminkäinen, the amorous hero of the *Kalevala*, to the Mediterranean island, whose beautiful princess, Chryseis, he takes back to Finland with him. The Finns call her Kyllikki; thereby Topelius had made a somewhat strained connection between his libretto and the eleventh canto of

Lönnrot's *Kalevala*, where Lemminkäinen carries off Kyllikki, the beauty of Saari ("the island"). The handmaiden of Chryseis, Anemotis, persuades the princess to abandon her Finnish husband; he sets out on new and dangerous adventures. Augusta Krook, who was present, a young girl, at an early performance, was overwhelmed: "I was entirely on Finland's side, and wildly hated Anemotis, who wished to lure Chryseis away from Lemminkäinen; [I] wept with mother Helka . . . The last scene in Finland, where the dead Lemminkäinen, lying beside Tuoni River, is awakened by his mother from the slumber of death, made an indelible impression upon me." The competition of Finland and Hellas was a notion that captured other youthful hearts; some years after the premiere of *The Princess of Cyprus*, the school-boy Aho — Johan Brofeldt then — predicted that Finland would be a new and better Greece: "They had the *Iliad* and we the *Kalevala*. But our heroes strove for greater goals than theirs." The audience in the new theater may not have been prepared to make such comparisons, but it sensed that it had been present at a major cultural event. However ludicrous *The Princess* might seem to eyes less blinded by patriotism (the performance was closed each night by "Our Country" and Quanten's "Suomi's Song"), it pointed to the future, to the employment of *Kalevala* materials by Sibelius and Gallen-Kallela and Eino Leino.

Some major theatrical events took place inside the "New Theater," but the house was "unlucky . . . from the beginning"; the phrase, as might be guessed, belongs to Sven Elmgren. A student wit described its qualities: "It consists of places where you can't see, places where you can't hear, and places where you can do neither the one nor the other." Personal and artistic tragedies of the cruelest sort were connected with its brief existence. Runeberg hoped to see a performance of his Greek tragedy, *Kungarne på Salamis* (*The Kings on Salamis*), in the new house, for which a troupe of professional actors had been engaged; but the play was not published until December of 1863, six months after the theater's destruction and two days before a stroke put an end to Runeberg's literary career. Worse had already happened: on November 26, 1862, a student named Josef Julius Wecksell, 24 years old, had witnessed the premiere of his drama about the Club War, *Daniel Hjort*; in *Hjort* the New Theater of Helsingfors had the honor of introducing a work generally conceded to be the best Swedish tragedy before Strindberg's *Master Olof*. At the time of the performance, however, poor Wecksell was already slipping into insanity: "It all sounds so familiar, but I can't remember where I've read it," he is supposed to have said. Shortly thereafter his father, the well-known hatmaker, sent him off to Bonn for treatment in the Endenich asylum, where Robert Schumann had passed away. The treatment was unsuccessful; Wecksell was returned to the institution at Lappviken — the "madhouse," as the list of city-sights in Edlund's Helsingfors guide of 1866 delicately calls it — and remained in confinement there from September, 1865, until his death in August, 1907. His fellow patient for nine months in 1871–72 was Aleksis Kivi, who was then released into his younger brother's custody; Kivi was lucky enough to die at Christmas, 1872, but Wecksell lived on and on, begging cigars from visitors, wearing the new student-caps his friends brought him, and imagining, on his worst days, that he was a spider.

Wecksell's hero, Daniel Hjort, betrays Åbo Castle to the forces of Duke Carl of Sweden, providing another of those cases in Finland's history (and literature) where a "traitor" deals with a foe in what he conceives to be his country's best interests, interests which may coincide with his own. At the climax of the play, the heroine Sigrid (daughter of the castle's commander, Arvid Stålarm, and beloved of the low-born Hjort) has to throw a torch across the stage; on opening night, the nervous actress hurled it out into the boxes instead. This time the theater was saved from burning, and survived long enough to allow the premiere of Runeberg's little comedy, *Kan ej*! (*Cannot!*); but in the spring, on the night of May 7–8, 1863, the interior of the theater was burned out. The fire department was able to keep the blaze from spreading; "but the flames smouldered for several days in the smoking ruins, and everyone talked with horror about the moment when the great candelabrum had come plunging down." The town's theatrical activity was forced to return to Engel's old wooden theater. Waste not, want not: in 1860, it had been dismantled and removed to a site north of Åbo Barracks, quickly getting the sobriquet of "Arcadia Theater" from the section of town, misleadingly named, in which it now lay. As it was being torn down prior to the move, pious folk heard that a nest of snakes had been found beneath its steps, and so it got the subsidiary nickname of "the devil's church." The puritans employing this hard term cannot very well have been Finnish enthusiasts; from 1873 until 1902, the Arcadia served as a home for the city's Finnish theater and opera. But, returning to the theatrical situation of 1863: it was worse than it had been before the New Theater's building, since the Arcadia was inconveniently located away from the center of town. The ruins of the New Theater, at the Esplanade's western end, were an eyesore, which had to be draped with black cloths on the occasion of Alexander's joyous summer visit, in order that the Czar's sensibilities not be offended. The town's musical fortunes had darkened together with its theatrical ones: the brilliant young conductor of the New Theater's orchestra, Filip von Schantz — whose *Kullervo* overture, also *Kalevala*-inspired, shared the opening bill with *The Princess of Cyprus* — had organized the burned theater's pit-men into a "Finnish Orchestra," taking them on tour to Denmark and Sweden. A white hope of music, as Wecksell had been in literature, von Schantz returned to Helsingfors in 1864 to devote himself to composition; the next summer, 30 years old, he fell prey to typhus, or "was devoured by a fiery soul," Yrjö Hirn wrote, "like Wecksell, Kivi, and Ingelius."

The theater was rebuilt with surprising swiftness, using plans provided by a professional theater architect, Nikolai Benois of Saint Petersburg, a choice criticized by patriots, until they realized how much he had improved the lot of the audience. The new dedication, on October 2, 1866, was more subdued than that of six years before; good things grow from modest beginnings. A permanent troupe, that of Vilhelm Åhman and Mauritz Pousette, which had already made a satisfactory impression during the Arcadia interlude, was engaged, and the "golden age" of Swedish theater in Helsingfors quietly began. The moving force was Nikolai Kiseleff, a brother of the Feodor who had aided the construction of Chiewitz's theater; with his money, his passion for the stage, and his inherent good taste, Nikolai was the kind genius, albeit a very proprietary one, of what he liked to call his "little ruin." His stars were from Sweden, of course: the intelligent and ambitious Charlotte Forsman-Raa, and her husband Frithjof Raa, who had both a touch of greatness and a terrible hankering for the bottle. Charlotte could play Ophelia, Goneril, Oehlenschläger's Valborg and Schiller's Maria Stuart in unforgettable fashion; her husband, the special pet of the ladies, was an ideal leading man, but liked to do all kinds of roles, from the splendid Gustaf Adolf of *Regina von Emmeritz* to the tormented Hjort of Wecksell's play. The first phase of the golden age was short-lived; Frithjof Raa had drunk himself to death by 1872, and was followed to his grave by a giant procession of mourners, including his dog Whisky. At the cemetery, unhappily, shameful events took place. Professor von Essen, turning out his theological rather than his witty side, held a nasty speech about the departed's flaws, as Gustaf Gustafsson, Åhman's successor and Raa's best friend, wept. Cygnaeus, who had promised to deliver the eulogy, became affronted at the crowd's failure to make way for his large person, and left — for once, without saying a word. The bereft Fru Raa departed for Sweden and Norway, where she found another husband; robbed of his two brightest lights, Kiseleff put down the director's burden in 1880.

One of the few deplorable points in Kiseleff's benevolent dictatorship had been his aversion to actors and actresses born in Finland, an aversion shared by his audiences. (The same tradition pertained in the demimonde of Helsingfors; the best bordellos were careful to employ only whores imported from Sweden.) Some exceptions had been made to the rule; but once hired — for show? — Finno-Swedish artists discovered that they were very little used. Victor Salin, whose "unmistakable talent" won the

approval of Raa, had so much time on his hands that he became a member
of the volunteer fire-department and, in this capacity, caught a mortal chill
in 1877; another aspirant, Adolf Lindfors from Borgå, grew restive after
seven years of idleness on contract, went to sea, returned, and joined the
Finnish theater, of which he forthwith became a star, despite certain difficulties with the language. On the whole, Helsingfors' "New Theater"
could be called a training ground for Swedish actors, that is, actors from
Sweden who wished to win their spurs in the provinces before going to
Stockholm: two of the greatest Swedish stage performers in the century's
last decades — August Lindberg, whom Kiseleff employed as Raa's successor, and Emil Hillberg — got invaluable experience in Finland.

Aided by Fredrik Berndtson, Kiseleff had served as his own artistic director, although his title, and ostensible duties, were rather of a financial
nature; he was the "executive director of the guarantee association" for
the New Theater. When he finally withdrew, after long having threatened
to do so, and after a perceptible decline of the theater's fortunes, the administration of the house passed to a three-man committee; what happened on the stage became the responsibility of a new "intendant," Oscar
Malmgren. Despite his being a native Swede, Malmgren followed a more
generous policy toward Finno-Swedish performers than Kiseleff had, in
part out of a sense of fairness, in part because the current crisis in the city's
theatrical life dictated a policy of financial moderation, and Swedish imports were relatively expensive. Nevertheless, Swedes still dominated the
roster; even the indigenous Finno-Swedish star, Fanny Grahn, had been
born in Helsingfors of native Swedish parents, and so she was perfectly
able, as the result of home experience, to speak with a "correct" Swedish
accent. (Her dramatic teachers had been expatriate Swedes, too: Fredrik
Berndtson and the actor Hjalmar Agardh, an old faithful in the New
Theater's troupe.) Fanny, the darling of Helsingfors, left the stage very
early, marrying Paul Sinebrychoff; she may have been miffed, too, by the
remarks of Pacius during the revival of *Kung Carls jagt*, in which she
played the 16-year-old king: "These damned actresses spoil everything,
they screech so much." (Another Finno-Swede with a much longer career
ahead of him was August Arppe, a notable Tartuffe, who later [1894–99]
became the New Theater's director.) Oscar Malmgren made a name for
himself not only as a cultivator of home-grown talents but as the importer
of distinguished guests: chief among these was a former member of Kiseleff's company, Emil Hillberg, whose "Iago" made the fastidious Hjalmar
Neiglick say that Hillberg was the greatest artist ever to have appeared on
a Helsingfors stage. Another of Malmgren's imports — who, like Hillberg,
packed the theater, but for altogether different reasons — was the Danish
author and would-be actor Herman Bang; people came to see him, in one

of his own plays and as Oswald in the third act of Ibsen's *Ghosts*, because they knew his reputation as an exotic and probably depraved creature. From Helsingfors (it was April, 1885) Bang wrote to his dear friend, Peter Nansen, that he had met and dined with a Princess "Kamrazim" — the most beautiful woman he had ever seen, and that, when the curtain went up for his "Oswald," "a thrill went through the house; never, I think, was an auditorium more quiet." (Under Malmgren, too, the social-problem dramas of Dr. Ferdinand [von] Wahlberg reached the boards, originally a German-speaker from Russia, Wahlberg had attended school and the university in Helsingfors and became a physician in the Finnish military.)

For all these successes, Malmgren eventually grew tired of the small budget and the large pieces of criticism he received from the press; his successor was still another Swede, Harald Molander (1886–93), whose particular merits lay in his interest in the modern repertoire — Ibsen, Bjørnson, Strindberg (*Master Olof*), Alexander L. Kielland, Hermann Sudermann — and occasionally in the works of Finno-Swedish authors, including not just Runeberg, Topelius, and Wecksell, but Tavaststjerna and even, once, 'Daniel Sten' (Ina Lange). Molander was lucky enough to have a leading lady capable of doing Ibsen's Hjørdis and Rebekka West and Fru Alving and Gina Ekdal, Bjørnson's Maria Stuart and the Leonarda of *En handske* (*A Gauntlet*), a play condemning the double standard ; the artist of such varied talents was Ida Reis-Brander, born in Stockholm of Jewish parents and a member of the troupe at the New Theater since 1877. After his brilliant beginning, though, Molander grew steadily more unpopular. The press had castigated Malmgren because, in order to make ends meet, he offered too much operetta; now the public was unhappy with Molander because he gave too little. Also, gossips fed delightedly on Molander's troubles with Ernst Brander, Ida Reis-Brander's husband; a handsome young man, Brander's acting was much too old-fashioned to suit Molander's taste, a fault which led to Brander's dismissal and eventual suicide. The reign of August Arppe, the first Finno-Swede in the post, was an attempt at retrenchment, and at pleasing all sides; by 1899, Arppe had had enough, departing for the "Swedish Local Theater" in Åbo, a praiseworthy institution which was the "genuine center of Finno-Swedish theatrical life," aboriginal and without pretensions. The New Theater was rechristened the Swedish Theater in 1887; it remained more a center for theater from Sweden than a genuine Finno-Swedish theater during the years after Arppe's departure, under the Swede Victor Castegren (1899–1904) and the Finno-Swede Konni Wetzer (1904–1916), respectable but hardly stirring times, in which economic considerations often overrode artistic ones. The directors salved their consciences by sometimes remarkable methods, Wetzer, for example, meeting the constant public demand for more operetta by hiring Danish guest-troupes for this purpose: it was well-known that the Danes were particularly skillful, or even artistic, in this light-hearted genre.

A continuing difficulty for the New Theater (or Swedish Theater) in the years both during and after its golden age was the opposition it met from Finnish forces in the national diet. Of the four estates, the peasants and the clergy had a clear Finnish-speaking majority, inclined to regard theatrical undertakings as the work of the devil, particularly when they took place in Swedish. Moral strictures were quickly forgotten, however, once a Finnish national theater was underway. By 1878, after only six years of existence, the Finnish Theater had achieved allocations as great as those accorded to the New Theater; eight years more, and the Finnish Theater had a subvention of 36,000 marks, to be used entirely as the directors saw fit, but the Swedes got only 24,000 marks, available only if half of it were to be spent on the support of an orchestra. The next year — 1887, when the New Theater became the Swedish Theater — *Nya Pressen*, always ready to defend Swedish interests, made no bones about the injustice of the situation: "As far as the allocation from the state is concerned, the Swedish Theater is a stepchild in comparison to the Finnish Theater, which has at its disposal — for theatrical purposes alone — state funds exceeding those accorded the Swedish Theater by 20,000 marks." The Finns could justify their actions by reference to past Finnish humiliations and present Swedish frivolity (the operetta), arguments not always free from pharisaism. In 1870, Anton Almberg (a name later changed to Jalava), the "official translator" of the peasant estate, wrote in *Uusi Suometar* that the New Theater in Helsingfors was not a "national institution" and so did not deserve a state allowance at all. Besides, "if one knows how to keep one's requirements within the limits of reason, allocations are not needed. However, if the Swedish-speaking public of Helsingfors has crossed these limits, if it has built a prideful theater for itself, the likes of which cannot be found anywhere else in Europe's largest cities [the theater had 750 seats, and standing room for about 150 more persons], if it has imported an exceedingly expensive theatrical troupe from Sweden, if it has equipped its wardrobe with splendid costumes and expensive apparatus — then the Finnish people do not need to be responsible for these immoderate expenditures." With his barrage of spitefulness Almberg, quite unintentionally, noticed an injustice done to Finland's Swedish speakers: the New Theater, its personnel drawn from Sweden, still did not nurture native theatrical talent, for all its presentation of plays by Finno-Swedish authors. His point, of course, was that the theater was essentially "foreign," and deserved to disappear, unless it could pay its own way. State funds should go only to a true "national theater of Finland" —

by Almberg's lights, a theater whose tongue was Finnish. In March, 1872, a group of seven peasant representatives from various parts of the country delivered a petition to their estate concerning the establishment of a Finnish national theater. The event caused some amusement in the Swedish-language press; Theodor Sederholm in *Helsingfors Dagblad* fell to wondering why some "old fellows from the backwoods," who had never given a moment's thought to esthetic questions, suddenly interested themselves in so lofty a project. The Finns were enraged at this superciliousness; the proposal made in the newspaper *Vikingen* — that a Finnish national theater should be put into the provinces, where Finnish predominated — scarcely helped to soothe them: at this time, it should be remembered, von Kothen had just ordered the removal of the Finnish lyceum to Tavastehus. More cutting still was the current Finno-Swedish witticism: why talk about founding a Finnish theater before there are any Finnish plays? Such hostility simply strengthened Finnish determination, and, exactly a year after the delivery of the petition, the Finnish Theater gave its first performance in Helsingfors, on the worn boards of the Arcadia.

This maiden effort, deserving of applause, immediately got besmirched by the sanctimonious attitude the Finns assumed toward the New Theater — in the claim that it was a theater for special amusement purposes, serving a special class. The claim was scarcely applicable to the theater in the best years of the Kiseleff era; the repertoire had included Goethe, Schiller, Shakespeare, Calderón, Molière, the Danes Oehlenschläger and Hertz, and the Norwegian Bjørnson. Despite the charges brought by a firebrand named Kaarlo Bergbom, in the Finnish journal *Kirjallinen Kuukauslehti* (*Literary Monthly*, a forerunner of *Valvoja*) and in the Fennomane Swedish paper, *Morgonbladet, Tidning för Politik, Ekonomi och Litteratur* (a forerunner of *Finland*), that "local plays" were neglected, the Kiseleff-Berndtson team had seen to it that the Swedish plays by Finlanders were produced: for example, *Drottning Filippa* of Gabriel Lagus or Runeberg's *Kungarne på Salamis*, as well as *Regina von Emmeritz* and *Daniel Hjort*. August Lindberg, whose standards of taste were not easily satisfied, recalled in later years that the "repertoire at the Swedish Theater [had been] overwhelmingly serious," and Rafael Hertzberg, who admired Kiseleff and served as an adviser to him, found fault mainly with the popular but crude "Stockholm farces," which he wished to have replaced with the subtle Danish *vaudevilles* of Johan Ludvig Heiberg and Christian Hostrup. Nonetheless, in the later years of Kiseleff's reign, there occurred that lamentable falling-off in quality and attendance already mentioned. In an effort at recuperation of finances, if not standards, it was decided to give the new Austrian operetta of Johan Strauss the younger, *Die Fledermaus*. The choice of the Strauss sensation should scarcely have been shocking to a public already familiar with the naughtiness of an Offenbach; but the Finns, swollen with virtuous indignation and national pride, decided to take advantage of the opportunity for revenge on the Swedes, long spoiled and (Finns took pleasure in the thought) surely decadent. The first two performances of *Die Fledermaus* went by without incident, save that the audience greeted them enthusiastically; during the third evening, on Sunday, November 19, 1876, the Finnish puritans struck. It had been rumored that a demonstration was in the offing, and measures had already been prepared to prevent or, if worst came to worst, to quell it. At the opening of the ball at Prince Orloffsky's, in Act Two, Finnish disgust burst forth in the form of whistles, shouts, and stamps. Detectives planted in the audience tried ineffectively to find the chief-noisemakers, among them one of the Järnefelt brothers, Kasper, and his lady love, Minni. Rector Topelius of the university (he had reached this lofty post) tried to calm the crowd — but did not try very hard, some said, because he was in sympathy with the rioters' cause; ladies fainted, or had hysterical seizures; and the singers on stage (demonstrating Finnish *sisu*, too, however Swedish they may have been) continued to shriek out their roles at the top of their lungs. When the curtain fell at act's end, the detectives, finally succeeding in their mission, had taken the offenders away, and *Die Fledermaus* was completed amidst the applause of the survivors. The next day Kiseleff, holding a party for his brave artists, announced that the inflammatory operetta had been removed from the repertoire at the request of Governor-General Adlerberg. It did not return until fifteen years had passed.

A certain counterproductivity lay in the Finns' actions: they rioted when the New (later Swedish) Theater displayed the very frivolity which was such a handy whipping-boy for their own cause. Their behavior contributed, as well, to the missing of an opportunity: the New Theater had begun its existence, it will be recalled, with a work which celebrated Finnish mythological themes in Swedish linguistic dress. Had there not been so much vindictiveness on the Finnish side, and so much snobbery on the Swedish, then the New Theater might perhaps have become a place of meeting for Finland's two cultures — as indeed it did, very briefly, during the press festival of the century's end, when Sibelius' *Finlandia* was first played at the retitled theater during a demonstration of unity against the Russian threat. Yet this is wishful guesswork; the development of a separate Finnish theater had meanwhile become a national cause, with its own epic of creation, destined forever to make Finnish hearts beat faster.

A stag dinner had been held in Kleineh's Hotel on November 12, 1868, discussing, as usual, the question of the creation of a Finnish culture; the diners decided to give an amateur performance of a play in Finnish. Someone — Kaarlo Bergbom? — suggested that Charlotte Forsman-

Raa, the star of the New Theater, should be persuaded to play the leading role, despite her lack of Finnish, and the littérateur Emil Nervander promised to compose a vehicle for her; it would have to be translated into Finnish, since Nervander had no command of the written language. Happily, Nervander did not have to make good on his offer; at a subsequent meeting in the Bergbom home, Kaarlo announced that he had just read a new one-act play by Aleksis Kivi — about Lea, the daughter (in Kivi's creative imagination, not Holy Writ) of the publican Zacchaeus, the man of Jericho who climbed a sycamore tree to behold Jesus. In Bergbom's opinion, this high-minded work was both the "fairest pearl in the crown of the Finnish muse" and, by virtue of its brevity and simple language, an ideal choice for amateurs. The problem was now to persuade Fru Raa; her Finnish consisted, as she willingly confessed, of words of greeting. Bergbom told her of the momentousness of the event; succumbing, she managed to memorize the sounds of the text, aided by a patient teacher and a Swedish translation. On May 3, 1869, on the stage of Arcadia Theater, a preliminary Finnish festival was held, which did not contain *Lea*; the pearl was kept hidden for another week, giving Fru Raa still more time to perfect her role. The intention of the first performance (without *Lea*) was to show, evidently, the variety of uses to which Finnish could be put: it opened with a "tableau and melodrama" employing a Finnish translation of "Molnets broder" ("The Cloud's Brother"), the Homeric-Ossianic third canto of Runeberg's *Fänrik Stål*, set to a musical background by Adolf Fredrik Lindblad, the Swedish composer; then came Topelius' comedy *Ett skärgårdsäventyr* (*An Adventure in the Skerries*), likewise translated into Finnish — an odd choice of text, since the Topelius trifle deals with Swedish speakers, including a member of the Swedish royal house, in eighteenth-century Finland. As a finale, the amateurs offered the Second Act of von Flotow's *Martha*, with the "Last Rose of Summer" and the good-night quartet put into the language of the *Kalevala*. Arcadia Theater was exchanged for New Theater on May 10, when the program was given with *Lea* in place of *Ett skärgårdsäventyr*; can there have been some symbolic import in the abandonment of Swedish froth for Finnish biblical idealism? The move to the house on the Esplanade took place not because of Finnish sentiments on Kiseleff's part, but because Fru Raa's contract did not allow her to play anywhere but within the New Theater's walls; Fru Raa did her role for nothing, but the theater's direction demanded a rental fee of 850 marks. Before beginning her first speech, Fru Raa almost fainted on stage, and had to be held up by Emilie Bergbom, Kaarlo's sister, who was also taking part; recovering, she gave a faultless recitation of the Finnish words she had learned. Her reward was a standing ovation by the public, many members of whom, to be sure, had a command of Finnish not much greater than Fru Raa's; in a speech at the post-performance party, Yrjö-Koskinen told his listeners and the world that "the victory which the Finnish language has won, thanks to Fru Raa, is no ordinary theatrical success, but rather a historical event."

It is interesting to pursue the subsequent fates of the contributors to the victory, "this true turning point in the development of our theatrical situation." Kivi, the author, did not attend the performance (the only staging, by the way, of any of his plays during his lifetime); he had already grown afraid of crowds, a symptom of the madness to which he would shortly succumb. Fru Raa became so enamored of her Finnish studies that her poor husband Frithjof lost contact with her altogether; when she was at home, he claimed, he could not talk to her ("all she does is jabber in Finnish"), and she spent the whole summer of 1870 inland at Keuru, improving her fluency. Seizing every opportunity to demonstrate her new self in public, she recited the great first-act monologue of Joan of Arc from Schiller's *Jungfrau*, turned into Finnish, appeared in the title role of Bergbom's *Paola Moroni* (originally written in Swedish but translated into Finnish for a gala Finnish-language dramatic evening, held at the New Theater), and made a tour of the provinces; upon her return to Helsingfors, she was attacked by the Swedish-language press for the exaggerated manner in which she now performed in her native tongue. The question arises: were her critics punishing her for disloyalty, or had she in fact learned a less subtle style of acting, in order to appeal to unsophisticated audiences? A new contract forbade her to appear in Finnish; unafraid, she continued to give private performances in her acquired tongue, and, in the spring of 1872, just before her husband's death, she hired Arcadia Theater, issuing personal invitations to her friends in order to avoid legal difficulties. Once she had left Finland, she longed to return to the scene of her greatest triumphs, but she discovered that the Swedes of Helsingfors no longer wanted her, and the Finns felt they had outgrown her. Neither Kiseleff nor Bergbom was willing to ask her to Helsingfors for performances in connection with the industrial exposition of 1876; she then invited herself, arranging another of her *soirées* at the Arcadia, with the scene between Daniel Hjort and his mother Katri (in Swedish) as her chief number: the evening was not a success. In 1880 she had a somewhat happier time at the Arcadia, offering new Finnish roles translated from the German, Schiller's *Maria Stuart* and Thusnelda in Kleist's *Die Hermannsschlacht*; nonetheless, she was unable to match the popularity of Ida Aalberg, a native speaker of Finnish 19 years her junior, who gave the first Helsingfors performance of Ibsen's *A Doll's House*. Making a final appearance in Finland's capital in 1894, as Kivi's Lea in celebration of the great day a quarter-century before, she made her Finnish listeners cringe.

"Although the words were familiar," wrote Helmi Krohn, daughter of the late Julius, "the sound was so strange and the pronunciation so foreign that the younger ones among us, at least, felt anxiety seize our hearts."

The Finnish Theater in Helsingfors was the creation of Kaarlo and Emilie Bergbom, in whose father's home the Raas, once upon a time, had been favorite guests. Kaarlo had possessed literary ambitions in Swedish, and, at 19, had composed a play, *Pombal och jesuiterne*, which was performed by the Åhman-Pousette troupe in 1865 and 1868; in the latter year, the would-be playwright also won a doctorate with a dissertation, written in Swedish, on the historical drama of Germany. Then a passion for Finnish overwhelmed him; he decided that it was his destiny to write in Finnish alone, a language he had learned as an adult. "An unparalled auto-da-fé" took place, "in which he burned his mother tongue, his poetry, his youthful dreams of being a dramatic author, and emerged as a Phoenix from the flames." This purple prose (belonging to his contemporary and sometime friend, Jac. Ahrenberg, the Finno-Swedish Plutarch) conceals some important factors: Kaarlo's elder sister Emilie, a fanatic on the language question and a woman of steel, often made decisions for Kaarlo, who was "a warm-hearted, introverted dreamer." Bergbom himself liked to claim that his determination to create a Finnish theater was forged by an experience he had during his brief membership (July-December, 1869) in the directorship of the New Theater. When he asked the wardrobe mistress about some particularly shabby costumes, she replied: "They're good enough for Finns." Such legends, or true tales, were inspirational material for the Bergboms and their followers, rich (notably Antti Ahlström of Björneborg) and poor. The Bergboms were lodged in the older theater, they struggled — during a brief time, which they made longer for rhetorical purposes — against financial difficulties, they lacked trained artists, they had few genuinely Finnish stage-texts. But they had the masses behind them, the Finns of Helsingfors, who stopped performances with their applause (Finnish acting during the Bergbom reign was anything but restrained), and the Finns from the countryside, for whom an evening at the Arcadia was a religious obligation. A guide to Helsingfors from 1889, written for just such provincials, passes over the Swedish Theater with the icy observation that its repertoire is mostly "conversation pieces, comedies, and operettas"; the Finnish Theater, in contrast, "devotes itself primarily to foreign and domestic classics, and the lyric stage (i.e. opera)." (Tickets started at 5.50 marks in the Swedish Theater, 3.50 in the Finnish Theater: were the Finns more democratic, or did their bargain prices result from a larger state-subvention?) The attitudes of the respective audiences of the rival institutions have often been compared. To the contemporary and anonymous author of *Statsrådet*, the Swedish Theater was a place for the exchange of gossip rather than a temple of the arts, and its handsome male leads, suave fellows from Sweden, cared more about amorous than thespian triumphs; the Finnish (Arcadia) Theater was airless and smelled bad, but its audience was devoted and proud, brooking no criticism. The "guests," such as the Councillor of State and his family, were carefully watched at the Arcadia, and they knew it: "The lorgnette of the Councillor's wife now had nothing critical about it (in contrast to her manipulation of it at the Swedish Theater); it expressed the most friendly attention." Yrjö Hirn, scholar and critic, is less cynical: "[in the Finnish Theater] . . . a mass, inspired as much perhaps by national zeal as by artistic interest, [in the Swedish Theater] a select crowd of critical observers, ranking everything offered to them, making high demands, and culpable of the charge that they wanted above all to be amused when they went to the theater."

The Arcadia became the property of the Bergboms' Finnish players in 1875, a year after Ida Aalberg — a girl from a poverty-stricken home in Janakkala, on the Helsingfors-Tavastehus railroad line — had joined the troupe; her previous experience had been in amateur theatricals, as Maria in Hannikainen's pioneer chestnut, *Silmänkääntäjä*. Until Ida Aalberg left the Finnish Theater in 1889, she was its star attraction, an actress of international calibre who created role after role in Finnish: from Ophelia to Aase in *Peer Gynt*, from Luise in Schiller's *Kabale und Liebe* to the gypsy girl Homsantuu in *Työmiehen vaimo* (*The Worker's Wife*) of Minna Canth, Finnish Finland's major creator of realistic drama in Ibsen's wake. Perhaps the most famous of Aalberg's many performances outside Finland, and in other tongues (she essayed German, Swedish, and even, unhappily, Danish), was her collaboration with the great Joseph Kainz at the Ostende Theater in Berlin, 1890; the music-student Sibelius, who saw her with Kainz in *Romeo and Juliet*, gave a report indicating that even the incomparable Ida had her physical limits: "During the first acts her German was impeccable, but exhaustion got the better of her, as the play went on, and in the final scenes she reached the point where her lines were almost incomprehensible." The account does not detract from her genius; Albert Edelfelt's portrait of Aalberg as Hedda Gabler makes the viewer aware of the excessive nervous energy which was a good part of her secret, and which sometimes consumed her. Aalberg continued to make guest appearances on her home stage; Hagar Olsson, in her novel about Helsingfors, *Chitambo*, writes that "she was such a great star that she gave only guest-performances at our National Theater, between her triumphs in Saint Petersburg and on the continent." "She was celebrated like a queen . . . tears ran down my cheeks, I shouted and cheered with the full power of my lungs" — that was the way Vega Maria Dyster, Hagar Olsson's *alter ego*, remembered Ida Aalberg's visits. Aalberg's place had to be taken, once Finland was no longer her home base; Vendla Rautio was her replacement, and the fugitive from the Swedish stage, Lindfors, was the chief among the male performers. Yet the Finnish Theater cared as much about repertoire as about stars: it emphasized, as the guidebook said, the classics of world literature and of the new Finnish stage — Kivi, Canth, Gustaf von Numers, Arvid Järnefelt. Whether Finnish playwrights could bear honest comparison with the poets so industriously translated into Finnish — Calderón, Shakespeare, Goethe, Schiller, or Bjørnson, Ibsen, Strindberg, Hauptmann — is a question not to be answered here; the Finnish people were proud that they had acquired stage-works of their own, just as they were proud of the Bergboms. "Cold and calculating" to the end, Emilie died in 1905, the year in which her brother, weakened by a stroke, retired from his post; together, they had brought their company from the Arcadia to a castle on Railroad Square, designed by Onni Alcides Törnquist (later Tarjanne) the "Suomen Kansallisteatteri" ("Finland's National Theater"). The apple of the nation's Finnish eye, the Theater was dedicated on the centennial of Lönnrot's birth, April 2, 1902.

13. "Concordia res parvae crescunt": Finland's Art

ACROSS RAILROAD SQUARE there had stood, since 1887, "the particularly handsome building" (Hertzberg's opinion, with which one need not agree) of the Ateneum, a work of the architect Theodor Höijer. It housed not only the collections of the Finnish Art Union, but the Union's art school and, in accordance with a proposal of C.G. Estlander, intended to gain the support of practical-minded businessmen, a school for applied arts as well. Estlander called it, in words modest and true, "the central point around which the vital interests of the plastic arts [in Finland] are united, making the artist humble in the knowledge that his art, too, is a child of general human endeavor, and raising the self-esteem of the artisan, by teaching him to ennoble his work through the sublime forms of art." In consideration of these mixed aims of the Ateneum, it is a small wonder that some of Finland's greatest artists, once they had achieved a measure of success, stayed far away from Railroad Square — the painter Edelfelt and the sculptors Walter Runeberg and Ville Vallgren in Paris, Gallen-Kallela in distant Ruovesi and even in still more distant British East Africa (1909–1911), and Helene Schjerfbeck in the Finnish countryside. The city became a center for the graphic and plastic arts simply because it was Finland's capital, and not because of an atmosphere otherwise particularly favorable to their development. The prehistory of the Ateneum had begun, one supposes, with the efforts of Professor Nils Abraham Gyldén, the classical philologist who had got the job Runeberg wanted at the university; Gyldén was abetted by two students, already well-known to the reader: Robert Tengström and Herman Kellgren, who, after spending a summer in Berlin, decided that their town also deserved a "collection of plastic works of art" for study purposes — not an "Altes Museum," perhaps, but something good enough for little Helsingfors. After taking up a collection among their fellows, the young men, with Gyldén's help, purchased copies of the Laocoon group, the Diana of Versailles, and the Belvedere Apollo, putting them on display in the sketching room of the university, together with some paintings bought from a Belgian traveling salesman — the city's first art show. Later, the statues were set out in the University Library, "where the students, with a certain pride, regarded them almost as their own work."

On January 27, 1846, a new step into the artistic future was taken. The Finnish Art Union was founded, with a "true aristocrat," Carl Johan Walleen, as its first chairman. The next year Topelius — inevitably? — became the secretary of the group, and then Cygnaeus, returned from his grand tour, joined the directorship; Walleen resigned in 1849, peeved that his opinions on art were not accepted as gospel. The purpose of the Finnish Art Union now became clear; the quasi-nation must have its national art, and esthetic standards must take second place to the blanket encouragement of Finnish-born artists, good or mediocre. At the Union's first exhibition, in March, 1846, 94 oil-paintings were displayed; among the exhibitors were Robert Wilhelm Ekman, lately returned to Åbo after almost 20 years in Sweden, France, and Italy, Berndt Abraham Godenhjelm, come back to Helsingfors after a similar period in Saint Petersburg, to serve as a teacher in the Union's drawing school (from 1848 until 1869); and the brothers Magnus, Wilhelm, and Ferdinand von Wright, as well as three painters already gone to their eternal reward — Alexander Laureus, Gustaf Wilhelm Finnberg, and, Finland's first known woman artist, Mathilda Rotkirch. The exhibitor most closely associated with Helsingfors was doubtless Magnus von Wright, whom Topelius remembered as one of the heroes of the Golden Age, together with Runeberg, Pacius, and Henrik Borgström. Born at the von Wright family estate, Haminanlax near Kuopio, in 1805, Magnus had made himself into a kind of Audubon for Sweden and Finland. (His younger brothers, Wilhelm and Ferdinand, shared his mixture of artistic and natural-scientific gifts: Wilhelm, who went over to Sweden as a boy of 18, in order to aid Magnus in the preparation of his *Svenska fåglar* [*Swedish Birds*], stayed in the wealthier land, and made his career there; Ferdinand, the junior of Magnus by 17 years, joined his brothers in Sweden, but did not thrive, any more than he would feel at home in Helsingfors later on; he preferred the isolation of Haminanlax, painting the wild life which remained his sole and never exhausted theme.) Unlike Wilhelm and Ferdinand, Magnus had a second string on his bow, as a recorder of the Helsingfors scene, although his life in the city was never a particularly happy one; returning from Sweden in the 1830's, he obtained a position as official cartographer, married, and set about fathering a throng of children. Beset by financial problems and increasing blindness, the poor man — "sensitive and conscientious" to a fault — was never able, after the youthful days of *Svenska fåglar*, to devote his full energies to any single task; nonetheless, and particularly in the last decade before his death (in 1868), he managed to do some 120 oil-paintings, including such small classics as the summertime "Helsingfors Yard" and "Annegatan 15 on a Cold Winter Morning." Thanks to Magnus von Wright — and, on a much more modest scale, to the drawing-teacher at Borgå gymnasium, Johan Knutson, a native Swede — the appearance of Helsingfors at the middle of the century has been preserved, captured by an artist's eye.

It is a pity that the white hope of Finland's art in the 1850's, Werner Holmberg, never got around to painting his home city. A student of Godenhjelm at the new art school, Holmberg had done his first serious work with landscapes from the interior of Finland; he left his native country in 1853 for studies in Germany, interrupted by summer trips to Norway and, once again, to the Finnish upland. He died in Düsseldorf on September 24, 1860, only 30 years old — "one of the worst losses," it was said, "ever suffered by Finland's art." Holmberg's successors and fellow students at Düsseldorf, Berndt Lindholm and Hjalmar Munsterhjelm, never equalled him; neither did the marine painter, Oscar Kleineh — Louis Kleineh's son, who wished to escape his father's restaurants and hotels, nor Fanny Churberg, who abandoned her Finnish landscapes and still-lifes for the Finnish language-cause and the rugs and tapestries of her "Friends of Finnish Handwork." Adolf von Becker, another child of Helsingfors, tried Düsseldorf like Holmberg and Kleineh but exchanged it for France; returning to Finland, he became a faithful academician, succeeding von Wright as art teacher at the university and establishing his own school. He is best known for his pupils, Gallen-Kallela and Schjerfbeck, the latter of whom can fairly be counted as his discovery, since her cat-drawings, done when she was ten, awakened the interest of the aleurophile von Becker. Something southern always clung to von Becker; upon his retirement he left Helsingfors for good, residing in France and Switzerland until his death in 1909.

A nation with paintings needed sculpture too. Visiting Stockholm in 1856, Fredrik Cygnaeus had persuaded a sculptor named Carl Aeneas Sjöstrand — already grown somewhat familiar with Finnish myth and legend through the efforts of the exile, Emil von Quanten — to go over to Finland for work (including busts of Runeberg and Lönnrot) and study; Sjöstrand liked the open field he found, but postponed the decision to move eastward for several years, which he spent in Munich, Rome (where he completed the Porthan statue commissioned by the Finnish Literary Society), and Stockholm again. In 1863 he finally committed himself to Finland altogether, having been appointed a teacher in the Art Union's school. Not only did he render figures and stories from Finnish mythology, among them "Kullervo's Curse" and "Väinömöinen's Song," both intended for the New Theater but never given a home in that increasingly more Swedish milieu; he also trained a generation of sculptors for Finland — Walter Runeberg, Johannes Takanen, Robert Stigell. The poet's third son, Walter Runeberg became Sjöstrand's successor as a kind of unofficial "sculptor of the nation," creating monument upon monument: his father's on the Esplanade, Alexander II's on Senate Square, and Per Brahe's before the cathedral in Åbo. Takanen's beginnings were as simple as Runeberg's were illustrious; a poor Finnish boy from Karelia, who had attracted attention by his wood-carvings, Takanen made his way over Sjöstrand's classes in Helsingfors and Bissen's in Copenhagen to Rome, the city in which he died, not quite 36, in 1885. A sculptor of a more individual quality than Sjöstrand or Runeberg, his embarrassed girl — "Nuova modella," unfinished — is more directly appealing than their Finnish heroes, ancient and modern. Stigell, a Swedish-speaker from Helsingfors, was born almost at sea, on Sveaborg, and left Sjöstrand's school to become an intermittent seaman, between periods of study in London and Naples. Maritime life provided the theme for the best-known of his works, "The Castaways," begun in 1889 and finished, after considerable creative agony, a decade later. Placed for all to see atop Observatory Hill, the statue serves as a reminder not just of Stigell's salty past but of other things: that he was very familiar with the Laocoon group; that he had taken a close look at Géricault's painting, "The Raft of the Medusa;" that Helsingfors itself possessed an old sea-faring tradition; and that Stigell, like his compatriots, was aware of the growing hazards which threatened Finland's vessel in the Russian sea.

Many artistic events of the middle and later century belong to popularization's realm. "Konstnärsgillet" ("The Artists' Guild") — or, in Finnish, rather less picturesquely, "Taiteilija-seura" ("The Artist-Society") —

was established at the suggestion of Topelius, a pleasant group and about as Bohemian as could be expected in Helsingfors of the day; its costume balls were the talk of the town, but the Guild's particular importance lay in the autumn exhibits it gave from 1891 on. One of the city's leading eccentrics and most efficient managers, Berndt Otto Schauman, August's brother, was appointed director of the ever-growing collections of the Art Union, a post he held, brilliantly and sometimes pugnaciously (his chief opponent was another cranky bachelor, Fredrik Cygnaeus) from 1869 until the opening of the new Ateneum in 1888. Berndt Otto was a remarkable mixture: one of those Finnish zealots who could not speak the language, an admirer of the late tyrant Nicholas, and a polyhistor, the last-named a valuable quality in the man responsible for collecting art treasures on a limited budget. Unintentionally, Schauman also provided amusement for the Helsingfors populace at large: he was called "Smack" because of the nervous noises he made with his lips, and the "monocle-peeker" because of the instrument he used to examine both paintings and fellow men. Like handsome Severin Falkman, Anders Ramsay's great and good friend, who had returned to Helsingfors from Paris to escape the Franco-Prussian War, Schauman lived up to the popular notion that members of the art world had to be colorful in and of themselves: Berndt Otto (no artist at all) was known for the practices just described, Falkman (who abandoned painting after the savage reception accorded his show of 1870) for the costumes, straight out of a historical novel, which he dared to wear even in everyday life.

In 1887, work on the "particularly handsome building" of the Ateneum was completed. The motto on the Ateneum's facade was "Concordia res parvae crescunt" ("Small things grow in harmony"); small things had in fact grown, nurtured by people of good will and modest talent, flourishing under the aegis of peace — here, for a change, the language question was forgotten. The busts of Raphael, Phidias, and Bramante above the Ateneum's main entrance made the market-women on Railroad Square nervous: "It's terrible the way all those chopped-off heads keep staring at us." If not the vegetable sellers, then other folk were learning to like art; near the close of Schauman's tenure (1884), the Art Union was able to attract 3,505 visitors for an exhibit. A catalogue was printed, and 700 copies in Swedish were sold, as opposed to 150 in Finnish.

A decade earlier, a particularly gifted product of the Art Union's drawing school and the university's (i.e. von Becker's) art classes had gone to Antwerp to study, transferring shortly to the École des Beaux-Arts in Paris. It was Albert Edelfelt, the son of the builder of the neo-Gothic railroad station, who must have felt particularly at home in the bright new

rooms the university had allotted to von Becker's classes; they were located in the university's chemical laboratory, another work of the elder
Edelfelt, and their brightness corresponded to Albert's own nature. He
was a child of light, a kind of humanist of the paintbrush, who wished to
reproduce with utmost clarity whatever interested him. In Paris, the young
man — become a close friend, by the way, of the Americans Julian Weir
and John Singer Sargent — quickly got himself known as the best talent,
and most agreeable company, in the Finnish artists' colony. Albert Edelfelt
had qualities reminiscent of the Gustavians — he detested provincialism,
he was polished, he sought the elegant and the beautiful. By the 1880's he
had won such fame that he got a commission to paint Louis Pasteur; the
famous portrait in the laboratory came, in time, to grace many an American drugstore. His innate aristocracy notwithstanding, Edelfelt was able to
appeal to inexperienced viewers of art; the most successful exhibit in the
early history of the Ateneum appears to have been the memorial display of
Edelfelt's works in 1910, viewed by 15,000 people. Another of Edelfelt's
qualities was his industry, something he had learned, he said, from his father.

In his relatively short life (he died in August, 1905, not very long after
his 51th birthday) he turned out an oeuvre as remarkable for its variety as
for its size: historical paintings, portraits ranging from "The One-Eyed
Karelian" to the singer Aino Ackté, from Juhani Aho to Nicholas II of
Russia, interiors, seascapes, and, in Helsingfors, where he maintained an
atelier on and off, his views of the city and its people — the Russian
drosky-man or *izvozchik*, the chattering ladies and the Russian officers on
the snow-covered Market, the prospect of Long Bridge (seen from his
studio on Broholmen), Kronohagen observed from that romantically
named island, Blåbärslandet, Blueberryland. Edelfelt was most at home in
Paris — the handsome traveler never missed a spring there — yet never
slighted his homeland: he painted Finnish and Finno-Swedish subjects, he
did the standard illustrations for *Fänrik Stål* (complaining that it was easy
enough to get relics "of those Asiatic relatives whom Castrén made the
mistake of digging up for us," but impossible to find a drum from the War
of 1808–09), and his last major work was the fresco for the aula of
Helsingfors University, the procession of Per Brahe with his suite, destroyed by bombs in 1944 and since restored. Edelfelt was a patriotic Finlander, then, although he could not speak Finnish at all well (a failing for
which he was sneered at by younger Finnish colleagues), and was surely
not someone to deny his Swedish heritage.

As Ahrenberg observed, Edelfelt had few imitators in Finnish art, Axel
Gallén had many. Gallen-Kallela (he removed the accent and Fennicized
the name in 1902) was eleven years younger than Edelfelt, whom he ad-

mired and in whose footsteps he followed for a time; like Edelfelt a pupil at the Swedish Normal Lyceum in Helsingfors, whither his mother had moved from Björneborg after his banker father's death, then a student at the Art Union, he went to Paris for further training. Here the resemblance stops. The winter sojourns in France were far less fruitful for Gallén than the summers at Enola; his marriage to Mary Slöör and his honeymoon trip to Karelia and the White Sea (in 1890) led him back, he liked to think, to the world of his Finnish forebears: " . . . in the north, beside the Arctic Circle, I found the vision I had dreamt of since I was a child." He began his series of paintings on Finnish peasant themes (one should compare his reverence for Finnish nudity in "Sauna" with the half-prurience, half-disgust he accords the Parisian nude in "Demasquée"); he began his long, long struggle with motifs from the *Kalevala*, ending only when he died. And then there are the portraits of the young heroes and heroines of Finnish culture: Sibelius, Ida Aalberg, and the *Symposion* of 1893, where the sturdy Gallén has the air of holding his liquor far better than his companions in the picture: Robert Kajanus, head in hand, young Sibelius, look stunned, the unidentified form sprawled on the table.

Although Gallén eventually settled down on the outskirts of the capital, in his strange stone castle at Alberga, he did not care to capture the city in his work; his spirit was miles and centuries away. Other artists liked Helsingfors better; for example, Gunnar Berndtson, Fredrik Berndtson's son and Edelfelt's friend, who got minor immortality for his silhouettes decorating the Chapel (a restaurant, nota bene, in the Esplanade) and his portraits of August Schauman and Eero Järnefelt. This Järnefelt, the painter among the gifted brothers, himself got a place in Finland's art somewhere between Edelfelt and Gallén, more introspective than the former, less heroically Finnish than the latter. Not above making quiet fun of the Finnish peasants he was impelled to admire (see "The Master and His Men," where the laborers are drunk or asleep), Järnefelt was a portraitist of small range but keenest perceptivity — revealing the fanaticism of the shy and scholarly Danielson-Kalmari, underlining the determination of Mathilda Wrede to aid the unfortunate, whether they wanted succor or not. Berndtson and Järnefelt do not show what Helsingfors looked like, but they populate it with living beings, great and small. Other artists of the age, Gallén, the early-dead August Uotila, the recluse Helene Schjerfbeck, looked at the city and did not like what they saw, or felt. Still a boy, Axel Gallén told the truth about shabby Fredriksgatan, a second-rate street in any northern European city; Uotila, whose favorite subject was Bretagne peasants, left a view of a nondescript Chapel; Schjerfbeck's convalescent girl could be recovering from the miseries of a Helsingfors winter. (A teacher at the Ateneum from 1896 to 1901, Schjerfbeck, the greatest of

Finland's women painters, had a pathological hatred of her native city —
"it has never given me any spiritual profit, has no content for me." Leaving her job, she went out to Hyvinge, and did not return to Helsingfors
until forced to do so by the Civil War of 1918.) When all is said and done,
it is Edelfelt, the *bon vivant* familiar with so many European capitals, who
has made posterity *see* the Helsingfors of those relatively peaceful years.
And Edelfelt's funeral, in the Nikolai-Church, was an occasion of mourning for all Helsingfors. Could a man of his background and interests win
the same tribute from the contemporary city? Edelfelt's museum is at
Borgå, the still almost half-Swedish town of Runeberg; Gallen-Kallela's
museum lies inside the city limits of the modern capital. The tradition
Edelfelt represented, and the Helsingfors he depicted, may be in greater
danger of entering the limbo of forgotten cultures than is Gallen-Kallela's
Kalevala-world.

That the sculptor Ville Vallgren shares the museum at Borgå with Albert Edelfelt is not improper: art-historians have noticed parallels between
them, just as they have between another sculptor, Emil Wikström, and
Gallen-Kallela: the first pair, both children of the 1850's, both with close
connections to Borgå, both Parisians by choice, both in love with beauty
and grace; the second pair born in the 1860's of families with a west Finnish peasant heritage, both devoted to Finnish nationalism, both possessed
of a brutal energy. Gallen-Kallela's description of "the naked, hairy fellow
inside [his] clothes" could apply as well to Wikström, just as Gallen-
Kallela's fresco, "Kullervo Goes Forth to War," shares a frightening vitality
with the frieze sculptures Wikström executed for Gustaf Nyström's otherwise serene House of Estates — or as Gallen-Kallela's ceramic,
"Väinämöinen's Head," shares its strength with the subsidiary group of
Wikström's Lönnrot statue: Väinämöinen, looking appropriately hoary,
rises from the belly of the sleeping giant Vipunen. (The statue stands, for
better or worse, across the street from Engel's Old Church, providing the
chance for a worthwhile comparison of the Neo-Classic and the National
Romantic spirits.) Yet one wonders if the double joining, of Vallgren and
Edelfelt, of Gallen-Kallela and Wikström, does justice to the participants.
Vallgren was far more the sensualist than Edelfelt (or Edelfelt, the aristocrat, hid his sensuality better, and refined it more); Vallgren allowed himself to become a rustic parody on the boulevardier, walking about that arty
suburb, Alberga, with his pig on a leash, and describing his own semi-
legendary self in his grotesque "memoir," *Ville Vallgrens ABC-bok*. In life,
and in sculpture, he had been very fond of round and pretty girls, not just
pigs; his third wife, Viivi Paarmio, generously supported and extended this
aspect of the Vallgren-tale with her *Sydämeni kirja* (*The Book of My Heart*,
1949). Far and away the best-known of Vallgren's works is the "Girl from

the Sea," or "Havis Amanda." as she is popularly called, at the harbor end
of the Esplanade; nicely if plumply curved, she has become the symbol of
"happy Helsingfors," the city of gay cafés and student pranks, the city
whose erstwhile existence the contemporary pessimist might well question.
Vallgren tells us in the *ABC-Book* that he first met young Edelfelt at the
industrial exposition of 1876: "Oh, what a handsome man and a great
artist he was . . . he had seen so much and traveled so widely!" Could it be
that Vallgren's subsequent life-style was born of affectionate envy? Emil
Wikström, however, had no reason to envy Gallen-Kallela, nor is there
evidence that he did; he stood on his own feet, possessing a feeling for
Finnish realities, and for the entirety of Finnish history, which Gallen-
Kallela, with his passion for stylization and for the primitive, apparently
lacked. Wikström's grasp of history made him ideally suited to his calling,
as a quasi-official creator of monuments for Helsingfors. He did the statue
of Lönnrot, but he was also able to do the bust of Pacius (from 1895) in
Kajsaniemi Park. (The fact that Pacius got his monument so early, before
either Lönnrot or Snellman — whose turn, again at Wikström's hands, did
not come until 1923 — caused discontent on the part of those who did
not wish to see any celebration of the "foreign element" in Finland's culture.) Wikström's frieze on the Estate House ignores neither the long
"Swedish time" in Finland's history nor the nineteenth century's Swedish-
language culture. Before the frieze was revealed to the public eye, the architect Nyström chose a couple of strophes from Runeberg's psalm,
"Fosterlandet" ("The Fatherland"), and Wikström had them engraved on
a copper plate; then, one dark night, he climbed up the scaffolding and,
worming his way along behind the figures of the frieze, fastened the inscription on the breast of "Faith's" symbolic representation. It was a daring act, both physically and because it aroused the ire of the new Russian
governor-general, Bobrikov; that a defense of Finland as a totality, rather
than a special preserve of Finns or Finno-Swedes, came from Wikström,
with Swedish name and Finnish blood, seemed both hopeful and appropriate.

14. A Musical Capital

THERE EXISTED A passably good soil for the growth of a common tradition
in Finland's music, blending Finno-Swedish and Finnish elements. When
the gossipy Ahrenberg called Pacius "a zealous Scandinavian, in contrast
to most Germans," he may have been thinking of such originally Baltic-

German Fennomanes as the Krohns or Elisabeth Järnefelt (née Clodt von Jürgensburg); but Pacius had managed to write music for Topelius' crazy-quilt phantasy on *Kalevala* themes. Even earlier, the unfortunate Ingelius had tried to employ Finland's history for inspiration, composing an over-ture to his own play, *Biskop Henrik och bonden Lalli* (*Bishop Henry and the Peasant Lalli*), and making a setting of the "Kulneff" canto from Fänrik Stål. In somewhat turbulent prose, Ingelius had predicted a splendid fu-ture for his nation's musical art: "Now there prevails in our land . . . a kind of restlessness, but the awakening will be beautiful." By the time he per-ished in a blizzard, in 1868 (an event immortalized by Topelius in verses which Fru Raa read at a meeting of the Artist's Guild: "And the night was cold in the forest waste, / The whistling snowstorm roared"), Ingelius had long been lost to musical creation; his place had been taken by von Schantz, whose sad story has already been told, and Karl Collan, the youngest of three gifted brothers who had come down to Helsingfors from the pastorage at Idensalmi. (The others were the schoolman, hunch-backed Fabian, and the imperial physician, Alexander.) Karl had been Ingelius' friend — both had been members of the "Sjuan" coterie (named "Seven" after the size of its membership), together with August Ahlqvist and Emil von Quanten. Like Ingelius (and like the Swede C.J.L. Almqvist, author and composer, "Sjuan's" idol), Collan could not make up his mind between music and letters; he won a reputation as a translator of Heine (another of the group's favorites) and, more important, of the *Kalevala* (1864–68) — young Albert Edelfelt owned a copy of Collan's Swedish version. As a musician, Collan is remembered for his songs, some of which, "Savolaisten laulu" ("Song of the Men of Savolax"), the "Vasa March," and the settings of poems by Runeberg ("Old Hurtig"), Topelius ("Sylvia's Song," "On Roine's Banks"), and Lars Stenbäck ("The Star"), became the property of both his homeland's language groups, whose folk-music he knew well. Collan was no genius, and as a practical musician could not measure up to his father-in-law, Pacius; much of his short life was spent in pedagogical and bibliographical pursuits (he was appointed university librarian in 1866), and there is no reason to believe that his early death (of cholera, at 43) caused "far greater hopes" to be buried be-neath the tombstone in the Lutheran cemetery, a stone on which four measures of the "Savolaisten laulu" were inscribed.

Pacius himself grew ever more prankish with the years, and more can-tankerous: filling Topelius' glass at the Artists' Guild when the great man was not looking, calling Bohuslav Hrimaly, the conductor of the orchestra at the Swedish Theater, "diesen lausigen, hochmütigen Kapellmeister." The epithet is supposed to have been hurled during the rehearsals for the revival of *Kung Carls jagt* in 1888. On this occasion, Pacius also wrote that he was too old to put up with new miseries. His crown prince had appeared in Helsingfors two decades before — another German, Richard Faltin, come from Danzig by way of Leipzig and Viborg, married, like Pacius, to the daughter of a good Finno-Swedish family, and possessing the same broad skills as the old master: he was able to keep up a many-sided life — as director, briefly, of the orchestra at the New Theater, as the music teacher of the university, as the organist at Nikolai Church, and (in the 1870's) as conductor at the Finnish Opera. He also founded a chorus, "The Song Union" (1871–1884), with which he continued a work begun by Pacius, the performance of oratorios. Here Faltin expanded the repertoire of Spohr, Mendelssohn, and Félicien David that Pacius had favored, adding newer fashions from the German homeland — Bach (rediscovered by Mendelssohn), Schumann, Liszt, Brahms. Like Pacius, too, Faltin was an industrious composer, but had come to Finland too late for easy victories; and, like Pacius, he was not altogether successful in the battle to establish a permanent orchestra in Helsingfors. He gave up the podium at the New Theater (whose orchestra, augmented, presented independent concerts) almost too quickly, leaving the job to one Nathan B. Emmanuel (remembered by the ladies because he had "pale and sensitive features, soulful eyes, and curly hair"), and to the Bohemian Hrimaly.

Confronted by those most skeptical of God's creatures, professional orchestral musicians, Faltin — described as a "timid, nervous man with a stammer" — had a harder time than Pacius, who had never been at loss for insult; Helsingfors gossip reported that Faltin despised and envied Emmanuel, despised him because he was Jewish, envied him because he was flamboyant enough to make the public forget that there were only 22 men in his symphony orchestra. However, for all his insecurity, Faltin made two contributions of singular importance to musical life in Helsingfors; as the leader of the Finnish Opera during its short life, he showed both the solidity of his musical gifts and his position in the language struggle. Faltin had not spent time in Sweden before coming to Finland, as Pacius had; in Viborg, he had been a welcome guest at the home of the German enthusiasts for Finnish, the Krohns. Shortly after coming to Helsingfors, he was invited to conduct an amateur performance of Weber's *Preciosa* (in Finnish) arranged by the new "Suomalainen seura" ("Finnish Society"), and so, like Fru Raa, felt a pioneer's affection for the Finnish cause; the next step was the conductorship at the quasi-professional operatic performances undertaken by the society at Arcadia Theater. No doubt the sensitive Faltin was offended when he read the condescending accounts in the Swedish press about the Finnish operas at the Arcadia; when *Il Trovatore* was given, Theodor Sederholm wrote in *Helsingfors Dagblad*: "A person whom I asked about the performance replied: 'Oh, it went quite smoothly, but two of the singers disturbed the ensemble — *their* work reminded one of the [musical] theater of a cultured nation'." Another, more positive factor in Faltin's devotion to the Finnish Opera was his friendship with Kaarlo Bergbom. Bergbom, so fanatical in undertakings of pure theater, revealed a different side of himself here — he had a genuine love for music, and hoped to lure a Swedish-speaking audience into the Arcadia's auditorium, imagining that they would listen to operas in Finnish, even though they boycotted Finnish plays. And Faltin — the outsider, who had come to the reasonable conclusion that the two language groups had better hang together, if they did not wish to hang separately — had an equally clear view of the opera as an instrument of reconciliation; "before we can say Jack Robinson," as the old councillor remarks in Järnefelt's novel *Veljekset* (*The Brothers*, 1900), "a third party will come along and take *his* share." Bergbom's plan, and Faltin's, was not unlike that of Sibelius a decade later: music was to be a link between Finn and Finno-Swede.

In its seven years (1873–80) the Finnish Opera developed a repertoire equivalent to that of a middle-line German or Austrian house of the period; it gave about 450 performances of 24 works — Gounod's *Faust* (which got the record of 55 performances) and his *Romeo and Juliet*, Donizetti's *Lucia* (46 performances), *The Daughter of the Regiment*, *Lucrezia Borgia*, and *Linda di Chamounix*, Verdi's *Trovatore* (44 performances), *Ernani*, *Traviata*. Mozart was represented, too (*Magic Flute* and *Don Giovanni*), Rossini (*The Barber of Seville*), and even *Fidelio* was given a try, as were Bellini's *Norma* and *La sonnambula*; then there were those 19th century favorites seldom heard today — Auber, Flotow, Halévy, Lortzing, Meyerbeer. Faltin was not the only conductor on the staff; he shared the podium with Lorenz Nikolai Achté, a Finn from Björneborg, who was also the troupe's leading bass-baritone, and he had the notorious Hrimaly as his substitute while he was on a study-trip to Germany in 1876–77. After his return, Faltin divided his duties with Martin Wegelius, a young Helsingfors musician, a veteran of training in Germany and (like Faltin after the latter's recent sojourn in Bayreuth) a Wagner-enthusiast. Of the male singers, none of the local performers appears to have risen above the level of mere competence, although the Opera was able to attract such guest stars as the Swede Ludvig Ericsson and the great Bohemian tenor, Josef Navratil. The ladies were more brilliant: Ida Basilier (one of those disturbers of mediocrity noted by Sederholm), Emmy Strömer (who married the variously gifted Achté and became the mother of the greatest of Finnish sopranos, Aino Ackté, who revised the spelling of her name), and Alma Fohström (who went from Helsingfors to a career on three continents, engagements at Kroll's, Covent Garden, and the Metropolitan, and a position at the Court Opera in Moscow). Despite such talents, it is likely that the reach of the Finnish Opera exceeded its grasp: it had to improvise, to work too swiftly — a sketch by Samuli Suomalainen in the journal *Liitto* (*Alliance*) shows Bergbom arranging to get a Finnish translation of the third act of *Fra Diavolo* "by eleven o'clock tomorrow" during a performance of *Lucia*. Nonetheless, like its sister, the Finnish Theater, it was borne along by enthusiasm, and managed to draw the new Finnish intelligentsia, as well as those Finno-Swedes for whom a love of opera was more important than the display of intransigence. Suomalainen's sketch tells about the crowd in the Arcadia's foyer between acts: old Snellman was there, Yrjö-Koskinen, Ahlqvist, Clas Herman Molander (Snellman's successor as the director of Finland's finances, a man neither Fennomane nor Suecomane, a patriot instead), Jaakko Forsman and his band from *Uusi Suometar*, the young teachers from "Suomalainen alkeisopisto." "Everyone is hopeful and lighthearted."

The Finnish Opera was killed in the language war. The liberal Rafael Hertzberg wrote: "[in Swedish quarters,] the Finnish Opera was regarded simply as an attempt to assassinate the Swedish Theater and Swedish culture . . . far from deserving encouragement, [it] ought instead to be opposed in every way, and destroyed. From this thought there arose the Swedish Opera. Now, Helsingfors had two opera companies at once — and both of them naturally had a rendezvous with ruin." Performing in the New (Swedish) Theater, the Swedish Opera, directed first by Emmanuel and then Hrimaly, went in for the light repertoire: Nicolai's *Merry Wives of Windsor*, Weber's *Freischütz*, Donizetti's *L'elisir d'amore*, Konradin Kreutzer's *Nachtlager in Granada* were some of its more estimable numbers. Its star was Emilie Mechelin, a sister of the imposing Leo Mechelin, who was now devoting *his* vocal talents to a career of statesmanship. (Guss Mattsson characterized Mechelin's oratory as a virtuoso musical performance.) In 1880, the Finnish and Swedish operas succumbed, victims of high costs and rivalry: Hertzberg reports that many patrons of the one theater refused, out of principle, to set foot in the other. Efforts at revival were made, but none succeeded: Emma Engdahl, a product of the Swedish Opera and the musical belle of the 1876 exposition, founded the Helsingfors Opera Society, which for two years (1888–1890) gave works sung to Swedish libretti; Emmy Achté had a try at Finnish opera again in 1891–92; Armas Järnefelt and his singer-wife Maikki offered Helsingfors a tablespoon full of Wagner in 1904–06. It was not until 1911 that something like a permanent opera for Finland's capital was founded. Edvard Fazer, the music-loving scion of the city's supreme candy-making family (originally Swiss, from Romanshorn), and Aino Ackté, returned from her triumph as Salomé at Covent Garden, set up a new company, opening with a performance on Kaarlo Bergbom's birthday, October 2. In 1914, it took the official name, "Suomalainen Ooppera," and, after the establishment of an independent Finland, moved into a new home, the former Russian theater on the Boulevard, not far from Sandvik Square.

The theater in which the new Finnish Opera found quarters had been built in 1876–79, at the command of Governor General Adlerberg, out of material taken from Bomarsund Fortress in Åland, reduced to rubble by the British fleet during the Crimean War. The handsome building was designed by the engineering corps on Sveaborg, with one Colonel Kasperoff in command; the Berlin theater-architect Hugo Gropius, called in for consultation too late in the game, suggested that the whole place be torn down and built over again — the fair exterior concealed a multitude of technical sins. The Russian Theater, as it was called, was intended for the edification and amusement of the officers stationed in and around Helsingfors; the Russian authorities generously allowed its occasional use for local audiences as well. The most glorious of these occasions was the premiere, in 1887, of Pacius' last opera, *Die Lorelei*, based on Geibel's stillborn drama. Faltin conducted, Emma Engdahl sang (or rather croaked in the early performances, since she was hoarse) and Pacius received thunderous ovations, together with the customary singing of "Our Country" by the audience. The scandals surrounding *Die Lorelei* are more interesting than the opera itself. From the start, the general director of the Swedish Theater, Professor Vilhelm Bolin, had refused to allow the premiere to take place at his institution, for reasons not altogether clear, and did his best to cut into *Die Lorelei*'s audience by scheduling a new operetta. Yet Pacius' fame (and the nation's gratitude) brought full houses; the run could have been extended if Bolin had not refused to allow the men from the Swedish Theater's pit to continue playing in the *Lorelei* orchestra. They were needed, he said, for the operetta. The orchestra had offered other problems too; its membership consisted principally of players in the Helsingfors Orchestral Association, founded five years before by a firebrand named Robert Kajanus, and Kajanus — who was envious of Faltin, according to Maria Collan, Pacius' daughter and the guiding spirit of the premiere — had not been much more cooperative than Bolin in providing good musicians. The story is instructive: Pacius and Faltin had given all their talents to the city and the nation; now the days of the German musical hegemony were over.

The opera experiments had shown, among other things, that Helsingfors needed a conservatory and a permanent orchestra, if decent musical standards were to be established and maintained. In 1882 Martin Wegelius established the Helsingfors Musical Institute, a private institution with some state aid; it was intended as a counterpart of the Ateneum's schools. The rector of the academy was Wegelius himself, who demanded that the best possible teachers be recruited — the most famous of them (save Sibelius) was the young Ferruccio Busoni, who taught piano from 1888 until 1890. Sibelius, a student at the academy from 1885 until he left for the continent in the autumn of 1889, said that: "Martin Wegelius lived solely for his Institute, and knew how to inspire his faculty and his pupils through his joy-in-work and his burning enthusiasm. During my later studies abroad I was able to determine that, thanks to Martin's personal contribution, the Institute stood on a perceptibly higher level than most of the comparable institutions abroad." That Wegelius sacrificed a career as a composer for his school, and that he wrote a series of textbooks (in which he demonstrated his first-rate stylistic abilities) for its use, are two further signs of his devotion. He had his limitations, of talent and of taste; he was a devoted Wagnerite, and Sibelius claimed (the listener to Sibelius' earlier orchestral works may think otherwise) that Wegelius tried in vain to inculcate his prize pupil with his affection. Brahms was left in outer darkness, Tchaikovsky inspired abuse, and Grieg was treated with skepticism, although Wegelius and Faltin had been pioneers in introducing the Norwegian's work to Helsingfors in the 1870's.

Another of the quirks of Wegelius, a peculiarly harmful one, was the unwritten law which forbade students at the Institute to attend the orchestral concerts of Robert Kajanus: the musical world of Helsingfors had not learned a lesson from the catastrophic opera feud. A few months after the founding of Wegelius' academy, Kajanus — from the same Helsingfors background as Wegelius, like him a student of Faltin and the Leipzig Conservatory, but ten years younger than the great pedagogue and of a radically different personality — had succeeded where so many others had failed; supported by the money of the merchant Klärich and the brewer Sinebrychoff, he established the Helsingfors Orchestral Association. (In 1895, the name was changed to the Philharmonic Society, in order to avoid giving the impression that the orchestra was made up of amateurs.) Kajanus not only knew how to attract benefactors, he knew how to attract paying crowds as well: during his first season he gave 8 symphony concerts with his 36 men, and simultaneously pleased a much broader public with his pop-concerts in Society House, where food and drink could be mixed with music. Hertzberg waxes very enthusiastic: "One comes here after the day's work to have a pleasant evening in good company, to meet friends, to chat, to laugh . . . All the solemnity, all the stiffness, those ill-reputed Finnish characteristics of ours, have disappeared, and . . . Helsingfors develops its *Gemütlichkeit* in full freedom." Wegelius could not conceal his contempt for such high-jinks. Furthermore, in another measure taken by Kajanus, Wegelius detected a direct threat to his academy. In 1885, deciding that Finland's orchestral needs should no longer be supplied with amateur players or imports from abroad, Kajanus opened a school for the training of orchestral musicians. The school's life did not run easily; the wind players in Kajanus' orchestra, appointed as faculty members, went on strike: they did not want to impart their secrets to future competitors. Kajanus' persuasiveness and the prospect of more money made them change their minds; the school existed until 1914, when it was absorbed by the Institute.

In 1900 the orchestra of Kajanus appeared at the World's Fair in Paris, increased to 70 players; there it introduced Finland's new music to the world, playing Sibelius' *First Symphony* and *Finlandia*, Armas Järnefelt's *Prelude* (it remains his sole surviving piece on non-Finnish concert programs), and Kajanus' own *Summer Memories*. Songs of Oskar Merikanto, the early-dead Ernst Mielck, and Järnefelt, sung by Aino Ackté, were also featured. In a second concert Kajanus included his *Finnish Rhapsody Number One*, Järnefelt's tone poem *Korsholm* (inspired by the five-hundredth anniversary of the building of the Ostrobothnian fortress), and more Sibelius — the *King Christian Suite*, the *Swan of Tuonela*, and *Lemminkäinen's Homeward Journey*. (A year later, *King Christian* served to introduce Sibelius to America: it was performed by the orchestra of another bilingual city, pre-1917 Cincinnati, conducted by Frank van der Stucken.) The orchestra's life, made so memorable by Sibelius premieres, was almost destroyed in 1912–13, assailed by the old disease of rivalry: a youngish lion from Viborg, the German-Finlander Georg Schnéevoigt, a cellist turned conductor, established the Helsingfors Symphony Orchestra, but was unable to lure all of Kajanus' musicians to his new, well-financed banner. Kajanus himself found aid, too; he got his membership increased to 62 men, the same size as Schnéevoigt's, and the "domestic" nature of his revised ensemble — in contrast to Schnéevoigt's, which depended to a great extent on foreign imports — was underlined by the hiring of two utterly authentic Finns, Toivo Kuula and Leevi Madetoja, as assistant conductors. (Both were composers of some stature, Kuula becoming known in particular as a writer of art-songs before his early and senseless death in the wake of Finland's Civil War — he was shot by a fellow officer at, of all things, a victory celebration in Viborg. Madetoja's contribution as a songwriter is also considerable, but his most memorable contribution to Finland's music is his *Pohjalaisia* [*Ostrobothnians*, 1924], which has come to be regarded as something of a national opera.) Wisdom prevailed in the orchestral war between Kajanus and Schnéevoigt, wisdom seconded by the outbreak of hostilities on the continent in 1914: a good many of Helsingfors' surplus musicians were recalled to Germany. The two bands were combined into one, called the Helsingfors City Orchestra, the rivals took turns at the podium, and the concertmaster, for a time, was Richard Burgin, subsequently to become the darling of Boston Symphony audiences. Thus the Kajanus-Schnéevoigt feud subsided, and Schnéevoigt's engagement as director of the Concert Association's orchestra in Stockholm put an end to the trouble. No harm had been done — which is more than can be said for the Wegelius-Kajanus conflict of some thirty years before; out of loyalty to Wegelius, the young Sibelius had gotten a chance for serious orchestral-concert going only upon his arrival in Berlin in 1889.

On September 7 of that year, Sibelius left Finland for his studies abroad; if *Storfursten* had sunk on the trip to Lübeck, a good portion of Finland's cultural future would have gone to the bottom with her. Eero Järnefelt, the painter, and Juhani Aho were on their way to Paris; Sibelius had been entrusted by Wegelius to the care of Docent Werner Söderhjelm, also en route to Berlin, with wife and two small sons. Söderhjelm found Sibelius to be "a nice and gifted boy [he was going on 24], but sometimes he annoys us by his so-called impracticality, which in most cases takes the form of sheer slovenliness." By 1891, after Berlin and Vienna, Sibelius was back in the homeland where, through the agency of his future in-laws, the Järnefelts, he became friendly with the *Päivälehti* circle; it included, among others, the Erkkos of newspaper fame, Juhani Aho, the writing and the painting Järnefelt sons, Gallén, and two other artists of some distinction — Pekka Halonen (the depicter of sober, close-cropped Finnish peasants) and Louis Sparre, a nobleman from Sweden who, according to Gallén, had become so ecstatic about Finnish Finland that he even swore in Finnish. (It is to be hoped that he controlled himself in the presence of his bride, Gustaf Mannerheim's younger sister Eva.) But, in Helsingfors, Sibelius also had gifted friends who were Finno-Swedish: the writers Karl August Tavaststjerna, Mikael Lybeck, Hjalmar Procopé. The first-named died young, at 37, misplaced as a newspaper editor in Björneborg: Sibelius made a sensitive comparison between him and Gallén — the author of *A Patriot without a Homeland* was given to darker moods than the artist who, having discovered the Finnish past, "saw the future in a brighter light." As for Sibelius, whose home-tongue as a boy was Swedish, whose school-tongue was Finnish, he did not, as a musician, know the anguished isolation of a Tavaststjerna, a Lybeck; both of Finland's worlds were his. In 1892, he wrote the tone poem *Kullervo*, based on the *Kalevala* and Kivi's tragedy, but at the same time he was at work on settings of Runeberg's poems; in 1892–93, he produced the tone poem with the clearly Scandinavian name, *En saga*, and the *Karelian Suite*, about the eastern borderlands, the *Kalevala*'s supposed home and a landscape Gallén loved; in 1894–95, he wrote the four legends for orchestra around the figure of

Lemminkäinen and put Tavaststjerna's verses to music. These two streams
in the production of Sibelius almost meet at the end of the 1890's, when
the "Athenians' Song" (to a text by the Swedish poet Viktor Rydberg)
and the First Symphony have their premiere together on April 26, 1899;
the former may be taken as an expression of a "Scandinavian" spirit of
bristling independence (for all its Greekish dress) and the latter as a
"symbolic picture of Finland's readiness for battle against the threat from
the east."

Such interpretations can be disputed: there is not much question,
however, about the meaning of certain famous events which took place
during the "Press Days" of early November, 1899, an organized protest
against the restrictions imposed on Finland's newspapers by the Russian
governor-general Bobrikov. The musical-dramatic program offered at the
Swedish Theater on November 4 reminds one of the house's inauguration
four decades earlier, when Topelius and Pacius let themselves be inspired
by the *Kalevala*. The evening opened with the march from *Tannhäuser*,
played by Kajanus and his men and intended, maybe, to put the audience
in the properly solemn yet brisk frame of mind. The music was followed
by verse prologues, the one in Swedish by Odo Morannal Reuter, the
other in Finnish by Larin-Kyösti; the main course was a series of
"historical tableaux," arranged by Kaarlo Bergbom, with text by Eino
Leino and music by Sibelius. The six scenes treated some epochs of Finnish myth and Finland's history — Väinämöinen pleasing the people of
Kalevala and Pohjola with his song; Bishop Henry baptizing the heathens;
Duke Johan's renaissance court at Åbo; Gustaf Adolf and his Finnish
shock troops (the "hakkapeliitat" of the Thirty Years' War); "The Great
Strife" of the eighteenth century's early decades, when Russian troops laid
waste a defenseless land; and "Finland's Awakening," whose musical setting in future would be called *Finlandia*. The tone poem became a mighty
weapon in the Finnish battle against a newly oppressive Russian regime; its
performance forbidden in Finland, it was played under innocuous names
(for example, "Phantasy" and "Impromptu") in other parts of the Russian
realm, and performed as a part of anti-Czarist demonstrations in western
Europe. As for its musical qualities, *Finlandia* has turned out to be the
hardiest of plants: rare is the bandmaster or choir-director who has ignored it.

Helsingfors was the scene, naturally enough, of Sibelius' greatest triumph as a "national" composer; but it was a city in which he — like
Helene Schjerfbeck — could not work. By the beginning of the new century, he told his biographer Ekman, he had decided that "it was necessary
for me to get away from Helsingfors. My art needed another atmosphere.
In Helsingfors, song died within me. In addition, there was the fact that I

was too sociable to refuse the many invitations . . . which disturbed my work. It was very difficult for me to say no. I had to get away." And get away he did, in September, 1904, to his new villa Ainola at Järvenpää north of Helsingfors, together with his wife Aino (after whom the house was named) and his children. He maintained his residence here, in the Finnish-speaking part of Nyland, for the rest of his life; as Otto Andersson remarks, "he was most frequently visible to the public of Helsingfors during the next years [c. 1905–1910] in connection with music written for productions at the Swedish Theater," Maeterlinck's *Pelléas et Mélisande*, Procopé's *Belsazars gästabud* (*Belshazzar's Feast*), Strindberg's *Svanevit* (*Snow White*), Shakespeare's *Twelfth Night*, and Mikael Lybeck's *Ödlan* (*The Lizard*), substantial evidence of the ability of theatrical works in Swedish, translated or original, to inspire him.

A whole literature of anecdotes has sprung up around the lure which Helsingfors "social" life — i.e., cafés and restaurants — exerted upon Sibelius during the 1890's, and then, later, when the train brought him down from his lair. Gallén's aforementioned painting, *Symposion*, has had its name borrowed, by biographers, for a special phase of this convivial life, a phase running — according to the master's memory — from about 1892 until 1895; the innocent outsider may wonder why Aino Sibelius (they had married in 1892) did not exert a stronger social attraction of her own during the first years of marital delights. The "Symposion" circle met sometimes at Catani's, on the North Esplanade, which had now passed into the hands of the vigorous grandson of the original owner: this John Catani, a gifted figure-skater, had decorated the walls of his "ladies' parlor" with a large picture of himself, dressed rococo-style and putting skates on a young beauty; or, if Catani's seemed too soft and feminine for the roisterers, then they passed to König's on Mikaelsgatan, an all-male restaurant (save for its waitresses, much pinched and patted) run by the *sous-chef* of the new and very popular Hotel Kämp — the former actor Carl König. "A cultural stamp lay on this old restaurant . . . winged, the hours there fled away, but they had not been wasted, they were small pearls on the string of memories"; Bertel Gripenberg's prose can perhaps be excused on the grounds that overwhelming emotions inspired it. Everyone in the group (according to Ekman) made his special contribution to the collective mood, "Gallén by his fantastic ideas, Kajanus by his polished speeches, often with some philosophical content, Sibelius by means of his lively conversation, hovering between jokes and the weightiest sort of seriousness." Just as he had in the summertime days of his youth at Lovisa, when Alma Söderhjelm saw him for the first time, and got those indelible impressions of hers, the composer took refuge at the piano when he had nothing to say. Maybe protesting too much, Sibelius claimed that strong drink played a smaller role than generally supposed during the heroic sittings at König's. What matters most about the "Symposion" hours is that Sibelius learned so much from them, and that he was perhaps more completely alive than he would ever be again. Eino Leino recorded a word-picture Juhani Aho had made of an older Sibelius, "a gray man in a gray suit, the air around him gray with cigar smoke." One appreciates the musical qualities of the works that came out of Ainola after 1905, the five later symphonies, the violin concerto, the *Oceanides, Tapiola*, the great songs, and the rest; but one may also be glad that the young Sibelius — the national artist, not the national monument in state-of-becoming — existed once upon a time.

15. Happy Helsingfors and Its Architects

JAC. AHRENBERG HAS a touching anecdote about the aged Anders Ramsay who, in the last springtime of his life (1910), insisted on taking a stroll through the city he loved with all his mendacious and arrogant heart. "He wanted to say farewell to Kajsaniemi, Hesperia, and Brunnsparken, wanted to go out to Gumtäkt, the great meadow where he had celebrated so many Flora-Days, he wanted to see the places . . . of the days of his youth . . ." Ahrenberg's imagination may have been over-exuberant here, as so often; but the tale has a meaning, nonetheless. The Helsingfors locales still magical for Ramsay (who was 78 at the time) belonged to a vanished, exclusive, and entirely Swedish-speaking world. In fact, even the Helsingfors of the 1890's had incurred the aristocrat's contempt; in the last volumes of his memoirs, Ramsay described a phenomenon with which the reader is already familiar: "From the interior of the land, the new railroad had brought down throngs of an element quite foreign to the city, easily detectible both by appearance and language. Even at places previously visited exclusively by the upper classes, it was not unusual to hear Finnish spoken." Sibelius recalled that the old man had said much the same thing to him as they sat together in the Chapel: "'It was different when I was young'," Ramsay muttered. "'Then, not just anybody could come into a better class restaurant'." (Sibelius added that, for the life of him, he could see nothing wrong with the crowd; he might have remembered the Ramsays were exceptional snobs, even when measured by Finno-Swedish standards. Another Ramsay, Vendla Gustafva, a born von Essen but nothing if not proud of the family into which she had married, claimed in all seriousness that the clan descended from Ramses II of Egypt.)

Whether or not this "happy Helsingfors" of the century's close pleased a Ramsay and his ilk, it delighted those whose hearts were young and gay. When Society House, its new banquet hall renovated and expanded, had its formal opening on October 14, 1888, Rafael Hertzberg read a poem, another of those pieces of celebratory verse with which the city's literary history is studded:

> Truly, proud Helsingfors has once again
> Made fast a jewel upon its queenly mantle,
> And these halls are now thrown open to become
> A center for our happy Helsingfors.

Until its functions as hotel and restaurant were ended (with another banquet, on April 2, 1913), Society House served as the site of the grandest social assemblies, and provided the stage on which the most popular entertainers appeared: when the Swedish cabaret singer, Sigge Wulff, came to Helsingfors in the 1890's, every seat in the banquet hall was taken. Society House was not the only large-scale breeding ground for merriment near the Esplanades; out on the greenstrip itself, on the so-called "Little Calf Pasture," there rose the summer restaurant "Kapellet" ("The Chapel"). (The grassy belt between the twin avenues was divided into three sections, like Gaul, with the "Little Calf Pasture" or "Little Esplanade" or simply "Calf Pasture," closest to the market, the "Runeberg Esplanade" — once called "Big Calf Pasture," but given its more elegant name after the erection of the poet's statue there in 1885 — in the middle, and the "Theater Esplanade," where the Swedish Theater stood, forming the western end.) The origin of the Chapel's name is a question much disputed by specialists on Helsingfors onomastics; it is sure that a little soft-drink kiosk already bore the name in the 1850's, and its condition gave Topelius reason to complain in his newspaper: "The Chapel in the Little Esplanade is turning more and more into a tumbledown chicken-house." A blasphemous and complicated explanation for the name runs as follows: a wit, recalling the original pasture-purposes of the land, dubbed the kiosk's owner the "pastor" of the "flock" of drinkers at his stand, which thus became the pastor's "chapel"; to later and less subtle minds, however, there was no doubt an association between "Kapellet" and the military bands — "kapell" in Swedish — which were the restaurant's stock in trade. In 1870, the kiosk gave way to the building designed by Hampus Dalström, the builder of the Old Student House; its first lessee was the grand old man of Helsingfors hotel life, Louis Kleineh. After some vicissitudes, it passed into the control of one Josef Wolontis, who got the idea of adding wind ensembles to good food and drink: the immortal Leander with the

Guards, Hrimaly with the musicians of Nyland's Battalion. (When the restaurant, expanded and with elaborately jig-sawed ornaments added, was re-opened in 1891, Hrimaly wrote a march for the occasion, "The New Chapel"; the designer of the bigger and better Chapel was Bruno Granholm, previously responsible for the expansion of Society House's hall.) A proverb — a surprising one in a city whose inhabitants dreamt all winter long of their summer homes in the country — was coined about the restaurant: "I don't know why people go to the country when they have the Chapel"; it may be that the Helsingfors practice of keeping wife and children in a distant rustic retreat, while the husband enjoyed the pleasures of grass-widowerhood, had something to do with the Chapel's legendary popularity. In the winter, the restaurant continued to serve a special clientele: its "Stammtische" were meeting places for various coteries, some financial, some journalistic, some held together by nothing more than a common interest in the bottle and the plate. Still extant today, and retaining something of its former lure, the Chapel once almost became a martyr of a despotic Russian's whim: in 1912, Governor-General Seyn, whose palace on the South Esplanade looked at the Chapel's back side, demanded that the hallowed hall be razed, since the smell of cooking crept through his official windows; the outbreak of World War One diverted Seyn to other cares. In truth, Seyn did a good turn for lovers of ginger-bread: the management of the Chapel had planned to replace the old wooden structure with a hardier building of modern design, and one of the young giants of Finnish architecture, Lars Sonck, had already submitted plans to the proper governmental bureau for approval; but Seyn — anxious to achieve the restaurant's total destruction — saw to it that they were lost in channels. Yet Sonck, despite his plan to make a substitute for Dalström's and Granholm's gloriously ornate shed, appreciated the Chapel's spiritual values. When a bluestocking complained to the press that "Havis Amanda," visible from the veranda, offended proper diners, Sonck retorted, in print, with a single line: "She doesn't offend me!" He spoke for the Chapel's entire male congregation.

Another of the Chapel's patrons, Guss Mattsson, observed that Runeberg, standing on his pedestal several hundred feet away, was no doubt glad to have "Havis Amanda's" charms as a constant feast for his old eyes. Coming to life, the national poet might have wanted to get down from his perch in order to visit the burgeoning Helsingfors which surrounded him. Two years before the Runeberg statue's unveiling (the solemn event took place in the rain, on the eight anniversary of the poet's death, May 6, 1885), the great Grönqvist Building, the marvel of its time, had been finished just across the street. It was the work of Theodor Höijer, who played Engel's role for Helsingfors during the concluding decades of the century. Not that Höijer had an Engel's purity of style; he combined monumental size and frivolous ornamentation in an almost sinful fashion. Describing another of Höijer's creations, the Kaleva building on Skillnaden, a sober historian of Helsingfors (Eino Suolahti) writes that "its lavishly rich facade and decorated cornices form an essential part of the Helsingfors which seemed to be about to acquire a Parisian air." Poor Höijer's works have not been treated reverently; of the buildings he designed, some have been torn down altogether — including Hotel Kämp and the Volunteer Fire Department's quarters at Centralgatan 7, for a while the home of the Finnish diet — and about 12 have been totally or partially rebuilt. The Ateneum still stands, as does the City Library (young Höijer is restrained here), the Norrmén Building on Skatudden, and the building at the corner of Mannerheimvägen and Kalevagatan which Höijer built for himself and his friend, the Swiss engineer Huber. Of the last-named work Ahrenberg (another architect) wrote: "From the foundation to the spire which once rose above its bay-window, it is covered over with ornamental decorations; the architects of Milan and Paris cannot outshine Höijer in richness, although they might do so in originality." The Grönqvist palace survives too, built at a cost of two million marks, and "with four hundred rooms equipped with fire-places. No fewer than 25 shops have found room in it at street level, and one can imagine what a wonderful sight will confront the evening stroller who beholds the ground floor all illuminated, with a flood of light streaming out of its lofty windows." The exuberant *fin-de-siècle* favored Höijer, but posterity, and preservation, have been kinder to Gustaf Nyström, who gave the city the academic classicism of the State Archives (1890), their neighbor, the House of Estates (1891), and the Nordic Union Bank on Alexandersgatan (1898), as well as the pleasant and practical Customs House on Skatudden, and the Market Hall beside South Harbor; nor should some of the other figures around Nyström be altogether forgotten: Ahrenberg (calmer as an architect than as an author), who made the annex of the post-office on Nikolaigatan (Snellmansgatan), the German Ludwig Bohnstedt, the creator of Finland's Bank on the same street, and Karl August Wrede, the designer of a rival to the Grönqvist Building, the "Wrede-Helenius House" with "its rich, palace-like facade" at the corner of the North Esplanade and Mikaelsgatan; at the same time, he gave his name to "Wrede's Passage," the elegant shortcut leading beside his edifice up to Alexandersgatan. (Later, the baron became the architect of religious edifices, for example, the chapel at the Deaconess Institute, the building-and-church of the Finnish Mission on Observatoriegatan, and the church of the inner-city mission, Betania; nor was this enough — a born-again Christian, he preached and wrote about his faith, publishing *Minnen från mitt arbete för Herren*

[*Memories from My Work for the Lord*, 1940], three years before he died at 83.) Less enthusiastic thoughts might be sent in the direction of the Swede Adolf Emil Melander, who wrought Saint John's Church (1890: he won an international competition) in Röddäldspark beside Högbergsgatan, its spire looming above the Helsingfors skyline; the Votiv-Kirche in Vienna and Helge Zettervall's All Saints' Church in Lund have a worthy rival in overwhelming neo-Gothic here, a pious excessiveness altogether different from Höijer's secular and, as it were, good-natured extravagance, or Wrede's gracefulness, which he retained even in his ecclesiastical buildings.

Surely, Höijer had the heart and the trust of the industrialist Grönqvist; for when Grönqvist underwrote Carl Kämp's plan to erect a new hotel in Helsingfors, directly beside the palace of offices and shops described above, he saw to it that Höijer was chosen as the architect. As usual when Höijer was on the job, the work went quickly; and in 1887 the hotel was opened: it had 75 rooms and "an elevator, by means of which one could travel through the whole house." A restaurateur named Gummesson, from Uleåborg, who took over the management a few years later, arrived at the historic decision that gave the house's various publics what they variously desired. The café-restaurant "Lower Kämp" became a favorite luncheon spot for the city's business men; the variety-restaurant, "Upper Kämp," "where the merry life was concentrated," offered entertainment. The latter's programs enchanted the Helsingfors public: the English quintet, "The Five Fishing Girls," cast out lines, baited with tiny panties, over the audience; Geo Jackson, a representative of American culture, encouraged his listeners to "Clap hands, clap hands, clap hands, holy Gee!", the cabaret artist Heinz Buda provided Berlinisms, in gesture and in word. The Kämp restaurants had the temerity to charge high prices, and Upper Kämp eventually succumbed to financial difficulties, being turned into a motion picture theater, the Eldorado, in 1910, but Lower Kämp flourished; twenty years still later, Upper Kämp, ending its film career, became a banquet hall. The flora of myth and legend surrounding Kämp's flourished, too, throughout half a century; the restaurant in the ground floor — serving, of course, not only clear financial heads at noon but cloudier ones at night — is said to have so enchanted Sibelius that he put Finnish words to Dyveke's dance ("Musette") in the King Christian Suite, "Minä menen Kämppiin takaisin" ("I'm going back to Kämp's"), and, during Finland's Winter War, it became known to the world at large as the watering place for international correspondents. Torn down in 1966, it was replaced by a great bank, the Kansallis-Osake-Pankki, albeit its facade was a copy of Höijer's design, an imitation which moved the wit

Henrik Tikkanen, a sometime faithful patron of Kämp, to write: "How much we have learned from Potemkin!"

Kämp, as a well lubricated cultural phenomenon, would deserve an essay in itself, but it did not stand alone, nor even in quadruple majesty with Catani's, König's, and that special case, the Chapel; Gambrini's was also popular (it had a giant samovar, out of whose spigots different kinds of brandy could be drawn), and "Operakällaren" ("The Opera Cellar," which in fact was in the Swedish Theater), and, feeding more exotic tastes, the Bodega Espanola on the neglected South Esplanade. For lighter and quieter refreshments, there were the city's cafés, Viennese neither in number nor atmosphere, but pleasant all the same. Fazer's, founded at the beginning of the 'nineties, ruled the field (in which Catani's and Kämp's had also competed before their transformation into full restaurants), and no wonder: Karl Fazer had the best of training, having studied sugar baking in imperial Saint Petersburg, and the strongest of support — from wealthy Karl Herman Renlund who, enormously fat, must have been a good judge of Fazer's wares. Yet Fazer was unable to lure all the customers away from familiar Ekberg, whose finest hour had come during the exposition of 1876. The goodies at Fazer's and Ekberg's were too good to stimulate intellectual life, though; literary Finlanders seem to require something stronger than coffee and cakes: Helsingfors has never quite had a Silberner Löffel, a Schwarzenberg. From a moral stand-point, one must approve the efforts made by August Ludvig Hartwall, Finland's king of soft drinks, to preach the advantages of "abstinence beverages" (i.e. his own products) for the capital and the land; he took his job so seriously that, in 1890, he made a research-trip to the continent in order to find out still more about the preparation of such brews. The newspaper article which announced his going bore the faintly ironic title, "Lycka till" (roughly, "Let us wish you all success"). By 1898, Hartwall's labors seemed about to bear fruit; a boycott of alcoholic beverages was proclaimed for the first of May. Marvelous to say, both the Finnish and the Swedish academic choruses pledged their support. (Should one be more astonished at their unanimity of purpose, or at the pledge itself?) Directly, a scene took place in the Chapel which boded ill for the temperance movement; a student lifted his glass, cried "Down with alcohol," and swallowed its contents. Hereafter the cancer (of teetotalism) lay dormant but still alive; in 1919, a prohibition law was passed by the Finnish Diet. In his book about Helsingfors of 1926, Ture Janson devoted a tragic chapter to the city's restaurant life, or what was left of it; "happy Helsingfors" had gone underground in order to survive, and Catani's — reputedly the noblest establishment of them all, where talk progressed undisturbed by music — voluntarily closed its doors forever, "too aristocratic to writhe beneath the dry whip."

16. The Russian Masters

PROHIBITION WAS THE tiniest of clouds, however, during those happy days, and even the Russians, for a long time, had been gracious and grateful masters; had not the charge of the Finnish Guards at Gorniy-Dubnyak, during the Russo-Turkish War of 1877–78, won the undying thankfulness of the czars? All seemed secure: writing his *Cartas finlandesas* in 1894, the Spanish consul (and gifted author) Angel Ganivet y Garcia observed a Finnish election: "To be sure, I am writing from Russia, but Russia . . . is a colossus; it comprises many provinces and vassal and autonomous states; and one of these is Finland, where I can say that, although I have my ears in a completely normal state, I presently have not heard a single groan. Rather, it seems to me that everyone lives quite contentedly in this stern and merciless climate." On the Esplanade, the prominent members of Finno-Swedish society held their corso, promenading from that popular rendezvous, "Edlund's Corner" (where Unionsgatan and the North Esplanade intersect), to Mikaelsgatan, and back again. On the less favored south side, the Finns walked — Yrjö-Koskinen, Jaakko Forsman, Löfberg-Lounasmaa, Danielson-Kalmari. Taking the parkland itself in possession, the regal Leo Mechelin had his morning stroll in the middle, heeding neither those who chose "the Swede's beloved street" to the north, nor "Finn-Footbridge" ("finnspång") to the south. And there was still another presence on the Esplanade, the governor-general, in the shadow of whose palace the Fennomanes strolled; but, since Berg's unlamented departure, it had been occupied by two men of good will and one who managed to scrape by on the popularity of his predecessors. In 1861, Platon Ivanovitch Rokassovsky had returned to the land which he liked, and which liked him; he had been convinced by his long prior stay in Finland as Menshikov's deputy that Finlanders, well treated, would be faithful unto death. It was during Rokassovsky's governorship that Alexander II paid the most glorious of all his visits to Helsingfors, for the diet's opening. Alexander was received with sheer adoration; in the crowd, a little boy was trampled to death by a gendarme's horse, and the story went around that Alexander, learning of the accident, said that he would have stayed at home rather than to cause the death of a child. Uttered or not, the remark suited Alexander's humane personality, and the notion the Finns had of him; like his representative Rokassovsky, he gained by the fact that he was a "family man." Returning from the maneuvers at Parola (where Snellman talked him into granting the Finnish language the rights it deserved), Alexander arrived at Helsingfors in a downpour; as he rode in his open carriage, exposing himself to the rain, someone cried "Lower your umbrellas," and the crowd obeyed immediately. Alexander was granted the same sort of adoration that the people of Helsingfors had for his friend Aurora Karamzin — he combined kindness with power. Learning of his assassination, as he rode through Saint Petersburg in his carriage on March 13, 1881, Helsingfors was stunned — it could not have happened in Finland.

The city mourned again, the same year, when it lost its second governor-general of pleasant mien and heart. For reasons of health Rokassovsky had retired in 1866; his replacement was Nikolai Adlerberg, a man probably more intelligent than Rokassovsky and destined to become as popular. "It was a mild and peaceful time, and a mild and peaceful governor-general ruled the country." Religion, or religions, could have been a stumbling block for Adlerberg. A born Lutheran, of Swedish extraction, Adlerberg had become a convert to the Orthodox faith, and practiced it zealously; he was likewise deeply in love with Russian culture. The Russian Theater was his work, as was the Russian Gymnasium; but, as Ahrenberg observed, "he did not wish to suppress the two domestic cultures, he rather wanted to elevate his own." A German and a Roman Catholic, Adlerberg's wife was also a source of some peril for him. Across from Saint Henry's Church (the work, it will be recalled, of Berg's Roman Catholic spouse), Madam Adlerberg opened a school for children of her faith, on money collected from co-religionists in distant Bavaria. The school directly became a mote in the eye of the city's Lutheran clergymen, who claimed that the teaching sisters were proselytizing the school's Protestant charges; the Russian military authorities complained that the pupils, mostly the children of troops stationed on Sveaborg, were being turned into little German patriots. Amalie Adlerberg's beauty and charity had already won her many friends in Helsingfors; and her husband, realizing that his subjects' memories of the Thirty Years' War were still curiously vivid, persuaded her not to allow her popularity, and his, to be spoiled by her project: the school was made to pass into oblivion. The good people of Helsingfors now were infinitely more tolerant of the many Orthodox believers in their midst than of the handful of Roman Catholics, in part because there was not much they could do about the Russians and their church, in part because the Orthodox priests provided an assortment of free entertainments. (In particular, the Russian Easter celebration on Skatudden had become an annual spectacle, if one is to believe the account of the pseudonymous "Jung Junior.") The longer Adlerberg stayed in Finland, the greater his understanding of the national mood grew, and the more clever his treatment of it; even the students came to love him, singing: "Hurrah for our governor-general, / He's our man, / And wields his sceptre o'er our land, / Our Dun-der-berg!" — the last line a play on his name and his deceptively stern manner. After Alexander III came to the throne, and Adlerberg submitted his resignation, a brother of the former governor-general made a prophecy; the time would soon come, he said, when the people of Finland would be glad if they could get him back.

The years of Alexander III's reign were paralleled, in Helsingfors, by the incumbency of Feodor Logginovitch Heiden, a native, as it were, of the city — born on Sveaborg in 1821, while his father was the music-loving commandant there. Heiden was inclined, at first, to follow in the footsteps of his immediate predecessors; Professor Rein sums up his initial behavior neatly: "[he] gave evidence of friendly feelings toward our land, and now and then caused rebuttals to appear in the Russian official newspapers against the [anti-Finnish] accusations of the [Russian] nationalist press." Heiden was especially popular among Finnish-speakers, because of the partiality he demonstrated for their cause; Yrjö-Koskinen was frequently a guest in his palace beside "Finn-Footbridge." In this behavior, some observers thought they detected a trace of divide-and-conquer; and they were correct. Like master, like man: the new Alexander was by no means as generously disposed toward Finland and its special status as his father had been. In the inexhaustible store of Ahrenberg's anecdotes about events historical or apocryphal, one tale concerns Alexander III's visit to Helsingfors in 1885. "It was a beautiful day . . . the harbor shone like a sheet of metal . . . Suddenly 'Our Country' resounded: everyone took off his hat, the empress herself [formerly Dagmar of Denmark] removing the caps from her boys' heads, but the emperor did not stir. Those of us standing in the rear noticed how she plucked at his sleeve — he did not stir. She whispered to him, she implored again and again." Only at the very end did he uncover. Rumor mongers (and Finnish enthusiasts?) had it that Alexander's antipathy to Finland was born on the day when, sailing through the Finnish skerries, he saw the Swedish flag flying beside the summer villa of a Helsingfors family. The influence which the nationalist Pobyedonostzev had upon him, the promulgation of measures undermining the sense of security which Finland had acquired during the reign of Alexander II, the incorporation of the Finnish postal system into Russia's, the dissolving of the Finnish committee in the imperial department of state, the statute commanding preferential treatment for Russian natives in the governor-general's office, the statute concerning better official employment for applicants with a command of Russian — all these events belong to the history of Finland, not just of Helsingfors. (With his keen

eye and his gift for the pungent phrase, Agathon Meurman summed up
Finland's growing anxiety on the first page of his tractate, *Finland förr och
nu* [*Finland Before and Now*], published in 1890, the year of the postal
manifesto: "The existence of this little people, happy within itself, beside
the Russian one, wounds Russian national sensibilities.") Pathetically, effort after effort was made to think the best of Alexander; encouragement
was found in the fact that he spent his summers along Finland's shores,
maintaining a spartan vacation home at Langinkoski, outside Kotka.
(Simplicity, even if affected, was a virtue in Finnish eyes.) As for Heiden,
he contributed his mite to the program of Russification by his proposals
for "Ordinances concerning the governmental procedures of the Grand
Duchy of Finland," which declared, i.a., that the Finnish diet only had an
advisory function, and that Russian was, in fact, the land's official
tongue — a trial balloon, but a frightening one. Fear was increased when
Heiden issued new press-regulations, granting the governor-general the
exclusive right to permit the publication of periodicals in Finland, and "to
have publication of a newspaper cancelled, temporarily or forever, in accordance with his opinion." Adding insult to injury, Heiden also forbade
newspaper editors to receive foreign journals in uncensored form.

On April 29, 1894, Alexander II's birthday, Walter Runeberg's statue
of the good emperor was unveiled on Senate Square. Heiden was annoyed
that he should have to share the speaker's desk with the leader of Finland's
constitutionalists, Leo Mechelin. It must have been an unforgettable tableau: the aristocratic and silver-tongued Mechelin opposite Heiden, "little
and dumpy and very gray," sensing the crowd's dislike but aware, still, that
he was the mightiest man in Finland. Five years later, matters had come to
such a pass that the people of Helsingfors — still wanting desperately,
many of them, to be loyal to Saint Petersburg — surrounded the pedestal
of the statue with flowers on the anniversary of Alexander II's death, and
stood in silence for a while. Then they sang "A Mighty Fortress" and
"Our Country." Juhani Aho wrote a patriotic story about it, "Kohtaus
Keisarin patsaalla" ("The Event Beside the Emperor's Statue"); hearing
the anthem's words, a policeman, a former soldier, salutes, in defiance of
new regulations. A lady in the crowd throws him a bouquet; and "picking
up the flowers, he placed them by the foot of the lion on the pedestal —
the lion of the law." That law (so citizens of Finland believed) had been
guaranteed by Alexander I, recognized by Alexander II, and abused by Alexander III; the last of these had died in the year of the statue's dedication. Now Nicholas II was Czar, bent on pursuing his father's course.
Albert Edelfelt, commissioned to do a portrait of the young ruler, had
thought he detected signs of hope for the future: Nicholas looked "well
brought up, a European." The painter had been led astray by his custom-

ary admiration for good manners, as he subsequently confessed. Edelfelt had also seen an acquaintance from Finland when he went to Moscow for Nicholas's coronation, an officer in the Chevalier Guard. To his mother, Edelfelt wrote that "Gustaf Mannerheim marched before the Czar's baldachin, his saber drawn, and had a very courtly air — really splendid." There were those in Finland who thought that Carl Robert Mannerheim's son served the Czar too well.

17. A Modern Epilogue

ALL THE WHILE, Helsingfors went its way toward modernity. Daniel Johan Wadén was not much more than a boy when, with an engineer's single-mindedness, he founded the first electrical shop in Helsingfors, and set about installing electric connections wherever a property owner was for-ward-looking enough to want them. By the turn of the century, thirty pri-vate electric-power concerns had sprung up; another nine years and the city established its own electric works, putting its various rivals out of business. Wadén gave the city another Pandora's box as well, its first tele-phone system (1882); in the catalogue, the initial name belonged to Hugo Standertskjöld, who had the reputation of being Finland's richest man. Here again a battle was joined between private concerns, if only two in this case; it ended, in 1891, with the establishment of the Helsingfors Telephone Union, owned not by the city but by the subscribers them-selves. (A unification had had to come quickly in the telephone's case, since the one private concern would not transmit calls to the other.) A fi-nal sign that Helsingfors was almost ready to enter the twentieth century came with the establishment of Helsingfors' "Streetcar and Omnibus Stock Company" in 1888 and the opening of regular horse-car lines in 1890, east and west between Sörnäs and Lappviksgatan, north and south between "ultima Tölö," as wags still called it, and Brunnsparken. (The or-ganizational genius was still another of those many Finlanders who had gone thorugh the Finnish Cadet School and served with distinction in the Russian military, Georg Fraser, retired as a colonel in 1887. In his long life, Fraser — dying only two years before the outbreak of the Winter War — became an advocate of the world-peace movement and of strict teetotalism.) By 1908, the horses were replaced by electric trolleys. The populace had some misgivings about the new contraptions, and despite Finnish stoicism, revealed their anxiety under stress. One dark day, as a streetcar was crossing Long Bridge on the way to Hagnäs Square, the lights went out. Someone shouted: "Now it's going to explode!"

III. 1898–1918

1. In Bobrikov's Days

OLD ZACHRIS TOPELIUS died in his home at Björkudden on March 12, 1898; eight days later, his body was brought into Helsingfors — by sleigh, over roads that had vanished beneath a new snow — for final services and interment. On March 21, after the ceremonies at Saint John's Church, the funeral procession set out through the streets of the capital, hung with mourning black; "the closer the clock came to four, the more the crowds on the sidewalks grew, until they formed an impenetrable wall, beginning at the church and ending only at the edge of the open grave" — a long way across Helsingfors, down Högbergsgatan to Lilla Robertsgatan, then along Georgsgatan to the Boulevard, then up Fredriksgatan to Lappviksgatan and the cemetery. (Elmer Diktonius' first childhood memory was of the "multitude of droskies" in the *cortège*.) When the mountain of wreaths, carried by 200 students, had been placed on the grave and the last hymns sung, there came another of those spontaneous performances of "Our Country"; then more snow began to fall, and the crowds went home. It was the end an age whose men, hesitantly or wholeheartedly, had trusted the emperors (now more and more frequently called czars), meanwhile loving their little country and hoping to maintain its special position nestled at Russia's side; Topelius had been the last survivor, his companion heroes having long since passed away — Runeberg in 1877, Snellman and Cygnaeus in 1881, Lönnrot in 1884, Pacius in 1891. Presently, the Russians meant to show Finland that a different time had come. On July 19, 1898, the Estates General were told that an extraordinary session would be held six months hence, to consider the incorporation of the Finnish military into the Russian army; on August 29, Nikolai Ivanovitch Bobrikov was appointed as governor-general, a man of sixty with a reputation for ruthlessness. Bobrikov assumed office in October; in an introductory speech delivered at his palace for members of the Senate and directors of governmental bureaus, he made a point of saying (in Russian, the only language he spoke) that: "Within the boundless reaches of the Russian Empire, there exists for all those people who stand beneath the mighty sceptre of the czar only *one* sort of allegiance and *one* sort of patriotism." Thiodolf Rein, who was present as the vice-chancellor of the university (a post from which he would later be temporarily removed, at Bobrikov's orders), noted laconically, after Alexis

Gripenberg, the director of Finland's prisons, had translated Bobrikov's words for him: "Unpleasant prospects."

Nicholas II had a largish reservoir of Finnish goodwill on which to draw, thanks to his grandfather; but, as old Emil Nervander said in a poem addressed to the czar, "You were rich, and gave our love away." "Chased it away" might have been a better phrase; on February 15, 1899, an imperial manifesto was read to the Senate by Bobrikov, freshly returned from a visit in Saint Petersburg, the "February Manifesto" by which — to make a long story short — Finland's constitution in effect was cancelled. The Estates General found themselves restricted to a giving of opinions only on those imperial laws which concerned "Finland alone," the czar and his councillors had complete charge of matters mutually concerning Russia and the Grand Duchy. The czar himself would decide which cases belonged to the imperial province, and which did not. Leo Mechelin said: "Now the door [has been] opened for whatever claims the Russians deign to make." Thus the "ofärdsår," the "sortokausi," the "time of oppression" began; its description falls properly into Finland's history, and not the history of Helsingfors alone. The humiliations followed swiftly, one on the heels of the other; the czar refused to accept a petition signed with more than 500,000 names, begging him to remember the promises of his forebears; the press of Finland was subjected to new and stern applications of the censorship law, with the result that, between 1899 and 1905, 25 newspapers, 10 in Swedish and 15 in Finnish, were "permanently discontinued." The most gallant of these victims were Axel Lille's *Nya Pressen*, forced to cease publication in the summer of 1900, and *Päivälehti*, the organ of the "Young Finns," which met the same fate four years later. (One is reminded of Juhani Aho's sketch, "Painajainen" ("The Nightmare"), about a man who dreamt he had discontinued all the newspapers of Finland.) The Russian efforts to do away with a separate Finnish military, begun even before the February manifesto, resulted in the dissolving of the Finnish battalions in 1900, with the exception of the Guards. Another of Finland's special military institutions, the cadet school at Fredrikshamn, whose notorious hazing had produced so many distinguished officers for the Russian army, survived until 1903, when it was closed at Bobrikov's behest. The question of what to do with draftees from Finland, which had had universal military service since 1878 (a by-product of the Russo-Turkish War, and its enthusiasms?), was treated in a somewhat more gingerly fashion by the Russians; for the time being Finland had only to supply such members as were needed for filling the vacancies in the Guards — thus, in 1902, a mere 280 men. What the future would hold, no one was sure, but it was feared that someday, the Russian foot having been placed in the door, citizens of Finland would be compelled to do military service in the Russian army proper. Other methods of Russification were boldly employed: the "language manifesto" of June 20, 1900, which gave Russian a predominant place "in certain of the administrative offices of the Grand Duchy"; the decree concerning the necessity of obtaining the governor-general's permission to hold "public meetings"; and the quaint decision to allow pedlars free movement in Finland, intended to afford easy circulation to Russian agitators. The last-named measures were approved by Nicholas a few days *after* the Estates General had ended its business in the early summer of 1900; it would not be summoned again for four years. By 1903, Bobrikov had what amounted to dictatorial powers; he could dissolve any institution or organization he regarded as "dangerous," and he could deprive persons "likely to cause trouble" of the right to reside in Finland — in other words, he could send his opponents into exile. Axel Lille had left Finland of his own volition, even before Bobrikov got the power to put him out; he was followed by other distinguished citizens of Helsingfors: among them, the constitutionalists Leo Mechelin and Rabbe Axel Wrede, the leader of the Young Finns, Jonas Castrén, and Eero Erkko of *Päivälehti*, Victor Magnus von Born, the chieftain of the Swedish Party, and the financier Carl Mannerheim, whose younger brother Gustaf — thanks to his good looks and knowledge of horse-flesh — graced the household troops of Bobrikov's master. (For the boulevardier Wenzel Hagelstam, the editor of the art-magazine *Ateneum*, the place to which he fled was so attractive that he left it only as an old man: Hagelstam remained in Paris, as the correspondent of *Hufvudstadsbladet*, from 1904 until 1923.)

The reactions to Russian oppression were many and varied. The Old Finns had followed a policy of "compliance" from the outset; Yrjö-Koskinen argued their case in an open letter to his friends, written on the occasion of his seventieth birthday: "a strong folk-spirit is the surest defence against external oppression," as the great Snellman himself had said once upon a time. The Finnish people should "look the truth in the eye, and, to the extent it turns out to be necessary, give way to the external pressures of history." Thus Snellman's Hegelianism continued to serve as a good excuse for odd behavior among his successors; Yrjö-Koskinen saw a chance, in the submission of the Finns to Russian despotism, to break the back of the Swedish Party, and so to let history take its Hegelian course here, too: "All connections with the so-called Swedish Party should be broken off, since [it] consists only of 'Vikings' [the reference is to Freudenthal's adherents and their long-dead paper], for whom the existence of the Finnish people is unimportant in comparison to the supremacy of the Swedish language." The performance of the septuagenarian, who also derided the Young Finns of Castrén as "a tail of the Swedish dog that wags in Finnish" (one of the classic insults of Finnish politics), must have provided considerable solace for Bobrikov. Pithy sayings bloomed handsomely in this atmosphere: the widower Agathon Meurman, enraged at Yrjö-Koskinen's successful attempts to obtain the promulgation of the February manifesto in the Senate, had damned his once beloved colleague with another deathless remark: "God took my wife, the Russians took my fatherland, the devil took my best friend." On February 18, 1901, the second anniversary of the promulgation, the members of the Senate were paid a visit at their homes by a crowd bent on insulting them for what was regarded as their pusillanimity of two years before; and lights were turned out all over Helsingfors, as a sign of lamentation at Finland's disgrace. Yrjö-Koskinen, the poor old man, was given an especially unfriendly serenade by a mob gathered in front of his house; he died on November 13, 1903, and was pursued even beyond the grave by the mocking voices. After the first phase of the "time of oppression" had ended, in March, 1906, a musical review called *Carnival* was presented at the Arcadia Theater, which had become the home of the Swedish Folk Theater, the latest tenant in the rickety old house. In *Carnival*'s second act there appeared, among others, the figure of one Bobban (Bobrikov's nickname among Finlanders) and a frail but fiery old man closely resembling the late Yrjö-Koskinen, as well as Old Scratch, who carried the first two down to hell. Once the review's contents were known, its performances were interrupted in the familiar style: students from "Suomalainen Nuija" whistled, stamped their feet, and uttered the long-winded battle cry: "Shall we allow one of the great men of the Finnish cause to be insulted in this fashion?" The ensuing riot convinced the direction that the shade of Yrjö-Koskinen should vanish from the Arcadia for good and all; in retrospect, Veikko Antero Koskenniemi, an accessory to the fact, justified mob rule by writing that not only the memory of Yrjö-Koskinen but the very stage of Kaarlo Bergbom's old theater had been desecrated by the performace. The language struggle did not subside, then, during these years of Russian threat; but healthy signs appeared — the alliance between the Swedish Party and the Young Finns, and the noble paraphrase which Jonas Castrén made upon the Fennomane slogan, "Yksi kieli, yksi mieli," "One tongue, one spirit." Now it should read, Castrén said: "Yksi mieli, vaikka kaksi kieltä," "One spirit, even though two tongues."

As the capital of the hard-pressed land, Helsingfors became by necessity the scene of decisive and sometimes dramatic events — the formation, for example, of "Kagalen" at Turholm Estate outside the city in August, 1901, an organization in which both Swedish and Finnish speakers took part, and which had a program of passive resistance to the Russians. (Its name was a Hebrew word used by the Russians as an insulting term for

Jewish secret societies inside Russia, and then transferred to anti-Russian forces in Finland, who received it as a badge of honor.) The main fruit, probably, of passive resistance was the "draft strike" of April, 1902, in which only 4.4% of the men summoned to report for military duty appeared — 57 out of a possible 855, and of the 57, 19 changed their minds and went away. The students of "Nyland's nation" had been particularly effective in organizing the demonstration; at the Nylanders' annual festival on April 2, 1902, the first to be held in their new building on Kaserngatan (designed, not inappropriately, by the magnificently named Swede, Karl Hård af Segerstad), Axel Lille — almost ready to go into Swedish exile — had publicly uttered the slogan, "Away from Russia — away from the tree whose shadow burns the earth, so that it bears only thorns and thistles." Unhappily, the throng of onlookers assembled outside the "Gardesmanege" on April 17 was more interested in excitement than in effective resistance to Russian designs; they managed to provoke the police (by this time infiltrated with recruits from Estonia who, the Russians assumed, would be more loyal to imperial authority than native Finns), and the result was scuffling and bloodied noses. On the evening of the next day, another incident took place on Senate Square; the crowd hurled insults at some passing senators, making the new "procurator," Eliel Johnsson — shortly to be ennobled as Soisalon-Soininen — the particular object of their invective. (It was the "procurator's" task, among other things, to determine the order in which matters were taken up by the Senate; Johnsson's predecessor, Woldemar Söderhjelm, had tried to postpone the promulgation of the February manifesto, intending to present his objections, taken from a constitutional standpoint, to the czar himself. "Transferred" out of his post, Söderhjelm resigned from the Senate altogether.) An insult cast at Johnsson was an insult cast at Bobrikov; the new governor of Nyland province, a Russian named Kaigorodov, called out the Cossacks. It was the first time this peculiarly Russian measure had been taken in Finland's capital — the Cossacks, probably bored with their long inactivity, were glad for the opportunity to exercise: they rode their horses up the magnificent and very steep stairs of Engel's great church, they swung their whips with a happy vengeance; but the Finns, persistent as always, kept surging back toward the statue of Alexander II from the corners of the square. The skirmishing continued for three hours, until evening; then the Cossacks were replaced by a company of the Guards, and the rioters, mollified, went home. Kaigorodov got a new nickname, Nagaikarodov, from the Russian "nagaika" or "whip," and the whole of Scandinavia was shocked by the employment of "Cossack methods" on its very doorstep.

During 1903, the strike against the draft was less effective, since Bobrikov now had the aid of his dictatorial powers, and of the Old Finns'
propaganda: ten students of draft age issued a statement in which they appealed to their contemporaries to follow the obedient line of Yrjö-
Koskinen and Johnsson. A victim of the 1903 draft was the mayor of
Helsingfors, Elias Öhman, a nephew of the Borgå publisher who had
given Runeberg the idea of writing *Fänrik Stål*; the city of Helsingfors had
refused to name members, or substitutes, for the draft board in 1902, and
Bobrikov saw to it that Öhman was removed from his post in March,
1903, on the eve of the new draft summons. Out at Lovisa, a physician,
Dr. K.O. Hoffström, shot himself rather than serve as an inspecting physician at the spring summons of 1904. In the long run, the country's pro-
verbial obstinacy triumphed; obligatory service in the Russian army never
became a reality in Finland and, after the sudden disbanding of the Finnish
Guards in 1905, the whole matter was conveniently forgotten. "When the
Russians observed the stubborn resistance, they deemed it unprofitable —
perhaps even dangerous, if one thought of the future — to train the
youths of Finland."

Quite naturally, thoughts had also arisen of a more active opposition to
Russian programs. Johannes Hoving, who eventually went to America as a
refugee from Bobrikov, tells of a meeting held at an elegant residence in
Brunnsparken sometime during the winter of 1900–01: a junior captain of
the fire-department, one Sjöblom, volunteered to shoot Bobrikov from a
window in the Grönqvist Building while the governor-general took his
afternoon stroll on the South Esplanade. In return, Sjöblom wanted
enough money to get out of the country, and the promise that his family
would be looked after. The plan came to naught; a continuation of passive
resistance was agreed upon by the thinnest of majorities. As Heiden once
observed, "the people of Finland want to have law in everything." Nor did
those who preached active resistance always inspire complete confidence.
One of their leaders was the much-published Konrad (or Konni) Zilliacus,
journalist, author, and adventurer, who had spent many years abroad (in
America, Japan, Egypt), only to be lured back to Finland — by the love of
country or the love of excitement? — in 1899, just in time to find his
place in history as a busy organizer of derring-do against the Russians; he
was able to satisfy his penchant for travel by making a specialty of gun-
running. Inside Finland, the plans to assassinate Bobrikov continued, giving birth to low comedy and high tragedy. An example on the former
score is the story of John William Nylander, a sea-captain from Ekenäs
(and, as time showed, a gifted writer of sea-stories), who, together with a
burly medical student named Lennart Hohenthal, waited by the statue of

The Castaways on Observatory Hill, prepared to drop a bomb on Bobrikov as he passed along the avenue below: the governor-general did not come.

The assassination was finally accomplished by an outsider, a member of no conspiratorial group. Eugen Schauman had been born in Kharkov, the son of a Finno-Swedish officer in the Russian army; sent back to Helsingfors as a boy, where he lived for a while with relatives, the August Schaumans, he had been teased by his schoolmates at "Nya svenska läroverket" because of his Russian accent in Swedish. Waldemar Schauman, the father, returned to Finland in 1889, to serve as chief of staff of the Finnish military; he then became governor of Vasa Province as General Järnefelt's successor in 1894, and appeared to have reached the apex of his career in 1898 with an appointment as senator and head of the Senate's military department. Unhappily, Bobrikov came to Helsingfors at the same time; on the eve of the February manifesto affair, the governor-general summoned General Schauman to a dinner, together with various "loyal" colleagues from the Senate, a summons which Schauman, as Bobrikov's military subordinate, believed he could not refuse. During the dinner, held in a salon whose windows afforded passers-by on Fabiansgatan a fine view of the proceedings, Bobrikov approached Schauman, gave him a moist Russian kiss, and said: "He is a wise fellow." The episode immediately became the talk of Helsingfors. General Schauman, sensing that he was compromised by Bobrikov's show of friendship, nonetheless continued to argue for Finland's rights as a part of his official task, until he was abruptly removed from his military post; a year later, in 1900, he resigned from the Senate altogether. His son Eugen was quite aware of the ugly light in which his father had been placed; and the young man appears to have felt that the blow he received from a Cossack whip during the draft riots was a humiliation of a related sort. According to by-standers, Schauman, slight of build, became so enraged that he pulled the soldier from his horse and knocked him to the pavement.

On June 16, 1904, at 11:00 in the morning, Eugen Schauman waited for Bobrikov to come to the Senate; as the governor-general climbed up the stairs, Schauman approached him, shot him three times with his Browning, and then turned the gun on himself, dying instantly. Bobrikov was less fortunate than his executioner; he walked through several chambers before he collapsed. Taken home and examined, he was discovered to have received "two gunshot wounds in the submaxillary region, as well as another wound near the navel." At his own request, Bobrikov was taken to the University's Surgical Clinic rather than the Russian Military Hospital; the emergency operation showed that the wound in the abdomen would probably be mortal. He died early the next morning. His medical care had been excellent — the attending physicians included Hjalmar von

Bonsdorff, Ali Krogius, and Richard Faltin, the musician's son — but the inner organs had been too severely damaged by the shot which, according to Faltin's report, "entered the abdominal cavity in a deformed and splintered condition." Faltin offered the opinion that the bullet had struck a metal object, a belt buckle, on its way into the victim's body; but Sigrid Schauman recalled a conversation she had with her elder brother a few weeks before the assassination. A friend, on leave from the Russo-Japanese War in Manchuria, had told him that "the man who gets a dum-dum bullet in his belly is finished." Bobrikov was given a state funeral in Saint Petersburg; Schauman was buried at the Malm Cemetery, an out-of-the-way place chosen by the Russian officials, in a macabre ceremony, during which the attendant police urinated within sight of the mourners.

In 1906, Schauman's body was removed to the family plot at Borgå, and given a more solemn and public interment; by this time the Russian pressure had lightened, a result, mainly, of the difficulties in which Russia found itself following the defeat by Japan. It is impossible to say what part Schauman's deed had played in the change of Russian policy in Finland; before he died, he sent the czar a letter in which he designated himself as His Majesty's most faithful subject, arguing that the assassination was intended to call the ruler's attention to "the true situation in the empire." If the czar got to read the letter, he should have been shaken by its contents, at least if he recalled them when another of his advisors, von Plehve, Russian secretary of the interior (and, simultaneously, secretary of state for Finland), was blown to bits by a Russian assassin's bomb in Saint Petersburg a little more than a month later; but there were reports that he wrote "a madman" on the envelope. As for the departed Bobrikov, he had thought all along that he was doing his duty to czar and country; a pathetic quality attaches to his deathbed question: "Pochemu?", "Why?" And there is, as well, something a little distasteful about the rejoicing which took place in Helsingfors on the night of June 16; never before had so much champagne been consumed in the city. Of course, the assassination called forth other reactions as well: thoughtful persons realized the gravity of what had happened; some feared reprisals, others, like Leo Mechelin, regarded the shooting as murder, however noble Schauman's motives may have been, and still others, in the Old Finnish camp, were horrified at the "Swedish act." Axel Lille, however, venerated Schauman's memory, and kept the young man's picture on his study wall, with the words written on it: "Fallen after a deed well-done for the fatherland."

Schauman's example found its imitators. The following winter, Lennart Hohenthal — most recently seen as he stood atop Observatory Hill, a bomb in his briefcase — performed an assassination in Helsingfors which showed what damage glory-seekers can do to the best of causes. "A splendid swimmer, strong as a bear, and a first-rate sailor," as Hoving described him, Hohenthal cut a fine figure as he approached the residence of the former Eliel Johnsson, now officially Soisalon-Soininen, on the morning of February 6, the day after Runeberg's birthday: Hohenthal was clad in the uniform of an officer in the Russian Lifeguards' Light Infantry. Speaking Russian, he deposited a visiting card and was allowed by the Finnish detective on duty to enter the office of the procurator. Once admitted to the lofty presence, he pulled out his revolver and shot Soisalon-Soininen several times; the procurator fell dead into the arms of his wife, who had run into the room. The victim's teen-aged son tried to catch the assassin, and was shot in the leg for his trouble; the detective, awake at last to his duty, shot Hohenthal in the same place. Captured, Hohenthal was put on trial and defended by Pehr Evind Svinhufvud, a prominent jurist and a member of the "Kagal"; condemned to life imprisonment, he escaped from the prison on Skatudden, aided by two members of Nyland's nation and a lovely young woman. The saga ends very happily: arriving in England, Hohenthal wedded his fair rescuer. The handsome fellow seems a great deal less heroic than Schauman, even as his victim is more wretched than Bobrikov. Thiodolf Rein offered the opinion that the procurator was simply too insignificant (this "boring and exceedingly solemn man," Alma Söderhjelm called him) to change anything in Finland; once the Russians had decided to take a gentler course in the Grand Duchy, Soisalon-Soininen could certainly not alter their intentions, although the death of a willing tool might have been used by them, under other circumstances, as an excuse for reprisals. The bereaved Old Finns had been given a "martyr, who fell a sacrifice for his patriotic deeds"; the fact that the illegal Finno-Swedish paper *Fria ord* (*Free Words*) praised Hohenthal's deed and compared it to Schauman's scarcely helped to bridge the chasm between Finland's various brands of patriots. Perhaps the unhappiest note of all was struck by the comrades of the dead procurator's son at "Suomalainen yhteiskoulu"; when the boy returned to classes after recovering from the wound suffered as he defended his father, they ostracized him.

Patriotism had slid over into blind pettiness, and the schoolboys' cruelty was as unnecessary as Hohenthal's bloody masquerade had been. In August, 1904, a new governor-general of a type altogether different from Bobrikov had come to Finland, Ivan Mihailovitch Obolenski, a man who liked the arts and, otherwise, seemed pleasantly lazy; the same month, the members of the Estates General were given notice that they would reconvene in December, and those exiles who belonged to the Estates General were officially urged to return to Finland, "not only as a right but as a duty," an invitation shortly extended to everyone else who had fled. When

Leo Mechelin climbed into his carriage outside the railroad station during
the Advent days of 1904, the delighted crowds unhitched the horses and
themselves pulled the great man to Society House, singing "Our Country" at the top of their lungs. Offering thanks for the thrilling ride, the regal Leo cried: "I am but a simple man, and yet I have been received as if I
were a king."

2. Prince Obolenski and the Great Strike

THE KING HAD returned to a capital that seemed to be on the eve of
brighter days. Obolenski's interests were artistic, not administrative; the
summer villa, Bjälbo in Mejlans, which Ahrenberg had redesigned for Bobrikov (and into which the hard-working despot had never set foot), had
to be done over in accordance with the tastes of the new governor-
general. Colonel Lvovski, Nyland's governor, told Ahrenberg: "it's like a
bivouac now . . . it must become a chalet for the Russian grand
seigneur — the prince is descended from the line of the Ruriks." (In independent Finland, Bjälbo would be the official summer residence of prime-
ministers.) Ahrenberg quickly discovered that the handsome Obolenski
gobbled up flattery; the sly architect assured his master that, with his good
looks, he appeared to come from northern Italy, or from Corsica, a suggestion with which Obolenski was in ready agreement. Whether Obolenski
concealed the military gifts of a Napoleon within him, will remain a mystery forever; he did possess something of the Corsican's magnetism. Upon
hearing Ahrenberg say that life in Finland had been a hell of late (an exaggerated description, if Bobrikov's dictatorship is compared with more recent versions in other lands), Obolenski rejoined that it had not been a
hell but rather a purgatory, and "tout sera beau encore." The prince interested himself in the beauty of Helsingfors: looking at Eliel Saarinen's
sketches for the new railroad station, he found its tower, "ce candelabre,"
quite horrible, and wished to have it removed. Here, Ahrenberg found
himself in the odd position of having to defend Saarinen's tower for reasons of patriotism and professional solidarity, concealing his personal belief
that it was "reprehensible" to erect "these ugly noses at all sorts of possible and impossible places in our classical city."

Obolenski's stay in Helsingfors could have been pleasant and even
amusing for everyone concerned, save the young lions of national-
romantic architecture; but the world was too much with him. In short order, he grew less friendly; his agents had informed him that the Finnish

Guards, partaking in the usual summer encampment at Krasnoye Selo, would mutiny upon their return to Finland, in support of a general uprising. The czar's abrupt decision to disband the glorious regiment, in September, appears to have been taken on Obolenski's advice. Nicholas himself had even better reason than his satrap to be distraught; imperial power had been threatened in Saint Petersburg and Lodz and Odessa.

The autumn of 1905 was uncommonly clement in Helsingfors, a circumstance which encouraged the next outdoor events: the general strike in Russia spilled over into Finland. Out of the turbulence of the strike-week, from Monday, October 30, 1905, until Monday, November 6, one happy fact emerges — no blood was shed. The good luck of Helsingfors, demonstrated in 1808 and in 1855, held again; it may have been aided by common sense in the right places. After the strike had been declared, during a meeting of the workers on Railroad Square at 2:00 on Monday, a struggle for power was played out between three (or perhaps four) factions with as many aims. The workers themselves had a particular goal of obtaining universal suffrage and a vaguer one of otherwise improving their lot, an improvement which took the shape, in some hot spirits, of toppling Russian authority, or Finland's bourgeoisie, or both. Loosely allied with the workers were the activists, determined to obtain independence for Finland at any cost. As ever, the constitutionalists wished to achieve the restoration of lawful procedures of government, something not yet attained, although the Russians had recently given considerable evidence of good will. The Russian officials had the ticklish job of maintaining control of city and country; but they could not be sure of the loyalty of their troops, and, still worse, were in the dark about the strength and intentions of their superiors in Saint Petersburg. In addition, they were concerned with saving their own skins if fighting broke out. Some Russian women and children resident in Helsingfors, among them Obolenski's ladies, made their way to the Uspenski Cathedral and the Naval Barracks on Skatudden; still others went out to Sveaborg, preferring potentially mutinous fellow countrymen to rebellious Finns. When the battleship *Slava* and four other vessels arrived from Reval on Friday of the troubled week, refugees of sufficient importance were taken on board, Obolenski — who had been through a great deal — among them.

A first crisis had occurred on Tuesday, October 31, Halloween in other lands. A crowd assembled at Railroad Square and marched on the governor-general's palace, in which members of the unpopular Senate had found refuge. (The crowd's threats against the senators were, in fact, unnecessary, since the Senate had already decided to request that it be dissolved; but the decision had not yet been made public.) The leader of the activists was a balding man in his late twenties, Arvid Mörne, whom literary history remembers as one of the great poets of Swedish Finland; only recently Mörne had beheld a lyric vision of the event which now became reality — a more complicated reality, to be sure, than he had dreamed, and a reality set against a less optimistic season of the year. Wrapped in euphoria, Mörne had seen the working man of Finland rise up before a vernal background, casting off his chains and his thralldom to a foreign past, which had compelled him to bleed on distant fields for causes quite alien to his own:

> Today the drums are beat no more, and pikes no more are drawn,
> The flag of red's unfurled against the springtime and the dawn.
> Where'er it's borne, in mighty waves a human floodtide streams,
> Because its cloth's a vision of the people's very dreams.
> For now at last they fight *their* fight, and now at last they know
> Whither through springtime's trees of green the flag of red will go.

In his autobiographical novel, *Ett liv* (*A Life*), Mörne later minimized the importance of his own role in the events of the strike-week, emphasizing instead the "awakening sense of youth in the people's soul." Nonetheless it was Mörne who held an impassioned speech on the steps of the palace, in which he proposed that a deputation be sent in to the governor-general, to ask both for his resignation (what a bold slap in the czar's face!) and that of the Senate; and it was Mörne who, once inside, confronted Obolenski, demanding to see the Senators to whom the Russians had given shelter. Very much in character, Obolenski retorted that he did not wish to inconvenience his guests; and Mörne, combining rudeness with rhetoric, made another oration: "The people, who strike and are hungry, have sent us here; they cannot pay heed to the requirements of good manners." Then he flung open the door of an adjoining room in which — some heavenly dramatist must have arranged the scene — the nervous Senators were seated. During all these magnificent and dangerous actions, Obolenski maintained a calm that aroused the admiration even of his opponents; he watched and listened "dispassionately, without changing his expression or his stance; a forced smile passed over his . . . swollen face only at the mention of his resignation." The reporter here is August Schauman's son, Georg, who was present as a member of the constitutionalist delegation in Obolenski's headquarters; despite Schauman's dislike for the Russian, he knew that the fate of Helsingfors rested in Obolenski's hands just now, and admired his self-control. The crowd outside on the Esplanade grew ever more restive; a false alarm, that the Cossacks were coming, caused a panic, the iron railing between the street and the Chapel broke, and a good many demonstrators tumbled over into the restaurant's property. (The next day 341 galoshes, 95 umbrellas, and 100 hats were found, signs that, in autumnal Helsingfors, fine weather or not, rioters must be properly dressed.) When, at last, the report was made from the steps that the Senate had asked to be dismissed, the crowd grew calm; having performed "Our Country," it trudged across the grass to Runeberg's statue, singing the "March of the Men of Björneborg" from *Fänrik Stål.* The people who, in Runeberg's words, had bled on Narva's heath, on Poland's sand, on Leipzig's plain and Lützen's ridges, had not been required to fight Obolenski's troopers on the Esplanade.

Another danger existed, to be sure: that the newly constituted "Red Guard" of the workers and the "Defence Corps" of university and technical students might collide; on Wednesday morning, Schauman, at once actor and observer, took a stroll through the city: "No newspapers, no traffic, men with white or red armbands everywhere, keeping order, women with a white cross passing out small change and food, and even medical students with a red cross — an ugly implication." Fearing for its safety, the regular police force had gone on strike; in order to fill the gap, the rival factions in the city had set up their own militias. On Monday evening, Matti Kurikka, the leader of the Social Democrats, had given his colleague, the tailor and political writer Kaarlo Luoto, permission to organize a "National Guard"; it had two sections, one for carrying out normal police functions, the other for "military purposes": this second section shortly got the sobriquet of "Red Guard." The "Student Defence Corps," however, regarded its own function solely as that of keeping order in the streets, since even the city's illumination had vanished: the gas and electric works were closed down. A member of the Worker's Central Strike Committee and a former officer in the disbanded Viborg Sharpshooters' Battalion, Captain Johan Kock, had emerged as the commander of the "National Guard," by reason of his military experience; he was enviously seconded by Eero Haapalainen, a student who had direct responsibility for the police section, and by Luoto of the military branch. In addition, Kock was in theoretical control of the Defence Corps; but its members were scarcely inclined to obey his commands. The former chief of police, Colonel Ivar Gordie, removed during the Bobrikov regime, would have been to the taste of the students and the city fathers, but he refused to take back his old post, knowing full well that the workers, on their side, would not follow him. Thus poor Kock, a nervous and kindly man, had duty after duty heaped upon him. A product like Kurikka of "Suomalainen alkeiskoulu" in Helsingfors, and Kurikka's close friend, Kock was a convinced and idealistic leftist; Georg Schauman met him, worn out and shaky, at the end of the strike. "Kock made a shy and pleasant impression on me. A number of his acquaintances have assured me that he is an honest man . . ." [The same claim could not be made, it turned out, for Luoto; in 1906 he was dismissed for embezzling the funds of the Red Guard.]

"Jonas Castrén knows Kock well and says that he is an idealist . . . but that his education was not especially good; he was mentally ill for a while." Even the liberal Schauman could not resist condescension toward the Finn; but Kock, like Obolenski of the bloated face and nervous manner, would keep control of himself and his men at the dangerous moment.

On Tuesday morning the newspapers, still appearing, had printed the manifesto by which Nicholas, or his minister Witte, took the edge off the demands of Russia's revolutionaries; the news helped inspire the march on Obolenski's residence later that day. Presuming that Nicholas would also accede to demands from Finland, the constitutionalists and their allies set to work on a proposal for a second imperial manifesto. The authors of the document were Leo Mechelin, whose motto was "Pro lege," Rabbe Axel Wrede, professor of law and the university's rector, whose initials were taken to mean "Rätt alltid warar" ("Justice lasts forever"), and E.N. Setälä, holder of the chair of Finno-Ugric studies and a leader of the Young Finns. At a preliminary meeting with Obolenski, immediately following the stirring hours when the activist Mörne had invaded the governor-general's salon, J.R. Danielson-Kalmari, the university's vice-chancellor and the bearer of the departed Yrjö-Koskinen's toga, had indicated that his Old Finns would be in agreement with Mechelin's proposal. By Wednesday afternoon, the constitutionalists gave the manifesto a final examination at a conclave in the House of Estates, and saw to its translation into Russian. Obolenski had promised that he would facilitate the handling of the document for the sake of peace, and he did, turning it over on Thursday to General Sjöman of the pilot service for transportation to Saint Petersburg. On board the pilot boat *Eläköön*, Sjöman steamed to Saint Petersburg as quickly as he could; other modes of communication between Helsingfors and the Russian capital had been cut off. Nicholas signed the document at 3:00 on Saturday morning, November 4, and Sjöman sped home again with his precious cargo. In giving his signature to the manifesto, Nicholas appeared to abandon the program of Russification pursued during the past decade; a sinister catch lay in the change that had been made before the czar would sign: the February manifesto of 1899 was suspended, not cancelled. Saturday evening, Obolenski summoned the chieftains of the various factions to his floating citadel, the *Slava*. The manifesto was read to them, and Obolenski took leave of his guests with some touching words. His days in Finland were over.

Early on, the workers had concluded that the establishment, as usual, had acted without consulting them. They had got a chance to partake of the manifesto's contents only at a general assembly in the Fire House on Wednesday, when the document was read aloud; the reader was Georg Schauman, who enjoyed the respect of the powerful Mechelin on the one hand and the radical forces on the other. (Ironically, because of his ability to understand a variety of factional viewpoints, Schauman in time became what Johannes Salminen has called "the great outsider" of Finland's politics.) The reading was interrupted again and again by the cries of the Social Democrats, in particular of the eccentric Jean Boldt, who screamed "Liar, Liar!" at Jonas Castrén, the chairman of the meeting; in a colorfully unreasonable juxtaposition, Boldt demanded the immediate creation of a national assembly and the abolition of saloons and whorehouses in Helsingfors. The manifesto contained some elements which should have been pleasing to the Social Democrats; it commissioned the Senate to work out a plan for the reorganization of the Estates General, "based on general and equal suffrage," as well as laws concerning freedom of expression, assembly, and the press. However, the workers felt no overwhelming trust of the Senate, a point of view which Mechelin, born with a silver spoon in his mouth, found ridiculous: "I have a good conscience," he said, "about always having been a democrat, if not a socialist." Having sampled power, the laboring man understandably wished to try a larger dose; he put his faith in the Tammerfors manifesto (so-called because it was drawn up in the factory city), which demanded, again, a national assembly and, prior to that, installation of an interim government, to be elected "by the individual votes of all men and women over 21." The election did in fact take place, on Saturday afternoon while the *Eläköön* was steaming toward Helsingfors with the manifesto signed by the czar. It was to no one's advantage, this election, since the persons elected never served, and the lengthy procedure caused Kock and his associates to arrive tardily at the meeting on the *Slava*. The perils of the election lay not in its slate (which contained 15 names from the right as opposed to 9 from the left, an indication that the workers either wished to be fair, or to have the appearance of fairness) but in its prelude and aftermath. The bumptious behavior of the Red Guard on election eve, Friday, made everyone anxious, and the anxiety was heightened by the arrival of the Russian ships from Reval, coupled with the show of strength given by the Russian military parade on Market Square: Friday was also the anniversary of Nicholas's coronation, and Obolenski did not let it pass without observation. Then, on Sunday, once the Strike Committee had agreed to an end of the strike and a printing of the manifesto, the Red Guard, embittered by what it thought was a betrayal of its aims, wanted to continue the work-stoppage. In agreement for once, Kock and Luoto urged the militants on.

The official conclusion of the strike was announced for 2:00 on Monday afternoon. The city's businessmen intended to open their shops for the morning trade; the Red Guard forbade them to do so, claiming that they at least must wait until the time agreed upon. Now capitalist and socialist stood eye to eye. Consul Stockmann took up a position outside his department store at the corner of Senate Square, declaring that, having closed his business without the workers' permission, he would open it likewise. At this dramatic and somewhat silly moment (Consul Stockmann could have done without the morning's profits) a detachment of the "Student Defence Corps" appeared, mostly unarmed but all singing; did they remember that November 6 was the day of the battle of Lützen, when Gustaf Adolf, the Swedish lion, had fallen for faith and fatherland? The members of the Red Guard who had been threatening valiant Stockmann swung round to meet the students; the men with red armbands maneuvered nicely, since veterans of the Finnish Guard were in their ranks. The great strike might have belatedly turned into a civil war then and there, had not Captain Kock emerged from the nearby police station. The former officer commanded his socialist troops to withdraw; the Red Guard marched away and the students, not knowing how lucky they were, followed suit. It was Kock's finest hour. At 1:30, the imperial manifesto was distributed in printed form on one side of Senate Square; on the other, Kock — mounted, a black slouch hat on his head — delivered formal thanks to his men. But he did not say goodbye. The Red Guard was one of the enduring products of the great strike, a good deal hardier than some of the constitutional gains the November manifesto had granted.

Briefly, the capital got still another piece of patriotic apparatus during the strike-week. Upon the arrival of news about Witte's manifesto (October 31), the old lion-banner of the Grand Duchy of Finland — a golden lion rampant on a red field — was hung from the windows of the Ateneum, and then flown over the University, the Senate, the City Hall, the Student House; two days later the flags were taken down, at the orders of Eero Haapalainen and Johan Kock. Were they removed to placate Obolenski, as Kock claimed? Or because they seemed to be symbols of an aristocratic tradition which the Social Democrats could not approve? Not only the Social Democrats; the clear-sighted and anxious Georg Schauman was likewise aware that they might irritate the Russians too much: "I thought that the hanging of these flags was stupid . . . Later, they were taken down at Obolenski's command." It had been a gallant gesture; but the Russians still ran the country.

3. Sveaborg, Hagnäs, Seyn: Mutiny and Afterwards

THE NEXT SUMMER Helsingfors tottered once again on the brink of violence and almost fell in; and, once again, as in the case of the great strike, the immediate impulse came from Russia — or from Russia's fortress in Helsingfors harbor. On July 30, 1906, some of the troops on Sveaborg mutinied. It happened very suddenly in the quietest part of the summer; people heard shooting and could scarcely believe it came from the mysterious realm at their doorstep. A Russian colonel, relaxing at his summer villa on Drumsö, got himself rowed out to Sveaborg in order to see what was afoot; as he clambered onto a jetty, soldiers seized him, hung a stone around his neck and cast him into the water to drown. In all haste, the battleships *Slava* and *Czarevitch* and the cruiser *Bogatir* were summoned from Reval; they shelled the batteries on Kungsholmen, held by the mutineers, and the ammunition dump there blew up, an event which broke windows and hurled sleepers from their beds in Helsingfors. At length the rebellious troops, who had seized three islands of the fortress complex and the Naval Barracks on Skatudden, gave up. Despite the difficulties of transport involved, the Red Guard of Helsingfors had tried to come to the mutineers' aid, and some of its members were taken prisoner at the surrender. Thinking to pry them free from the Russian military authorities, and perhaps hoping to recuperate his own sinking political fortunes, Johan Kock called for another general strike, but the response was poor indeed: Finnish summer days are precious, and the city's labor force preferred to use them for recreation. The affair should have ended then, yet it did not; in order to run the city's streetcars, people from the community of Esbo, Swedish-speakers, were brought in; these "espoolaiset," as the Finns called them, were hated both in their capacity as strike-breakers and, it seems, Swedes. At Hagnäs Square, on the southern reaches of Berghäll, the workers' stronghold, the trolleys were stopped by a detachment of the Red Guard, augmented by Russian sailors. The Defence Corps, left over from the great strike, was called out in order to get traffic moving again; here, as in the skirmish at Stockmann's the previous autumn, the Corps' spirit was willing but its weapons too few. After the defence corpsmen had delivered their demand that the trolleys be allowed to move, the Red Guard, determined to use its advantage this time, opened fire. When the smoke had cleared, seven members of the Defence Corps, including its

commander, were dead, together with two of their opponents, and one
policeman, who had been a bystander. At length, Russian troops were
called out to restore order. It presaged the Civil War of 1918, Finlanders
fighting Finlanders out of political conviction. As an aftermath of the
Hagnäs affair, the Defence Corps decided to disband, and the Red Guard
was forbidden to exist by order of the Senate; both organizations came to
life again in 1917, prepared to engage in an immeasurably bloodier encounter. Johan Kock disappeared from Finland's history, fleeing in
woman's disguise — a Bonnie Prince Charlie of the left — to America. A
judgment of Juhani Aho was hurled after him: "Is it possible that such a
madman could have persuaded thousands of people to follow him?" No
one was more intolerant of Finnish failings than the patriot Aho. (Kock
died in Fitchburg, Massachusetts, in 1915; Matti Kurikka, who became a
newspaper man and farmer in Rhode Island, passed away a few months
later.)

Now, at last, Finland seemed to have come out of the storm, stronger
than before. The Senate dominated by Old Finns had been replaced by
Leo Mechelin's constitutionalist body. The final session of the quadripartite Estates General had taken place, closing in September, 1906, with
pomp and circumstance. Victor Magnus von Born gave a purple speech to
his fellow nobles: "Finland's knighthood and nobility has today taken its
place at the head of its land's representatives for the last time, and our
exalted task in the official life of the homeland is concluded. In a few
fleeting moments the tale of the Swedish-Finnish Estates General will have
come to its end, and we almost hear the rustling of history's page as it is
turned." He was surely right; the Finno-Swedes, who had controlled the
four estates under the old system, would now, by the proportional mode
of election, be masters at the most of only an eighth of the voices in the
single-chamber house. The new diet was elected in the spring of 1907,
and, at about the same time, the workers of Helsingfors, perhaps aware of
the moment's symbolic value, laid the cornerstone of their new headquarters on Broholmen, near Hagnäs Square of recent memory. It was called
"The House of the Workers," "Työväen talo" or "Folkets hus," and to
Runar Schildt's eye it was "threatening and gray — the fortified headquarters of a new age"; no doubt it looked cheerier to the inhabitants of Berghäll and Sörnäs. When the elections for the diet were held, it became clear
that, for the nonce, the main contestants in Helsingfors itself were the
city's prosperous Swedes, and the workers, largely Finnish-speaking: the
one side realized that it had to struggle to keep its power, the other that it
had a chance of getting a place in the sun. Even though the proportion of
Swedish speakers in the city's population was declining with some rapidity
(from 42.5% in 1900 to 35.1% in 1910), the recently established Swedish

People's Party, the work of Axel Lille, got 38.3% of the votes cast in Helsingfors in 1907, and so momentarily emerged as the city's largest political entity. The Social Democrats came in second, with 32.1%, and the Old Finns, past behavior not forgotten, as a poor third, with 18.7%. Amusingly enough, the Old Finns swallowed their own hyperconservative tenets (in national politics they were called "the party of pastors and peasants") in order to curry some favor with the Social Democrats, largely their brothers in language. What was it Georg Schauman said of Danielson-Kalmari? "He would creep before the workers, as before the Russians, for the sake of the Finnish language and its supremacy."

The spot of clear weather, such as it was, vanished before it was fairly begun. A well-intentioned and generous man, Nikolai Gerard, was Obolenski's successor as governor-general; in the autumn of 1907, Frans Albert Seyn, once chief of staff to Bobrikov, was appointed as Gerard's adjutant, without Gerard being consulted in the matter; a few months more, and Gerard was relieved of his post, amidst the indications of friendship Helsingfors traditionally gave to the "good governors." (After the Russian revolution, Gerard was given sanctuary by the government of the Republic of Finland at the Halila sanitorium, once upon a time the Karelian summer home of the Clodt von Jürgensburg family.) General Vladimir Boeckman took Gerard's place; likewise deemed to be overindulgent by Saint Petersburg, he gave way in November, 1909, to the waiting Seyn.

The second phase of the "time of oppression," under Seyn's leadership, was less dramatic than the first. The popularly elected diet, although often shunted aside or dissolved, gave the populace the sense of having its voice heard; furthermore, Russians did not set to work with the same frank brutality as in the days of Bobrikov. The question of military service, for example, was handled by the payment of tribute: Finland's citizens were freed from the draft, for the time being at any rate, but the Grand Duchy had to make a substantial contribution of money each year to the military establishment of the empire. At the opening of the First World War, an access of jingoism gave fresh fuel to the czar's policy of Russification, and, in November, 1914, a program was published in Finland's newspapers, composed by "the special committee for Russian affairs." Under 38 headings, projected measures were described which would surely have put an end to Finland's peculiar status. One example will serve to illustrate the program's spirit; the educational system of Finland was to be made responsible to the Russian ministry of "popular enlightenment." Waspish as always, Alma Söderhjelm said that the people of Finland had lived for a century on the empty words of Alexander I, and on the illusions growing out of them. It might be rejoined that, empty or not, the words and the illusions had offered protection of a sort. But now their magic had run out.

4. Berlin, Grönköping, Tashkent

"HELSINGFORS GREW UP under the aegis of Swedish initiative and Swedish progressiveness; then Finnish cultural life, recently awakened, injected its strong impulses into the circulatory system of the city; and in the next phase Russian power was ready to suffuse everything . . . after the turn of the century, the outward appearance of Helsingfors raced with giant strides toward Russification." The description is by Ture Janson, looking back from the 1920's across the city's history. Russians were no novelty in Helsingfors; but now, the establishment of the naval base at Skatudden and the radical expansion of Russian military installations around the city made it impossible for the population to forget who was the master of Finland's capital. Not everyone found the Russian presence abhorrent. For young Vicke Pettersson, the son of the poet of Skatudden, it was simply a part of life. The Petterssons did not live on Skatudden any longer, having moved to Gasverksgatan (Gas Works' Street), a homely stub of pavement named after the establishment to its east; parallel to it, on the west, there was Henriksgatan. Gas Works' Street lay "about where the new post office now stands. Here, as on Skatudden, the Russians were always present; Åbo Barracks stood on the other side of Henrik's Esplanade," a boulevard which maintained the ample simplicity of nineteenth century Helsingfors. "Big and broad, with its greening lindens, it was a fine street, although lined mostly with low wooden houses. The few stone buildings, as well as the red walls of Åbo Barracks, seemed enormously high, and the Old Student Union was like a palace. In the simple leather shop of the Lindgren family [relatives of the Petterssons], there was a great deal to look at . . . many strange grownups came and went, foreign languages were spoken. One could often see Russian . . . soldiers there, buying half-sole leather for their boots. From my childhood years, I have . . . a very strong impression of the Russian strain in the city's life. There were swarms of officers, splendidly decked out, gendarmes, shabbily clad soldiers, academy students in their uniforms, Russian street-cleaners, gardeners, pedlars, ice-cream vendors, Tartars, and — especially — Jews. I also have a vivid memory of a good-sized fight on Henrik's Esplanade between Russian sailors and local artisans." As in the past, one saw the *izvozchiki*, the drosky-drivers who were out in every kind of weather; they did not necessarily have Russian as their mother tongue, but — until the days of Bobrikov, at any rate, when a reaction against everything smacking of Russia took place — they wore the dress of Russian drosky-men, with a shiny cylindrical hat in the summer, a huge bear-skin cap in the winter.

A shimmer of undeniable romance hung over this Russified Helsingfors — romantic to those who see it now, from afar, because it affords a last view of a dying czarist world, and romantic to those who lived in its midst because (whatever perils it offered to Finland) it was a world spiced with the exotic. This "late czarist" Helsingfors was captured best of all, one supposes, by Runar Schildt, who wrote that Helsingfors was no longer "a little Swedish provincial town, with a university, and a society strictly limited to some few hundred persons," but an "odd mixture of Berlin, Grönköping [the small town of Swedish legend, a kind of Podunk], and Tashkent, with 'true Finnish' lickers of Russian platters, trilingual street-signs, and national architecture from the turn of the century." The elderly colonel who thinks these thoughts in Schildt's story "Perdita" affects contempt for Helsingfors in its latest transformation, and Finno-Swede that he is, aims an especially sharp kick at the Old Finns and their heirs, the Suometarians; nonetheless the colonel, like his creator, cannot resist the city's new lure. All of a sudden, Helsingfors was imbued with a hectic air of decadence, a veiled and erotic softness: "Inside Djurgården they met droskies bearing happy people of the night, automobiles came rushing from another direction with a glimmer of uniforms, a bobbing plume, a fur boa waving" (in "Den svagare," "The Weaker One"). Not all the eroticism was veiled, of course, not all the danger vague and delightful. The journalist Guss Mattsson, another classic of this Helsingfors, tells a nocturnal story different from Schildt's. Returning from work after midnight, he sees a woman "frozen with fear, in a big hat, staring at me in a porcelain way," and hears a cry somewhere for police. Three or four men run away, their victim lies stabbed on the street. Once the ambulance has come, the "editor" takes a drosky the rest of the way home. "'I wonder if he died?,' the driver asked softly when I paid. 'Ehkäpä,' 'Perhaps,' [I] said, and went inside. And the night was filled with questions and empty of answers." (The "I dag" column is from August 27, 1913.) Neither Mattsson nor Schildt survived the age they described. Mattsson died of tuberculosis in 1914; Schildt, thinking his literary gift was gone, shot himself in 1925.

5.   The Lonely Swedes

AT FIRST GLANCE, the situation of the Finno-Swedes in Helsingfors bears a
certain resemblance to that of the Russians; they were still in command of
municipal life, as the Russians were in command of military strength, and
their tenure, like that of the Russians, was almost up. However, individual
Russians came and went, enjoying (if they were officers) the performances
in the "well-proportioned and dignified" Russian Theater, populating (if
they were officers) the tables of the Chapel on a summer's day. The
Finno-Swedes were the builders of the city and its backbone, its best defenders, they believed, as they had been the best defenders of the land.
They gloried in the heritage; in his memoirs Torsten Helsingius wrote
that, even as a boy, he had been proudly aware that "members of his
group had led the defence of Finland's rights." Small thanks were got for
their sacrifices; all too many Finns said in real life what Arvid Järnefelt's
zealous Uno (in *Veljekset*) says in fiction: "'All [the Finno-Swedes] ought
to be loaded into a boat and taken over to Sweden'" — Snellman's old
theory, crudely put. To be sure, some Finns, like Järnefelt himself, were
critical of such rantings; but reflective Finno-Swedes, hearing them, could
fall into cynicism or despair. In 1907, Gustaf Alm (the pseudonym of a
schoolteacher, Richard Malmberg) published *Höstdagar* (*Autumn Days*),
a title meant to lead the reader's mind not only to the decline of the
Finno-Swedes in Helsingfors but to the irritable mood of the city during
its dreariest season — falling leaves, gales from the Gulf of Finland, failing
daylight, gloom unrelieved. Alm has an ill word for everyone; the ugliest
of his grotesques are the fanatical Finns, who rejoice in visions of "that
patriotic day, when crows will feast on Swedish cadavers." A resumé of the
novel's climax will show its savage tone. One evening the idealist (and
Swede-hater) Säynävä goes for a stroll with his friend Lohisaari; a Finnish
laborer, taking Säynävä for a "gentleman," a member of the establishment,
crushes his skull with a rock. Lohisaari has always been more the oppor-
tunist than Säynävä, arguing that the Finns must make use of the Finno-
Swedes until they need them no longer; in the melée he steals the money
of his mortally injured comrade and spends it at a house of ill fame in
Rödbergen. Even the Finnish extras on Alm's stage are vicious or stupid;
the crowd helps the murderer to escape from the police.

Finns are not the only recipients of Alm's wrath, although they get the
brunt of it. Swedes from Sweden condescend to Finno-Swedes, and

Finno-Swedes, feeling somehow inferior, do not know whether to rebel against their criticisms or not. A "genuine" Swede named Angelica makes cruel fun of Helsingfors and its Finno-Swedes; the city "'gives the impression of being an enormous pig with gold-rimmed glasses on its snout. That's the way you all are; can't you learn to live life as it's presented to you, instead of thinking up schemes and theories for everything?'" Frivolous and superbly ignorant of the historical burden under which Finland (and Finno-Swedes) labor, Angelica has put her finger on one sore spot just the same: the city's Finno-Swedish society had indeed demonstrated a tendency to draw lines around itself, to live by rules rather than impulses, to abandon itself to sheer selfishness. The little novel of Torsten Helsingius, *Dagdrivare* (*Idlers*, 1914), gave its name to the school of dispirited and cynical Helsingfors literature that came in the wake of *Höstdagar*, waiting for the end, sensitive Finno-Swedes would become aimless beaux-esprits, strolling through the city which had ungratefully dismissed them. Yet idlers have their own arrogance; in the words of Alm, and then of Schildt, Helsingius, Henrik Hildén, one may detect a special estheticizing variety of that Finno-Swedish haughtiness which drove Finns to blind fury and silly excess. Yet it is Schildt's particular awareness of the hauteur, and of the failing self-confidence which accompanied it, that makes his novellas little masterpieces not only of Finno-Swedish but of Scandinavian literature.

Sometimes the malaise of the idlers was more apparent than real. A sonnet, "Staden" ("The City"), in Ture Janson's *Mitt Helsingfors* (*My Helsingfors*, 1913) opens with the often quoted quatrain:

> In one's own town to be a foreigner,
> standing locked out forever from the ring
> of unity, which makes one glad and sure —
> to be excluded and to be a nothing.

Like Guss Mattsson, Janson was from Åbo; the remainder of the poem indicates that Janson's burden is the difficulty experienced by any outsider in gaining entrance to an established society, a society belonging to a limited number of families. In other words, the poem has nothing to do with the language problem of Helsingfors; it could apply as well, say, to patrician Bergen or Basel. All the same, the poem's opening has often been read in another way, as a description of the isolation of the Swedish linguistic minority in a city grown steadily more Finnish. Still another familiar poem in the collection, "Sydväst, sydväst . . ." ("Southwester"), describes the prevailing wind, which drives the waves of the Gulf of Finland in toward Brunnsparken:

Southwester, southwester, which gains in force and gains,
give color to the soul of Finland's Swedes!
Our mood, too dark and too much hardened, needs
a greater flexibility, more light.
We're at one with the sea and with its might,
so let us be inspired by union's band —
for us, the sea's the only fatherland.

Somewhat over-dramatically put, perhaps: the Finno-Swedes have their backs to the water. Fleetingly read, the poem appealed to the Finno-Swedish taste for a "Viking heroism" in face of overwhelming odds, a taste often flattered by Bertel Gripenberg, among other skalds, "Svensk sång" ("Swedish Song"): "Sing loud, oh Swedish mother tongue, in our destruction's hour!" Careful examination would again prove the interpretation to be wrong. By means of rhetoric, Janson has captured an audience in order to make it listen to a message of some hopefulness: achieving unity and flexibility, the Swedes of Finland may survive. Otherwise, only a museum will remain: the House of Nobles (he says in the poem of that name), where von Born declaimed his farewell to Finno-Swedish glories, is "a frozen dream . . . an abandoned palace and a dead one."

Axel Olof Freudenthal had preached unity to Finland's Swedes, Axel Lille had preached it, and Ture Janson preached it once again. But Janson's job was hardest: his intent was to make the Finno-Swedish working man of Helsingfors aware of himself and his rights, and simultaneously to inject him into the consciousness of more prosperous folks, as Freudenthal had tried to remind the well-to-do Swedish speakers of the town that they had a responsibility toward their linguistic brethren in the countryside. Two novels in particular, whose titles speak for themselves, were used by Janson to argue his case, *Inga medmänniskor* (*No Fellow Men*, 1911) and *De ensamma svenskarna* (*The Lonely Swedes*, 1916). The books have a common theme: "As soon as the Finno-Swedes left the coast, they were in a foreign country. And their own group was divided into 'upper class' and 'lower class'." Gunnar Holming, in *Inga medmänniskor*, tries to reach the "lower class" at the Swedish Youth Club in Sörnäs; he finds his task well-nigh hopeless: "The adolescent boys were made ugly by their slovenly and sprawling behavior, and they spoke a language neither Swedish nor Finnish." Bernt Bjelke, in *De ensamma svenskarna*, goes into the breach once more; an elementary school teacher, he gives himself up wholeheartedly "to Finno-Swedish poverty in the heart of the capital." Shortly, he comes close to despair: "There were moments when he asked himself if he were the only Swede in Finland" who knew something about the problems of the Swedish-speaking poor; he almost abandons the fight when his wife goes home to Sweden, acceding, he believes, to her father's wishes. (A noteworthy sub-theme in the book is the condescension of his Swedish father-in-law, and his compatriots, toward Finno-Swedes: "They made fun of their hard accent, and the lack of smoothness in their manner.") *The Lonely Swedes* has a happy and artificial ending: the absent wife studies pedagogy in Sweden, the better to help her husband. Upon her return, Bernt is beside himself with joy, but cannot forget history: "For the first time, Sweden has come to Finland's aid." In real life, matters did not turn out so brightly. Janson moved to Sweden in the late 1920's, spending the rest of his life there as a rootless and rather unsuccessful man of letters. His valedictory to Helsingfors ends with a chapter on unity's failure: "The Swedish workers of Helsingfors are a rejected and abandoned group, stationed at an outpost in a different linguistic milieu, and constantly presented with opportunities either to betray or assert their national character." If they follow the latter course, clinging to their Swedishness, they will get no thanks for it from the Swedish-speaking upper classes, whose indifference and ingratitude are a heritage from "the old Finno-Swedish bureaucracy."

Janson's fate should be compared with that of Arvid Mörne, who appears in a vignette of *The Lonely Swedes*. "At the podium he saw young Swedish Finland's poet, tall and stately, the very figure of a youthful chieftain." The Mörne portrayed here was closer, certainly, to the bold leader of 1905 than to the tormented self-doubter of the "dead years"; the phrase is the title of a collection of Mörne's verse from 1910. After the great strike, Mörne had continued his efforts on behalf of Finland's democratization while, at the same time, as the director of a countryside adult-education center (from 1899 to 1909), as curator of Nyland's Nation (from 1911), and the heir of Freudenthal's tradition, he was a champion of the whole Swedish-speaking population of Finland. Disappointment followed disappointment: he was deeply distrusted by the Swedish middle class from which he had sprung, looked at askance by the workers because of his background, hated by Finnish zealots (although he was a close and appreciative student of Finnish letters) because of his adamance in the language question. During the Civil War, hearing of atrocities committed in the name of the red flag he once had praised, he wrote a poem condemning it as "a banner of blood." Unlike Janson's talent, the genius of Mörne grew stronger because of the tests to which it was submitted; staying in Finland, Mörne reached his full stature as a lyricist in the last quarter-century of his life. He died at 70, in 1946.

As a postscript, the tantalizing and unanswerable question remains: did the fight put up by Janson (and, less polemically, by Sigrid Backman in her Rödbergen novels), for the loneliest of Swedes, the working men of Helsingfors, bear any fruits? It could be replied that, if the estimates of historians are correct, a momentary solidarity of the Swedish speakers came about during the Civil War; Krister Wahlbäck says that the "number of Swedes on the Red side during the war of 1918 was extremely small." However, if language blood proved thicker than the water of a social program in that cruel conflict, the "lower class" was not showered with rewards for its loyality — the point Janson made as he took his farewell of Helsingfors. The Swedish-speaking proletariat continued to go its quiet and somewhat melancholy way into limbo: "the Swedish working man in Finland does not lust after the glory of power; in his boldest dream, he dreams of his own garden plot."

6. Finns Ascendant

THE FINNS OF Helsingfors also had their differences, both of a political and a social nature; but they were held together by the faith that the future was theirs. A comparison of the new Finnish-language travelers' guide to Helsingfors from 1910 with that of 1889 offers an object lesson on the advances they had made in self-esteem. The guide of 1910 contains 239 pages plus advertisements, as compared to the skimpy 100 pages of two decades before; and, an important symptom, Stockmann has learned to appreciate the Finnish customer — the guide contains a large spread from the greatest of the city's department stores, as well as announcements from a multitude of firms with Finnish names. The serious tone of the guide of 1889 still prevails in 1910; in the latter case even greater attention is paid to the city's architectural marvels, the contents of the Ateneum, the Botanical Gardens, the Zoological Museum of the university. The man from the back country who purchased the guide must have felt that its prime intention was to create a nation of instant scholars. The newest national shrine, Bergbom's Kansallisteatteri, gets the saga of its long gestation retold, together with an enthusiastic account of its present power and glory; but the Swedish Theater — the guide's malice is lightly disguised as objectivity — has gone downhill since the great days of the Raas. In Helsingfors, the guide of 1910 implies, one can be a Finn and proud of it; on the hundredth anniversary of Snellman's birth, May 12, 1906 ("What are the world's Napoleons compared to him?," a character in Järnefelt inquires), a mass change of Swedish surnames into Finnish ones took place, a display of onomastic zeal repeated from year to year, encouraged by the propaganda of such organizations as the "Helsingin kansallismielinen nuoriso," the "Nationally Minded Youth of Helsingfors." Its leaflets proclaimed: "The Fennicization of a Swedish name is the plainest sign of a courageous national spirit."

Finnish nervousness in the presence of the capital made way for affection, affection to which Eino Leino gave voice. Born Armas Eino Lönnbohm at Paldamo in north central Finland, Eino Leino had come to Helsingfors in 1895 after finishing his schooling at Tavastehus. His boyish, open manner captivated all who met him: he passed back and forth between the Finnish and Swedish camps with remarkable ease. Oddly, in his prose, as in that of Talvio and Ilmari Kianto (who wrote a sketch bearing the revelatory title "Kirottu Helsinki" ["Damned Helsingfors," 1904]), a favorite theme is the Finn's foundering on the shoals of the city. Yet even as Eino Leino's characters descend into the depths of *la vie de bohème*, they enjoy the city which affords the opportunity; there is no moral indignation here. In his lyrics — infinitely superior to his novels — Leino paid tribute to Helsingfors with an artistic validity matched only by Schildt in his novellas. Leino captures Helsingfors in autumn mist (a mist symbolic, to be sure, of Russian oppression), and Helsingfors in winter dress, in the ingressus of the poem "Helsinki helmilöissä":

> All of Helsingfors is clad in pearl-clothes,
> all the parks are shining white with hoarfrost,
> gaslights burning now, and arc-lights shining,
> the Esplanade aglitter like a castle,
> a fairy castle, a court inside the mountain,
> where the maids of Hiisi hold their wedding.

The poet from the Finnish uplands (whose most widely read work remains the *Kalevala*-inspired *Helkavirsiä* [*Helka Hymns*, 1905 and 1916]) describes Ehrenström's Esplanade in trochaic pentameter, suggestive of the Finnish epic, and uses a reference to the maids of Hiisi (the evil demon of the *Kalevala*) — and the juxtaposition works. Celebrating Helsingfors as a city of the sea, in the suite, "Meren kaupunki," Leino does not harangue a section of its population, as Janson does in "Sydväst, sydväst." Instead, he conjures up its beauty. The suite opens thus:

> You see the town before you like a sea-shell,
> through which the spirit of the sea is speaking,
> with a rush and roar that sounds forever.
> All lovely, when the summer sun is sinking,
> and fairer still when leaves are turning russet,
> and loveliest of all, when dressed in hoarfrost
> it lies beneath the white moonlight of winter.

Unfortunately, Leino loved nocturnal Helsingfors too well; "it was impossible to visit any popular Helsingfors restaurant without stumbling onto Leino," his friend V. A. Koskenniemi recalled. Koskenniemi himself had gone through early years of student-loneliness, reflected in his first collection of verse, until he fitted himself into the new Finnish intelligent-sia of the city, learning to know the "spiritual nobility" (as opposed to nobility of birth) of such a man as Talvio's husband, the Slavic philologist Jooseppi Julius Mikkola. A hint of disapproval can be detected in Koskenniemi's reminiscences of Leino, who refused to be respectable, to be fitted in. After the collapse of a first marriage in 1908, and a long trip abroad, Leino began to slip perceptibly downward, rather like the people in his prose works: from 1911 to 1913 he published his quadripartite "slave novels," about unfortunates variously addicted to work, money, women, and gambling. No one knew where he got the time, or the clarity of mind, to continue his many-sided literary production and his journalis-tic activity; he patently enjoyed his circle of hangers-on as much as they enjoyed him, with his priest's collar and romantic cape. (Like his contem-porary, Captain Kock, he had a weakness for costumes.) Acquaintances from the past detected a falling-off in the quality of the revelers at Leino's table, just as there was in the quality of his work. Life in the restaurants of Helsingfors was no longer a joy but a necessity; Leino had avoided do-mesticity like a plague. Going home with him from König's one night, Koskenniemi was shocked at the wretchedness of his quarters, a room rented from a mailcarrier. He could still get entrée to better circles, if he wanted it; but more and more, wherever he was, he played the clown or the sacrificial beast. Ville Vallgren, himself a Bohemian within the limits of health and wisdom, tells in his *ABC Book* about Leino's midsummer eve visit to the Vallgren studio at Alberga. The guests decided to have a bull-fight, but "it was hard to find someone to play the bull. The lot fell to Leino."

Prim Koskenniemi saw Leino for the last time in 1921, at the funeral of Juhani Aho, held in the chapel of the Deaconess Institute, hard by the legendary villa of Mikkola and Talvio on Djurgårdsvägen. Leino came late to the services and appeared to sleep through them; afterwards he button-holed Koskenniemi in order to talk — not about the departed master of Finnish prose but about the six-hundredth anniversary of Dante's death. He must have looked much as he did in the portrait which Antti Favén did of him two years later, where his very face seems ready to dissolve, drip-ping downward off the canvas. Leino died in 1926, a few months after the suicide of Schildt; in an obituary for the restaurant life of Helsingfors, killed (or rendered intellectually impotent) by the Prohibition Act, Ture Janson paid a special tribute to Leino, "a small restaurant coterie" all by himself; "there was no truer or nobler connecting link between Swedish and Finnish than he." It is fitting that his statue, looking raffish, stands on the Esplanade, near Runeberg's estimable replica; indeed, Leino has a greater right to be there, since his devotion to Helsingfors was immeasurably deeper than Runeberg's.

7. Printer's Ink

IN THE ABOVE-mentioned novel of Torsten Helsingius, *Dagdrivare*, the hero and his comrades are unable to settle down to any serious task. Young Otto spends a great deal of time at an estate near Helsingfors, he drinks too much, he goes to bordellos and the movies (this last a sign of new times); about to pull himself together for love of fair and decent Märta, he discovers that he has syphilis. Grown older, Helsingius was embarrassed both by the contents of his youthful work and its popularity; in his memoirs, he took pains to show how well the members of the "idler" group had turned out in real life. (Several of their number joined the 27th Prussian Light Infantry in Germany and graduated to Mannerheim's army in the Civil War, others served as best they could in organizations behind the Red lines; all subsequently became pillars of society, soldiers in the armed forces of the Republic of Finland, authors, teachers, businessmen.) Long before the World War and its Finnish sideshow provided a chance for action, however, the young men of Helsingfors, Swedes and Finns alike, had been at work on a task which lay close at hand: bringing the city into the twentieth century. It would be incorrect to imagine a whole generation of jaded Finno-Swedes, frittering away the years before 1914 in hopeless lassitude, just as it would be incorrect to think that the city's energetic Finns spent themselves in painful adjustment to the metropolis. The burgeoning of the city's book-dealers and publishers is a case in point. After the Åbo fire of 1827, the ancient academic printing house of the Frenckell family, founded in 1642, moved to Helsingfors, where it directly made a cultural contribution as the publisher of Runeberg's *Helsingfors Morgonblad*; its great rival was the house of Gustaf Otto Wasenius, established in Helsingfors in 1823, which began the publication of *Helsingfors Tidningar* in 1829 (the paper would have its great days, as had been seen, under the editorship of Topelius, from 1841 to 1860). The Wasenius bookstore flourished for decades as the city's most-favored shop (and had its sentimental customers up until the 1960's when it was moved from the North Esplanade to a corner of the Academic Bookstore and then vanished altogether). Meanwhile, out at Borgå, the works of Runeberg and Topelius, as well as Fredrik Berndtson, were brought out by the house of

Constantin Öhman, sometime clerk at Wasenius's; Öhman's great project was the forerunner, in fascicles, of the coffee-table book, *Finland framställdt i teckningar* of 1845–1852. Öhman's early death, in Vienna in 1848, put an end of sorts to the Borgå project; but a Helsingfors branch, founded the same year, had the shortlived role of being a Finnish-language bookstore in the capital, run by Herman Kellgren and the unfortunate Paavo Tikkanen. (In 1855, Theodor Sederholm [mentioned above in connection with the newspaper *Helsingfors Dagblad*] purchased the Öhman bookstore in Helsingfors, and became the publisher of the first edition of Runeberg's collected works.)

Meanwhile, in 1863, the bookstore of Frenckell and Sons was taken over by Gustaf Wilhelm Edlund who, in time, not only published the collected works of Runeberg, Topelius, and Cygnaeus, but maintained the store at the above-mentioned "Edlund's Corner," a meeting-place offering a view, Ture Janson suggested in a poem, that seemed a "glimpse of a metropolis," with the glittering spray of "a waltz's happy waves" from the Chapel across the Esplanade. (As a coincidence, it may be mentioned that Edlund's nephew, Thomas Fredrik Wulff, long emplyed in his uncle's store, left "the land's most distinguished bookdealer" in 1890, to found the stationery business which gave a name to "Wulff's Corner," at the intersection of the North Esplanade and Östra Henriksgatan, now a part of Stockman's giant emporium.) In 1893, Edlund set a capstone to his publishing activity with the great volume, *Finland i XIX seklet*, a salute — edited by C.G. Estlander — to Finland's progress during the Russian time; it was translated into six languages. Yet Edlund also erected an invaluable monument to the past (and particularly the Finland-Swedish past) with Tor Carpelan's *Finsk biografisk handbok* (1903–1905). But he was evenhanded: it had been proceeded by the pioneering Finnish-language *Biografinen nimikirja* (*Biographical Namebook*) of 1879–1883.

Nonetheless time, and energetic young men, were catching up with Edlund. In 1890, the spirit of the long-dead Kellgren-Tikkanen undertaking was taken up by a young Finnish enthusiast, Alvar Renqvist, a friend of the *Päivälehti* circle and the Järnefelts; he established the Otava publishing house, whose intention — the name means the Pleiades or Great Bear — was to bring out Finnish-language literature of high quality; the great firm has remained in the hands of the family (which in 1935 changed its name to Reenpää) ever since. In 1893, the remarkably active Renqvist (from Viborg) became the firm's managing director, the same year he — with Gösta Branders — established the Academic Bookstore (Akademiska bokhandeln/ Akateeminen kirjakauppa), meant to be "a truly firstclass, effective, and well-ordered bookshop," and "a favored place for the new Finnish-language literature." Then, in 1896, Renqvist, looking for new worlds to conquer, left the bookstore in the hands of Branders, to devote himself to the newly founded Finnish bank, Kansallis-Osake-Pankki, returning (in 1904) whole-heartedly to Otava, turning it into Finland's perhaps most prestigious Finnish-language publishing house. For its centennial in 1990, an observer from Sweden, Per Gedin, wrote: "Alvar Renqvist published every specimen he could find of the new Finnish intellectualism, including the scores of Jean Sibelius." Taking over the Academic Bookstore entire, Branders — refusing to be left in Renqvist's dust — made it into a place where not just the latest Finnish and Finno-Swedish literature but also the rest of European letters could be had. (These were days when the three core countries of Scandinavia, Denmark, Norway, and Sweden, were at a literary zenith.) Under Branders' leadership, the store became one of the largest in the world.

At little Borgå, meanwhile, events had again taken place that would have an immediate bearing on the capital's publishing life. In 1853, the Borgå merchant Gustaf Leopold Söderström purchased Öhman's shop there, and, in 1860, set up his own printing house to go with it. By 1878, his son Werner, aged eighteen, decided to enter the publishing trade himself, and launched a concern whose major project was a Finnish translation of Georg Weber's four-volume *Lehrbuch der Weltgeschichte* (1882 ff.). Like his contemporary Renqvist, Söderström *filius* strongly believed in the encouragement of Finnish-language belles-lettres and other works; taking over his father's printing house in 1888, he concentrated entirely, from 1891, on works in Finnish, bringing out Juhani Aho, Arvid Järnefelt, and other debutants of Finnish-language realism. However, the firm's activity was hampered at first by Söderström's hesitation to publish "morally defect" literature, and it was not until 1904, when the firm was turned into a stock company, under the name "Werner Söderström Oy", directed by Jalmari Jäntti, that it came fully into its own, bringing out works of the (then) shocking 'Johannes Linnankoski' (Vihtori Peltonen), as well as Eino Leino, Maila Talvio, and V.A. Koskenniemi. (It also issued the nationalistic and Fennomane reference-work about Finnish Finland, *Oma Maa* [*Own Land*, first edition 1907–1912].)

The Swedish branch of the Söderström undertaking in its turn (1891) was moved to Helsingfors under the name "Söderström & Co.". (Helsingfors would also become, in time, the administrative headquarters for the Finnish house, while printing remained in Borgå.) Directed by Werner Söderström's brother Lennart, "Söderström & Co." published, in its early years, Tavaststjerna, Jac. Ahrenberg, and a new star, Mikael Lybeck; a generation or so later, it became the publisher of such modernists as Rabbe Enckell and Gunnar Björling. A great success of its early years was the edition, with illustrations by Albert Edelfelt, of *Fänrik Ståls sägner*

(1898–1900). Yet Söderström & Co. did not hold the Finland-Swedish stage alone, of course; Wentzel Hagelstam began his publishing activity in 1891 in Fredrikshamn (producing translations of Aho, among others) and then moved into the capital, where, following a familiar pattern, he established a bookstore and issued the journal *Ateneum*. (The store, now for second-hand books, still exists.) And then, continuing the centripetal movement toward Helsingfors, Holger Schildt — a nephew of Werner Söderström himself — founded his own house at Borgå in 1913, moving to the capital in 1917, where he purchased and incorporated the holdings of G.W. Edlund. With his cousin, Runar Schildt, as one of his leading authors (and his editorial reader), his firm became a major nurturer of Finland-Swedish literature. Its lists included, or came to include, such older voices as Mörne's and Gripenberg's, the collected works of the late Guss Mattsson, and the exceedingly popular verse of the golden boy, Jarl Hemmer. From Karelia, in 1916, the unknown Edith Södergran sent her *Dikter* to Schildt's and turned out, after her death, to be the house's luminous martyr-figure, much celebrated by such other modernists and Schildt-authors as Hagar Olsson and Elmer Diktonius — but their story belongs to the 1920's and beyond. Six years after Runar Schildt's suicide, Holger Schildt left Finland for Sweden; the house remained, and kept much of its creative tradition.

The cultural life of Helsingfors was further enriched during the century's first decade by the appearance of several new Swedish and Finnish journals, noteworthy because of their standards and their range of interest. Founded in 1901 by the music critic Karl Flodin, the magazine *Euterpe* was intended to have a musical content; when the editorship passed into the hands of Gustaf Strengell, architect by profession and polyhistor by inclination, the horizons of the journal were radically expanded. Among its leading lights were: Werner Söderhjelm and his brother Torsten, the latter a cultural historian who died all too young; Gunnar Castrén, the grandson of Mathias Alexander and a literary critic of icy lucidity; Rolf Lagerborg, trained as a philosopher and psychologist, but, in time, a writer on everything under the sun; and Olaf Homén, whose apprenticeship as a drama critic, served on *Euterpe*, prepared him for the most brilliant career in this line of endeavor Helsingfors had ever seen. Working for Guss Mattsson's short-lived *Dagens Tidning* (1911–14) and then for *Dagens Press* (the result of a union between the Mattsson paper and *Nya Pressen*), Homén produced the oeuvre collected in three volumes as *Från Helsingfors teatrar* (*From the Theaters of Helsingfors*, 1915–19). Lyric poetry was presented too; Arvid Mörne gave some verse to *Euterpe* but the house-poet of the organ was, *hélas*, Bertel Gripenberg, who exhibited many flowers from his hothouse in its pages:

"The Swan to Leda" ("I snuggle soft against your marble knees"), for example, and "Herod at the Harp" ("Salome makes love with steel and blood"). The review section was particularly good: notably, Finnish belles-lettres were given a very fair share of space, these critiques falling principally to Homén; but Werner Söderhjelm's words on Linnankoski's sensational novel, *Laulu tulipunaisesta kukasta* (*Song of the Fire-red Flower*, 1905), can be regarded as the germ-cell of Söderhjelm's mono- graph on Linnankoski from 1918. Although *Euterpe* never abandoned its literary emphasis (how could it, with such a stable of talents), it at- tracted representatives of the other arts as well, notably, thanks to Strengell, the city's vigorous young architects — Sigurd Frosterus chief among them.

After the passing of *Euterpe* in 1905, which aimed too high and found its subscription lists too low, the gap it left was filled by *Argus*, of which the moving spirits were Werner Söderhjelm and Guss Mattsson. (Mattsson had poked fun at the virtuoso ways of *Euterpe* and the Euterpists in Rafael Lindqvist's *Fyren* [*The Lighthouse*], a comic paper of which Mattsson was editor for a time — and which, for the rest, offered "cultivated humor and satire," in the forgiving opinion of Gunnar Castrén, a sometime victim.) As Sven Willner has neatly put it, Mattsson, a trained chemist, was a repre- sentative of C.P. Snow's two cultures. *Euterpe* had gone in heavily for the arts; in order to correct this bias, Mattsson provided scientific articles for *Argus* from his own indefatigable pen. After three years, *Argus* was done to death by the Russian censor in 1911; it was immediately succeeded by *Nya Argus*, which survives until the present, maintaining the initial policy of broad content and genuine substance. Still another journal in this Finno-Swedish blooming was *Framtid* (*Future*), an activist weekly appear- ing from 1906 to 1910; a successor of *Fria ord*, the "illegal paper" of Bo- brikov's day, it carried on its political activity above ground — its stars were Arvid Mörne, Konni Zilliacus, and, again, Gunnar Castrén. Mean- while, the Finns had established an answer to *Euterpe* in 1907; or perhaps it was more the retort of conservative Finnish minds to the Young Finns, who had made *Valvoja* their cultural organ. The former group became the sponsor of *Aika* (*The Time*), a literary and political monthly, which took its editor, Gunnar Suolahti, from still another Finnish magazine, *Raataja* (*The Drudge*), the mouthpiece of students with Old Finnish sympathies. Suolahti, a "cultural aristocrat" not unlike many of the Euterpists, selected V.A. Koskenniemi, 21 years old, as his right-hand man and special advisor in literary matters. The program of *Aika* (apart from its political tenden- cies, which appear to have interested Suolahti rather little) was that the Finnish nation still lacked authentic "European" culture, a fault Suolahti and Koskenniemi meant to correct in short order. It may be revelatory that, as an historian, Suolahti's research took him again and again into the eighteenth century, when Finland was clearly dominated by Swedish culture; Koskenniemi's "other homelands" were classical antiquity and Goethe's Germany. (Afterward, while professor of literary history at the University of Turku, Koskenniemi also found Hitler's Third Reich attractive, and was an officer of Josef Goebbels' *Europäischer Reichsschriftstellerverbund*.) *Aika*, of which Koskenniemi was the chief editor from 1912 until 1922, ceased publication in 1923; Finnish cultural life no longer needed the prop it had provided.

8. The Great Role

THE FINNS BUSILY collected the prerequisites of culture on every front. Even as Koskenniemi, later on, provided them with translations of his beloved Goethe and Grillparzer, and with a long and instructive essay-series, in the fashion of Paul Elmer More, on books and authors (*Kirjoja ja kirjailijoita*, 1916–31), so the Finnish National Theater, "the most national of all national shrines," remained the object of Finnish veneration, notwithstanding the distinctly petty squabbles that took place inside its massive walls. The theater had four directors in the first dozen years following Bergbom's retirement; a romantic to the end, the old man had cut a brave and pathetic figure as he walked the streets of Helsingfors during the great strike, whistling the Marseillaise. The wittiest of Bergbom's successors, Jalmari Finne, lasted only a season; but he captured the institution's mood perfectly with his paraphrase on the Latin motto of the Ateneum across the square. There, Finne said, art flourished beneath the words, "Concordia res parvae crescunt"; here, on the theater, the inscription should read: "Discordia res maximae dilabuntur" ("The greatest things are ruined by discord"). Discordant or not, the theater retained its constantly high-hearted public, which was fed an ever larger and more dignified repertoire. From its imposing new home at Regeringsgatan number one, the "Suomalaisen kirjallisuuden seura" ("Finnish Literary Society") saw to it that the nation was supplied not only with an endless flow of Finnish folksong and folkpoetry, but with "official translations" of Racine, Molière, Lessing, Goethe, Schiller, and, the pinnacle, Shakespeare. Paavo Cajander's version of the bard, begun in 1879, was completed in 1913; the translator died upon completing his enormous task. The Finnish National Theater also got its history — somewhat prematurely, it might seem to the outsider — under the auspices of the same Literary Society; Professor Eliel

Aspelin-Haapkylä, a founding father of *Aika* and C.G. Estlander's successor as professor of esthetics and modern literature, published a four-volume account (1906–1910) of the theater's miseries and grandeurs. Finnish theatrical life in Helsingfors was bedecked with the tokens of respectability; on the practical side, it was expanded by the establishment of a popular stage group in 1907, "Kansan Näyttämö" ("The People's Theater"), which got its first home in the ever more Fennicized Old Student Union.

Swedish theatrical life in Helsingfors could have borrowed the motto which Jalmari Finne proposed. At the Swedish Theater, the administration continued to keep the native idiom from being spoken on its stage; at Åbo, in 1894, the "Swedish Local Theater" was founded, "poor in coin but rich in hopes." Its principal scene of activity at the beginning was the provincial towns, and its first leader was Anton Franck, a native Finno-Swede from Björneborg, a veteran of the Swedish Theater in Helsingfors where, with his accent, he had not become a stunning success. In 1898, Franck left the post; a year later he was called back to Helsingfors to direct a newly constituted "People's Theater," sponsored by the funds of "Konstnärsgillet," "Arbetets vänner" ("Labor's Friends"), and other Helsingfors institutions interested in giving all levels of the Swedish population in Helsingfors edification and amusement. The theater's activity began with a performance, in translation, of a Finnish play, Minna Canth's *Roinilan talossa* (*At Roinila Farm*), held in the Finnish stronghold, the Old Student Union; two years later it moved, taking up abode in the Arcadia Theater of long and varied history. At length, in 1907, the Arcadia Theater was condemned by the fire-prevention authorities; the "People's Theater" was given permission to appear, when it could be fitted into the schedule, on the boards of the Swedish Theater. The favor was, in fact, a very small one, and grudgingly given; even after the combination, in 1913, of the Swedish Theater and the "People's Theater" into a single institution with two departments, "Swedish" and "domestic," the "domestic" (i.e. Finno-Swedish) division received the small end of the stick. For two years, Runar Schildt was its director, and his experiences no doubt confirmed him in his already dark view of life; the Finno-Swedish players were assigned an awkward time for their performances (4:00 to 7:00 on Monday, Friday and Sunday), charged lower prices (a sign, in the cultured public's eye, that they were offering second-rate stuff), and had to entrust the important plays to their "Swedish" big brothers.

Most of the actors and actresses of the "domestic" division had reached considerable competence. In 1908, young Nicken Rönngren, who had got a reputation for his dramatic recitals, was appointed teacher at the newly established dramatic school of the Swedish Theater; the products of

his gifted instruction were understandably anxious to spend their careers
on better vehicles than farces and hand-me-downs. Out of these pressures
arose the "great theatrical war" of 1913–16, grandiloquently named but a
matter of some consequence to the participants. In order to further the
interests of the new professionals, who had learned "to speak Finland's
Swedish clearly, carefully, and intelligently," the Swedish Theatrical Union
of Finland was born, led by Rönngren, Mina Cygnaeus (the widow of
Gustaf Cygnaeus, who had been the mainstay of Swedish theatrical activities in Åbo), and Julius Hirn, the drama critic of *Nya Pressen*. Through
fund-raising, polite intrigue, and, not least, newspaper skirmishes ("no
stage has ever been doused with so much polemical blood," Ture Janson
claimed), the supporters of Finno-Swedish dramatic art were triumphant,
and Olaf Homén's judgment of 1904 in *Euterpe* — "the old Swedish
Theater is an institution that has outlived itself" — came true. Although
ending in victory for the side of right, the little war indicated the strength
possessed by Swedish conservative forces in Helsingfors; the struggle was
lengthened by the determination of Arthur Frenckell, the editor (and
owner) of *Hufvudstadsbladet*, to keep the Swedish Theater what it histori-
cally had been, an excellent provincial showcase for artists from Sweden
rather than a national stage for Finno-Swedes — which it now at long last
became. After three years under the directorship of the Dane, Adam
Poulsen, interrupted by the Civil War, Nicken Rönngren was appointed as
manager, having been secretary of the theater's administration in the interim. Prompted by Rönngren, Poulsen had been sympathetic to Finno-
Swedish aspirations; the last and greatest triumph of the Dane's regime
was, remarkably, a staging of Kivi's classical comedy, *Nummisuutarit* in
the translation of Per Åke Laurén, *Sockenskomakarne* (1917), with a young
man from Pyttis, Axel Slangus, as the stubborn innocent, Esko. Upon
Rönngren's coming to the helm, Slangus, his former pupil, created the
role of Armas Fager — the braggart, sly and stupid and pathetic, killed by
his own dreams — in Runar Schildt's play, *Den stora rollen* (*The Great
Role*, 1923), about the Red days of 1918 in Helsingfors.

9.   "The golden age of Finland's art"

THE ATENEUM, ONCE peaceful, also became a battleground of cultural
progress. The artists who followed after Edelfelt and Gallen-Kallela had a
harder time of it, be it from life itself or from art critics. Going directly
from elementary school at Lapinlahti in northern Savolax — the home of

Juhani Aho — to drawing instruction in Helsingfors, Pekka Halonen had made Paris his next stop, where he became the student of Gauguin, just returned from Tahiti, a primitive world different in climate, at any rate, from the Finnish backwoods. Halonen's short-clipped peasants and wild Finnish woods were a success, in good part because of their picturesque novelty, yet he was unable to advance beyond stereotypes; what would have happened to the international repute of Sibelius, if the composer had had to depend on "national" music alone? Hugo Simberg, however, a Finno-Swede (the son of a teacher in the military academy at Fredrik-shamn), suffered precisely because of the eccentric quality of his vision; his grotesques aroused the horrified perplexity of Casimir Leino, writing in *Päivälehti*: "I can't say either one thing or the other about the artist's 'paintings,' representing 'The Poor Devil with Twins' and 'The Poor Devil with his Playmates' . . . I suppose that they are put on display so that each of us can form his own opinions about them." The broad public was surely better able to swallow Halonen's honest toilers of the fields and forests than Simberg's hordes of stylized "poor devils," imps humiliated, tricked, abused by life. No doubt a strain of personal complaint lies in all Simberg's figures: when he died of a stroke at 44, in 1917, he felt that he had been altogether forgotten. His strange caricature-painting of Sibelius, Kajanus, and a large blue crow, represented in Punch-and-Judy style, from 1911, may be an expression of resentment at the vagaries of national esteem. Simberg was the victim of his own narrow but immutable genius; he was also the victim, like Halonen to an extent, of the "revolution" which took place in Finland's painting after 1908, in consequence of the cruel dissection French critics made of the Finnish art on display in Paris. Finland's artists had been encouraged, all too much, by the delight with which their pavilion at the Paris World's Fair of 1900 had been received, a phenomenon comparable to the triumph of Finland's music at the same exhibition. At that time, another poor boy from Savolax who had made his way to Helsingfors as an apprentice house-painter, Juho Rissanen, had become a special darling of the critics; he had been warned by Gustave Geoffroy, the champion of impressionism, against abandoning the world he had portrayed with his "Blind Old Women." Full of momentary enthusiasm, Geoffroy sent a rhetorical plea in Rissanen's direction: "Oh Rissanen, painter of peasant life, do not ever come to Paris, stay in the world you depict in so solemn a manner, and which you love so much!" Eight years later, however, the painters of Finland were taken to task precisely because they were outside the continental idiom — they must, in brief, learn how to paint, abandoning the "dark and impure colors" of their earlier work.

A group of artists, calling itself "Septem," was formed, with the intention of correcting Finland's art in accordance with the devastating criticism it had just received. Its chief representative was Magnus Enckell, already the owner of a considerable reputation as a cunning portraitist (witness the painting of the near-sighted Thiodolf Rein), who now stepped forth as a chief advocate of the "pure palette," using only the colors of the solar spectrum, in accordance with French Neo-Impressionist theory. In a way, it was odd that this "triumph of clear, pure color" should have come about through Enckell's efforts, since in his earlier works Enckell had been an austere colorist, as paintings such as his "Awakening" from 1893 (a boy rousing himself from sleep) or "The Netmaker" from 1894 (more a sturdy young parson than a toiler of the sea) will show; but travels and studies in Spain and Italy had helped to prepare him for the revolution, a final inspiration of which had come from France. The members of "Septem," apart from Enckell, were the Belgian (of English background) Alfred William Finch, brought to Finland by Count Louis Sparre, now the director of Iris Art Industries in Borgå; Verner Thomé, whose light and airy "Boys on the Beach" of 1904 anticipates the color-ideals of "Septem"; Yrjö Ollila, whose best-known picture, "Watering Horses" from 1919, is filled with a hot sunlight seldom felt on Finnish strand; Mikko Oinonen, who made a specialty of flowers; Juho Rissanen, who felt uncomfortable with "Septem's" strictures and left it, still seeking his lost naiveté; and Ellen Thesleff, for whom, as for Enckell, the experience of quattrocento Italy had been of prime importance: her "Tuscan Landscape" from 1908 was a parade-piece (if such a noisy noun is applicable to her quiet art) of the new direction. (In subsequent years, Ellen Thesleff's place among the seven was taken by the variously gifted Per Åke Laurén, who not only translated Aleksis Kivi but also painted *sujets* from the author's works, and Rissanen's by Uuno Alanko, not only a painter but an engineer and architect.) By the background and character of its two leading members, Enckell and Finch, the "Septem" group was cosmopolitan and more interested in the application of certain techniques than in the subject matter; its topics were often French (see the early paintings of Thomé and Oinonen), or at least had an implied "southernness" about them. The Helsingfors paintings of Enckell from 1908–09, "Cofferdam" and "The Dock at Skatudden," could as well be located somewhere in France: only the outline of Nikolai-Church in the background of these works offers a key to their locale. The opinion that the "Septem" artists are the spiritual descendants of Albert Edelfelt may be accepted only with reservations, reservations which will arise after one has compared the pictures of Helsingfors by the earlier artist, where the *genius loci* means a great deal, to those of Enckell, where it does not.

The triumph of "Septem", and the "victorious procession of the colors of the rainbow," as Sigurd Frosterus, its champion in the essay, called it, was distinctly healthy, by reason of "Septem's" concentration on painting as an art and not just an expression of national sentiments. The group's hegemony was relatively brief; its antagonists (who could loosely be called impressionists) were the painters of the "November" group, named after the month of their first common exhibition. The leader of this new band — a Finnish leader, by the way, not a Finno-Swede, as Enckell was — came from a simple background. Tyko Konstantin Sallinen was the son of a tailor. The father led a wandering life, which brought him and his family to Helsingfors in the 1880's; later, he lived at Haparanda in the far north of Sweden. The boy Sallinen tried his luck at tailoring in Stockholm, then joined his peripatetic family at Tammerfors; here, he was stabbed on the street by an unknown assailant. The wound was not mortal; as a somewhat overage student in the drawing school at Helsingfors (supporting himself by working at his father's craft in a department store), he went his troublesome way, in art and in life. Albert Edelfelt, appointed chairman of the Art Union, found him altogether baffling. A few years later, when Sallinen had grown in assurance and bad manners, he reportedly threw the Artists' Guild into chaos by publicly calling Gallen-Kallela a "paskahousut," thereby employing one of Finnish childhood's favorite terms of scatological insult; ejected from the society, Sallinen made a rapid trip to the Finnish settlements of Upper Michigan. Gallen-Kallela could have consoled himself by reflecting that he had been treated no worse than the members of Sallinen's immediate family; Tyko was notorious for the abuse he heaped upon his pig-faced model and wife, who (verbal mayhem aside) can scarcely have been flattered by the portraits her ill-tempered and faithless husband did of her. It might seem that the poor woman's features were put on double display in the painting of two superbly unattractive Finnish girls, "The Washerwomen," with which Sallinen, in the spring of 1912, won the attention of the art critics of Helsingfors; their responses ranged from Nils Wasastjerna's verdict on artist and public in *Nya Pressen* ("no doubt he's laughing on the inside at the people who take these pictures seriously") to the mild praise of Lennart Wennervirta in *Aika*, who found Sallinen to be a man "with a temperament and a future." In Guss Mattsson's *Dagens Tidning*, Gösta Stenman was more specific: to him, Sallinen was "a strongly individual artist, representing new values in our art." It was Stenman who, upon Sallinen's return to Finland after his American escapades, helped the artist to find some necessary peace and quiet at Hyvinge, whither Sallinen had fled, together with his painter friend Jalmari Ruokokoski, from the temptations of the artist's café, Brondin's, on the South Esplanade. Visitors to Hyvinge quickly observed that Sallinen and Ruokokoski had found liquid refreshments in their hermitage. Stenman, too, arranged the November exhibit of 1916 that gave the group around Sallinen its name.

If the Novembrists had a common style — and, placed alongside the "Septem" artists, they scarcely appear to have one, so varied are they in their manner — then it was, as Tito Colliander said, "a harsher and more secretive kind of painting, surely, even gloomy in its gravity, and dramatic — therefore more 'Finnish' . . ." This heavy Finnishness of the Novembrists, perhaps more easily sensed than defined, is not inclined to romanticize or flatter, as did the art of Gallen-Kallela's heyday; witness the defiant or stolid old people of Ruokokoski, a defiance shared by Sallinen in his self-portrait and in his picture of "Pekka's Hilma," witness Juho Mäkelä's and Eero Nelimarkka's somber Ostrobothnian flatlands, Marcus Collin's overwhelming or brooding scenes of skerry life and death, Anton Lindforss' sad-faced girls, Ilmari Aalto's quizzical "Man in a Fur Cap," the dead "town-scapes" of Ragnar Ekelund, Alvar Cawén's stark cubism, used to such ominous effect in his picture of the Russian battleships moored around Skatudden. What the Finnish art-historian Onni Okkonen said of the Novembrists was direct and to the point, like their paintings: "They wished to avoid beautification, but they gave expression to a poetic concept all their own." Or Ragnar Robert Eklund's verdict on Sallinen might be applied to each of the Novembrists — "his brutality is never very far from tenderness." (R.R. Eklund was an Ostrobothnian poet and, transplanted to Helsingfors, a newspaper man; his lyrics could be illustrated by a Mäkelä or a Collin.) This new Finnish art, both of the "Septem" and the "November" groups (in the latter case, even before it had got its collective name), was given a chance to reach a broad public very quickly, it is gratifying to note, by the efforts of the man who held the directorship of the Ateneum from 1914 until 1918, Gustaf Strengell, sometime "Euterpist," architect and art critic. In Nils-Gustaf Hahl's formulation, Strengell lived "in hate and love," doing nothing by halves; he combined bohemianism with a passion for mathematical exactness. Under him, the Ateneum was transformed from a storehouse of national treasures, such as they were, to a modern art museum, a museum designed to please Strengell's taste if not that of all the members of his public. Whatever conservative voices in Helsingfors were raised against him (and his post entailed, after all, a certain responsibility to the past), he was an ideal director of the Ateneum's museum during critical years of a time Erik Kruskopf has called "the genuine golden age of Finland's art."

10. "Backwoods Symphonies in Stone"

IN 1922, FOUR years after his abrupt retirement from the directorship of the art museum, Strengell published a book called *Staden som konstverk* (*The City as a Work of Art*). It was scarcely an empty title; since the turn of the century, Helsingfors had been under the scrutiny of a dedicated band of architects who were determined to change the city's face, or at least to give it features it had not possessed before. Their new style of building, in its first phases, was dubbed "national romanticism," a term familiar from other creative fields; it undertook to do in stone what Sibelius had done in music, what Gallen-Kallela had done in painting, and what Leino's *Helkavirsiä* would shortly do in words. The question immediately arose — think of Obolenski's objection to Saarinen's new railroad station — as to whether quasi-mediaeval piles, inspired by Karelian peasant houses, by Finland's few castles (especially Olofsborg at Nyslott), and Finnish country churches, could be comfortable companions for the Neoclassicism of Engel's Helsingfors. The products of this late-come archaism contrasted far more sharply with what Engel had wrought than did the works of Chiewitz and the elder Edelfelt, of Sjöström and Höijer and Nyström. National romanticism was an assertion of Finland's special spirit, born of a time in which such assertions were altogether understandable; it may also be taken — in Helsingfors — as a declaration of "Finnishness" in a city that, heretofore, had shown few architectural signs that it was the capital of a Finnish hinterland. Somehow, it seems appropriate that national romantic buildings began to dot Helsingfors in a decade when the city's Finnish-speaking population at last surpassed the Swedish speakers in numbers. However, men of unimpeachably "Finnish" backgrounds were few and far between in the ranks of the national romantic architects. Finnish was the home language of Eliel Saarinen, the son of a pastor at Rantasalmi, in Sankt Michel's county, but he married twice across the language line, and was a fluent and willing speaker of Swedish; of his two colleagues in the famous firm of "Gesellius, Lindgren, and Saarinen," the former was from Helsingfors, a Finno-Swede of German extraction, while the latter came from Tavastehus, like Sibelius, and, like the composer, commanded Swedish and Finnish. Lars Sonck — who, after Saarinen and Lindgren, might be reckoned the third genius of the movement — was again from a parsonage, in Ostrobothnia; he spoke Swedish natively, as did the brothers Bertel and Valter Jung, Valter

Thomé, and Karl Lindahl — the last-named, indeed, had been born at
Jönköping in Sweden. Onni Alcides Törnqvist-Tarjanne, the creator of the
Finnish National Theater, was an exception to the rule; none save an ardent exponent of Finnishness could have furnished the Finns with their
dramatic shrine.

An initial triumph of Finland's national romantic architecture came at
the Paris World's Fair of 1900, where the Finnish Pavilion, a creation of
Saarinen, offered an apt setting for Finnish music and Finnish art. At
home, one "poem in stone" after another went up, with towers and
crenellations, asymmetrically placed windows, half-oval doors, and unex-
pected bay-windows. The firm starring Saarinen and Lindgren created the
facades of the Pohjola Building (which aroused the amused contempt of a
Swedish architect in Alm's *Höstdagar*), the National Museum, and a
wealth of private buildings, among them the wonders of Skatudden,
"Olofsborg" and "Eol"; it won a prize with its plans for the new Railroad
Station, a project much transformed by Saarinen after the firm was dissolved. Lars Sonck designed the Telephone Company's headquarters
(making jokesters ask why the exchange should be hidden behind terrifying battlements), the hospital at the edge of a new section of town, Eira,
west of Brunnsparken (Eira Hospital is still thought to be the city's most
charming milieu for an illness), and the church in Berghäll, shutting off
Unionsgatan at the northern end, as Engel's Observatory does in the
south. Berghäll Church may not have brought faith to the section's
working men, but it inspired Guss Mattson to a description of national
romantic architecture, seen without the spectacles of patriotic pride: "The
rest of Christiandom is accustomed to enter its churches beneath the
tower, but the most northerly Christians of Helsingfors [a reference to
Berghäll's location north of the city's center] are confronted at that point
by a nicely swollen belly, and have to sneak in by the kitchen door." Not
only Saarinen, Lindgren, and Sonck dotted the Helsingfors landscape with
their overwhelming phantasies. Valter Thomé and Karl Lindahl designed
"Sampo," the student union of the Technical University, the training
place of the majority of the new architects; in "Sampo" — named after the
marvelous and mysterious machine of the *Kalevala* — the desire of the
national romantic movement to create a whole building, down to the interior friezes, is still readily (though, by now, somewhat dingily) discerni-
ble, as it formerly was in the Private Bank, a work of Sonck and Valter
Jung. Mortality among the buildings of national romanticism has been
high, some representatives having disappeared altogether: such was the
fate of "Nordbanken" on Unionsgatan, designed by Gesellius, Lindgren,
and Saarinen, a lighter and more elegant building than its brothers, but
one lasting only thirty years, from 1904 until 1934. Others have been

quite transformed; the building of the Finnish Steamship Company on Unionsgatan, by Harald Neovius, has lost much of its original character through repair and rebuilding — yet those typical bay windows can still be spotted.

"Gesellius, Lindgren, and Saarinen" came to pieces in a friendly way, while national romanticism was still in full bloom. Saarinen interested himself, from 1907 on, more and more in international and domestic competitions, winning one of his many prizes in 1908 for a design of a new diet-building, to be placed on the slope of Observatory Hill. Realizing the earlier plan of Frans Anatolius Sjöström, the monument would have corresponded, in magnificent visibility, to Sonck's church due north along Unionsgatan. For better or worse, the diet was never built — not in Saarinen's form nor in the location he proposed. When the parliament of the Finnish Republic got its home, in 1931, it was the work of Johan Sigfrid Sirén, and had landed on the knoll where the Arcadia Theater had ended its days, across from the railroad yards. Lindgren struck out on his own two years before Saarinen, giving Helsingfors a set of imposing structures — the "New Student Union" of 1910, coupled to the "Old Student House" like an elephant to a gazelle; the "Suomi Building," an insurance company headquarters at Andrégatan (Lönnrotsgatan) and Georgsgatan, which likewise dwarfs a graceful neighbor, Engel's wooden church in the park opposite (the facades were by Lindgren, the plans by Törnqvist-Tarjanne); and another insurance-house, again on Henriksgatan, the Kaleva Building of grayish-red granite, a fitting companion to the massive Student Union next door. Critics were enthusiastic about the new Lindgren, who had abandoned the wilder excesses of national romanticism without giving up its strength; in *The Architect*, Sigurd Frosterus — calling the outside world's attention to Finland's recently acquired treasures in the building art — wrote that "the Suomi Building is the most distinguished work of Lindgren so far, enriching the city with a sight which far surpasses the norms of the day." As for Sonck, he continued his work with energy unabated, designing the pillared "Hypoteksforening" ("Mortgage Union") of 1908 (a year which also found him at work on a spiritual task, Berghäll Church), the "Stock Exchange" of 1911, in which he grew more monumental, and the giant storehouse on Skatudden, beside Nyström's modest customs office. In these later works of Lindgren and Sonck, as well as in the revisions undertaken by Saarinen in the railroad station plans (so grand and complicated a venture that the building was not completed until 1919, even as Sonck's storehouse went on from 1913 until 1928), it became evident that the "architect-poets" had grown tired of their "backwoods symphonies in stone." Their style fell prey to wide-spread copying, some of it worthy (as in the case of the firm of Usko Nyström,

Petrelius, and Penttilä), some not; looking at the imitations, Saarinen wrote of a "chaos of form" and a "hunger for profit." The fathers of the movement were therefore constrained to change to a manner related but different, massive still, but much simpler and sterner. The intoxication was over. Good and bad national romanticism remained the style by which Finland's architecture was best-known abroad, until Alvar Aalto and Erik Bryggman won their international reputations in the 1930's. But Helsingfors had visually profited. A German guidebook of 1927 claimed that the city "offers architectonic beauties in a genuinely astonishing abundance . . . [they] compete with one another in beauty of style and grandeur, so that the glance of the foreigner who walks through its streets is captivated again and again."

11. City Planning

AS NATIONAL ROMANTICISM went down the primrose path, its creators — and especially Saarinen — turned their attention to a new and related discipline, city planning; it seemed as though the spirit of Ehrenström had returned. In 1907, Bertel Jung, Armas Lindgren, and Lars Sonck submitted a plan for Eira to the municipal government. With its elevated position beside the sea, Eira could well become one of the loveliest parts of Helsingfors, second not even to neighboring Brunnsparken. The plan would turn Eira into a genuine "garden town"; all the houses would be of a relatively uniform size and would meet high esthetic standards. Unhappily, Eira fell instead into too small a space, and regulations concerning height were applied with the greatest tolerance. Nonetheless, many of the buildings put up in Eira, and sometimes their settings, bear witness to good taste: Selim A. Lindqvist's graceful little Villa Ensi, is pleasant to regard even today, as are many of the apartments and homes that grace the section — here too the facile and elegant Lindqvist was very active.

Shortly the city-planners tried again, Bertel Jung with thoughts for a redoing of the residential parts of Brunnsparken (as the first architect in Finland to specialize in city planning, he was well equipped for the job), and Saarinen with a plan for a "new city" out at Munksnäs-Haga, far to the north-west of the center of Helsingfors, on the shores of Bredviken. The plan was published in 1915, with contributions by various hands, including those of the brilliant Strengell, who presented cogent reasons for planning new sections well in advance of their being taken into use: if Helsingfors continued to grow as rapidly as it had in the recent past, then, without preparation, impossible problems of domicile and transportation would arise. In earlier days — Saarinen's argument in *his* part of the book on Munksnäs-Haga — "a complete subjectivism and arbitrariness had prevailed; every builder, like every architect, thought only of himself; no one cared about architectural co-operation." As proof, Saarinen adduced some photographs of horrors recently perpetrated in Eira. Saarinen envisioned a different and better fate for Munksnäs; a pleasant sameness of design (within reason) would prevail, and each subsection would have its own style and character. "The beach-section will be inhabited by the well-to-do, the blocks around Hoplax station and north of the railroad by the middle class," and, "toward the west, in the direction of Sockenbacka, there will be an industrial tract, with dwellings for workers."

In 1918, Saarinen's plan for "Greater Helsingfors," sponsored by the public-spirited Julius Tallberg, came out; it had been completed in the first flush of Finland's independence, and made awed reference to the possibility of Helsingfors becoming a "royal city," the residence of Friedrich Karl of Hessia, Kaiser Wilhelm's brother-in-law, presently touted as Finland's king. Other thoughts in it are likewise dizzying: Saarinen proposed the removal of the railroad station, not yet completed in its present site, to Fredriksberg, far away, on the other side of Tölö Bay (which would be filled in completely, thus finishing the work started by Ehrenström), beyond the parklands of Djurgården; the station would then be joined to the city's center by a mighty thoroughfare, ninety meters across, to be called "King's Avenue." (The germ of the plan is supposed to have sprung in the mind of a convict, who submitted it to the city fathers with a proposal that he and his colleagues would provide the labor; Tallberg, admiring boldness, passed the suggestion along to Saarinen and his fellow workers.) Had the plan been carried out — and, like so many of Saarinen's dreams, it was not — the city would have been more imposing in its layout than it presently is; and the dreadful traffic problems posed by the combination of hilly terrain, inlets, and narrow peninsula might well have been ameliorated. Yet Engel's Helsingfors, by such a removal of the city's center-of-gravity northward, could have lost at least some of its vitality, becoming more a museum than an integral part of the city's life. Was it disappointment at the failure to realize this plan and others which helped Saarinen decide to leave for America? He was a man who put heart and soul in his work, and for whom no detail was too small; Per Nyström, a Munksnäs enthusiast, tells how Saarinen, preparing the giant model of his "new town," carved out the main buildings himself, assigning the dwelling houses to his assistants.

Whatever the cause of Saarinen's departure (in 1922) may have been, Helsingfors lost its most fecund planner's mind, just as, upon the death of

Julius Tallberg a year before, it had lost the most brillant and generous of its businessmen. Like Saarinen, Tallberg realized that the population of Helsingfors would grow ever more rapidly. In 1911 he had purchased the island of Drumsö, west of the main peninsula, for 750,000 marks, after the previous owners, offering it to the city for 900,000 marks, had been refused; Tallberg then proposed to sell it to Helsingfors for precisely the amount he had paid, cognizant of the fact that the island, a summer vacation spot in those simpler days, would provide residential room shortly to be needed by the city. Blind to its future needs, Helsingfors rebuffed him. Parodying Tallberg's expansive manner, Guss Mattsson nonetheless paid him an extraordinary compliment. In Mattsson's feuilleton, the directors of "Brändö Company" phoned Tallberg to offer him their property, complete with special streetcar-line, elegant villas, and a casino from the drawing board of Armas Lindgren. (Brändö, an island to the east of the peninsula, was controlled by a private concern.) The company's proposition went as follows: "'Mr. Tallberg, we've heard that you're in the market for used islands. We're a company that could offer you a very nice one, almost as good as new, just a little ragged around the edges.'" And Tallberg's reply: "'I understand. Well, perhaps you'll send it up to me for inspection some day soon, and then we'll find out whether it's suitable or not.'" Men of Saarinen's and Tallberg's heroic measure may cause the skeptic to smile; yet some melancholy clings to them as well, for they came too late. What would Saarinen and Tallberg have done with Helsingfors, if given an opportunity like that which fate and Alexander I afforded Ehrenström and Engel?

Still another show of the same bold optimism about the future of Helsingfors is to be found in the plans of Amos Anderson, a country boy from Kimito who had made good in the business life of the big city. Anderson — in later years director and chief editor of *Hufvudstadsbladet* and Maecenas of the Swedish Theater — dreamed of a revival of Helsingfors as a vacation spot; the golden age of Brunnsparken would return, on an even grander, albeit more democratic, scale. Anderson first published his plans in 1909, then revised them in 1915. In the first edition, written while anti-Finnish sentiment was high in Russian nationalistic circles, he argued that a by-product of increased Russian tourism was to be had; the Russians would form their impressions of Finland at first-hand, rather than being misled by their newspapers. (Anderson took it for granted that the good folk of Helsingfors would make a favorable impression on the contemporary guests from the east, just as they had on Grot some eighty years before.) By the time the second edition of Anderson's panegyric to his adopted city appeared, the outbreak of war had compelled the Russians to go abroad to Finland if they went abroad at all; Anderson was convinced that they would find Helsingfors to be "a lovely city, whose location is doubtless one of the most beautiful in the north." But in March, 1917, the Russian revolution began; eventually, some of those Russians who might have been paying guests in Finland came instead as penniless refugees. Helsingfors itself had other problems than tourism to worry about. In the March days, a veritable hunt after Russian officers took place in the streets of Helsingfors, a spectacle the citizens watched with very mixed sentiments, gratified patriotism, human sympathy, and anxiety for their own skin among them; much of what happened on Sveaborg, in Åbo Barracks, and on the ships in the naval harbor remained a mystery, no doubt a bloody one. As in the early days of the war, a German invasion of Finland was feared; Kerenski's government poured new and not very well disciplined units into the country and the city. By August, there were some 25,000 men on Sveaborg and in the city's other military establishments.

12. On the Eve, 1917

A SPRINGTIME OF somewhat confused jubilance was followed by a summer of anxiety. By the manifesto of March 20, the interim government had restored to Finland the constitutional rights it once enjoyed. "The lion-banners waved over Helsingfors," as they had so briefly during the great strike of 1905. "Hearts were full at the sight. The manifesto had come. Legality was restored. And on the streets, people passed back and forth with garlands of flowers around their necks, as if at a masquerade." This is the way Erik Grotenfelt described "the springtime of freedom" in his book, *Det nya fosterlandet* (*The New Fatherland*, 1918), a novel written in the very midst of the events described. A few days later, Kerenski himself appeared in Helsingfors, to assure the populace of his good will and his government's; his visit coincided with the return of Pehr Evind Svinhufvud from his exile in Siberia, whither he had been sent in November, 1914, at the order of Governor-general Seyn. (A judge, Svinhufvud had been unwilling to recognize the Russian procurator's right to review a legal decision he had reached.) Delight at Kerenski's announced good intentions was mingled with some innocent merriment at the buss the Russian planted on the cheek of Antti Oskari Tokoi. A sometime mineworker in America, Tokoi had more recently (1913) been a successful speaker of the diet, to the considerable surprise of those who distrusted Social Democrats. Now, as head of his party, which had the majority in the diet, Tokoi was briefly a man of vital importance — and a man who lived, for the rest, in Berghäll, the worker's stronghold. The euphoria, and the smiles, quickly passed; lack of foodstuffs caused demonstration after demonstration on Senate Square; and, on Easter Sunday, Tokoi himself had to calm the masses; a little later, the quondam fortification-workers, mostly armed, appropriated the contents of the stands on Market Square, at prices they themselves determined. Hereupon, a rationing system was introduced; and queues became a common sight in the capital. With considerable regret, Grotenfelt, who had an eye for almost everything around him but the despair — and the simultaneous sense of strength — which filled the city's masses, lamented the damage done to the city's customarily idyllic summer atmosphere: "But this summer it seemed as though the earlier air of peace and quiet had been taken away . . . by harsh hands. All those places that for many, many years had been the goal of the pilgrimages of lonely wanderers, were desecrated by clamorous mobs." The wanderers were changed, too: "they were pulled along by the storm and cast into the great herd of men, and themselves became fumbling, struggling, yearning and searching creatures."

Several hundred members of the Red Guard, disbanded a decade ago, assembled in Kajsaniemi Park on May 12, 1917, with the express intention of taking up where they had left off; on August 17, the Helsingfors Defence Corps, after several weeks of training, came out into the open too. The occasion was an outbreak of civil disorder. The city fathers found themselves besieged by Finnish working men and Russian sailors as they met in Lars Sonck's new Stock Exchange: the besiegers, demanding a minimum hourly wage of 2:50 marks, were driven away shortly after midnight by athletic young men with white arm bands around their arms — former policemen, members of the Kronohagen Sports Club, and others. Thus the two forces which had confronted one another before Stockmann's and at the Hagnäs trolley-stop were locked in dubious battle once more; the initial victory of the youths at the Stock Exchange, armed with billy-clubs, inspired false confidence. A regular police-force presumably could have prevented such a clash, but it had been disbanded, as a representative of czarist power. Indeed, the preservation of the general public's safety had become a steadily more serious problem; women did not like to go out after dark, and Djurgården was to be avoided at all costs. Idealists among the Russian troops thought that the behavior of some of their fellows was scarcely appropriate for representatives of the revolution; a letter to the editor of the short-lived newspaper, *Helsingfors Izvestia*, was filled with indignation: "I am given to understand that the behavior of our soldiers and sailors in Djurgården even goes beyond drunkenness and petit larceny," the author wrote, in a quaint turn of phrase perhaps intended to spare the reader's blushes. "I should like to ask the company-committees and ship-committees to explain the nature of freedom more frequently to their comrades, who apparently do not know what they are doing." Experimenting with liberty, the Russian enlisted men were not to blame for all the unpleasant occurrences; cessation of work on the chain of fortifications around Helsingfors "sent an army of unemployed, gathered from all over the country and comprising elements of a low cultural standard, flooding out across the city."

Public turbulence was accompanied by political confusion. On July 18, having assured themselves of the support of the Socialist parties in Russia, the Social Democrats pushed the so-called "law of authority" through the diet, by which the diet itself became the "highest authority" in Finland. The government in Petrograd could see to foreign and military affairs. Two weeks later, the diet was dissolved, at the wish of Kerenski; the next-to-last of the Russian governor-generals, Stahovitch, announced that he would use armed force if the Social Democrats, who did not intend to give up their position of power without a struggle, refused to prepare for a new election. On August 29, Kullervo Manner, the Speaker of the dissolved diet, called for a plenary session; Stahovitch retorted by sending troopers of the 14th Hussars to the Heimola Building (the former headquarters of the Old Finnish Party, now used as the diet's meeting place), with orders to turn the members of the diet away. The show of force worked, but only for a time. Within three weeks, Stahovitch retired from his post; his place was taken by Nikolai Nekrasov, whose reign, if it may be called that, lasted from the end of September until news of the October (Bolshevik) revolution arrived. The main event witnessed by Nekrasov was the election of a new diet, on October 1–2; when the votes were counted, it was learned that the Social Democrats had lost their majority.

The radical faction in the Social Democratic party then decided on "direct action" in the fashion just practised in Russia; a first demonstration of this dangerous course was the strike of November 13–20, an event much bloodier than its forerunner of 1905. Some 15 people were murdered in the environs of Helsingfors, and 36 in the whole land: the deeds had the air of reprisals against those unhappy souls considered to be the tools of the establishment. Many of the victims were Swedish-speakers. A widow Sahlström in Fredriksberg, whose two sons had been killed on the steps of their home by men who spoke Finnish, said: "I believe that the Russians would have shown more mercy." Learning that members of the Red Guard laughed, when, out in Malm, the wife of a mortally wounded man asked them to bear their victim indoors, Juhani Aho wrote in *Haja-mietteitä kapinaviikoilta* (*Stray Thoughts from the Weeks of Rebellion*): "I hear that genuine Finnish laughter, crude and piercing, the like of which I've never heard from any other people." What had become of the "patience and mildness, the simplicity and piety," that Runeberg knew? The shocked members of the middle and upper classes called it "the bloody week"; they would see much worse in short order. Nor would their fears have been allayed by a speech held at the extraordinary congress of the Social Democratic party in Helsingfors on November 25–27, immediately in the strike's wake, a speech the moderate Social Democrats themselves found upsetting in the extreme. The orator was a Georgian, Josef Dzhugashvili-Stalin, who had what might be called sentimental ties to Finland; he had first met Lenin at the Social Democratic party congress in Tammerfors in 1905. Presently, through his interpreter, he said: "In an atmosphere such as this, only Danton's tactics — boldness, boldness, and again boldness — can help. If you want our aid, you'll get it, from hands outstreched in friendship."

13. War of Liberation, Civil War, Finnish Revolution

IT WAS ALSO of considerable significance, for those who could read the signs, that the proclamation of Finland's independence, presented to the diet on December 4, was supported by the bourgeois parties in its more extreme form, which simply ignored the existence of a government in Russia. The Speaker of the previous diet, with its "law of authority," Kullervo Manner, presented the Social Democratic alternative, to the effect that "independence must be sought by conciliatory means, in the form of an agreement with Russia." The parties of the right wing won, and on December 6 Finland suddenly became an independent nation. Positions were reversed: the side that had been hesitant about a break with Russia in July wanted speedy action in December, and vice versa. The exchange, and its motivations, fed one of those protracted debates that make the study of Finland's history so tortuous and so fascinating. Those advancing the claims of "the White faction" would interpret the Social Democratic switch as a symptom of the latter group's wish to stick to Russia, now that the Bolsheviks were in the saddle; prolocutors of the Social Democrats would say that their faction likewise wanted independence, but only after negotiations with Lenin's government, which had taken (the Social Democrats had been assured) a standpoint favorable to an independent Finland. A difference of opinion would also exist on the name of the armed conflict which followed hard on the heels of the declaration of independence. Was it "The War of Independence," as it was called by

persons of a conservative camp, who thereby implied that the Reds were
Bolshevik tools, wishing alliance with the new Russia? Or was it "The Civil
War," a name indicating a conflict between Finlanders of differing political
and social ideologies? Or was it "The Finnish Revolution"? Just so, the
character of the war's main figure has given rise to strikingly disparate interpretations: was he a savior of his young nation, or an opportunistic adventurer, or a "butcher," plain out, as the insulting ditties of the Reds
called him?

A veteran officer, Gustaf Mannerheim had served Nicholas with distinction against the entente forces in Poland, in Galicia, in the Carpathi-
ans, in Bessarabia; even after March, 1917, he had continued as
commander on the Transylvanian front, promoted to lieutenant-general
and in charge of the Sixth Corps of Cavalry. A riding mishap gave him an
excuse to resign his post; since September he had been resting in Odessa,
but the Bolshevik revolution made him decide to abandon his pleasant
hotel and the city's good weather. Accompanied by a youthful Finno-
Swedish hussar, Martin Franck, he went northward by train; his companion records that, despite the perils such bravery entailed, he refused to remove his officer's insignia, "traveling in the full uniform of a general."
After an eight-day journey, "in which our lives often hung by a hair," the
pair reached Petrograd; the general stayed here for a week, coolly deter-
mining the political lay of the land. Then he climbed on board another
train, and continued his journey to Helsingfors, arriving on December 17.
Immediately after Christmas, he made a final excursion to Petrograd, in
order to aid old friends caught in the growing terror there, returning to
Finland's capital in time for a New Year's celebration at the home of his
sister Sophie. The other guests were perhaps more notable than the retired
general of an empire gone to smash — Professor Faltin (the physician who
had cared for Mannerheim during the Manchurian campaign), A.W.
Finch, Magnus Enckell. But Mannerheim's stock rose immediately. A
"military committee" had been formed early in 1917, a private group
comprised mostly of former officers in Finland's military before it was dissolved during the "years of oppression"; the committee meant to organize
a defence force for Finland, with its newly achieved but doubtful independence. On January 7, 1918, the Senate, aware that an armed conflict
was imminent, recognized the committee as an organ of state; a week
later, Mannerheim was elected as its chairman. His predecessor had been
another officer returned from Russia, Claës Charpentier, who graciously
made way for the younger man. (Charpentier possessed one skill not
shared by his replacement — he spoke fluent Finnish.) Mannerheim's personality and gifts were well-known to the committeemen, for most of
them were alumni of the Fredrikshamn military academy, from which

Mannerheim had been expelled once upon a time. The vigor he displayed as a young cadet and a field officer stood him in good stead now; he told the committee, which had assumed the comfortable ways of a gentlemen's club, that it must act directly if it intended to act at all. A matter of prime importance was to establish a military base far away from the capital; Helsingfors was destined, like Petrograd before it, to fall into Red hands. After an interview with Svinhufvud, in which Mannerheim convinced the Senate's procurator that a White army could be stamped out of the earth, the general set out by train for Vasa, in Ostrobothnia, where the Red Guard was weak, and communication with the western world relatively easy. The overnight trip was as perilous, in Mannerheim's opinion, as the journey from the Ukraine to Petrograd; Mannerheim needed both the help of false papers (made out to a traveling salesman, Gustaf Malmberg) and of a quick-thinking railroad man to get past the Russian soldiers who inspected the train at Tammerfors. In Vasa, Mannerheim got word that Russian military trains were on their way thither, with reinforcements. Ignoring a call for patience from Svinhufvud, who expressed hopes that he could persuade the Russians to refrain from intervention, Mannerheim ordered an attack on the five Russian garrisons around Vasa; and his peasant troops, "a handful of men unafraid" in Mannerheim's bristling description, got the Russians to surrender. Mannerheim's assault began at 3:00 on Monday morning, January 28; at 11:00 the previous evening, a red lantern was hung on the tower of the People's House in Helsingfors, a signal for the Red Guard to march down from Berghäll and occupy the city. Its commander was Eero Haapalainen, whose desire for action, thwarted back in 1905, presently found only a mild fulfillment. The Defence Corps of Helsingfors saw directly that it was quite outnumbered and outgunned by the Red Guards and (if they wished to pitch in) the Russian soldiers and sailors. All the Whites had, in fact, was music: the *Jägarmarsch* or *Jääkärien marssi* of Sibelius, a setting of Heikki Nurmio's poem, written while Nurmio was stationed in Libau with the 27th Light Infantry, and dedicated to the Finlanders serving in the German army. It had its first public performance in Finland on January 19, in the aula of Helsingfors University. The words of Heikki Nurmio, to which the White supporters had listened so intently at their patriotic concert, suddenly became empty: "Häme, Karjala, Vieran rannat ja maa, / Yks, suuri Suomen valta" ("Tavastland, Karelia, shores and land of the White Sea, / Great and united is Finland's rule"). The Reds held the southern part of the country, its major cities and its industry.

The supremacy of the Red Guard in Helsingfors lasted about two-and-one-half months; during this time, the city slowly ceased to function. The directorship of the civil service union decided at a secret meeting on January 29 to ask its membership not to aid the Reds, and their request was widely followed, with the result that the postal and telegraph service no longer was in operation, and the railroads ran only when the Reds could find willing personnel. Schools and banks were shut; since the gold reserve of Finland's Bank was in Kuopio, behind the White lines, the Reds used the bank's printing establishment, in Helsingfors, to turn out new bills. State-owned and private factories, as well as the larger places of business, closed down. The closings — dictated mostly by an unwillingness to co-operate with the Reds — were not altogether wise: the unemployed were readily recruited into the Red Guard. A particularly depressing factor, for the city's White sympathizers, was the lack of news. Mimeographed copies of *Fria ord* or *Vapaa Sana*, a title and spirit borrowed from the days of Bobrikov's oppression, were eagerly read, whenever they could be obtained: the paper got its information from hidden telegraph stations and radio senders. The press of the side in power blossomed. In Swedish, remarkably, there appeared three papers (*Arbetet, Finlands Folkkommissariats Notisblad,* and *Arbetarnas Notisblad*) and, in Finnish, *Työmies* flourished as never before, supposedly attaining some 90,000 subscribers before the fall of the Red regime; it was seconded by the organ of the people's commissariat, *Työväen Tiedonantaja* (*Workers' Intelligencer*). Red and White alike, the population of the city was better supplied with worthless currency and newsprint than with food. The Red government tried hard to keep life in the city running as normally as possible, a task made much more difficult by the hesitance of the moderate Social Democrats to assume positions of authority; the Council of People's Commissars dispatched several trains to Russia, loaded with agricultural machinery to be exchanged for grain, but only one of the expeditions returned. Word got around that some people in Helsingfors were hoarding victuals, as indeed they were; the Red Guard entered private homes in a combined search for food and firearms. The lucky owners of a food supply used all their wits, naturally enough, in efforts at concealment; large brass curtain rods became caches. Foragers, foolhardy or simply hungry, went out into the countryside on the few trains still leaving Helsingfors; the way home could be extremely uncomfortable. The Red Guard carefully inspected packs and valises.

Other travelers left or tried to leave the city for good and all, young men determined to make their way to Mannerheim's army or, a more practicable idea, to join one of the Defence Corps groups near the capital; during February, these bands provided a certain irritation for the Red leadership. Older men departed too: Senator Edvard Hjelt got out of Helsingfors on a train filled with Swedish citizens bound for Björneborg, and Svinhufvud made a daring attempt at escape by seaplane, which had to return to its base at Hermanstad after mechanical difficulties arose. Never say die: disguised as an engineer, Svinhufvud then sailed off on the ice-breaker *Tarmo*, ostensibly to investigate the ships frozen fast in the Gulf of Finland. Having concealed themselves on board, members of the Defence Corps seized the *Tarmo* and set its course for Reval. Once on the continent, Svinhufvud and his companion, Senator Jalmari Castrén, had easy going to Berlin, and thence north again to Ostrobothnia. Other people entered Helsingfors: hearing of Red atrocities, White sympathizers in rural districts decided that there was greater safety in numbers. Among the refugees from nearby were Jean Sibelius and his family. The home at Järvenpää had been ransacked in February; upon the intercession of Robert Kajanus, the composer was persuaded to join his brother Christian at Lappvik Asylum, of which the latter was the director. (The psychiatrist had demonstrated the quick Sibelius tongue in response to a demand that he receive patients from the Red Guards in his hospital. He had no space, Dr. Sibelius retorted, and, besides: "You're all crazy anyway.")

The road to the capital could end in death; after the collapse of the Defence Corps operations near Borgå, a number of its members crept back into Helsingfors. Some succeeded in reaching their homes, thanks to luck or the persuasive quality of their friendly conversations with Red sentries, but other corpsmen, about 20 of them, were shot in the streets of Kronohagen or on the ice of North Harbor. The Defence Corps detachment based at Sigurds Estate near the hamlet of Kyrkslätt withdrew southward toward Porkala; outnumbered and outfought, they surrendered, and were saved from massacre by the intercession of an attaché from the Swedish legation in Helsingfors. Transported to the capital, they were imprisoned at the Swedish Reallyceum building, where they had considerable propaganda value as an object lesson in the humanity of the Reds. The People's Commissars attempted to prevent murder and atrocity; yet, under such disorganized conditions, they were scarcely able to stop individual acts of cruelty. An estimated 30 people were slain in Helsingfors during the Red regime, not counting the youths returning from the Borgå-Pellinge enterprise. Some were taken while smuggling weapons and executed out of hand, like Thorvald Schwindt and Osvald Häggman; others were the victims of political murder, like Antti Mikkola, shot on the ice of Tölö Bay because, a member of the diet, he had championed the establishment of a military force; still other deaths resulted from chance, as in the case of a young physician, Gösta Schybergson, killed (the story goes) because he laughed, his murderers imagined, at their pronunciation of the "b" sound, which turns into a "p" in Finnish; they were inquiring after a head nurse named Blom, suspected of harboring members of the Defence Corps. (The anecdote about Schybergson's death, whether true or not, reveals a great deal about attitudes prevalent on both sides.) Investigators of the "Red Terror" (as opposed to the "White Terror" which followed the war) have observed that the Red atrocities aroused particular indignation because they often involved prominent people. Such was Mikkola's case; such were the executions, in the forest near Vichtis, of the Thomé brothers, the forester William and the architects Valter and Ivar; such was the shooting in his Eira residence of Oskar Rosenquist, director of the Swedish Commercial School, thought to be a distributor of *Fria ord*; and such was the death of an aged general in retirement, Carl Silverhjelm, who refused to admit the Red Guard to his apartment. He held them off single-handed for three hours, a man of 76 with a pistol against machine guns, until he took his own life.

At a secret meeting in the Old Student House in February, a White Guard for Helsingfors was organized; its purpose was an eventual uprising against the Reds. Well supplied with money, it began to collect weapons wherever it could; its gunrunners showed their bravery again and again, young women among them. Its drills, on stocking feet in dimly-lit apartments, had a mildly hopeless air about them, until the news came, via the secret receivers, that on April 3 the "Baltic Division," 9,500 troops of the German army under General Rüdiger von der Goltz, had landed at Hangö. (The Kaiser's government had more than willingly accepted the invitation of the White government's representatives to participate in the conflict.) In his memoirs, von der Goltz, with typical German modesty, wrote that: "the mere appearance of German steel helmets caused the Red opposition to melt away." The German advance eastward was hampered a little by the bicycle companies attached to von der Goltz's expeditionary force — the bicycle was not the most effective means of military transport on Finnish roads early in April. Red Guard units, five companies in all, were sent out from Helsingfors; these poor fellows had little chance agains the "sieggewohnte deutsche Truppen." (Twenty-one companies had already been dispatched toward Lembois, to help in the fighting around Tammerfors, but that city fell to the army of Mannerheim on April 5, after a brave defence.) By April 8, the Russian fleet in Helsingfors had got steam up and sailed away to Kronstadt, voluntarily improving upon the Hangö agreement by which the admiral of the Russian Baltic Fleet promised that the crews of his ships and the garrisons of his fortresses would not intervene in the fighting; in return, the Germans would eventually see to it that the Russians got home safely. The mariners decided not to wait and see if the Germans would keep their promise. As for Sveaborg, its guns might still have posed a threat to von der Goltz's men as they entered the capital, since units of the Red Guard had taken over parts of the fortress; but the cannon had been taken care of by a daring ruse on the part of an engineer named Allan Staffans and his helpers. The little band appeared at Sveaborg under the pretext of seeing to questions of reparations and storage under the terms of the Brest-Litovsk Treaty, and, aided by anti-Bolshevik officers of Polish birth, made most of the armaments on Sveaborg usable.

The newspapers of the Council of People's Commissars put the best possible light on the German landing: "A weak force of White Guards has been set ashore in Hangö harbor, of whom a few members wear German uniforms." All the same, "workers' companies" were quickly formed, to aid in the defence of the city, and, even as they were being set up, the commissars started to flee (April 5), followed two days later by the Red general staff: the report had arrived that the Germans had also landed at Lovisa, to the east, and the commanders did not wish to be cut off from Russia. Two days more, and Captain Sigurd af Ekström of the Swedish legation reported to the Germans that the Red forces in Helsingfors were prepared to surrender; von der Goltz replied that he would guarantee their safety until they had been turned over to Finnish courts. The reply was not satisfactory — the members of the Red Guard had the not wholly unreasonable desire to be treated as prisoners of war. After much hesitation and argument, the Reds decided to fight for the city. It was hopeless: apart from the German troops now at Alberga, where Ville Vallgren had once promenaded with his pig, there were the German war ships the icebreaker *Sampo* had brought into the harbor on the evening of April 11. Last but hardly least, four battalions of the White Guard waited inside Helsingfors, ready to rise up from their manifold hiding places upon signal. They had their own plans for taking the city without German aid, a notion which would have made von der Goltz smile — later on, he said diplomatically that the White Guard was "essential for the morale of the population."

On the morning of April 12, the final German advance began; in the afternoon, amid some confusion, the White Guard appeared on the streets. By four o'clock, a German prong had reached the National Museum, but Åbo Barracks proved a hard nut to crack; during the night, it was set on fire by artillery. Guided by members of the White Guard, smaller German detachments were sent out in various directions, one going around by the back way, over Sandviken, to Saint John's Church and then north to the former Barracks of the Finnish Guard, another taking the Swedish Theater. The Finnish National Theater fell, and the edges of Kronohagen were reached; meanwhile 400 German sailors captured Skatudden. The Reds were still in control of Berghäll, of course, and of Kronohagen; but, the next day, their last strength flickered out. The Red's headquarters, the old governor-general's palace, dubbed "Smolna" in imitation of Lenin's seat in Petrograd, came under siege and surrendered.

The imperial residence, the main guardhouse, and Borgström's tobacco factory — all places with memories of the age of Engel clinging to them — were bombarded into submission by the battleships anchored in South Harbor; the defenders of Borgström's were women. Stiff resistance was still to be met in Berghäll; the "Worker's House" was shelled by field artillery from across Tölö Bay and caught on fire; the last way of retreat through Hermanstad was cut off. At 2:00 on the afternoon of April 13, white flags were hung from the tower of Sonck's Berghäll Church and other prominent places.

14. Victory

THE GERMANS HAD a military band with them, and, wasting no time, held a victory parade through the city on the 14th; a report was spread that Red snipers were concealed along the route, and the White Guards, thirsting for action, went out in search of these largely imaginary spoil-sports. "Das ist aber ein komischer Krieg," a German officer was heard to say. The German soldiers and White Guards killed during the capture of the city were buried in the park of Old Church, in graves dug at night by Red prisoners; the work was directed by Birger Brunila, chief of city planning in Helsingfors. At the funeral service for the 54 Germans, Rector Waldemar Ruin of the university read a poem cataloguing the manifold virtues of the saviors and their nation; beside them, three days later, were placed the bodies of the 19 White Guards who had fallen: their names — among them a Pitkänen, a Westerlund, a Leontjeff, a Campbell — told something about their backgrounds, and the city from which they came. The members of the expeditionary force received the hospitality of a grateful populace; they had their headquarters, its entrance smartly flanked by mounted sentries, in Hotel Kämp, and they were feted, at least the officers among them, in the city's best homes. (Near the town of Lahtis, not far from Helsingfors, German troops had seen much more serious fighting than in the capital; on May 1–2, they confronted the main Red army, fleeing eastward from southwestern Finland, and took some 20,000 prisoners.) The troops' behavior toward everyone except the Red prisoners was unimpeachable. A young girl named Monica Ehrström, daughter of a professor of medicine at the university, recorded in her diary, quite without sentiment, how the Germans had made the Reds run the gauntlet across Market Square, "jumping over the bodies of [other] Red bandits." The day before, as fighting still went on, little Monica had seen something else that was memorable; as the Germans removed their captives from the Swedish Theater, they "hit them with their gunbutts, and the Reds howled and held their hands outstretched." One German soldier's opinion of the Reds was that "only the Belgians were worse." Presently, no one said in public, and few said in private, what the authoress named Sigrid Backman, the daughter of a Helsingfors streetcar conductor, concluded: "The Red War — no one was to blame for it." Meanwhile, the banquets went on. At his villa on Drumsö, Julius Tallberg asked von der Goltz, "Herr General, essen Sie Fil?", and the general, confused by the homonyms ("fil" is Swedish for yogurt, and "viel" is German for much), thought for a moment that he and his colleagues had been overeating. Von der Goltz, for the rest, resided in some luxury at Bjälbo, the former summer residence of the governors-general.

On May 16, Mannerheim and his White army, their part of the campaign completed, staged a formal entry into the city; the General, on his stallion Neptune, and in his white fur cap, cut the finest figure. He was followed by his men, or at least the most presentable detachments from among them; it was the first parade of what Bertel Gripenberg called "Finland's army, the army long dreamt of in secret." The veterans drew up on Senate Square; having addressed the Senate in its chamber, Mannerheim emerged, accompanied by Pehr Evind Svinhufvud and the other senators, to meet the members of the diet, assembled beside the statue of Alexander II, as the band played "Our Country." Then the music changed to "The March of the Men of Björneborg," and Mannerheim inspected rank and file, followed by Svinhufvud and his suite. After saluting the German officers stationed before the University, the General turned to a final task: the exchange of speeches with Alfred Norrmén, banker and chairman of the city council, who had the honor of informing Mannerheim that Helsingfors, in gratitude, wished to give a million marks to the widows and children of his army's slain. Mannerheim received the check with a speech of thanks which contained a hint, as the general's biographer Stig Jägerskiöld remarks, that von der Goltz's expeditionary force could now be removed: "May the city's inhabitants hereafter sleep soundly in the knowledge that the steady tread of our own sentries never again will cease to resound on the streets of the capital." It was a subtle way of getting back at Svinhufvud who, Mannerheim believed, had broken his pledge not to call for foreign aid. The day's ceremonies next included a divine service in Nikolai Church; as the general ascended the steps, he could be admired by the representatives of Finland's womanhood who lined them, clad all in white. God having got His due, the performance came to an end with a review of the troops, who marched past the statue of Runeberg on the Esplanade; the General, mounted again, took the salute in the poet's immediate vicinity. Before the month was out, Mannerheim had resigned his command and departed for Stockholm; on May 18, Svinhufvud had been selected "director of the country" by the diet. The German question, in all its aspects and nuances, was probably the cause for Mannerheim's sudden departure from this "promised land of intrigue," as a Swedish diplomat called Finland. Mannerheim was somewhat unpopular with the young veterans of German training because of his anti-German feelings, not always well hidden, and because he had been a Russian general, at home in the company of officers from a like background. And he was a Swedish-speaker, a quality which did not recommend him to Finns of a certain stamp. These had found a substitute hero in Aarne Sihvo, a sometime member of the Prussian 27th Light Infantry and an officer who had performed brilliantly in the Karelian campaign at the war's conclusions; on the very day of Mannerheim's victory parade, Sihvo had proudly informed the readership of *Uusi Suometar* and *Uusi Päivä* that not a word of Swedish had sullied his lips during his days of command.

Four days prior to the parade, Svinhufvud had officially taken possession of Sveaborg for Finland; the lion-banner was raised above the Carpelan bastion. A poetess in Karelia, Edith Södergran, saw photographs of the event in the newspapers, and wrote:

> Does not our wonderful citadel arise from the sea in Helsingfors?
> Do not the sentries stand there with blue and red banners the world has
>   not seen?
> Do not they stand there, leaned on their spears, looking out over the sea,
> With the granite of fate in their features, turned into stone?

It is estimated that, principally during April and May, some 8,390 persons were summarily executed in acts of punishment or revenge for the 'Red terror' accompanying the war itself. Sveaborg was used as an internment camp for Red prisoners; of the 80,000 men and women held in such camps throughout southern Finland, about 12,500 are estimated to have died, mainly of undernourishment and disease. The enormously wealthy Hjalmar Linder, a friend of Mannerheim (and son of the obscurantist Constantin Linder), published an article in *Hufvudstadbladet* for May 28, 1918, condemning the excesses that had already taken place: "Despite the interdict of the commander-in-chief, the executions go on without pause." And: "Red madness has been succeeded by White terror." Linder's home truths aroused such hatred against him that he left Finland forever; three years later, he killed himself in Marseille.

During the summer, too, monarchists continued to beat the drums for Friedrich Karl of Hessia, who began, with his family, to take Finnish lessons. The sometime Heidenstrauch mansion, subsequently the imperial residence in Helsingfors, was to be fitted out as his palace, and rumor had it that he would call himself Väinö I. On October 9, 1918, Finland's parliament voted to tender him the crown; on a visit to Reval, then occupied by German troops, the estimable prince caught a brief glimpse of the Helsingfors skyline across the Gulf of Finland, but got no closer to his intended realm than that. The sudden collapse of the Kaiser's Germany put an end to the royal phantasy; prudently, Friedrich Karl released Finland from any obligation it might have toward him and, after a plebiscite, Finland officially became a republic.

However foolish the notion of an imported German king — sitting on a freshly baked Finnish throne in a capital where considerable power, intellectual and financial, still lay with Swedish-speakers — may seem to rational eyes, it nonetheless has a certain bizarre or perverse aptness. In a wistful essay, Lorenz von Numers remarks on the cosmopolitan feeling, for all its provinciality, Helsingfors possessed during the century's first decades, and even — for a brief time — after the "War of Liberation" of 1918. Not lovable or charming, Helsingfors' sometime linguistic and cultural variety made it a place with a special bouquet, a capital (Baltic, Scandinavian, North European?) of some singularity. Today, of course, 'Helsingfors' has long since passed from international geographical usage, replaced by its Finnish derivative, Helsinki.

A Glossary of Streets and Places

(In accordance with Swedish and Finnish practice, å, ä, and ö have been placed at the end of the alphabet.)

Swedish:	Finnish:
Abborfors	Ahvenkoski
Abrahamsholmen	Abrahaminluoto
Alberga	Leppävaara
Albertsgatan	Albertinkatu
Alexandersgatan	Aleksanterinkatu
Andrégatan: see Lönnrotsgatan	Antinkatu
Annegatan	Annankatu
Armfeltsvägen	Armfeltinkatu
Berghäll	Kallio
Bjälbo	Kesäranta
Björkudden	Koivuniemi
Björneborg	Pori
Blåbärslandet	Mustikkamaa
Borgå	Porvoo
Botby	Puotila
Brahestad	Raahe
Bredviken	Laajalahti
Broholmen	Siltasaari
Brunnsgatan	Kaivokatu
Brunnsparken	Kaivopuisto
Brändö	Kulosaari
Centralgatan	Keskuskatu
Djurgården	Eläintarha
Djurgardsvägen	Eläintarhantie
Drumsö	Lauttasaari
Ehrenströmsvägen	Ehrenströmintie
Ekenäs	Tammisaari
Elisabetsgatan	Liisankatu
Engelsplatsen	Engelinaukio

Swedish:	*Finnish:*
Esbo	Espoo
Fabiansgatan	Fabianinkatu
Fredriksberg	Pasila
Fredriksgatan	Fredrikinkatu
Fredrikshamn	Hamina
Fredsgatan	Rauhankatu
Gamlakarleby	Kokkola
Gammelstaden	Vanhakaupunki
Gardesmanegen	Kaartinmaneesi
Gasverksgatan	Kaasutehtaankatu
Georgsgatan	Yrjönkatu
Glogatan	Kluuvikatu
Gloet	Kluuvi
Gräsviken	Ruoholahti
Gumtäkt	Kumpula
Haga	Haaga
Hagasund	Hakasalmi
Hagasundsgatan	Hakasalmenkatu
Hagnäs	Hakaniemi
Hagnäs torg	Hakaniementori
Haminanlax	Haminalahti
Hangö	Hanko
Helsinge	Helsingin maalaiskunta
Henriksgatan: see Mannerheimvägen	Henrikinkatu, Heikinkatu
Hermanstad	Hermanni
Hertonäs	Herttoniemi
Hoplax	Huopalahti
Hyvinge	Hyvinkää
Högholmen	Korkeasaari
Idensalmi	Iisalmi
Jakobstad	Pietarsaari
Jungfrustigen	Neitsytpolku
Kajsaniemi	Kaisaniemi
Kalevagatan	Kalevankatu
Kampen	Kamppi
Kaserngatan	Kasarmikatu
Katrinegatan	Katriinankatu

Swedish:	*Finnish:*
Kervo	Kerava
Kimito	Kemiö
Korsholm	Korsholma
Kronohagen	Kruununhaka
Kungsholmen	Kuninkaansaari
Kymmene älv	Kymijoki
Kyrkslätt	Kirkkonummi
Lappviken	Lapinlahti
Lappviksgatan	Lapinlahdenkatu
Lembois	Lempäälä
Lilla Robertsgatan	Pieni Roobertinkatu
Lilla Östersvartö	Pikku Musta
Lindnäs	Linnainen
Lovisa	Loviisa
Ludvigsgatan	Ludviginkatu
Långören	Särkkä
Malm	Malmi
Malmgård	Malminkartano
Manegegatan	Maneesikatu
Mannerheimvägen	Mannerheimintie
Mejlans	Meilahti
Mikaelsgatan	Mikonkatu
Munksnäs	Munkkiniemi
Nikolaigatan: see Snellmansgatan	Nikolainkatu
Notsjö	Nuutajärvi
Nummis	Nummi
Nyland	Uusimaa
Nylandsgatan	Uudenmaankatu
Nystad	Uusikaupunki
Nyslott	Savonlinna
Olofsborg	Olavinlinna
Paldamo	Paltamo
Pargas	Parainen
Pellinge	Pellinki
Pernå	Pernaja
Porkala	Porkkala
Pyttis	Pyhtää

Swedish:	*Finnish:*
Regeringsgatan	Hallituskatu
Rehbindervägen	Rehbinderintie
Reval	Tallinna
Richardsgatan	Rickardinkatu
Rödbergen	Punavuori
Röddälden	Punanotko
Röddäldsparken	Punanotkon puisto
Sandhamn	Santahamina
Sandviken	Hietalahti
Sandvikstorget	Hietalahdentori
Sankt Michel	Mikkeli
Savolax	Savo
Sibbo	Sipoo
Skatudden	Katajanokka
Skillnaden	Erottaja
Snellmansgatan	Snellmaninkatu
Sockenbacka	Pitäjänmäki
Sofiegatan	Sofiankatu
Sordavala	Sortavala
Stora Robertsgatan	Iso Roobertinkatu
Stora Räntan	Harakka
Stora Östersvartö	Iso Mustasaari
Sveaborg	Viapori;
	Suomenlinna (after 1919)
Södra Magasinsgatan	Eteläinen Makasiinikatu
Sörnäs	Sörnäinen
Tammerfors	Tampere
Tavastehus	Hämeenlinna
Tavastland	Häme
Tavastvägen	Hämeentie
Tölö	Töölö
Turholm	Tullisaari
Uleåborg	Oulu
Ulrikasborg	Ullanlinna
Unionsgatan	Unioninkatu
Vanda å	Vantaanjoki
Vargön	Susisaari

Swedish:	*Finnish:*
Vasa	Vaasa
Viborg	Viipuri
Vichtis	Vihti
Vilhelmsgatan	Vilhonkatu
Villmanstrand	Lappeenranta
Vladimirsgatan: see Kalevagatan	Vladimirinkatu
Västra Chauséen	Läntinen Viertotie
Åbo	Turku
Åland	Ahvenanmaa

Three Language Glossary

English:	Swedish:	Finnish:
Arcadia Theater	Arkadiateatern	Arkadia-teatteri
Barracks Square	Kaserntorget	Kasarmitori
Bath House	Badhuset	(Ullanlinnan) kylpylä
Boulevard	Bulevarden	Bulevardi
Emperor's Shallows	Kejsargrunden	Keisarinluoto
Empress' Stone	Kejsarinnans sten	Keisarinnan kivi
Finnish Art Union	Finska konstföreningen	Suomen taideyhdistys
(Finnish) National Theater	Finska Nationalteatern	Suomen Kansallisteatteri
Finnish Naval Barracks	Finska sjöequipaget	Suomen meriväen kasarmi
Finnish Literary Society	Finska litteratur-sällskapet	Suomen kirjallisuuden seura
Friends of Finnish Handwork	Finska handarbetets vänner	Suomen käsityön ystävät
German Church	Tyska kyrkan	Saksalainen kirkko
Glo Inlet	Gloviken	Kluuvilahti
Glo Well	Globrunnen	Kluuvikaivo
Guards' Barracks	Gardeskasernen	Kaartinkasarmi
Holy Trinity Church	Heliga treenighetskyrkan	Pyhän kolminaisuuden kirkko
House of Estates	Ständerhuset	Säätytalo
House of Nobles	Riddarhuset	Ritarihuone
House of the (Working) People	Folkets hus	Työväentalo
Karelia	Karelen	Karjala
Long Bridge	Långa bron	Pitkäsilta
Main Watch	Högvakten	Päävartio
Market Place	Salutorget	Kauppatori
National Museum	Nationalmuseum	Kansallismuseo
Nikolai-Church	Nikolai kyrkan	Nikolainkirkko
(Cathedral	Domkyrkan	Tuomiokirkko)

English:	Swedish:	Finnish:
(Great Church	Storkyrkan	Iso kirkko)
North Esplanade	Norra Esplanadgatan	Pohjoinen Esplanaadikatu
North Harbor	Norra hamnen	Pohjoissatama
Observatory Hill	Observatorieberget	Tähtitornin vuori
Old Church	Gamla kyrkan	Vanha kirkko
Old Clinic	Gamla kliniken	Vanha klinikka
Ostrobothnia	Österbotten	Pohjanmaa
Railroad Square	Järnvägstorget	Rautatientori
Saint Henry's Church	Sankt Henriks kyrka	Pyhän Henrikin kirkko
Senate Square	Senatstorget	Senaatintori
Society House	Societetshuset	Seurahuone
(City Hall	Stadshuset	Kaupungintalo)
South Esplanade	Södra Esplanadgatan	Eteläinen Esplanaadikatu
South Harbor	Södra hamnen	Eteläsatama
Spa House	Brunnhuset	Kaivohuone
Student Union	Studenthuset	Ylioppilastalo
Swedish Theater	Svenska Teatern	Ruotsalainen Teatteri
Triangle	Trekanten	Kolmikulma
Tölö Bay	Tölöviken	Töölönlahti
Tölö Inn	Tölö värdshus	Töölö ravintola
University Botanical Garden	Universitetets botaniska trädgård	Yliopiston kasvitieteelinen puutarha
University Library	Universitetsbiblioteket	Yliopiston kirjasto
Ursin's Cliff	Ursins klippa	Ursinin kallio
Uspenski Cathedral	Uspenski katedralen	Uspenski katedraali

Select Bibliography

Åkerblom, Rudolph Waldemar. *Minnen från Skatudden eller det Helsingfors som går: Penneteckningar.* Helsingfors: 1873.

Åström, Sven-Erik, ed. *Helsingfors i forna tider II: Tre Helsingforsskildrare: Rudolf Åkerblom, Victor Pettersson d. ä., Victor Pettersson d.y.* Helsingfors: 1958.

Ackté, Aino. *Minnen och upplevelser*, I. Helsingfors: 1925.

Aho, Juhani (until 1906 Brofeldt). *Helsinkiin.* Porvoo: 1889. (*Till Helsingfors*, tr. anon. Fredrikshamn: 1893.)

Aho, Juhani. *Yksin.* Porvoo: 1890. (*Ensam*, tr. anon. Viborg: 1891.)

Aho, Juhani. "Maan sydämeen" and "Wilhelmiina Wäisänen". In: *Lastuja I.* Porvoo: 1891. (*Spånor: Berättelser och bilder*, tr. Werner Söderhjelm och N. Tötterman. Borgå: 1891.)

Aho, Juhani. "Kohtaus Keisarin patsaalla" and "Painajainen". In: *Katajainen kansani.* Porvoo: 1900. (*Enris: Andra samlingen*, tr. anon. Helsingfors: 1900.)

Aho, Juhani. *En idéernas man: Biografi öfver August Fredrik Soldan.* Helsingfors: 1901.

Aho, Juhani. *Hajamietteitä kapinaviikoilta.* Porvoo: 1919–1920.

Aho, Juhani. *Muistatko?* Helsinki: 1921. (*Minns du?* tr. Bertel Gripenberg. Helsingfors: 1921.)

Ahrenberg, Jac. *Människor som jag känt*, I-VI. Helsingfors: 1904–1914. (I: 'Carl Robert Sederholm,' 'Berndt Otto Schauman'; II: 'Vladimir Svertschkoff,' 'Nikolai Adlerberg', 'Severin Gabriel Falkman', 'Fanny Churberg'; III: 'Albert Edelfelt', 'Z. Topelius', 'Robert Lagerborg'; IV: 'F.L. Heiden', 'Fredrik Pacius'; V: 'Anders Ramsay', 'Carl Gustaf Estlander', 'Ivan Mihailovitsch Obolenski', 'Kaarlo Bergbom'; VI: 'Julius Krohn', 'Carl Theodor Höijer', 'Robert Konstantin Stigell'.)

Ahtela, H. (ps. Einar Reuter). *Helene Schjerfbeck: Kamppailu kauneudesta.* Helsinki: 1953.

Alho, Asmo & Uljas Rauanheimo. *Helsinki ennen meitä: Vanhojen kuvien kertomaa.* Helsinki: 1962.

Allardt, Marita, Erik Häggman, Richard Malmberg, Joel Rundt, eds. *Boken om Helsingfors, utgiven av Helsingforssamfundet.* Helsingfors: 1937.

Alm, Gustav (Richard Malmberg). *Höstdagar*. Helsingfors: 1907.

Anderson, Amos. *Helsingfors som bad-, rekreations- och turistort*. Helsingfors: 1909/1915.

Andersson, Otto. *Den unge Pacius och musiklivet på 1830-talet*. Helsingfors: 1938.

Andersson, Otto. *Jean Sibelius och Svenska teatern*. Åbo: 1956.

Andersson, Otto. *Den unge Amos Anderson: Några minnen*. Helsingfors: 1965.

Appelberg, Hanna & Eilif. *Helene Schjerfbeck: En biografisk konturteckning*. Helsingfors: 1949.

Aspelin, Eliel. *Johannes Takanen, elämä ja teokset*. Helsingfors: 1888.

Aspelin-Haapkylä, Eliel. *Werner Holmberg, hans lefnad och verk*. Helsingfors: 1890.

Aspelin-Haapkylä, Eliel. *Päiväkirja 1905–1917*, ed. E. Saarenheimo. Helsinki: 1980.

Aspelin-Haapkylä, Eliel. *Suomalaisen teatterin historia*, I-IV. Helsinki: 1906–1910.

Bäcksbacka, Leonard. *Ellen Thesleff*. Helsingfors: 1955.

Bang, Herman. *Vandreaar: Fortalt i Breve til Peter Nansen*. Copenhagen: 1918. (Letter of April 10, 1885.)

Barck, P.O. *Arvid Mörne och sekelskiftets Finland*. Helsingfors & Copenhagen: 1953.

Barck, P.O. & Henrik Schauman. "Från storstrejken 1905: Georg Schaumans anteckningar utgivna och kommenterade." *Historiska och litteraturhistoriska studier* 36 (1961):189–220.

Bergroth, Hugo. *Om grunderna för fastställandet av ett svenskt scenspråk för Finland*. Helsingfors: 1917.

Berndtson, Fredrik. *Notiser om Helsingfors för resande, isynnerhet bad- och brunnsgäster*. Helsingfors: 1843.

Berndtson, Fredrik. *Panorama af Helsingfors*. Helsingfors: 1848.

Björkstén, Carita. "Fredrik Berndtson." *Nyländska öden*, II: 47–106. Ekenäs: 1966.

Blomstedt, Yrjö. *Johan Albrecht Ehrenström: Gustavian och stadsbyggare*. Helsingfors: 1966.

Bonsdorff, Lars Gabriel von. *Lars Gabriel von Haartman*. Helsingfors: 1946.

Bruun, Patrick. "August Maximilian Myhrberg: Legend och verklighet." *Historiska och litteraturhistoriska studier* 38 (1963): 145–247.

Brunila, Bruno. *Arkitekter och annat folk.* Helsingfors: 1966.

Castrén, Gunnar. "Robert Tengström." *Förhandlingar och uppsatser* 17 (1903): 22–90.

Castrén, Gunnar. *Herman Kellgren: Ett bidrag till 1840- och 1850-talens kulturhistoria.* Helsingfors: 1945.

Castrén, Gunnar. "Vårt land." *Historiska och litteraturhistoriska studier* 30 (1954): 154–169.

Cawén, Ragni, ed. *Alvar Cawén.* Borgå & Helsingfors: 1958.

Christ-Janer, Albert. *Eliel Saarinen.* Chicago, 1949.

Collan, Fab[ian]. *Finsk språklära: Förra delen: Formläran.* Helsingfors:1847. (The second part did not appear.)

Collan-Beaurain, Maria. *Fredrik Pacius.* Helsingfors: 1921.

Colliander, Erland. *Svenska inhemska teatern 1894–1919.* Helsingfors: 1920.

Colliander, Tito. *T.K. Sallinen.* Helsingfors: 1948.

Cronström, Ingegerd Lundén. *Här är Helsingfors.* Helsingfors: 1964.

Dahlström, Fabian. *Sibelius-Akademien 1882–1982.* Helsingfors: 1982.

Dahlström, Svante. *Den inhemska teateridén.* Helsingfors: 1915.

Dahlström, Svante. *Svenska teaterns framtid.* Helsingfors: 1915.

Damstén, B. *Stockmann genom hundra år.* Helsingfors: 1961.

Degerholm, Emilie. *Vid svenska scenen i Helsingfors,* I-II: *Minnen och bilder.* Helsingfors: 1900–1903.

Diktonius, Elmer. "Bakom spegeln". In: *Medborgare [i republiken Finland],* II. Helsingfors: 1940.

Edelfelt, Berta, ed. *Ur Albert Edelfelts brev,* I-V. Helsingfors: 1917–1930.

Edlund, E.O. *Helsingfors: Historiska, topografiska och statistiska notiser om Finlands nuvarande hufvudstad.* Helsingfors: 1866.

Ehrenström, Johan Albrecht. *Efterlämnade historiska anteckningar,* I-II. Uppsala: 1882–1883.

Ekman, Karl. *Jean Sibelius: En konstnärs liv och personlighet.* Helsingfors: 1935.

Elmgren, S.G. "Sveaborgs bombardering 1855." *Historiallinen arkisto,* X (1889): 249–265.

Elmgren, Sven. *S.G. Elmgrenin muistiinpanot. Päiväkirjat 1853–1868,* ed. Aarno Maliniemi. Helsinki: 1939.

Enckell, Carl. *Finska Kadettkåren 1812–1887.* Fredrikshamn: 1890.

Enckell, Carl. *Finska Kadettkåren 1887–1903: fortsättning af arbetet under samma rubrik för åren 1812–1887, med kort öfversigt öfver denna period.* Utgiven med en inledning av J.E.O. Screen. Helsingfors: 1990.

Ervamaa, J. R.W. *Ekmanin ja C.E. Sjöstrandin Kalevalaaiheinen taide.* Helsinki: 1981.

Estlander, Bernhard. *Elva årtionden ur Finlands historia,* I-V. Helsingfors: 1919, revised 1929.

Estlander, Carl Gustaf et al., eds. *Finland i 19de seklet.* Helsingfors & Stockholm: 1893.

Estlander, Carl Gustaf. *Ungdomsminnen.* Helsingfors: 1918.

Estlander, Ernst. *Friherre Viktor Magnus von Born: Hans person och politiska verksamhet skildrade i samband med svensk nationalitetsrörelse.* Helsingfors: 1931.

Faltin, Richard Wilhelm Gottlieb. *Mitt liv.* Helsingfors: 1961.

Federley, Berndt. *R.A. Wrede: Lantdagsmannen och rättskämpen. 1877–1904.* Borgå: 1958.

Finlandia 1924 årsbok. Helsingfors: 1924. (Kaarlo Blomstedt, 'Helsingfors stads öden,' Birger Brunila, 'Stor-Helsingfors,' Y. Weilin, 'Helsingfors-minnen från åren 1885–1888.')

Flodin, Karl. *Finska musiker och andra uppsatser i musik.* Helsingfors: 1900.

Flodin, Karl. *Martin Wegelius: Levnadsteckning.* Helsingfors: 1922.

Flodin, Karl. *Musikliv och reseminnen.* Helsingfors: 1931.

Flodin, Karl & Otto Ehrström. *Richard Faltin och hans samtid.* Helsingfors: 1934.

Forsman (Koskimies), Rafael. *Fredrik Cygnaeus kirjailiana ja ajanilmiönä.* Porvoo: 1923.

Fosterländskt Album, I-III. Utgivet af H[erman] Kellgren, R[obert] Tengström, K[onstantin] Tigerstedt. Helsingfors: 1845–1847.

Franzén, Frans Michael. "Resan till jubelfesten i Helsingfors 1840." In: *Samlade dikter,* II: 137–151. Örebro: 1868.

Frenckell, Ester-Margaret von. *Offentliga nöjen och privata i Helsingfors 1812–1827.* Helsingfors: 1943.

Frenckell, Ester-Margaret von. *Offentliga nöjen och privata i Helsingfors 1827–1832.* Helsingfors: 1947.

Frenckell, Ester-Margaret von. *Sju magra år med Thalia: Offentliga nöjen och privata i Helsingfors 1827–1833.* Helsingfors: 1952.

Frenckell, Ester-Margaret von. *ABC för teaterpubliken.* Helsingfors: 1972.

Frenckell, Ester-Margaret von. "Teaterliv i Helsingfors på 1830-talet." *Historiska och litteraturhistoriska studier* 20 (1944): 18–36.

Frosterus, Sigurd. *Ab Stockmann Oy.* Helsingfors: 1931.

Gabriels, A. *Antti Fawén: Tjugotre porträtt.* Helsingfors: 1930.

Gadolin, Brita. *Barnsdomsminnen från sekelskiftet.* Helsingfors: 1969.

Ganivet y Garcia, Angel. *Cartas finlandesas.* Madrid: 1905.

Gedin, Per. "Family Business 1890–1990." *Books from Finland* (1990): 155–159. (The Reenpää family and Otava.)

Ginström, Egidius. *Julius Tallberg och hans verk.* Helsingfors: 1930.

Ginström, Egidius. *Hufvudstadsbladet under 50 år, 1864–1914.* Helsingfors: 1964.

Granfelt, Otto Hjalmar. *Friherre Rabbe Axel Wrede: Universitetslärare och vetenskapsman. Domare. Akademiekansler.* Lovisa: 1951.

Gripenberg, Bertel. "Herodes vid harpan." In: *Dikter.* Helsingfors: 1903.

Gripenberg, Bertel. "Svensk sång," "Svanen till Leda." In: *Gallergrinden.* Helsingfors: 1905.

Gripenberg, Bertel. "Den drömda armén." In: *Under fanan.* Helsingfors: 1918.

Gripenberg, Bertel. *Det var de tiderna.* Helsingfors: 1943.

Gripenberg, Gustaf Adolf. *Finska kadettkåren och dess kamratskap.* Helsingfors: 1912.

Grot, Jakov. *Utdrag ur J. Grots brevväxling med P. Pletnjov angående finska förhållanden vid medlet av 1800-talet,* I-II. Översättning av Walter Groundstroem. Helsingfors: 1912/1915.

Grotenfelt, Erik. *Det nya fosterlandet.* Stockholm: 1918.

Gulin, Helmi. *Karl August Wrede: Ungdomsvärld och livsgärning.* Helsingfors: 1948.

Haapanen, Toivo. *Finlands musikhistoria,* tr. Otto Ehrström. Helsingfors: 1956.

Hällström, Gustaf Gabriel. *Clima Helsingforsiae.* Helsingfors: 1840.

Hämäläinen, Pekka Kalevi. *Nationalitetskampen och språkstriden i Finland 1917–1939.* Helsingfors: 1968.

Hämäläinen, Pekka Kalevi. *In Time of Storm: Revolution, Civil War, and the Ethnolinguistic Issue in Finland.* Albany: 1979.

Hagelstam, Wentzel. "Angel Ganivet y Garcia" and "Flykten från Finland." In: *Personer och minnen.* Helsingfors: 1923.

Hahl, Nils-Gustav. *Samling Gösta Stenman: Finländsk konst.* Helsingfors: 1932.

Hahl, Nils-Gustav. *Om konst och konstindustri.* Helsingfors: 1942.

Hakkila, Esko Kalervo. *Mikko Oinonen: Karjalan saloilta taiteen parnassolle.* Helsinki: 1941.

Hartman, Torsten. *De tre gustavianerna.* Helsingfors: 1899. (Johan Fredrik Aminoff, Gustaf Mauritz Armfelt, Johan Albrecht Ehrenström.)

Hartman, Torsten. *Då Helsingfors blev hufvudstad.* Helsingfors: 1912.

Havu, Ilmari. *Lauantaiseura ja sen miehet.* Helsinki: 1945.

Heikel, Axel Olai. *Brunnsparkens historia 1834–1886.* Helsingfors: 1919.

Heikel, Ivar August. *Helsingfors universitet 1640–1940.* Helsingfors: 1940.

Heikel, Ivar August. *Minnen från min studenttid och mina studieår.* Helsingfors: 1946.

Heikinheimo, Ilmari. *Kaarle Aksel Gottlund: Elämä ja toiminta,* I. Porvoo: 1933.

Heinricius, G. *Anteckningar om Immanuel Ilmoni enligt bref och dagböcker.* Helsingfors: 1912.

Heiskanen, Seppo. *Kuvia Helsingistä.* Helsinki: 1983.

Helenius, Ilmari et al., eds. *Helsingin valtaus 12.4.1918. Helsingfors intagning.* Helsinki-Helsingfors: 1938.

Helsingfors i forna tider: Årsbok för Helsingfors stads historia I. Helsingfors: 1938.
    (A.W. Rancken, 'Signet och vapen för Helsingfors stad,' Gunvor Kerkkonen, 'Helsingfors kungsgård — Viks ladugård,' Berndt Aminoff, 'Drag ur Gloets historia,' Henrik Ramsay, 'Helsingfors ångbåtsförbindelser 1837–1887,' Nils-Erik Wickberg, 'Familjen Andsten,' Vicke Pettersson, 'Där riksdaghuset och posthuset nu står: Försvunnen idyll i Arkadia.')

Helsingfors med omgivningar och Borgå. Helsingfors: 1928. (Turistföreningens resehandböcker.)

Helsingfors stads historia, II-IV. Helsingfors: 1950–1966.
    (II. Eirik Hornborg, 'Perioden 1721–1809.' III:1: Carolus Lindberg & Gabriel Rein, 'Stadsplanering och byggnadsverksamhet,' Gabriel Rein, 'Helsingfors som landets huvudstad,' Eirik Hornborg, 'Militär och krigshändelser,' Martti Kovero, 'Helsingfors som trafikstad,' Martti Kovero, 'Helsingfors som handelsstad,' Martti Kovero, 'Industrin. III:2: Heikki Waris, 'Huvudstadssamhället,' Heikki Waris, 'Fattigdom och fattigvård,' Onni Wiherheimo & Gabriel Rein, 'Kommunalt liv,' Gabriel Rein, 'Helsingfors stads representanter vid lantdagarna,' Martti Ruuth,

'Helsingfors som kulturcentrum.' IV:1: Birger Brunila & Marius af Schultén, 'Stadsplan och byggnadskonst,' Itsakki Laati, 'De politiska händelsernas scen,' T.V. Viljanen, 'Kriget går fram över Helsingfors,' Martti Kovero, 'Helsingfors som trafikcentrum,' Martti Kovero, 'Helsingfors som handelsstad,' Martti Kovero, 'Helsingfors som industristad,' Reino Lento, 'Näringslivet under första världskriget.' IV:2: Sven-Erik Åström, 'Stadssamhällets omdaning,' Itsakki Laati, 'Det kommunala livet,' Paavo Virkunnen, 'Församlingarna,' Aarne Anttila, 'Kulturlivet.')

Helsingin opas. Helsinki: 1910.

Helsingius, Gustaf Adolf. *Hågkomster*, I-II. Helsingfors: 1927–1929.

Helsingius, Torsten. *Dagdrivare*. Helsingfors: 1914.

Helsingius, Torsten. *Det var*. Helsingfors: 1947.

Hertzberg, Rafael. *Helsingfors för trehundra år sedan och i våra dagar*. Med teckningar av Alex Federley. Helsingfors: 1888.

Hertzberg, Rafael. *Finska konstnärer*. Helsingfors: 1883.

Hildén, Henrik. *Strövtåg i Helsingforstrakten*. Helsingfors: 1927.

Hintze, Bertel. *Robert Wilhelm Ekman, 1808–1873: En Konsthistorisk studie*. Helsingfors: 1926.

Hintze, Bertel. *Albert Edelfelt*, I-III. Helsingfors: 1942–1944, rev. 1949.

Hirn, Marta. *Sveaborg genom två sekler: Ett bildverk med text*. Helsingfors: 1948.

Hirn, Marta, ed. *Finland framställt i teckningar*. Helsingfors: 1950, revised 1988.

Hirn, Sven. *Operett i Finland 1860–1918*. Helsingfors: 1992.

Hirn, Yrjö. *Akademiska bokhandeln 1893–1943*. Helsingfors: 1943.

Hirn, Yrjö, C.A. Nordman, Hilding Ekelund, Marius af Schultén, eds. *Vår stad: En bok om Helsingfors*. Helsingfors: 1947.

Hirn, Yrjö. "Den stora teaterstriden år 1857." *Historiska och litteraturhistoriska studier* 23 (1947): 1–77.

Hirn, Yrjö. *Teatrar och teaterstrider i 1800-talets Finland*. Helsingfors: 1949.

Homén, Olaf. *Från Helsingfors teatrar*, I-III. Helsingfors: 1915, 1918,1919.

Hornborg, Eirik. *När riket sprängdes*. Helsingfors: 1955.

Hornborg, Eirik. *Finlands hävder IV: Tiden 1809–1919*. Helsingfors: 1933.

Hornborg, Eirik. *Man i ledet: Minnen och episoder 1899–1927*. Helsingfors: 1959.

Hornborg, Harald. *'Wulffska hörnet' under 50 år*. Helsingfors: 1940.

Hoving, Johannes. *Sextio år: Mitt livs dagbok.* Uppsala: 1928.

Hoving, Victor. *En viborgare i Helsingfors och Stockholm.* Stockholm: 1945.

Hoving, Victor. *Henrik Borgström: En storborgare i det gamla Helsingfors.* Helsingfors: 1949.

Hoving, Victor. *Karl Fazer 1891–1951.* Helsingfors: 1951.

Huldén, Anders. *Finlands kungaäventyr 1918.* Helsingfors: 1989.

Hultin, Herman. *Gamla kyrkan vid hundra år 1826–1926.* Helsingfors: 1926.

Hytonen, Viljo. "Paavo Tikkanen." In: *Suomalaisuuden merkkimiehiä,* 2 (1917): 3–55.

Jägerskiöld, Stig. *Den unge Mannerheim.* Helsingfors: 1964.

Jägerskiöld, Stig. *Gustaf Mannerheim 1906–1917.* Helsingfors: 1965.

Järnefelt, Arvid. *Isänmaa.* Porvoo: 1893. (*Fosterlandet,* tr. Ernst Gråsten. Fredrikshamn: 1893.)

Järnefelt, Arvid. *Veljekset.* Porvoo: 1900. (*Bröderna,* tr. anon. Helsingfors: 1900.)

Järnefelt, Arvid. *Vanhempieni-romaani.* Porvoo: 1927–1929. (*Mina föräldrars roman,* I, tr. Bertel Gripenberg. Helsingfors: 1929. Completed by Thomas Warburton. Helsingfors: 1988.)

Janson, Ture. "Staden," "Sydväst, sydväst . . . ," and "Riddarhuset." In: *Mitt Helsingfors.* Helsingfors: 1913.

Janson, Ture. *Boken om Helsingfors.* Helsingfors: 1926.

Janson, Ture. *I huvudstadens virvlar: Helsingforsfilm i tolv öden.* Helsingfors: 1928.

Janson, Ture. *Inga medmänniskor: Fragmentarisk berättelse.* Åbo: 1911.

Janson, Ture. *De ensamma svenskarna.* Borgå: 1916.

Joukkahainen [sic]: *Läsning i vexlande ämnen, Utgifven af Österbottningar: Första Häftet.* Helsingfors: 1843.

Joukahainen: Ströskrift utgifven af Österbottniska Afdelningen: Andra Häftet. Helsingfors: 1845.

Jung, Bertel. *Ett förslag till stadsplan för 'Stor-Helsingfors.'* Utarbetat av Eliel Saarinen m.fl. Helsingfors: 1918.

'Jung Junior' (Rafael Hertzberg). *Statsrådet: Silhuetter, klippta ur Helsingfors-lifvet.* Helsingfors: 1887.

Kianto, Ilmari. "Kirottu Helsinki". In: *Nuoren miehen kädestä: Kokoelma mielialoja.* Helsinki: 1904.

Klinge, Matti. *Ylioppilaskunnan historia*, I-IV. Helsinki: 1966–67, 1978. (*Studenter och idéer: Studentkåren vid Helsingfors universitet 1828–1960*, I-IV, tr. Bertel Kihlman. Helsingfors: 1969–1979.)

Koroleff, Herman. *Den goda gamla tiden*. Helsingfors: 1953.

Koskenniemi, Veikko Antero. *Onnen antimet*. Helsinki: 1935. (*Lyckans håvor: Blad ur min levnadsbok*, tr. Einar Spjut. Helsingfors & Uppsala: 1943.)

Koskenniemi, Veikko Antero. *Vuosisadanalun ylioppilas*. Helsinki: 1947. (*Student när seklet var ungt*, tr. Hjalmar Dahl. Helsingfors: 1948.)

Koskenniemi, Veikko Antero. *Werner Söderström*. Porvoo: 1950.

Koskimies, Rafael & Pekka Tarkka. *Otavan historia*, I-II. Helsinki: 1946,1980.

Koskimies, Rafael. *Helsinki ja Härjänvatsa: Muistelua*. Helsinki: 1953.

Koskimies, Rafael. *Suomen Kansallisteatteri. I: 1902–1917*. Helsinki: 1953.

Krohn, Aarni. *Tsaarin Helsinki: Idyllistä itsenäisyyteen*. Helsinki: 1967.

Krohn, Eino. *Gösta Stenman: Upptäckare i konstens värld*. Helsingfors: 1970.

Krook, Augusta. *Mitt Helsingfors: Ungdomsminnen*. Helsingfors: 1950.

Kuvia Helsingistä/ Vyer från Helsingfors. Helsinki: n.d. (1912?).

Kylävaara, Keijo. *Finland 1917: Ett reportage om det självständiga Finlands födelseår*. Helsingfors: 1967.

Lagerborg, Rolf. *Sanningen om Casimir von Kothen*. Helsingfors: 1953.

Lagus, Hugo. *En gammal akademisk släkt*. Helsingfors: 1936.

Lagus, Wilhelm. *Från pojkåren och gymnasiet: Hågkomster*. Helsingfors: 1904.

Leino, Eino (until 1906 Lönnbohm). "Helsinki helmilöissä" in *Pyhä kevät*. Helsinki: 1901; "Meren kaupunki" in *Halla*. Helsinki: 1908.

Léouzon Le Duc, Louis Antoine. *La Finlande, son histoire primitive, sa mythologie, sa poésie épique, avec la traduction complète de sa grande épopée 'Le Kalewala,' son génie national, sa condition politique et sociale depuis la conquête russe*. Paris: 1845.

Léouzon Le Duc, Louis Antoine. *La Baltique*. Paris: 1855.

Lille, Martha. *Min far [Axel Lille] i närbild*. Helsingfors: 1965.

Lindberg, Vivi. *v. Wrightarna på Haminanlaks*. Helsingfors: 1926.

Lindström, Aune. *Taiteilijaveljekset von Wright*. Helsinki: 1932.

Lindström, Aune. *Pekka Halonen, elämä ja teokset*. Porvoo: 1957.

Lindström, Aune. *Konstmuseet i Ateneum 1863–1963*. Helsingfors: 1963.

Lördagsqvällens jul- och teaterkalender. Helsingfors: 1891–1892–1893.

Lüchou, Marianne. *Rollerna talar.* Helsingfors: 1951. (Nicken Rönngren, Axel Slangus.)

Lüchou, Marianne. *Svenska teatern i Helsingfors: Repertoar, Styrelser och teaterchefer, Konstnärlig personal 1860–1975.* Helsingfors: 1977.

Mårtenson, Gunnar, ed. *Vår hufvudstad Helsingfors.* Helsingfors: 1950.

Mårtenson, Gunnar. *Historiallinen Helsinki/ Det historiska Helsingfors.* Helsinki: 1968.

Maasalo, Kai. *Suomalaisia sävellyksiä: I: Tulindbergistä Sibeliukseen.* Porvoo: 1965.

Maasalo, Kai. *Suomalaisia sävellyksiä: II: Melartinista Kilpiseen.* Porvoo: 1969.

Marmier, Xavier. *Lettres sur la Russie, la Finlande, et la Pologne.* Paris: 1843.

Mattsson, Gustaf (Guss). *Så rulla våra öden: Kåserier Dec. 1911-Juli 1912.* Inledning och kommentar av Gunnel Steinby. Borgå: 1971.

Mattsson, Gustaf (Guss). *Valda skrifter: 'I dag' kåserier,* I-V. Helsingfors: 1919.

Meissner, Carl. *Carl Ludwig Engel.* Berlin: 1937. (Forschungen zur deutschen Kunstgeschichte, 20.)

Meurman, Agathon. *Finland förr och nu: Betraktelser.* Helsingfors: 1890.

Mörne, Arvid. 'Den röda fanan.' In: *Ny tid.* Helsingfors: 1903.

Mörne, Arvid. "Studier i Finlands press 1854–1856." *Förhandlingar och uppsatser* 26 (1912): 109–196.

Mörne, Arvid. *Från 'Saima' till 'Vikingen': En studie över den svenska nationalitetsidéns utveckling i Finlands press.* Helsingfors: 1916.

Mörne, Arvid. *Ett liv.* Helsingfors: 1925.

Mörne, Arvid. "Liberala meningsyttringar i finländska pressen före 1860-talet." *Historiska och litteraturhistoriska studier* 2 (1926): 178–218.

Mörne, Arvid. "Liberalismens genombrott i den finländska pressen." *Historiska och litteraturhistoriska studier* 6 (1930): 121–184.

Mörne, Arvid. "Kring Emil von Qvantens 'Fennomani och skandinavism'." *Historiska och litteraturhistoriska studier* 8 (1932): 1–85.

Mörne, Arvid. *Axel Olof Freudenthal: Liv och gärning.* Helsingfors: 1936.

Mueller-Reichau, Gerhard. *Finnland.* (Unter Mitwirkung der Deutsch-Finnischen Vereinigung von 1918.) Berlin, 1928, pp.1–22.

Mustelin, Olof. "Ateneum 1898–1903: Några anteckningar om finlandssvenska kulturtidskrifter kring sekelskiftet 1900." *Historisk Tidskrift för Finland* 47 (1962): 1–24.

Mustelin, Olof. *Euterpe: Tidskriften och kretsen kring den.* Helsingfors: 1963.

Mustelin, Olof. "Då studenterna inte ville sjunga 'Vårt land': En episod från år 1880 återspeglad i finlandssvensk press." *Historiska och litteraturhistoriska studier* 42 (1967):169–197.

Mustelin, Olof. *En förläggare och några av hans författare: Kring Holger Schildts förläggardebut 1913–1917.* Helsingfors: 1983.

Nervander, Emil. *I de dödas stad.* Helsingfors: 1883. (Helsingfors' cemeteries.)

Nervander, Emil. *Helsingfors med omgivningar.* Helsingfors: 1889.

Nervander, Emil. "I anledning af 'Vårt lands' halfsekelfest den 13 maj 1898." *Blad ur Finlands kulturhistoria.* Helsingfors: 1900, pp. 381–392.

Nervander, Emil. *Ett konstnärslif: Severin Falkman.* Helsingfors: 1902.

Nikula, Oskar. *Sveaborg: En vägvisare.* Helsingfors: 1939.

Nordenson, Eva, ed. *Finskt sekelskifte.* Stockholm: 1971.

(Matti Klinge, 'Finland efter 1809', Marika Hausen, 'Finlands paviljong på världsutställningen i Paris,' Leena Maunula, 'Konstindustrin och 'den finska stilen,' Aune Lindström, 'Kalevalaromantiken i Akseli Gallen-Kallelas konst,' Sakari Saarikivi, 'Hugo Simberg: En finsk symbolist,' Gustaf Strengell, 'Nya skönhetsvärden.')

Nordenstreng, Sigurd. *L. Mechelin: Hans statsmannagärning och politiska personlighet,* I-II. Helsingfors: 1936, 1937.

Nordmann, Petrus. *Bidrag till Helsingfors stads historia,* I-V. Helsingfors: 1905–1908.

Nordström, W.E., Olof Mustelin, & Gunvor Nordström, gen. eds. *Finländska gestalter,* I-XI. Ekenäs: 1961–1976.

(I: Olof Mustelin, 'Axel Olof Freudenthal,' Axel Öhman, 'Axel Lille,' Eric Anthoni, 'Leo Mechelin,' Berndt Federley, 'R.A. Wrede och Robert Hermanson,' Bertel von Bonsdorff, 'Robert Tigerstedt.'; II: Ingrid af Schultén, 'Mathilda Wrede,' Ernst von Born, 'Viktor Magnus von Born,' Olof Mustelin, 'C.G. Estlander,' ; IV: Olof Mustelin, 'Ivar August Heikel,' J.O. Tallqvist, 'Gunnar Castrén' ; V: Sven Willner, 'Guss Mattsson,' Henrik Cederlöf, 'Runar Schildt,' Olof Mustelin, 'Theodor Sederholm'; VI: Ester-Margaret von Frenckell, 'Nicken Rönngren,' Sven Willner, 'P.E. Svinhufvud,' W.E. Nordström, 'Hjalmar Linder'; VII: W.E. Nordström, 'Alma Söderhjelm,' Sven Willner, 'Bertel Gripenberg,' Gösta Cavonius,

'V.T. Rosenqvist'; IX: Sven Willner, 'Werner Söderhjelm,' Erik Bergh, 'Severin Falkman.')

Numers, Lorenz. "Kring det baltiska." In: *Månen är en säl.* Stockholm: 1952, pp.114–123.

Numers, Lorenz von. "'Fennica'." In: *De hemliga rummen.* Stockholm: 1980, pp.111–123.

Numers, Lorenz von. "Vid Senatstorget." In: *Oting: Historietter*, pp.94–101. Stockholm: 1968. (Translated in: G.C. Schoolfield, *Swedo-Finnish Short Stories.* New York & Boston: 1974, pp.267–276.)

Nyberg, Paul. *Zachris Topelius: En biografisk skildring.* Helsingfors: 1949.

Nyberg, Paul & Victor Hoving, eds. *Människor och minnen: Personliga hågkomster och släkthistoriska skildringar*, I-VII. Helsingfors: 1942–1957. (II: Erik Therman, 'Wentzel Hagelstam'; III: Carl von Bonsdorff, 'Hågkomster från skolan och universitet' ; IV: Nils Wasastjerna, 'Norra Hamnen och Norra Kajen,' Elsa von Born, 'J.J. Tikkanen och konstnärerna'; V: Estrid Furuhjelm, 'Femtiotvå år med Nylands nation'; VI: Edvard Bergh, 'En skvallerkrönika från Helsingfors 1855: Dagboksanteckningar'; VII: Martha Lille, 'Sångerskan Emma Engdahl,' Vicke Pettersson, 'Helsingfors då jag var barn'.)

Nyberg, Stig-Björn. "Den Öhmanska bokhandeln 1839–49: En studie i bokhandelns- och förlagsförhållanden i Finland under 1840-talet." *Historiska och litteraturhistoriska studier* 57 (1982): 81–136.

Nyström, Per. *Tolv kapitel om Munksnäs.* Helsingfors: 1945.

Odelberg, Vilhelm. *Viceadmiral Carl Olof Cronstedt: Levnadsteckning och tidsskildring.* Helsingfors: 1958.

Odelberg, Wilhelm. *Sveaborgs gåta: En studie i defaitism.* Helsingfors: 1958.

Öller, Ragnar. "En finländsk romanskrivare från 1850-talet: Några blad om romanskriveriet i vårt land och om en av dess första idkare." *Förhandlingar och uppsatser* 33 (1919): 6–187.

Okkonen, Onni. *Juha Rissanen: Elämäkertaa ja taidetta.* Helsinki: 1927.

Okkonen, Onni. *Suomen taiteen historia I-II.* Porvoo & Helsinki: 1945.

Okkonen, Onni. *A. Gallen-Kallela, elämä ja taide.* Helsinki: 1949.

Olsson, Hagar. *Chitambo: Romanen om Vega Maria.* Helsingfors: 1933.

Paavolainen, Jaakko. *Röd och vit terror: Finlands nationella tragedi.* Översatt av Tuuli Forsgren. Stockholm: 1986.

Palmgrén, E.G. *Helsingfors 1800–1900: Byggnadsverksamhet och tomtvärde.* Helsingfors: 1907.

Pettersson, Victor d.ä. *Bilder ur Skatuddslifvet i forna dagar.* Helsingfors: 1881.

Pettersson, Victor d.ä. *Den gamle polisgevaldigerns berättelser: Bilder ur Helsingforslifvet.* Helsingfors: 1884.

Puokka, Jaakko. *Magnus Enckell: Ihminen ja taiteilija.* Helsinki: 1949.

Qvarnström, Ingrid. *Ett legendomspunnet liv: Aurora Karamsin och hennes samtid.* Helsingfors: 1937.

Qvarnström, Ingrid. *Svensk teater i Finland,* I-II. Helsingfors: 1946, 1947.

Ramsay, Anders. *Från barnaår till silverhår,* I-VIII. Helsingfors: 1927.

Rancken, Arne Wilhelm. *Helsingfors från småstad till storstad.* Helsingfors: 1932. ('Namnet Helsingfors'; 'Helsingfors karta'; 'Den stora nyregleringen'; 'Esplanadernas historia'; 'Ulrikasborgsbergen'; 'Eldens framfart'.)

Rancken, Arne Wilhelm. *Helsingfors genom fyra sekler.* Helsingfors: 1926.

Rancken, Arne Wilhelm. *Sveaborg: Dess tillkomst och öden.* Helsingfors: 1933.

Rancken, Arne Wilhelm. *Helsingfors, stad och landsbyggd.* Helsingfors: 1937.

Rein, Thiodolf. *Johan Vilhelm Snellman,* I-II. Andra illustrerade reviderade upplagan. Helsingfors: 1904. (*Juhana Vilhelm Snellmanin elämä.* Helsinki: 1904–1905.)

Rein, Thiodolf. *Lefnadsminnen.* Helsingfors: 1919.

Reuter, J.N. *'Kagalen': Ett bidrag till Finlands historia 1899–1905,* I-II. Helsingfors: 1928, 1930.

Reuter, Einar. *Helene Schjerfbeck.* Stockholm: 1953.

Reuter, Odo Morannal. *Finland i ord och bild.* Stockholm: 1901, pp.9–136.

Ringbom, Nils-Eric. *Helsingfors orkesterföretag 1882–1932.* Helsingfors: 1932.

Rosas, John. *Fredrik Pacius som tonsättare.* Helsingfors: 1949.

Rosas, John. "Musikaliska sällskapet och Symfoniföreningen i Helsingfors 1827–1853." *Historiska och litteraturhistoriska studier* 27–28 (1952): 425–498.

Runeberg, Fredrika. *Anteckningar om Runeberg/ Min pennas saga,* ed. Karin Allardt Ekelund. Helsingfors: 1946.

Runeberg, Johan Ludvig. "Vårt land." In: *Fänrik Ståls sägner: En samling sånger* (1848).

Runeberg, Johan Ludvig. "Sveaborg." Written in 1846 and circulated in manuscript. First printed in Runeberg's *Efterlemnade Skrifter* (1878), and since then included as the penultimate canto of *Fänrik Ståls sägner*, I (1848).

Runeberg, Carl Michael. *Finland under Orientaliska kriget*. Borgå: 1962.

Ruth, Martti. *Storkyrkan i Helsingfors: Hundra år*. Helsingfors: 1952.

Saarinen, Eliel et al. *Munksnäs-Haga och Stor-Helsingfors: Stadsplansstudier och förslag*. Helsingfors: 1915.

Saarinen, Eliel et al. *Munkkiniemi-Haaga ja Suur-Helsinki*. Helsinki: 1915.

Saarikivi, Sakari. *Hugo Simberg, hans liv och verk*. Helsingfors: 1951.

Saarikivi, Sakari et al., eds. *Düsseldorf ja Pohjola*. Helsinki: 1976.

Salminen, Johannes. "Emil Zilliacus och drömmen om Hellas." In: *Pelare av eld*. Helsingfors: 1967, pp.80–89.

Salminen, Johannes. "Georg Schauman — den store outsidern." In: *Pelare av eld*. Helsingfors: 1967, pp.125–137.

Salminen, Johannes. "Georg August Wallins orient." In: *Minnet av Alexandria*. Helsingfors: 1988, pp.103–115.

Schauman, August. *Nu och förr*. Helsingfors: 1886.

Schauman, August. *Från sex årtionden i Finland: Levnadsminnen*, I-II. Helsingfors: 1922.

Schauman, Sigrid. *Min bror Eugen*. Helsingfors: 1964.

Schildt, Runar. "Den svagare," "Perdita," and "Sinande källor." In: *Perdita och andra noveller*. Helsingfors: 1918. ("Sinande källor" translated as "Failing Sources" in G.C. Schoolfield, *Swedo-Finnish Short Stories*. New York & Boston: 1974, pp.107–119.)

Schildt, Runar. "Karamsinska hästen." In: *Hemkomsten och andra noveller*. Helsingfors: 1919.

af Schultén, Marius. *Helsingfors, stad vid havet*. Helsingfors: 1956.

af Schultén, Marius. *Benois teaterhus*. Helsingfors: 1970.

Schybergson, Emil. *K.H. Renlund*. Helsingfors: 1915.

Sommerschield, Finn Edvard, ed. *Akademiska sångföreningen 1838–1938*. Helsingfors: 1938.

Snellman, Lina. *Till öfverstinnan Karamzins minne*. Helsingfors: 1909.

Södergran, Edith. "Fragment." In: *Septemberlyran*. Helsingfors: 1918. (Usually called the "Petersburg fragment" in the secondary literature on Södergran.)

Söderhjelm, Alma. *Min värld*, I-III. Stockholm: 1929–1931.

Söderhjelm, Henning. *Unga år*. Helsingfors: 1962.

Söderhjelm, Henning. *Werner Söderhjelm*. Helsingfors: 1960.

Söderhjelm, Werner. *Profiler*. Helsingfors: 1923. (Edelfelt, Hjalmar Neiglick, Jean Sibelius et al.)

Sohlman, August. *Det unga Finland: En kulturhistorisk betraktelse*. Stockholm: 1855.

Soikkanen, Hannu. *Dokument från finska inbördeskriget*. Översättning av Finn Sommerschield. Stockholm: 1980. (Revised and abbreviated version of: *Kansalaissota dokumentteina*. Helsinki: 1967–1969.)

Somerkivi, Urho. *Helsingfors folkskolors historia*. Helsingfors: 1979.

'Sphinx' (Rafael Hertzberg). *Helsingfors-Monaco: Skildring ur vårt hufvudstadslif*. Helsingfors: 1887.

Steinby, Gunnel. *Oss väl och ingen illa: Guss Mattsson publicisten och kemisten 1902–1914*. Helsingfors: 1976.

Steinby, Gunnel. *Journalister och publicister i svensk press i Finland under tvåhundra år*. Åbo: 1981.

Steinby, Torsten. *Finlands tidningspress*. Stockholm: 1964.

Steinby, Torsten. *Amos Anderson*. Helsingfors: 1979.

Steinby, Torsten. *Johan Jakob Nervander (1805–1848)*. Helsingfors: 1991.

'Sten, Daniel' (Ina Lange). *Luba: En studie*. Helsingfors: 1889.

Stenberg, A.W. *Boklådor och bokhandlare i Helsingfors, Borgå och Viborg*. Helsingfors: 1942.

Stenius, Sigurd. *Boken om Drumsö*. Helsingfors: 1947.

Stigell, Jarl. *Robert Stigell*. Ekenäs: 1977. (*Finländska gestalter*, NF, 1.)

Stjernschantz, Göran. *Ett förlag och dess författare. Söderström & Co. Förlags Ab 1891–1991*. Helsingfors: 1991.

Strengell, Gustaf. *Finska mästare*. Helsingfors: 1906.

Strengell, Gustaf. *Staden som konstverk*. Helsingfors: 1922.

Suolahti, Eino E. *Helsingin neljä vuosisataa*. Helsinki: 1949.

Suolahti, Eino E. *Helsingfors 1550–1950*. Helsingfors: 1950.

Suolahti, Gunnar, Carl von Bonsdorff, Gunnar Castrén, V. Tarkiainen, eds. *Från universitetets första tider i Helsingfors*. Helsingfors: 1928.

Suomalainen, Yrjö. *Robert Kajanus: Hänen elämänsä ja toimintansa*. Helsinki: 1952.

Talvio, Maila. *Niniven lapset*. Helsinki: 1915. (*Ninives barn*, tr. Holger Nohrström. Helsingfors: 1915.)

Tanner, Väinö. *Näin Helsingin kasvavan.* Helsinki: 1947. (*Mina pojkår: Minnen från 1880- och 1890-talens Helsingfors,* tr. Lars Hjalmarsson Dahl. Stockholm: 1948.)

Tanner, Väinö. *Det vita skräckväldet i Finland: Förskräckliga sanningar om den borgerliga diktaturen: Ett officiellt dokument.* Stockholm: 1919.

Tavaststjerna, Karl August. *Barndomsvänner.* Helsingfors: 1988. (Reprint of first edition, 1886.)

Tavaststjerna, Karl August. *En patriot utan fosterland.* Helsingfors: 1896.

Tawaststjerna, Erik. *Jean Sibelius,* I-V, tr. Tuomas Anhava and Erkki Salmenhaara. Helsinki: 1965–1988.

Tawaststjerna, Erik. *Jean Sibelius,* I. Helsingfors & Stockholm: 1968.

Tawaststjerna, Erik. *Jean Sibelius,* II: *Åren 1904–1914.* Helsingfors & Stockholm: 1991.

Tawaststjerna, Erik. *Jean Sibelius,* I, tr. Robert Layton. London: 1976.

Tawaststjerna, Erik. *Jean Sibelius,* II: *1904–1914,* tr. Robert Layton. London: 1986.

Tengström, R[obert], ed. *Finsk anthologi eller samling af valda skaldestycken af Finska författare från äldre till nyare tider, jemte korta karakteristiker och biografiska notiser: Första delen: Öfversättningar af Finska folksånger.* Helsingfors: 1845. (The announced second part did not appear.)

Terho, Olavi et al. *Helsingfors gatunamn.* Helsingfors: 1971.

Tikkanen, Henrik. *Mitt Helsingfors.* Helsingfors: 1972.

Törnegren, Carl Wilhelm. *Teckning af den svenska vitterhetens äldre öden i Finland intill Franzén: Litterära soiréer i Helsingfors under hösten 1849.* Helsingfors: 1849.

Törngren, Adolf. "C.W. Törnegrens brev från Krimkrigets dagar." *Historiska och litteraturhistoriska studier* 10 (1934): 241–340.

Törngren, Adolf. "Ur friherre Emil Stjernvall-Walleens brev till Aurore Karamzine." *Historiska och litteraturhistoriska studier* 15 (1939): 136–270.

Törngren, Adolf. *Från Finlands strid för rätt och frihet: Personliga upplevelser åren 1901–1914.* Helsingfors: 1942.

Tolvanen, Jouko. *Carl Eneas Sjöstrand : Suomen uudemman kuvanveistotaiteen uranuurtaja.* Helsinki: 1952.

Topelius, Zachris. "Sång, tillegnad de med allernådigste tillstädjelse den 21 Juni 1844 vid Kejserliga Alexanders-Universitetet i Finland promoverade sextioen philosophiae magistrar." Helsingfors: 1844.

Topelius, Zachris. "Finlands namn." *Ljungblommor*, 2. Helsingfors, 1860. (First printed in *Helsingfors Tidningar*, May 20, 1848.)

Topelius, Zachris. *Efter femtio år: Skådespel i tre akter med prolog.* Stockholm & Helsingfors: 1851.

Topelius, Zachris. *Text till Sångpartierna i Kung Carls jagt. Opera i tre akter af Fredrik Pacius.* Helsingfors: 1852.

Topelius, Zachris. *Fältskärns berättelser: 1.cykeln: Konungens ring. Svärdet och plogen. Eld och vatten.* Helsingfors: 1853. (Revised version of publication in *Helsingfors Tidningar*, 1851–1852.)

Topelius, Zachris. *Regina von Emmeritz: Skådespel i fem akter.* Musiken af J.A. Söderman Jr. Helsingfors: 1854.

Topelius, Zachris. *Vincent Vågbrytaren. Helsingfors Tidningar* (1860). In book form, *Vinterqvällar*, I. Helsingfors & Stockholm: 1880.

Topelius, Zachris. *Ett skärgårdsäventyr & Prinsessan af Cypern.* In: *Dramatiska dikter*, 1. samling. Stockholm: 1861.

Topelius, Zachris. *Dagböcker*, I-IV, ed. Paul Nyberg. Helsingfors: 1918–1924.

Topelius, Zachris. *Självbiografiska anteckningar*, ed. Paul Nyberg. Helsingfors: 1922.

Topelius, Zachris. *Fästmansbrev*, ed. Paul Nyberg. Helsingfors: 1948.

Topelius, Zachris. *Konstnärsbrev*, I-II, ed. Paul Nyberg. Tammerfors: 1956,1960.

I: Z. Topelius brevväxling med C.J.L. Almqvist, J.L. Runeberg, Fredrika Runeberg, Fredrik Cygnaeus, Fredrik Pacius, Conrad Greve, J.A. Josephson. II: Z. Topelius brevväxling med Fredrika Bremer, Bernhard von Beskow, Johan Ludvig Heiberg, Johanne Luise Heiberg, Carl Anton Wetterbergh, Herman Sätherberg, Karl Robert Malmström, Ludvig Leonard Laurén.

Topelius, Zachris. *Anteckningar från det Helsingfors som gått.* Helsingfors: 1968.

Urbans, Runar. *Oy Hartwall Ab: Banbrytaren i Finland för mineralvatten och läskedrycker: En krönika till 125-års-jubiléet.* Helsingfors: 1961.

Valbäck, F.J. *En afton i Kaisaniemi: Romantiserad skildring ur Helsingforslifvet.* Helsingfors: 1892.

Vallgren, Viivi. *Sydämeni kirja.* Helsinki: 1949.

Vallgren, Ville. *Ville Vallgrens ABC-bok med bilder.* Helsingfors: 1916.

Vasenius, Valfrid. *Helsingforsvägvisare för resande och historisk-statistisk öfversigt.* Helsingfors: 1876.

Venäläisyys Helsingissä/Ryskt i Helsingfors/The Russian Style in Helsinki. Helsinki: 1984. (Exhibit catalogue, Helsinki City Museum.)

von der Goltz, Rüdiger. *Meine Sendung in Finnland und im Baltikum.* Leipzig: 1920.

Wahlbäck, Krister. *Från Mannerheim till Kekkonen: Huvudlinjer i finländsk politik 1917–1967.* Stockholm: 1967.

Wallin, Georg August. *Bref och anteckningar.* Utg. jämte en lefnadsteckning af Knut Tallqvist. Helsingfors: 1905.

Wasastjerna, Nils. *Finsk arkitektur: Exteriörer och interiörer.* Helsingfors: 1908.

Wasastjerna, Nils. *En krönika om Helsingfors.* Helsingfors: 1941. ('Det första teaterhuset', 'Det gamla societetshuset', 'Esplanadkapellet', 'Runebergsesplanaden'.)

Wasastjerna, Nils. *Helsingfors: Tre kulturverk.* Helsingfors: 1948. ('Svenska teater,' 'Den stora industriutställningen,' 'Ateneum'.)

Wecksell, Josef Julius. *Daniel Hjort: Sorgespel i fem akter med fyra tablåer.* Helsingfors: 1863.

Wennervirta, Ludvig. *Eero Järnefelt ja hänen aikansa 1863–1937.* Helsinki: 1950.

Westermarck, Helena. *Mina levnadsminnen.* Åbo: 1941.

Westermarck, R. *Några upplysningar om gamla Helsingfors.* Helsingfors: 1878.

Weckström, Tor. *Chiewitz teaterhus.* Helsingfors: 1966.

Wiberg, Albert. "Då Helsingfors skulle få sitt första offentliga bibliotek." *Historiska och litteraturhistoriska studier* 18–19 (1943): 313–336.

Wichmann, V.K.E. *Svenskt studentliv i Finland för 50 år sedan.* Lovisa: 1932.

Wickberg, Nils-Erik. *Empirestudier.* Helsingfors: 1945.

Wickberg, Nils-Erik. *Carl Ludvig Engel.* Helsinki: 1970, Helsingfors: 1973.

Wickberg, Nils-Erik. *Senatintori/ Senatstorget/ The Senate Square/ Der Senatsplat: Helsinki-Helsingfors.* Rungsted & Helsinki: 1981.

Wrede, Johan, Helena Solstrand, & Ulla Terling-Hasán. *Kommentar till Fänrik Ståls sägner. Samlade skrifter av Johan Ludvig Runeberg,* XIV:1. Helsingfors: 1983.

Zweigbergk, Otto von. *Finska studier: Ögonblicksbilder från Finland januari–februari 1894.* Stockholm: 1894.

Zilliacus, Benedikt (text) & Tikkanen, Henrik (illustrations). *Vi ser på Helsingfors.* Helsingfors: 1952.

Zilliacus, Clas & Henrik Knif. *Opinionens tryck: En studie över pressens bildningsskede i Finland.* Helsingfors: 1985.

Zilliacus, Konni. *I societeten: En Helsingfors-berättelse.* Helsingfors: 1895.

See also the numerous articles by various hands in:

Entisaikain Helsinki: Helsingin Historiayhdistyksen Vuosikirja, I-X: 1936–1980.

Helsingfors-Samfundet: Årsbok/ Helsinki-Seura: Vuosikirja, I-XI: 1965–1976.

Narinkka: Helsingin kaupunginmuseon vuosikirja/ Helsingfors stadsmuseets årsbok, 1976–.

Index

Persons

Buildings, Places, Streets